Education Governance for the Twenty-First Century

Education Governance for the Twenty-First Century

Overcoming the Structural Barriers to School Reform

Paul Manna
Patrick McGuinn
editors

In collaboration with
THOMAS B. FORDHAM INSTITUTE
and
CENTER FOR AMERICAN PROGRESS
Washington, D.C.

BROOKINGS INSTITUTION PRESS
Washington, D.C.

Copyright © 2013
THE BROOKINGS INSTITUTION
1775 Massachusetts Avenue, N.W.
Washington, D.C. 20036
www.brookings.edu

Published with financial support from
    The Carnegie Corporation of New York
    The Doris and Donald Fisher Fund
    The Eli and Edythe Broad Foundation
    The Lynde and Harry Bradley Foundation

Library of Congress Cataloging-in-Publication data
Education governance for the twenty-first century : overcoming the structural barriers to school reform / Paul Manna and Patrick McGuinn, editors.
        p.   cm.
    Includes bibliographical references and index.
    ISBN 978-0-8157-2394-3 (pbk. : alk. paper)
    1. Education and state—United States.   I. Manna, Paul, editor of compilation.   II. McGuinn, Patrick J., editor of compilation.   III. Finn, Chester E., Jr., 1944–   How current education governance distorts financial decisionmaking.
    LC89.E257 2013
    379—dc23   2012045316

9 8 7 6 5 4 3 2 1

Printed on acid-free paper

Typeset in Minion

Composition by R. Lynn Rivenbark
Macon, Georgia

Printed by R. R. Donnelley
Harrisonburg, Virginia

Contents

Acknowledgments

The editors and contributors would like to acknowledge the extraordinary assistance and support they received from many different individuals and groups during the development and production of this book.

The Carnegie Corporation of New York, the Doris and Donald Fisher Fund, the Lynde and Harry Bradley Foundation, and the Eli and Edythe Broad Foundation provided invaluable financial support.

The chapters benefited from the keen insights of the following conference discussants who commented on draft chapters and author presentations on December 1, 2011, in Washington, D.C.: Margaret Goertz, Chris Cerf, Marc Tucker, Paul Pastorek, and Jon Schnur.

The Thomas B. Fordham Institute thanks Janie Scull and Amber M. Winkler for their keen edits of paper drafts and Daniela Fairchild for her overall project management.

The Center for American Progress thanks Raegen Miller, Diana Epstein, Ulrich Boser, and Juliana Herman for their substantive contributions and smart editorial suggestions.

Steven Wilson offers thanks to Josue Cofresi for research assistance and to Kathryn Ciffolillo for editing.

Kathryn McDermott acknowledges the Center for Public Policy, University of Massachusetts Amherst, for financial support; Alan Dallmann and Anna Fung-Morley for research assistance; and the following individuals for reviewing earlier drafts: Michael Hock, Dane Linn, Chris Minnich, Jeff Nellhaus, Mike Petrilli, Janie Scull, Mike Smith, and Stephanie Shifton.

Jeffrey Henig would like to acknowledge the Institute for Advanced Study and the Spencer Foundation for support that has contributed to his chapter; Elizabeth Chu, a doctoral student in education policy at Teachers College, who provided extremely valuable research assistance; and helpful feedback at various stages from Dorothy Shipps, Patrick McGuinn, and Paul Manna.

Sir Michael Barber is grateful to Alys Barber, who edited and proofread his chapter and made numerous improvements to the language and flow of the writing.

Sandra Vergari acknowledges anonymous reviewers and Shama Gamkhar, Kathryn Harrison, Paul Manna, and Carol Weissert for comments on prior drafts; additional special thanks to Thomas Skotzke.

Barry Rabe offers thanks to Frank Thompson, Patrick McGuinn, and Paul Manna for helpful input on his chapter.

Paul Manna would like to thank the Spencer Foundation for its financial support of his work on education governance.

Patrick McGuinn would like to acknowledge the support of the Institute for Advanced Study in Princeton and the Spencer Foundation's Education, Democracy, and Justice workshops—led by Danielle Allen and Rob Reich—which offered him the opportunity to reflect on many of the themes explored in this volume.

As editors, Patrick McGuinn and Paul Manna owe many thanks to numerous people who helped bring this book across the finish line. First, they are grateful to the leadership teams at the Thomas B. Fordham Institute and the Center for American Progress—Checker Finn, Mike Petrilli, Amber Winkler, and Cindy Brown—for their confidence in choosing them to lead this project and their constant support in helping them to carry it out. Second, they thank the superb collection of contributors who accepted invitations to write chapters for this book. Third, they thank Daniela Fairchild of the Fordham Institute for her tireless work in keeping the project's many trains running on schedule, and at Brookings, they thank Christopher Kelaher, Janet Walker, an anonymous peer reviewer, and the rest of the production team for believing in the book and helping improve it every step of the way. Finally, for the enduring, endless, and unconditional love and support they always provide, McGuinn offers thanks to his wife, Ilana, and daughters, Bailey, Carigan, Haven, and Payton; and Manna thanks his wife, Lisa, and his son, Theo. As parents and former high school teachers, the editors hope that this book will advance the conversation about how the United States can improve its system of K–12 education and expand educational opportunities for all children.

PATRICK MCGUINN *and* PAUL MANNA

1

Education Governance in America: Who Leads When Everyone Is in Charge?

"The buck stops here!" So stated the famous sign displayed on President Harry Truman's desk in the Oval Office. In embracing that phrase, Truman asserted boldly that as America's leader, a wartime president for much of his tenure, he was unambiguously in charge and prepared to make tough decisions to protect the nation's interests. In short, Truman believed it was his duty to govern. Although the leadership style of "Give 'em Hell" Harry has inspired generations of officials across levels of government, the complexity of governing America's diverse society means that even the most energized leaders may fail to meet the standard that Truman's mantra suggests. In no policy area is governance in the United States more complex than in elementary and secondary education, where multiple actors and institutions have some formal say over what happens in the nation's classrooms. As a result, bold local, state, and federal education leaders who assert their own rights and duties to govern often find themselves attacked from all sides as their rivals for control target their ideas.

Consider for a moment the governing tasks that confront the nation's school principals, who lead America's nearly 100,000 public schools. Like the president, school principals are chief executives, charged with managing and attempting to lead their organizations, albeit on a much smaller scale. Although governing from the president's perch in the White House, or even the governor's mansion in the state capital or the mayor's chair in city hall, may be a daunting task, school principals face challenging management tasks of their own. That is especially true in three areas that matter most to chief executives: making personnel decisions, setting financial priorities, and exercising autonomy.[1]

Principals work under several constraints as they try to execute such functions. Does the buck stop on the principal's desk when it comes to hiring the teachers that principals and their administrative teams believe can do the best job? Not really. Can principals flexibly manage school budgets to accommodate a

1

pressing need or seize an emerging opportunity that could enhance opportunities for students? Perhaps on the margins, but in general, not so much. Do they wield decisive authority to set the academic and other priorities of their respective schools? Well, somewhat, but a litany of other leaders, some working in local communities and others in more distant state capitals and the federal government, also govern these matters. Those limits on the principal's power even apply to more basic school functions such as maintaining order and developing conduct codes for student behavior.[2] One reason these constraints exist is that opinions differ about the proper level of authority that principals should possess. Although principals themselves might prefer to have the flexibility of private sector chief executive officers, they are still public officials, so some constraints do seem appropriate to most people.

In practice, the buck seems to be always on the move in the nation's system of education governance. Such dynamics pose great challenges for anyone who has some interest in how schools operate. This includes principals and teachers, who work side by side with students every day; ordinary citizens, who seek to understand how their tax dollars are being used to support public education; innovators in the high technology and nonprofit sectors, who have promising ideas about how to improve the way schools work; and American politicians and industry leaders, who worry about the nation's competitive edge and struggle to understand what can be done to improve the education experiences of the nation's students. As overall achievement remains flat and achievement gaps between student groups persist, self-defined reformers inside and outside traditional education circles express much frustration at the seemingly slow pace of change that present governing arrangements foster. Nor do individuals and organizations with some of the most enduring legacies and attachments to prevailing modes of governance, such as local school boards and teacher unions, offer ringing endorsements of the status quo. In short, nobody seems satisfied with how the nation governs its schools. But what is to be done?

Before analyzing why prevailing modes of education governance breed such frustration and inspire calls for change, it is important to address a more fundamental issue. Who governs American schools, and with what results? That strikingly simple yet important question has received scant attention, even as concerns about the nation's students have grown. That is a stunning oversight, given that several decades of intense American school reform efforts, focusing on specific policy changes, have produced at best marginal gains in student achievement. During that same time, reports from academic researchers, governments at all levels, and think tanks that inhabit all corners of the political spectrum have concluded that the country's education system produces neither the academic excellence nor equality of opportunity required for its students to succeed in the rapidly changing and shrinking world. This book begins with the premise that the structure of American education governance—highly fragmented, decentralized, politicized, and bureaucratic—contributes to these problems by undercutting the development and sustenance of changes needed to improve the education opportunities and academic performance of students. Although governance reforms alone cannot help all the nation's young people reach higher levels and erase achievement gaps between advantaged students (typically white and from higher-income families) and their disadvantaged peers (frequently racial, ethnic, or linguistic minorities and those from low-income families), it is hard to imagine much dramatic improvement occurring without some fundamental rethinking of how the nation governs its schools.

Why so little attention on education governance, then, if it is central to constructing a system of schooling that can meet the demands of the current century? One reason is that politicians and journalists often see governance as an arid, somewhat academic topic, better suited for ivory-tower debates or exchanges in scholarly journals. Questions about governance tend not to lend themselves to stark narratives that pit "us" against "them" or that line up neatly along the liberal to conservative spectrum that so many public officials and reporters use to organize the political world in their rhetoric and their articles. In contrast, other areas with compelling storylines, such as controversies over school accountability, student testing, teacher compensation, and the teaching of evolution, tend to fit into these more convenient narrative boxes and therefore provide much more interesting fodder for debate. The chapters in this volume reach beyond these headline-grabbing topics to illuminate why the understudied issue of education governance should be atop the list of anyone interested in the present and future of American education. In so doing, the book embeds specific policy issues, such as standards, teachers, and testing, in a larger context by focusing needed attention on the governance forest without getting lost in these policy trees.

Three key questions guide the analysis. First, how do existing governing institutions and relationships shape the content of education policy and school operations? Second, to what extent and in what ways has governance either assisted or stymied efforts to bring about systemic improvements? Third, how might reform of education governance promote positive changes in policy and ultimately improve student success?

This book demonstrates that choices about education governance can be at least as important, perhaps even more so, as the specific policy decisions that elected officials and civil servants make and implement each day. At the same time, the chapters disabuse readers of the notion that there exists an ideal governance arrangement that, if adopted, will automatically propel American schools and students to higher levels of performance. As in any complex area, panaceas do not exist, despite occasional claims to the contrary.[3] Still, this book does show that governance choices help to create conditions that can influence many things, including how teachers and principals use their time, whether promising new educational practices or organizational forms can gain traction, the degree to which parents and community members can understand how well schools are performing, and, above all, the opportunities that the nation's students enjoy in the classroom. Meeting the needs of all these groups, and the many others concerned about education in the United States, is no easy task. This book shows that the nation's fragmented and patchwork system of education governance has lowered the probability that any of these groups will be well served.

Contours of Education Governance in America

A striking feature of American governance in nearly all policy areas is federalism—the allocation of constitutional authority across federal and state governments. And nowhere is the impact of federalism more profound than in education. Several of America's international rivals have governments that centrally establish and administer education policy, including the creation of a single national curriculum and testing system. The multilevel and fragmented education governance structure and strong tradition of local control in the United States have made the creation of coherent policy in education much more complicated, both politically and administratively. In fact, saying that the United States has a "system" of education governance overstates the degree of coherence that exists, given the multiple centers of power that influence teacher preparation and licensing, school curriculum, accountability for performance, and budgeting, among other things. In short, education governance in America truly is a "tangled web," as one prior book on the subject has argued.[4]

The lack of coherence in the nation's system of education governance is largely the result of two factors. The first involves ongoing disagreements over the best way to govern the nation's schools to serve both public and private ends. Divergent views exist on whether education should be considered a public good that benefits everyone or a private good that primarily serves individual needs. Such differences of opinion are not surprising in a nation as large and diverse as the United States. These disagreements result in governance proposals that swing from extreme centralization, wherein the federal government would make most consequential decisions about funding and standards, to the most decentralized libertarian-style approaches, in which parents would shop for schools in a market-based system. The present reality and the bulk of proposals for change reside between these two extremes and recognize that education serves both public and private ends. What sort of system can strike the best balance between centralization and decentralization to advance public and private interests? Based on the empirical evidence to date, that question remains unresolved. And so the debates rage on.

The second main factor is that proposals about how to reform governance swirl in the nation's system of federalism and separation of powers (across legislative, executive, and judicial functions) and, if not shot down completely, emerge after leaders strike compromises based on competing plans. No governance proposal exits the process of political debate, legislative logrolling, and rule making in its pure or initially intended form. Ideas from numerous proposals are blended, sometimes with many lumps remaining, and layered onto or mixed with current arrangements. The result is a strange overall governance recipe or Rube Goldberg–like contraption (pick your favorite metaphor) that may barely resemble the initial governance proposals that began the debate. When asked whether this is the best that the country can do, even as the demands of citizenship and global competition become ever more challenging, large majorities say no, even though few clear answers exist about what might work better on a broad scale in a nation as large and diverse as the United States.

The simplest way to begin summarizing the complex web of education governance that has emerged is to note that the United States possesses nearly 100,000 public schools, which are overseen by almost 14,000 school districts, fifty state governments, and one federal government. Looking more deeply at the local, state, and federal layers and outside government at the private and nonprofit actors involved reveals why the system is so complex. Locally, though nearly all school boards are elected, electoral processes vary widely, the basis of representation can depend on whether school board elections are at large or based on wards, and the evidence shows that those procedural and structural choices matter.[5] In addition, a small but growing number of public charter schools exist, amounting to approximately 5 percent of all public schools.[6] Depending on state law, charters may be granted and overseen by a diverse set of institutions, including state universities, local school districts themselves, and, in some cases, mayors' offices.[7] Furthermore, in a very small (but growing) number of cities, and most notably in larger urban areas, the mayor possesses the authority to run the schools. Practically speaking, that power can include the ability to name the superintendent, reorganize the entire system, and implement various strategies to turn around struggling schools.[8]

State institutions that govern education also are numerous and diverse.[9] In addition to governors, state legislatures, and state courts, every state has a state education agency headed by a leader, commonly called the state superintendent or chief state school officer. Those leaders are responsible for administering state and federal policy by providing oversight and guidance to local education authorities, affecting essentially all dimensions of school operations. That latter role of interpreting and helping local districts carry out federal requirements is becoming increasingly important in light of the growing federal interest in education that exists alongside federal dependence on state governments for implementation of national initiatives. Governance of education truly is an intergovernmental endeavor. Depending on the state, the state education chief might be elected by the public at large, appointed by the governor, or appointed by the state board of education. Sometimes governors themselves maintain their own secretaries of education, typically cabinet-level officials who serve as the governor's point person for education inside the administration.

State governments also maintain an array of boards that govern different aspects of education. All states except Minnesota and Wisconsin have multipurpose state education boards. These bodies make policy for an entire state much like school districts do for local communities. Members of state education boards may be elected at large or on a district basis, be appointed by the governor, or attain their seats in other ways. Their duties include making substantive policy in areas such as defining state academic standards, establishing the cut scores that determine how well students must perform on state tests to be deemed proficient, and, in some states, defining requirements of public school teaching certification. Some states possess separate specialized boards, too, which address areas such as higher education, teacher policy, and vocational learning. Twenty-nine states have enacted takeover laws that permit the state to assume direct operational control of a school district or individual school, thereby bypassing the locally elected officials discussed above.

Finally, consider the federal level. Although federal involvement in education has received increasing attention since the No Child Left Behind Act became law in 2002, the federal government has no direct constitutional authority in this area, except in protecting civil and other rights of students. The vast majority of responsibility, money, personnel, and other resources that contribute to schooling in the United States comes from state and local governments; that has been true historically, and it remains true today. Operationally, the federal government gains much of its power in schools when states or local school districts accept federal money, which comes with strings attached that define federal priorities, a practice that the courts have deemed permissible.[10] The federal financial contribution typically totals 8 to 10 percent of what the nation spends on K–12 schooling.

The U.S. Department of Education is the federal agency primarily responsible for managing and administering federal education policy, but other agencies play additional supporting roles, contributing to the network of actors involved. For example, the largest federal program for prekindergarten education, Head Start, is administered by the U.S. Department of Health and Human Services, and the national school lunch program is run by the U.S. Department of Agriculture. The federal education department is a relatively small operation, and its main function is to dispense money and oversee expenditures from several dozen grant programs that attempt to address federal objectives.[11] Additionally, the federal courts have played a consequential role in the nation's schools, in particular on questions relating to educational equity, discrimination, and the personal rights of students in school, such as speech, religious expression, due process, and privacy.

Because education governance involves more than government actors, it is important to consider some of the groups and individuals outside government that also play key roles. Federal, state, and local agencies often employ private contractors, such as companies that develop tests, to help manage and implement policy. Others also exist in the private and nonprofit sectors, such as education management organizations and charter school networks, including large ones like the Knowledge Is Power Program (KIPP) and Green Dot, which run schools across several different districts and states. Technology companies and private foundations have also begun to take an increasingly active role in the operation of local schools, often entering communities as partners with local districts or, in the case of virtual schools, providing students with options that enable them to earn school credits outside traditional geographically bounded school attendance zones and districts. These groups represent a handful of the nongovernmental organizations that play some sort of governing role in American education. Subsequent chapters explore others, as well.

Fragmentation, Confusion, and Dissatisfaction

Owing to this complicated array of institutions, American public schools operate in a complex and challenging environment, with multiple sources of funding and numerous masters who sometimes possess conflicting priorities and demand incongruous results. Federalism has produced dramatic variation across and within each state, while a historical attachment to localism has left superintendents, principals, and elected school board members to make most major decisions about personnel, programming, and budgets. The massive number of school districts nationwide makes it difficult for federal and state officials to provide effective oversight and for local officials to leverage their collective efforts. At the same time, individual school leaders have lost discretionary power in the face of the many mandates from district, state, and federal policymakers. The hierarchical organization of American public schools has often produced a compliance culture that stifles the ability and willingness of school teachers and leaders to improve school practice organically or to faithfully or effectively implement external reforms.

Insiders who work in the diverse institutions that oversee education and outsiders hoping to advance new ideas regularly express frustration with existing arrangements. Local school officials, teachers, and their unions lament the apparent loss of flexibility that has come with accelerating standardization and testing. These groups often favor greater decentralization and control, which they see as a means to more accurately incorporate into schools on-the-ground wisdom and insights and to reflect local values and priorities. State administrators, board members, legislators, and governors struggle to advance their own initiatives while responding to mandates from state courts and the federal government.

Those working outside the traditional system who offer new methods for instructing children, organizing schools, integrating technology, and ushering teachers into the profession are often stymied as they try to implement their initiatives and bring them to scale within the complex web of institutions and rules that govern education. Even where new institutions have emerged that appear to break with prior practices, as with boards that authorize and oversee charter schools or collaborative efforts such as the Common Core State Standards Initiative, which attempts to define more uniform sets of student expectations, many questions remain about whether these arrangements can deliver on their ambitious promises absent broader structural changes in education governance.

In short, while public officials, advocates, and researchers may disagree on how to improve governance, there is considerable consensus that such improvements could help the nation make progress toward achieving its urgent education goals. With such agreement that the nation can—and must—govern education better, the moment is ripe for a comprehensive assessment of the strengths and weaknesses of what remains of the old, what has emerged of the new, and what alternatives to current governing arrangements might produce better education outcomes for children. It is our great hope that the analysis in this book can inform future attempts to adapt the country's nineteenth- and twentieth-century education governance structures to the changed demands of the twenty-first century.

Governance versus Policy

Scholars working around the globe in a diverse range of areas, including social welfare, labor, the environment, and energy, have considered the relationship between governance and policy and how both intersect to influence people's lives.[12] Although this book distinguishes between governance and policy, it is a fuzzy region of overlap rather than a bright line that separates the two. Still, maintaining a working distinction is useful because it clarifies that choices about governance and about policy are not necessarily the same thing. A key conclusion of this book, in fact, turns on that distinction. We hold that a challenge for education reformers is to harmonize governance and policy choices to foster conditions that maximize the opportunities for all students to have rigorous and inspiring experiences in school, experiences that will help enrich their lives and allow them to become adults who contribute to the nation's democracy and economy. To clarify the distinction between governance and policy, we offer the following specific definitions.

Governance refers to the process by which formal institutions and actors wield power and make decisions that influence the conditions under which people live in a society. Those institutions may be representative bodies, such as legislatures, school boards, and the governor's office of a particular state. They also include institutions of government that make rules and implement policies, such as bureaucracies, and others, including courts, that offer judgments about whether certain policies are appropriate, given constitutional and other statutory commitments. It has become increasingly common for the institutions that govern to include private and nonprofit actors working alongside their public (read *government*) counterparts.[13] Frequently, groups outside government are ushered into the system by granting or contract relationships. A common example in education is the use of education management organizations that run public schools in some large cities. The links that connect these various institutions and actors may imply lines of authority, as when one organization employs another to complete some task, or they may imply looser lines of collaboration, communication, or common interest. The former occurs, for example, when the U.S. Department of Education offers grants to state education departments to carry out some federal objective.[14] The latter scenario arises when school districts, law enforcement agencies, and philanthropic groups, including churches and foundations, collaborate on specific projects—sometimes formally, by jointly administering a federal or state grant, but also informally, too—that help young people stay out of trouble and succeed in school.[15]

In contrast to governance, *policy* refers to the array of initiatives, programs, laws, regulations, and rules that the governance system chooses to produce.[16] Policies can be quite broad or narrow. Much social science research and popular discussion have examined the degree to which certain education policy initiatives will improve the nation's schools. Consider these specific policy questions that have received increasing attention during the past decade: Are grant competitions a better way to distribute education funds than traditional formula allocations? Should teachers be evaluated based in part on student performance? If so, how should that performance be measured, and what elements should the evaluation include? Do students need to be tested in all (or many) grade levels for accountability systems to work? Should schools that struggle to perform receive additional funding, be subject to restaffing, or embrace new organizational designs? Should these schools be closed altogether and their students given opportunities to attend school somewhere else? Policies addressing these questions might result from the choices that elected officials working in legislatures and the executive branch of government produce, such as a law like No Child Left Behind that requires all students to take standardized tests in reading and math in grades three through eight. Other policies might emerge in the form of regulations by which government bureaucracies, including local school district offices, state education agencies, and the federal education department, fill in the gaps needed to implement laws or court rulings. Furthermore, in states that allow collective bargaining between teacher unions (a nongovernmental actor) and district school boards (nearly always elected by the public), teacher contracts that emerge from union-board negotiations define numerous policies that dictate how schools and districts will handle personnel and other matters.

One reason the lines between governance and policy discussions can get blurry is that policy choices often have direct governance implications. This can happen when policies fundamentally alter the relationship between institutions and the actors that govern them. For example, some state laws allow for the creation of public charter schools, which operate without the same regulatory and other requirements as traditional public schools. In contrast to the typical school principals described in the opening pages of this chapter, charter school principals generally have much more discretion because they do not work for traditional school districts and are often not bound by the terms of a collectively bargained contract. Another recent example involves state laws that have empowered mayors to run a handful of schools or the entire local school system. Those policy changes have dramatically undercut the historically dominant governance role of school boards and the superintendents those boards hire. State charter laws or laws that provide for mayoral control can substantially alter the array of actors that govern public schools, resulting in new relationships within the governance system.

The chapters in this volume argue that understanding how specific education policies perform requires careful analysis of the broader governing arrangements that influence their content and implementation. In other words, all policies emerge from and reside within systems of governance. Recognizing the distinction is important because it helps to identify the factors that contribute to the most important outcomes in education, namely, how well students do in school and the degree to which school helps prepare students for their adult lives. It could be that the same policy produces much different results in the presence of different governing arrangements. In that case, a policy change would be ill advised, whereas a governance change might improve performance. It also may be that a variety of policies perform quite well regardless of the governance system in place. Helping readers to think through these possible scenarios, and cultivating more careful and nuanced discussions about the relationships between governance and policy, is one of this book's main contributions.

Plan of the Volume

Taken together, the chapters that follow provide a comprehensive overview of the operation and effects of education governance in the United States. The book's approach is comprehensive in that the numerous diverse institutions and actors involved receive detailed attention, which contrasts with much work on governance that tends to focus on a relatively narrower set of players or topics.[17] Although this prior work does illuminate how particular institutions govern, produce education policy, and influence school behavior, its discussion is nevertheless limited because it accounts for only a small number of governing institutions that influence the way the nation's schools operate. Notably, with few exceptions these works also tend to emphasize the role of government actors in education governance while understating the role of nongovernmental groups that are playing increasingly important roles.

These chapters also provide a powerful comparative perspective that other analyses of governance, in education or other policy fields, typically lack. Some of our authors offer comparative perspectives by examining the United States in light of broader concerns about governance and specific reforms in other nations around the world. The analysis includes a comparison of education governance with governance in other sectors such as health care and environmental policy, both of which involve complicated policy networks and often hard-to-measure or relatively long-term outcomes, much like education. An additional comparative perspective our authors bring is the juxtaposition of scholarly writers and those who work more directly in the policy world (including those who have had experience in both). These perspectives serve to check each other, as does the fact that the authors were chosen for their knowledge and expertise, not because they adhere to any unified vision of what governance should look like. Although all chapters in this volume approach the issue of education governance with a healthy skepticism—no author believes that prevailing arrangements are perfect, and several believe it is downright dysfunctional—the contributors come at the issue from a wide variety of professional and ideological perspectives; readers will find no groupthink in the ensuing pages.

The book is organized into four parts. Part 1 sizes up the education governance problem as it presently exists in the United States. What are the shortcomings of the current system? How might they affect students and the schools they attend? In chapter 2, Chester Finn and Michael Petrilli of the Thomas B. Fordham Institute begin the discussion with a forceful critique of the present governance system. They take sharp aim at the nation's tradition of local control and the numerous ways it undercuts coherence, excellence, and educational equity.

In chapter 3, the University of Washington's Marguerite Roza tracks the many sources of funds that contribute to the nearly $600 billion K–12 education industry in the United States. Roza notes that local school boards possess much power to spend this money but operate under numerous constraints as they develop and fund the programs that these revenues make possible. A major problem with present patterns of governance for finance, she notes, is the lack of coherent approaches that accurately account for the cost of providing education services to children and the inability of current approaches to adjust revenue and expenditure streams as broader economic conditions change.

Next, in chapter 4, the journalist and *Education Week* writer Michelle Davis examines the challenges confronting public officials who operate within the current system of governance and attempt to adapt policy to meet shifting demands and to leverage new opportunities. As Davis shows, these challenges emerge for leaders across levels of government, in urban and rural settings, and in states that allow and in those that prohibit collective bargaining for teachers. No matter where these potential innovators operate, it seems, systems of governance create a thicket of obstacles that are difficult to navigate.

In chapter 5, Steven Wilson examines similar sets of constraints, but in contrast to Davis's chapter, he considers innovators working outside the system. Wilson, who is the chief executive officer of Ascend Learning, a charter school management organization in New York City, focuses on innovators in three areas: charter schools, nontraditional teacher preparation, and digital learning. He explains that although innovators who have worked outside the traditional lines of education have seen their initiatives gain momentum in recent years, they still struggle amid prevailing education practices that long-standing governance arrangements help to maintain. Yet as word has spread of these disruptive innovations and the educational opportunities they create, public support for the powerful alliance of interest groups that maintains the governance status quo is beginning to erode, a trend that Wilson predicts will continue into the future.

Although patterns of education governance have remained resilient, numerous trends are in motion that have already begun to alter patterns and practices across federal, state, and local governments. The chapters in part 2 examine these traditional institutions that are now in flux. That analysis begins in chapter 6, where Frederick Hess of the American Enterprise Institute and Olivia Meeks of the District of Columbia Public Schools examine some of the tensions between traditional models of local control and alternative models that have been proposed and implemented in some contexts, including mayoral leadership. The chapter pushes beyond assessing these prevailing trends, though, and offers reasons that future changes may produce even more dramatic departures from current practice, including the separation of education governance from local geographic boundaries.

Kathryn McDermott of the University of Massachusetts at Amherst examines state-level dynamics in chapter 7, focusing on emerging models of interstate governance that have the potential to influence how future standards, testing, and accountability policies unfold. The role of networks involving many states and nongovernmental organizations receives much attention here as McDermott analyzes the various state consortiums that have emerged from the Common Core State Standards Initiative. She compares that effort with a smaller one with a longer track record, the New England Common Assessment Program, to describe the current features and likely future paths for interstate governance.

In chapter 8, Kenneth Wong of Brown University examines the evolving federal role and the various education federalisms that this evolution has produced during the past several decades. Wong zeroes in on how initiatives such as No Child Left Behind and Race to the Top have helped move the nation from a "categorical federalism," focused on redistribution of funds, to new phases of "performance-based federalism" that now are designed to promote accountability for improved outcomes and institutional innovation as well as redistribution. The chapter considers how sustainable this new federalism may be as it confronts and tries to alter prevailing approaches to governance.

Jeffrey Henig of Columbia University provides a broad perspective that cuts across levels of government in chapter 9. His analysis examines how presidents, governors, and mayors—what he calls "education executives"—have begun to take on new governing roles in education. An important development fostered by increased executive interest, Henig explains, is the erosion of barriers that have kept education isolated as a special, exceptional, function of government.

The book's field of vision expands in part 3, where authors provide valuable comparative perspectives that help to place American education governance in broader contexts. These comparisons begin in chapter 10, where Sir Michael Barber of Pearson derives lessons for the United States based on his personal experience as an education official in England and as a consultant to numerous countries and organizations around the world. As Barber sees it, the United States and England seek similar ends, such as improved student performance and enhanced equity in outcomes, but he notes how their different governance contexts have led them to pursue these goals in different ways. Still, especially important in both nations (and any nation, really) is the need to cultivate an effective "mediating layer" that helps harmonize the interests of central authorities with the real-time challenges on the ground that teachers, principals, and innovators face each day as they teach and deliver other services to students.

In chapter 11, Sandra Vergari of the State University of New York at Albany offers another comparative perspective in her analysis of education governance in the United States and Canada. Vergari's analysis provides a useful contrast between what she calls national and federal education policy, the former emerging from the collaborative work of subnational governments and the latter the product of assertive central-government action. Her examination shows that provincial education leaders in Canada wield tremendous power compared with national leaders and local officials in Canadian school districts. Strong provincial leadership has produced a relatively coherent approach to schooling across the country that stands in marked contrast to the more fragmented approaches present in the United States.

Chapter 12, written by Michael Mintrom, of Monash University and the Australia and the New Zealand School of Government, and Richard Walley, of the New Zealand Ministry of Education, examines a handful of high-performing nations, relating their governance systems to student outcomes. The chapter shows how different governing institutions and relationships contribute to policy content and student performance. The authors note that the direct links between governance and achievement are weak, yet it is clear that governance approaches, whatever they are, can contribute to success as long as they make education effectiveness their central mission. The chapter derives six broad lessons that have the potential to help reformers connect governance changes to this key goal.

In chapter 13, Barry Rabe of the University of Michigan returns the focus to the United States but continues the comparative approach of part 3 by considering what insights one might draw for education governance by examining health care and environmental policy. Specifically, Rabe describes how two key policies, Medicaid and the Clean Air Act, are governed in the nation's federal system. He also analyzes the implications that governance has had on policy development and health and environmental outcomes, while comparing these developments with education. Rabe sees similarities and differences across these three policy areas, in particular, their complex intergovernmental structures and shared governance arrangements.

Part 4 considers paths forward and offers some specific governance reforms that would break with current practices. Cynthia Brown of the Center for American Progress begins this discussion in chapter 14, where she builds on Roza's earlier analysis of the mechanisms of school funding by demonstrating how these practices undercut equity. Brown argues that the nation should move toward a system that maintains the federal redistributive role while also centralizing the governance of education finance at the state level.

In chapter 15, Paul Hill of the University of Washington proposes a new model of education governance, essentially starting from scratch, that aims to cultivate fresh incentives and opportunities for managers and political overseers of schools. The model retains important yet specific and limited roles for elected officials and simultaneously provides school leaders with more flexibility to govern along with higher performance expectations. The model also attempts to limit the influence of organized interests on school governance while empowering parents and placing them in an even more important role.

In chapter 16, Kenneth Meier, of Texas A&M University and the Cardiff School of Business (U.K.), provides an assessment of the broad theoretical assumptions that the previous chapters have either embraced or implied. He shows that approaches to governance reform depend on how the governance problem is conceptualized. Different theories of the problem can produce divergent proposals grounded in different theories of action. Meier concludes by noting that regardless of the governance path chosen, a constellation of supporting policies, which he advocates, can help make numerous governance reforms more effective. He also emphasizes that regardless of the governance system, success is unlikely to occur if local districts and schools fail to develop and keep talented system- and school-level managers.

Finally, in chapter 17 we identify several lines of agreement and disagreement, and enduring questions that emerge from the diverse perspectives and bodies of evidence that our talented authors have assembled. Ultimately, we conclude that although no perfect or ideal form of education governance exists, anyone interested in improving student opportunities and performance in the United States absolutely must consider the ways in which governance influences how specific programs or policies are carried out. Although it may be difficult to find direct evidence that specific approaches to governance contribute to positive outcomes, it is relatively easy to see how certain approaches, when they encounter specific conditions on the ground, can get in the way and even do harm. The chapters in this book explain why this is true and what the United States might do to better harmonize its system of education governance with those ground-level conditions to achieve the country's stated goals of providing excellent and equitable school experiences for all students while maintaining a system that is transparent to politicians and accountable to the broader public.

Notes

1. On matters such as hiring people to staff the White House, helping to set the nation's budget agenda, and adopting policy initiatives with the stroke of a pen, as when Truman signed Executive Order 9981 that legally ended racial discrimination in the U.S. military, presidents wield much power. For an examination of the reach and limits of executive power in government, see James Q. Wilson, *Bureaucracy: What Government Agencies Do and Why They Do It* (New York: Basic Books, 1989).

2. Although variation in state and local policies gives some principals more power to make these decisions—as in large urban districts in Texas, where they have much power to hire and fire teachers (see chapter 16 in this volume)—the typical American principal operates under the sorts of constraints described here.

3. In their classic work on school choice, for example, John E. Chubb and Terry M. Moe note, "Without being too literal about it, we think reformers would do well to entertain the notion that choice *is* a panacea. . . . [Choice] has the capacity *all by itself* to bring about the kind of transformation that, for years, reformers have been seeking to engineer in myriad other ways" (emphasis in original). Chubb and Moe, *Politics, Markets, and America's Schools* (Brookings Press, 1990), p. 217.

4. Noel Epstein, ed., *Who's in Charge Here? The Tangled Web of School Governance and Policy* (Washington and Denver, Colo.: Brookings Press and Education Commission of the States, 2004), p. 1. See also Frederick M. Wirt and Michael W. Kirst, *The Political Dynamics of American Education*, 4th ed. (Berkeley, Calif.: McCutchan, 2009), and David T. Conley, *Who Governs Our Schools?: Changing Roles and Responsibilities* (Teachers College Press, 2003).

5. Kenneth J. Meier and others, "Structural Choices and Representational Biases: The Post-Election Color of Representation," *American Journal of Political Science* 49, no. 4 (2005): 758–68.

6. National Center for Education Statistics, *Digest of Education Statistics, 2010* (U.S. Department of Education, 2011), table 100.

7. See National Association of Charter School Authorizers, "Authorizer Comparison," 2012 (www.qualitycharters.org).

8. Kenneth K. Wong and others, *The Education Mayor: Improving America's Schools* (Georgetown University Press, 2007).

9. Arnold F. Shober, *Splintered Accountability: State Governance and Education Reform* (State University of New York Press, 2010); Wirt and Kirst, *The Political Dynamics of American Education*.

10. James E. Ryan, "The Tenth Amendment and Other Paper Tigers: The Legal Boundaries of Education Governance," in *Who's in Charge Here?* edited by Epstein, pp. 42–74.

11. Patrick J. McGuinn, *No Child Left Behind and the Transformation of Federal Education Policy, 1965–2005* (University Press of Kansas, 2006).

12. Barry Rabe, ed., *Greenhouse Governance: Addressing Climate Change in America* (Brookings Press, 2010); Carolyn J. Heinrich and Laurence E. Lynn, eds., *Governance and Performance: New Perspectives* (Georgetown University Press, 2000); Kenneth J. Meier and Laurence J. O'Toole, *Bureaucracy in a Democratic State: A Governance Perspective* (Johns Hopkins University Press, 2006); Simona Piattoni, *The Theory of Multi-Level Governance: Conceptual, Empirical, and Normative Challenges* (Oxford University Press, 2010).

13. Lester M. Salamon, ed., *The Tools of Government* (Oxford University Press, 2000); Meier and O'Toole, *Bureaucracy in a Democratic State*.

14. The classic statement on this sort of relationship is Martha Derthick, *The Influence of Federal Grants* (Harvard University Press, 1970). A recent example in education is Paul Manna, *Collision Course: Federal Education Policy Meets State and Local Realities* (Washington: CQ Press, 2011).

15. Robert Agranoff, *Managing within Networks: Adding Value to Public Organizations* (Georgetown University Press, 2007).

16. One could also add the nuance that policies are also suggested by the absence of these laws, initiatives, and programs. Scholars of agenda setting have noted that choosing

to ignore an issue or a potential topic of concern also implies a set of policy priorities (for example, "Our policy in area X is that we have no policy"). See, for example, Frank R. Baumgartner and Bryan D. Jones, *Agendas and Instability in American Politics* (University of Chicago Press, 1993); John W. Kingdon, *Agendas, Alternatives, and Public Policies* (HarperCollins, 1984).

17. Examples include William G. Howell, ed., *Besieged: School Boards and the Future of American Politics* (Brookings Press, 2005); Jeffrey R. Henig and Wilbur C. Rich, eds., *Mayors in the Middle: Politics, Race, and Mayoral Control of Urban Schools* (Princeton University Press, 2004); Eric A. Hanushek and Alfred A. Lindseth, *Schoolhouses, Courthouses, and Statehouses: Solving the Funding-Achievement Puzzle in America's Public Schools* (Princeton University Press, 2009); Patrick J. McGuinn, *No Child Left Behind and the Transformation of Federal Education Policy, 1965–2005* (University Press of Kansas, 2006); and Paul Manna, *School's In: Federalism and the National Education Agenda* (Georgetown University Press, 2006); Shober, *Splintered Accountability*. Exceptions include Wirt and Kirst, *The Political Dynamics of American Education*; Conley, *Who Governs Our Schools?*; and Epstein, *Who's in Charge Here?*

PART I

The Problem

CHESTER E. FINN JR. *and* MICHAEL J. PETRILLI

2

The Failures of U.S. Education Governance Today

To anyone concerned with the state of America's schools, one of the more alarming experiences of the past few decades has been seeing waves of important reforms and promising innovations crash on the rocks of failure. Charter schools have popped up all over the landscape; vouchers are being implemented in more and more places; massive federal initiatives like No Child Left Behind and Race to the Top have invested billions of dollars in fixing our schools. Yet America's student achievement results remain dismal, especially at the twelfth-grade level. Millions of children still cannot read satisfactorily, do math at an acceptable level, or perform other skills needed to obtain jobs in the modern world economy.[1]

Why this persistent failure? One major cause is our flawed, archaic, and inefficient system for organizing and operating public schools. Our current approach to school management is a Rube Goldberg-esque construct, sometimes compared to a marble cake, involving multiple, overlapping layers: the federal government, the states, and local school districts, each with ill-defined responsibilities and often conflicting interests.[2] As a result, over the past fifty years, obsolescence, clumsiness, and misalignment have come to define the governance of public education. This development is not, in itself, anyone's fault. It is simply what happens when opportunities and needs change but structures do not. The system of schooling we have today is the legacy of the nineteenth century, and it is hopelessly outmoded in the twenty-first.

Perhaps the foremost failing of that system is its fragmented and multipolar decisionmaking; there are too many cooks in the education kitchen, and nobody is really in charge. We bow to the mantra of local control, yet in fact, nearly every major decision affecting the education of our children is shaped (and misshaped) by at least four separate levels of governance: Washington, the state capital, the local district, and the individual school building itself.[3] And that is without even considering intermediate units (such as the regional education service centers seen in Texas, New York, Ohio, and elsewhere), the courts (which exert enormous influence on our schools), parents and guardians, or the degree to which all of these parties' decisions influence the nature and quality of a child's schooling.

Such fragmented governance does confer a measure of stability on the system, but it is the stability of inertia and gridlock, whereby dozens of interest groups, influencers, and decisionmakers can block change and in which forging the kind of coalition or consensus that might facilitate it is exceptionally difficult. This would be reasonable if the opportunity, productivity, and efficacy of our education system were satisfactory, but at a time when the demand for reform and improvement and equity and greater effectiveness is heard from so many quarters, education stability through inertia and fragmentation is not good for our children or our nation. Those who disagree with this analysis will invoke democracy in defense of the present arrangement, will assert that different communities have different education priorities, will argue that Americans, by and large, have the schools they want (or, perhaps, deserve), and will cite poll data indicating that most parents are satisfied with their own children's schools.[4]

No one's commitment to democracy trumps the authors'. But when it yields an education system that pays greater deference to the desires and interests of its employees, vendors, and other adult beneficiaries than to those of the families and communities it serves, it is a shabby form of democracy, indeed—and one that cries out for serious makeover.

Democracy creates obstacles to smart policy in other domains, too. Take, for example, the need to close superfluous military bases in recent years. The normal legislative process provided too many opportunities for members of Congress to maintain unneeded bases in their own districts,[5] so thoughtful people figured out a new approach—the base-closing commission—to solve this particular problem. That commission did not spell the end of democracy, but it did provide an alternative route to the common good. Such an alternative is needed in education.

Considering the extent to which our method of school governance is responsible for what ails American education today, it has received surprisingly little attention. Efforts to address the problem elicit either boredom—governance is not sexy, like extended learning time, last-in first-out, merit pay, and vouchers—or eye rolling, as many argue that even if the structure and governance of our K–12 system pose problems, trying to fix them is politically futile and therefore not worth spending much time on. Yet to fail to confront these malfunctions in the governance of public education is to accept the glum fact that even the most urgent and earnest of other reform efforts cannot make a dent in America's achievement deficit, produce quality alternatives to the traditional monopoly, or defeat the adult interests that benefit from that monopoly.

We cannot afford such complacency. Only by seeking to understand how we came to operate schools in such a haphazard way, what particular ills face our governance structures now, and how they might be reformed in the years ahead can we restore sanity and efficiency to America's public schools. We begin at the district level—the first layer of this misshapen cake.

Whence the School District?

America's unique brand of education localism dates to the nineteenth century and even earlier, when individual towns and families paid essentially all the costs of operating whatever schools they had. Indeed, education in the early days was entirely a local affair, and so quite varied. Some towns had schools, others did not; some paid for them with taxes, others with bushels of wheat, church tithes, or tuition charges levied on parents. Just as individual communities decided whether and how to operate schools, so did individual families determine which, if any, of their sons and daughters would attend school (and for how long). Children who were poor ordinarily got little or no schooling unless someone took pity on them and paid for their education.[6]

This started to change in the mid-nineteenth century, when states began requiring children to attend school, at least for a few primary grades. Massachusetts led the way in 1852, and New York followed a year later. By 1918, every state had some sort of compulsory-attendance law on the books. With such requirements came an obligation on the state's part to ensure that schools were available so that these requirements could be fulfilled; this drew states into both the financing and governance of primary and, in time, secondary education.[7]

The strongest imprint on today's school governance structures, however, may have been left by the Progressive Era—when it was deemed important to keep politics out of education so as to avoid the taint of patronage and party. According to the prevailing wisdom of the day, it was better to entrust the supervision of public education to expert professionals and independent, nonpartisan boards that would attract disinterested community leaders to tend to this vital civic function. The mayor and aldermen were to be kept at bay, lest public education become entwined with other government functions and agencies and thus become contaminated by politics and cronyism. (Indeed, this was a reasonable concern at the time.)

At the state level, too, the governance structures devised for education were meant to serve as a buffer from conventional politics. Most states established their own boards of education, some with members appointed by the governor to fixed terms, others elected. Each of these boards then hired a commissioner or superintendent of education, ordinarily a career professional, to head the education department—a state agency, to be sure, but seldom part of the governor's cabinet and rarely subject to his direct control. This meant that governors had minimal or nonexistent roles in education—even though it would eventually become among the biggest ticket items in a state's budget.

A few of these state-level structures predated the Progressives. For instance, the New York Board of Regents—whose members were (and still are) appointed by the legislature—was launched in 1784 (though its original mandate was just higher education). Massachusetts created its state board of education—focused on primary and secondary schooling—in 1837, a response to Governor Edward Everett's admonition to lawmakers that, though locally operated "common" schools were all well and good,

> the school houses might, in many cases, be rendered more commodious. Provision ought to be made for affording the advantages of education, throughout the whole year, to all of a proper age to receive it. Teachers well qualified to give elementary instruction in all the branches of useful knowledge, should be employed; and small school libraries, maps, globes, and requisite scientific apparatus should be furnished. I submit to the Legislature, whether the creation of a board of commissioners of schools, to serve without salary, with authority to appoint a secretary, on a reasonable compensation, to be paid from the school fund, would not be of great utility.[8]

The very first secretary of that board of commissioners was Horace Mann, often called the father of public education in the United States and, arguably, the first great centralizer of control over that education and the first eminent invader of its local control.

In the years that followed, as state constitutions were written and rewritten, they included provisions that explicitly tasked the states with responsibility for educating their own citizens. The wording of these clauses varies considerably; typical examples are Ohio's charge to its legislature to "secure a thorough and efficient system of common schools throughout the state" and Texas's assignment to its lawmakers to "establish and make suitable provision for the support and maintenance of an efficient system of public free schools." Whatever the phrasing, every state constitution now includes some provision to this effect.[9]

But though states bear formal responsibility for public education, all save Hawaii have opted to deliver schooling through local education agencies (LEAs), or school districts. The states did, however, retain direct control of teacher credentialing, ostensibly seeking to value professionalism and uniformity in this field over the patronage and unevenness of qualifications that they supposed would take over at the local level. Today, one can readily see how that retention of control acts as a severe constraint on local schools' decisionmaking.

The states did not create LEAs from scratch: They inherited them from the earlier era of community-based, locally financed education. And their configurations vary as greatly as do our communities. In some states, they coincide with counties; in others, they are coterminous with cities or townships. Rarely, however, are LEAs actually governed directly by these political entities.

Because of this history, and due in part to differences among states, LEAs vary greatly in size and number. Today, Illinois has 870 of them, Maryland just twenty-four. The agencies have also been shaped by decades of consolidation. In 1930, for instance, the United States contained a staggering 130,000 LEAs, many responsible for just one school each. Today, we have only one-tenth that number: 13,629 LEAs in 2009–10, responsible for 98,917 schools. This would suggest that, on average, each district in America is responsible for seven schools. But any such average is deeply deceptive, as some school systems (mostly in large cities) enroll more than 200,000 students each, while about half of America's LEAs educate fewer than 1,000 students apiece.[10]

Save for charter schools, a few specialized schools run directly by states, and federally operated schools for military children and Native Americans, LEAs administer America's public schools. They do so through a central office presided over by a superintendent—almost always a career educator—and his or her staff, which usually functions as a typical public sector bureaucracy with one unit in charge of transportation, another responsible for personnel, and so on. Except in the handful of cities where the superintendent reports to the mayor, or those in which the mayor appoints the governing board, the LEA's administrative team is answerable to an elected board of education or school committee. Typically, these school boards consist of seven or nine members; there are some 90,000 such officials nationwide.

The powers of these boards vary from place to place. Part of this variation stems from the fact that some states are more prescriptive than others when it comes to public education; it is also the result of differing approaches to raising revenue. School boards in some jurisdictions have their own authority to levy taxes, though more often school budgets and the local taxes that support them are subject to approval either by other local bodies—such as city councils and county supervisors—or by voters in a referendum.

Because today's LEA and school board structures arose organically from eighteenth- and nineteenth-century arrangements—and because these entities are thoroughly familiar and ubiquitous—their usefulness is rarely questioned. We hardly ever bother to ask how well this system is working, much less whether children, taxpayers, and the cause of American competitiveness might be better served by a different setup (and on the rare occasion when scholars do, the answers are grim).[11] We just take for granted that this is how public education works.

Structural Roadblocks

Such complacency is deeply harmful. Today, this system produces ever more failure; indeed, it is telling that America's education agenda has shifted from running schools to reforming them. And in the course of that historic shift, the customary governance structures emerge as major obstacles. On reflection, however, it should hardly be surprising that governing bodies that produced the current dysfunction are none too eager—or competent—when the time comes to make significant changes.

Examples of how current school governance structures hinder reform abound. Consider, for instance, the emerging practice of digital learning. Information and communications technologies are transforming the development and delivery of education; already, scores of online schools have opened—some as charters, some operated as franchises of national for-profit firms, some (such as the Florida Virtual School) run as integral parts of the state education system. The biggest of these schools operate throughout the states in which they are located—but they could just as easily be operated interstate or nationwide. After all, political borders do not constrain the delivery of online courses into children's homes, day care centers, churches, or brick-and-mortar schools.

But which government should write the ground rules for cyberschooling and hold its vendors to account for their results? Who would set distance learning's academic requirements and assessments? Who would pay for kids to attend them or—in an even more complicated scenario—to take separate courses from several of them, to assemble a curriculum tailored to each student? Districts? States? The federal government? Encumbered by the old LEA model and its geographically bounded jurisdictions, we have no governance mechanism well suited to answering these questions. Thus the potential for distance learning as an alternative to underperforming schools remains barely tapped, and its financing and rule making remain absurdly complicated.[12]

Consider also the challenges of teacher preparation. Today, teachers are certified by states, but districts and individual charter schools employ them. Washington, meantime, superimposes rules of its own—federal law requires a "highly qualified" teacher in every classroom—while national nonprofits like Teach for America circumvent some of these restrictions and recruit and place instructors all over the country. Graduates of our roughly 1,200 teacher-training programs move around, too—but the state in which each program is located sets its own curriculum, meaning that graduates of such programs may not in fact be fully prepared for the teaching jobs they will ultimately hold. (The adoption of the Common Core standards by forty-six states plus the District of Columbia may change that.) Further confusing matters is the fact that many of these programs are accredited by a national organization (the National Council for Accreditation of Teacher Education)—but some opt for other accreditors or get by with none at all. Added to this are the new complexities of virtual teacher preparation programs, such as those operating under the aegis of the University of Southern California or Kaplan University (a for-profit enterprise). Because of our patchwork governance system, there is little uniformity in teacher preparation, dubious quality control, and limited portability of credentials and skills.[13]

We know that the effectiveness of those teachers matters hugely in student learning, and we also know that it varies enormously from classroom to classroom. A child-centered education system would take for granted that those leading schools have the authority, as well as the responsibility, to maximize the number of highly effective instructors within their walls and minimize the number of duds. Yet tenure laws, last-in first-out provisions, and union contracts—which are also, in effect, part of the governance system—block school principals from replacing duds with superstars while conferring job security on individuals whose presence in the building is bad for kids.

Another example is school finance. Several promising reform proposals focus on how schools are funded—such as those aiming to force accountability and improve incentives by tying dollars to students and then allowing the money to go where the students go. But complicating such proposals is the fact that school funding today is sorely tangled. Nationwide, state taxes generate about 47 cents of the public school dollar, local taxes (mostly levied on property) yield about 43 cents, and Uncle Sam kicks in the remaining dime.[14] This distribution varies greatly, however; there are places where the state portion barely reaches one-third (such as in Florida, Missouri, Nebraska, and South Dakota), while other states (like New Mexico, Vermont, and Hawaii) cover more than 70 percent. These amounts vary even more widely within states. The public schools of Beachwood, Ohio, spend about $20,000 per pupil; seventy miles down the highway, the Strasburg schools spend less than half as much. Despite round after round of equity lawsuits (many of them successful)—as well as the supposed cushion provided by statewide "foundation funding" levels—the financing of schools across the country is woefully uneven and confused.[15] None of this should be surprising in a system in which local school district boundaries are often demarcated along major socioeconomic and ethnic divides.

Current governance structures also pose an obstacle to charter schooling. These independently operated public schools are meant to provide alternatives to district schools and in most places are designed to function as their competitors—giving choices to families, offering an escape hatch to kids trapped in dreadful schools, and creating at least a partial marketplace within what has long been a near monopoly. In fact, making every school a charter school is one possible remedy for the governance problems that now burden us.[16] Yet more than half of America's charter schools owe their very licenses to operate to the school systems they are supposed to compete with. In most states, would-be charter operators have nowhere else to turn for such licenses. Unsurprisingly, most school district bureaucracies abhor these upstart rivals; using their power and influence over local and state politicians, they do all they can to contain the growth of charters and, where possible, to eradicate them.

Even the signature education reform effort of the past two decades—the imposition of rigorous academic standards and accountability for meeting them—has been stymied by our dysfunctional approach to school governance.[17] This structure makes it almost impossible to address the question of what happens to school districts that fail to meet statewide standards and the further challenge of especially bad schools—dropout factories that fail completely in their most basic mission. After all, who is responsible for fixing them? The federal government? States? Districts—the selfsame districts that allowed these schools to fail in the first place, sometimes year after year? What reason is there to believe that these districts would move, or would know how, to set things right?

Given these obstacles, it is no accident that all the major education reforms of the past quarter century have come from outside the traditional school governance structures. Whether one looks at the development of academic standards, the imposition of testing-and-accountability regimes, the spread of school choice in its many variants, innovations in teacher preparation, or major changes in how teachers are evaluated and compensated, the impetus almost never originates with state or local boards of education or the people who work for them. Rather, such initiatives have come from governors and business leaders, from mayors and national commissions, from private foundations, and even from the White House. Although it may seem odd to describe such influentials as outside school governance, in reality the separate reporting-and-control structures of public education mean that mayors and governors and such are given remarkably little say over what happens within it—unless they take extraordinary action to gain greater influence.[18]

The Implementation Conundrum

Ardent outsiders can catalyze all manner of reforms, but putting those reforms into practice—and bringing them to scale—generally depends on the traditional management structure of public education. Such is the nature of the system. For it is those enduring structures that write the detailed regulations, manage the money, run the schools, and employ the people who work in them. And that is where any reform momentum slows to a creep. The traditional structure is typically lethargic, bureaucratic, and set in its ways; while people within it may have experience managing schools and complying with the rules they write, seldom do they have the capacity to innovate, to make judgments about matters beyond their customary duties, or to stage successful interventions in failing districts, schools, or classrooms. (This is true for most public sector bureaucracies, shielded as they are from market forces and encouraged as they are to avoid risking public embarrassments.)

Moreover, many of these people fiercely oppose the policies they are being asked—by "outsiders"—to implement.[19] It thus seems that, regardless of the innovative solutions emerging from foundations and think tanks—and no matter how many promising policies are propagated from Washington and state capitals—our current approach to governing schools will remain an all but insurmountable roadblock to the possibility of reform actually occurring with integrity, speed, and thoroughness.

By what right do we, the authors, take it on ourselves to identify the reforms that the system needs? Yes, it is immodest, maybe even arrogant, and one could again respond that America's democratic institutions have produced the kind of education system that the citizenry wants. Perhaps so. But that is an argument that can be made about many spheres of contemporary public policy that are working poorly.[20] One can say, if one wants to exonerate the status quo, that the current gridlocked circumstance, for all its costs and failings, is the price of democracy. But one could also say that it is the product of governmental structures and political influence networks that have lost track entirely of the common weal and now operate mainly to serve the interests of their own constituents and influentials. That is our view of public education in 2012. One need not endorse our particular reform agenda, but one must contemplate the possibility that any changes of any significance will founder on the same structural shoals.

Adults versus Change

These traditional structures are not just stolid and change averse. Over the decades, they have been organized, shaped, infiltrated, and manipulated so that they now exist principally to serve the material interests of adults. Many of these adult interest groups derive enormous benefit from the status quo and are thus fiercely opposed to changes that disrupt it.

Teacher unions head the list of such organizations but by no means complete it. School custodians, too, have unions. So do school principals. Although one might expect these educators to be classified as management, contracts in cities such as Providence, Las Vegas, and Baltimore clearly treat principals as employees allowed to organize. And behind the unions are queued more rent seekers: textbook publishers, tutoring firms, uniform manufacturers, bus companies, food service and building security businesses, as well as all manner of data-processing, information technology, and communications outfits, most of which hold longstanding contracts with public school systems. Colleges of education, local universities, and civil rights organizations also have stakes in how those systems work, whom they employ, and where they obtain guidance and expertise.

What gives these adult interests traction? Often it is habit, bureaucratic routine, multiyear contracts, and regulatory regimes that limit the options from which LEAs can select, thereby reducing the threat of competition. But political clout matters enormously, too. The unions generally accumulate such clout by helping union-friendly candidates get elected to school boards, a feat made easier in the many jurisdictions where such elections are nonpartisan, often uncontested, and conducted on random dates that do not coincide with other elections and thus draw few voters.[21] In such circumstances, any organized interest group that can mobilize its members and supporters has an excellent chance of prevailing at the polls. Time after time, we have seen examples—in Los Angeles, San Diego, and elsewhere—of unions mustering their members and their allies to ensure the electoral defeat of board members and superintendents who pressed aggressively for reforms the groups find objectionable. Even where the reformers have secured the votes to safeguard their slate of board members through another election or two, they are all but certain to lose the war eventually. The reformers will weary, leave town, grow old, or turn to other matters, whereas the union will always be there, ready to seize the first opportunity to restore the status quo ante.

Much the same thing happens at the state level. Through the use of savvy candidate recruitment, campaign contributions, shoe leather, publicity, and voter mobilization, it is often possible for unions to sway key legislative elections. This king-making power then intimidates both incumbent and aspiring lawmakers, steering them toward policies the unions favor. The unions frequently fend off, defeat, or marginalize those who defy their interests. Although most recipients of such help are Democrats, in jurisdictions where Republicans wield long-term influence in the state house, the unions have found ways to befriend—or defang—some of their customary opponents, too.

Still, state-level politics remains more difficult to influence. Those elections generally are contested, partisan, and held on regular election days, when voter turnout is strong. Concerned business leaders, taxpayer groups, and new, reform-oriented advocacy organizations can serve as counterweights to union influence. But at the local level, employee interest groups reign supreme. And nowhere is this truer than in America's big school systems, including (but not limited to) much of urban America.

Our cities (and many large suburban and countywide districts, as well) are demographically and economically heterogeneous, containing multiple communities and groups with conflicting priorities, needs, and dreams—especially when it comes to the education of children. And a large proportion of the nation's children are educated in such school systems: 35 percent of American students are enrolled in the 281 districts that have 25,000 or more pupils, and a majority of all students (54 percent)—including the overwhelming majority of poor and minority students—are accounted for by fewer than 900 districts.[22] This means that about 7,000 individual school board members are responsible for the education of more than half the country's children.

In far too many of these communities today, there is only mockery of the Progressive ideal that school board members will focus on the welfare of children and community, free of the stain of politics, and able to rise above party and patronage to advance the public interest.[23] In far too many places, well-educated, civic-minded, and reasonably prosperous people find district-level politics daunting and painful. Many have foresworn the public school system itself, moving to smaller districts, enrolling their children in private or charter schools, or busying themselves with other kinds of community service—service that is less onerous and more likely to result in gratitude than in hostility.

Particularly in large districts, school board service has grown demanding—according to 70 percent of the board members in such districts, it consumes more than twenty-five hours a month—and is poorly compensated. Although a slight majority of large American school systems pay board members a stipend, few stipends exceed $10,000 a year. Serving on such boards can also bring unpleasantness: long, boring evenings listening to public testimony; onerous (and costly) election campaigns; the risk of name-calling, picketing, and racial acrimony; painful responsibilities such as deciding whether to close and "reconstitute" neighborhood schools; and agendas that are laden with micromanagerial issues and short on decisions about fundamental policy and direction. Even if a school board member feels that fundamental policy needs to be addressed, he or she most likely knows that to make waves is to risk being booted out of office.[24]

Under these circumstances, who would want to serve on a school board? A look at many big-district boards provides the answer: aspiring politicians, union puppets, individuals with some cause or scheme they yearn to inflict on everyone's children, and former employees of the system with scores to settle. As a result, able, well-meaning, even reform-minded superintendents with commendable plans to improve their schools are often undermined or overruled by their own board members. Is it any wonder that the average tenure of urban superintendents is just 3.6 years?[25] This frequent turnover exacerbates yet another challenge to school reform: the tendency of any bureaucratic system to wait out the latest attempt to fix it, mindful that in a year or two that plan's author will have moved on and life will then revert to the old modus vivendi or that yet another reform notion will be tried, only to prove similarly short lived.[26]

Even when there is a decent board and competent superintendent, the ability to alter the system in any meaningful way is limited. The neediest youngsters quite likely require additional help from other agencies that answer to the mayor or city manager, not to the school system. Preschools, if there are any, answer to their own organizations or shareholders. The state—or, now, a multistate consortium—decides what the academic standards will be, what assessments will be used, and what makes for an acceptable level of achievement. The state also decides who gets licensed to lead or teach in its public schools, meaning that colleges of education feel scant obligation to tailor their offerings or prepare their graduates for work in a locally reformed system.

Too Many Cooks, Too Many Kitchens

Despite America's romantic attachment to local control, the reality is that the way it works today represents the worst of both worlds. On one hand, district-level power constrains individual schools; its standardizing, bureaucratic, and political force ties the hands of principals, keeping them from doing what is best for their pupils with regard to budget, staffing, and curriculum. On the other, local control is not strong enough to clear the obstacles that state and federal governments place before reform-minded board members and superintendents in the relatively few situations where these can even be observed.

Sure, remarkable individuals can sometimes make it work, at least for a while: Michelle Rhee (backed by Adrian Fenty) in the District of Columbia, Joel Klein (backed by Michael Bloomberg) in New York, Arne Duncan (backed by Richard Daley) in Chicago, and Jerry Weast (abetted by a rising budget) in Montgomery County, Maryland, stand out. Readers can surely cite additional examples. But these are the exceptions that prove the rule. The rule is that education policy decisions are made in so many places, each with some capacity to initiate change but with even greater capacity to block it, that there is really nobody in charge.

Some describe education governance in the United States as a marble cake (because the jurisdictions and zones of control of different governments and agencies are so jumbled). Still others favor the image of a loosely coupled train, where movement at one end does not necessarily produce any motion at the other. We find a more apt analogy in a vast restaurant or food court with multiple kitchens, each thronged with many cooks yet with no head chef in command of even a single kitchen, much less the entire enterprise.

Consider so seemingly straightforward a decision as which person will be employed to fill a seventh-grade teacher opening at the Lincoln School, located in, let us say, Metropolis, West Carolina. One might suppose that Lincoln's principal, or perhaps the top instructional staff at that school, should decide which candidate is the most likely to succeed in that particular classroom. But under the typical circumstance, the most the principal might be able to do is reject wholly unsuitable candidates. (And often not that, considering seniority and "bumping rights" within the district, its collective-bargaining contract, and, frequently, state law.) The superintendent's human resources office does most of the vetting and placing, but it is shackled by the contract, by West Carolina's inflexible licensure practices (which may be set by an "independent"—and probably union- and education school–dominated—professional standards board), by seniority rules that are probably enshrined in both contract and state law, and by uniform salary schedules that mean the new teacher (assuming similar credentials) will be paid the same fixed amount whether the subject most needed at Lincoln is math or physical education.

Washington gets into the act, too, with "highly qualified teacher" requirements that constrain individual schools. By the end of the process, at least a dozen different governing units impede the principal's authority to staff his or her school with the ablest (and best suited) teachers available.

Teacher selection is but one of many examples of the "too many cooks" problem. Much the same litany can be invoked for special education, for the budgeting and control of a school's funds, and for approved approaches to school discipline. (Not to mention a more literal "too many cooks" issue: what to serve for lunch in the school cafeteria.)

What great leader or change agent would want to become a school principal under these circumstances? Or a local superintendent? Or even a teacher? Well, maybe in a comfy (and probably smug) suburban setting; but not in the places that most need outstanding talent.

American education does not need czars or dictators. Separation of powers and systems of checks and balances are important elements of our democracy. Children and communities do differ, and there needs to be flexibility in the system to adapt and adjust to singular circumstances, changing priorities, and dissimilar needs. But today, our public education system lacks flexibility and nimbleness of all sorts. Surely that is not the education the creators of universal public schooling had in mind. And it is most definitely not what our children need at this point in the nation's history.

Notes

1. U.S. Department of Education, "The Nation's Report Card: Findings in Brief," November 2011 (http://nces.ed.gov/nationsreportcard/pdf/main2011/2012459.pdf).

2. Noel Epstein, ed., *Who's in Charge Here? The Tangled Web of School Governance and Policy* (Denver, Colo.: Education Commission of the States, 2004).

3. There are, of course, exceptions, such as Hawaii, which operates a single statewide school system, and charter schools that answer to authorities other than local districts.

4. Phi Delta Kappa International, "Highlights of the 2011 Phi Delta Kappa/Gallup Poll," September 2011 (www.pdkintl.org/poll/media/PDK-Poll-Report-2011.pdf).

5. R. Douglas Arnold, *The Logic of Congressional Action* (Yale University Press, 1990).

6. Lawrence Cremin, *American Education: The National Experience* (New York: Harper Collins, 1980); Carol Kaestle, *Pillars of the Republic: Common Schools and American Society, 1780–1860* (New York: Hill and Wang, 1983); Michael Katz, *Reconstructing American Education* (Harvard University Press, 1987), pp. 24–57.

7. National Center for Education Statistics, *Digest of Education Statistics, 2003* (U.S. Department of Education, 2004).

8. Massachusetts General Court records for 1837, Senate no. 1, p. 17, in Chester E. Finn Jr. "How to Run Public Schools in the 21st Century," *Defining Ideas*, June 22, 2001 (www.hoover.org/publications/defining-ideas/article/83137).

9. See Ohio Constitution, art. 6, sec. 2, "School Funds" (www.legislature.state.oh.us/constitution.cfm?Part=6&ExpandSections=Yes), and Texas Constitution, art. 7, sec. 1, "Support and Maintenance of System of Public Free Schools" (www.statutes.legis.state.tx.us/Docs/CN/htm/CN.7.htm).

10. U.S. Department of Education, "Numbers and Types of Public Elementary and Secondary Local Education Agencies from the Common Core of Data: School Year 2009–10," May 2011 (http://nces.ed.gov/pubs2011/2011346.pdf) and U.S. Department of Education, "Numbers and Types of Public Elementary and Secondary Schools from the Common Core of Data: School Year 2009–10," April 2011 (http://nces.ed.gov/pubs2011/2011345.pdf).

11. William G. Howell, ed., *Besieged: School Boards and the Future of Education Politics* (Brookings Press, 2005).

12. Terry M. Moe and John E. Chubb, *Liberating Learning: Technology, Politics, and the Future of American Education* (San Francisco: Jossey-Bass, 2009).

13. Dan Goldhaber and Jane Hannaway, eds., *Creating a New Teaching Profession* (Washington: Urban Institute Press, 2009).

14. U.S. Department of Commerce, "Public Education Finances: 2009," May 2011 (www2.census.gov/govs/school/09f33pub.pdf).

15. Eric A. Hanushek and Alfred A Lindseth, *Schoolhouses, Courthouses, and State-houses: Solving the Funding-Achievement Puzzle in America's Public Schools* (Princeton University Press, 2009). These issues are explained in greater detail in chapters 3 and 14 of this volume.

16. Also see chapter 15, this volume.

17. Paul Manna, *Collision Course: Federal Education Policy Meets State and Local Realities* (Washington: CQ Press, 2011).

18. Some are starting to push for this power; see chapter 9 in this volume.

19. Not that individual capacity and drive to innovate would necessarily be enough; the agents expected to implement reforms often face crosscutting legislated policies that hamstring any effort to change the status quo, as Michelle Davis notes in chapter 4 of this volume.

20. Consider, for example, health care financing, immigration, the condition of our infrastructure, the federal deficit, and the tax code.

21. Terry M. Moe, *Special Interest: Teachers Unions and America's Public Schools* (Brookings Press, 2011).

22. Information collected from the U.S. Department of Education's National Center for Education Statistics.

23. Chester E. Finn Jr., "The End of the Education Debate," *National Affairs* (Winter 2010) (www.nationalaffairs.com/publications/detail/the-end-of-the-education-debate); Thomas Toch, "Who Rules," *Wilson Quarterly* (Autumn 2011) (www.wilsonquarterly.com/article.cfm?aid=2013).

24. Frederick M. Hess and Olivia Meeks, *Governance in the Accountability Era* (Alexandria, Va.: National School Boards Association, 2010).

25. Council of the Great City Schools, "Urban School Superintendents: Characteristics, Tenure, and Salary," Fall 2010 (www.cgcs.org/cms/lib/DC00001581/Centricity/Domain/4/Supt_Survey2010.pdf).

26. Frederick M. Hess, *Spinning Wheels: The Politics of Urban School Reform* (Brookings Press, 1998).

MARGUERITE ROZA

3

How Current Education Governance Distorts Financial Decisionmaking

By any terms, public K–12 education is a sizable operation. The $584 billion U.S. public elementary and secondary system takes in more money than even the largest U.S. corporations—more than ExxonMobil, Fannie Mae, AIG, or Hewlett Packard. Its 6 million–member workforce is four times the size of total active military personnel. Funds for public education come in from different sources, the largest share generated by states (48 percent) and then by local revenues (44 percent), and the smallest (8 percent) from federal allocations. Unlike any of the companies or federally controlled operations (like the military), public education is a vastly decentralized operation without a single leader at the helm who can serve as a spokesperson for its resource decisions.

So who decides how to spend all this money? On the face of it, school boards do. Each district's school board has responsibility for adopting and approving a budget that includes all funds (even those generated at different governmental levels) and that, when taken as a whole, sets the plan for accomplishing the financial goals of the local school district. School district budgets are no trivial matter, in large part because a school district's use of resources is an expression of the implicit strategy at hand, whether the school board members recognize it or not.

There are nearly 14,000 school boards in the country, each with some five to nine board members, totaling approximately 90,000 board members. District budgets vary dramatically in size, but in illustration of their scale, the average school board decides how to spend roughly $50 million in public education funds, and the median student is served in a district where the board controls just over $100 million.[1] In the largest districts, the budgets top out in the billions, with a $4.8 billion school district budget in Chicago and a $9 billion budget for the school district in Los Angeles.

For most board members, the post is their first elected position, and experience managing an eight-figure budget is generally not a mandatory prerequisite. Whether the district is large or small, the responsibility for the investment in each student is substantial. Each school board decides how to apply $10,500 a year per student for each of their thirteen years of schooling. That total is a $136,500 investment for each student who attends an average public school from kindergarten through twelfth grade. The board decides what services are offered, how they are offered, and at what prices.

The financial responsibility of district boards, and their appointed superintendents, is not lost on the host of other stakeholders in the public education apparatus. At this point, those familiar with public education finance may cry foul to a characterization of school board members as standing center stage in resource allocation decisions, pointing out that state and federal policymakers, too, play heavy roles in the allocation of funds. And indeed, they do. With more than half the funds generated at the state and federal levels, it is no surprise that policymakers at those levels are prone to use various carrots and sticks, as well as mandates or prescriptions that affect the manner in which funds are applied at the local level. Some state leaders might point out that the courts also exert their influence on resource allocation decisions. Given that public education sits squarely in the political sphere, one might argue that other influencers such as parent groups, labor unions, and community groups play a heavy role in driving resource decisions. Again, this is all true.

So while school boards (and their hired district leaders) own the decisions, the role of other key players in the system has evolved to influence those decisions. The result is that school boards operate amid a confluence of multilayered forces that are imposed from above (with federal and state layers), as well as from within the system (by labor, parent, and community groups), and actively shape the allocation of resources. Thus assigning ownership over resource decisions to school boards does not do much to clarify the multidimensional manner in which resource decisions are actually made and, more important, how well the current system works to deploy resources. The existing structure for resource decisions has serious flaws that render it effectively dysfunctional against the expectations for an operation this size.

The Tangled Web of Forces That Shape Districts' Spending Decisions

State and federal formulas are well-established vehicles for dictating use of resources. Up through the 1960s, responsibility for funding public education rested primarily on local governments, since local taxes amounted to more than half of all education revenues. Districts had considerable flexibility in how resources were allocated, as the state and federal governments were minor (and often silent) funders. With its 1965 landmark Elementary and Secondary Education Act, the federal government redefined its role in funding education in an attempt to leverage the school system to address the ill effects of childhood poverty. Federal funds remained a small portion of the overall spending picture, but they came with requirements for how districts were to use these monies to ensure that poor students would benefit.

In the 1970s increased responsibility for funding began to shift to states. The subsequent decades witnessed a set of legal challenges that established increased state responsibility for funding public education and for funding it at an "adequate" and "equitable" level. In many states, the legal challenges asked courts to spell out how much states should be spending and how those funds should be distributed across districts. The New Jersey Supreme Court's rulings in *Abbott* v. *Burke* go further than many rulings in that they specify the types of investments that must be made (for example, improved Head Start programs) and in which districts. Although the effect of such legal challenges varied across states, on average states steadily increased their financial support to districts such that the state share of public education funding jumped from 39 percent in 1970 to 50 percent in 2000.

Since the mid-1960s, as they have increased their financial support for education, both federal and state governments have sought ways to ensure that their funds are put to good use. At the state level, the players include the legislatures, governors' offices, and state education agencies, each adding a layer of influence over the spending decisions that undeniably rest with school boards. The result of a flurry of state and federal activity has been an increased level of influence over district spending decisions.

At the federal level, the influence comes primarily through requirements associated with restricted funds, known as categorical grants and earmarks. These revenue streams come with rules about how the grants are to be administered, which students can benefit, what can be purchased, how resources can be distributed, and how the funds then can be accounted for.[2] While many in the system bemoan the federal constraints, as Melissa Junge and Sheara Krvaric have shown, most federal allocations require state administration of those funds, and in practice, state education agencies layer on additional restrictions as part of their administering of the funds.[3] As Junge and Krvaric's analysis demonstrates, since states would be required to repay federal funds if not used appropriately, the state agencies play a risk avoidance role in that they impose additional restraints to avoid triggering any complications with federal compliance. By the time the federal funds reach districts, then, they bring with them both federal constraints and state education agency constraints on how they are to be used.

State funds too can include categorical allocations, but state-level actors also rely on other forms of state leverage on district allocation decisions. While nearly all states (usually through legislation) use some basic formula that ties distribution of funds to student enrollment and local revenue capacity, many of these formulas contain additional fine print that effectively shapes how a district can use state funds.[4] For example, formula allocations may take the form of per student allocations, flat grants, competitive grants, staff allocations, funds for specific services, reimbursements of costs, cost sharing, and targeted allocations. A key difference is whether the state allocation works primarily to increase spending in the district, to restrict the use of funds so they only benefit a certain student type, or to specify exactly what program or service is provided with the funds. Most state legislatures have also added grandfathering or "hold harmless" provisions, which tend to trump other formulas intended to ensure that a change in district qualifications will not result in fewer dollars for the district, even when the student population decreases (as students move to charters or with demographic shifts).

Sometimes the legislature allocates a pot of funds for some purpose (school improvement, science education, or professional development, for example) and then tasks the state education agencies with expending the funds. The agency in some cases then chooses what gets purchased (principal coaches, professional development in science education) and then offers these options to districts, whose leaders may or may not accept (or incorporate) them into their programs.

A governor's office is sometimes an active player in pushing an agenda that ultimately shapes district expenditures. Reducing class size and raising starting pay for teachers are the kinds of mandates that often originate at the gubernatorial level and have the effect of influencing district-level spending choices.

Of course, state influence over district spending decisions extends beyond the details contained in finance formulas and deep into state regulations that define the parameters of schooling (minimum number of days, hours, subjects) and various terms of employment (minimum qualifications, pay for qualifications, pension terms, for example). State and federal revenues are combined with locally raised funds, some of which create similar restrictions on use. For instance, when local levies specify that funds will be used for arts, athletics, or crossing guards, similar restrictions apply.

The confluence of different funding formulas and their corresponding restrictions creates a challenge for district leaders tasked with developing the budget. The sum total for districts is a complicated financial matrix, where revenues from different sources must be combined and then doled out in ways that work to provide approved services, while being accounted for separately into dozens and dozens of fund accounts.[5] For instance, the staff paid for by the federal Title I program for poverty must clock their time and effort to ensure that federal funds have been properly deployed on poor students. The separate pots of money work as funding silos and savings in one silo cannot be applied to services paid for by another. Funds spent on transportation or special education cannot be commingled with other funds for different purposes. In an effort to avoid commingling, larger districts create departments that align with the various silos for things such as special education, Native American education, technology, and reading coaches, each with separate staff who focus only on their funded initiative.

This multilayered revenue structure creates challenges for district leaders tasked with creating a thoughtful comprehensive spending plan. But the challenges do not stop there, as additional spending pressures are applied at the local level. In addition to the prescriptions that come with the revenues, districts adopt additional restraints on their own spending decisions through long-term promises to employee labor groups by means of employment contracts and pension arrangements. Multiyear contracts might run five years into the future and might include not only terms of compensation but also directives for how services are to be delivered. Teacher contracts, for instance, often specify the schoolday schedule, class-size limits, substitute-staffing arrangements, use of aides, teacher training policies, lunch supervision duties, teacher evaluation, teacher placement, and the list goes on.

In one sense, these contract terms are effectively self-imposed, since each contract takes effect only once it receives a district signature. At the same time, many of the contract terms are industry standard (such as formulaic teacher pay scales based on years of experience and continuing professional education), and making bolder changes to the basic contract can be politically challenging.[6] While longer-term contracts work to create continuity for employees who operate in a revolving door of district leadership, they also work to limit decisions of future district leaders, who might find themselves in charge during the second year of a five-year contract. As some districts manage ten or more contracts (including those for teachers, principals, aides, custodians, bus drivers, food service personnel, and building maintenance staff, to name a few), differing expiration dates makes it nearly impossible to make a change in one contract if there are implications for other contracts (such as the school schedule).

Labor groups are not the only force at work at the local level. Parents, community members, and district staff influence spending in both organized and informal ways. Parents band together to block school closures and prevent budget cuts to cherished programs. Opportunistic principals and other staff who know how to work the current system can be consistent drivers of unintended variations in spending across schools. Some work their magic to skate through budget cuts or to get the most from the social services department working in the central office. There are parent-teacher clubs that make sure that the salary for the grant-funded specialist stays on the district budget when the grant ends.

Perhaps most powerful are the district practices, policies, and habits that create inertia for doing approximately the same thing year after year. Much has been written about how schools today resemble the schools of 1980, before the dramatic advancements in technology. In elementary schools, a group of some twenty-five nine-year olds are assigned to a teacher who takes them through a curriculum over 180 six-hour days. High schools are still divided into seven or eight fifty-minute periods, and each class (be it trigonometry or photography) meets for exactly the same duration all year long. Teachers for every subject carry roughly the same student load and are all paid on a uniform compensation system that rewards only longevity and graduate course work. Each school has a counselor, a librarian, a physical education teacher, and so on.

These habits are buried in the district policies that allocate resources to schools. Perhaps in part because of some of the forces named above, school district leaders see their resource allocation task as deciding how many staff to hire and for what positions. During budgeting season, the process involves a staff-based formula to allocate full-time staff to schools based on increments of student enrollment, such as a teacher for every twenty-five students and a vice principal when enrollment exceeds 400.[7] Additional staff can be allocated case by case and might include a music teacher for a specific magnet school or a technology specialist at an innovative high school. Many districts then add staff to cover special programs for needier students and assign the costs to categorical funds. The terms of staff compensation are not changed in any meaningful way from one year to the next, except to add across-the-board cost-of-living adjustments, cover the rising costs of health benefits, or add or subtract a day of training now and again. Job categories stay fixed from year to year, and once hired, staff members with the same job title are treated as interchangeable, seniority being the deciding factor in placement.[8] Technology and staffing purchases cannot be swapped, as those funds often draw from different funds.

Although some of these practices may indeed be the best way to serve students, it is not clear that the system regularly reevaluates those decisions in light of other potential alternatives in service delivery.[9] For instance, the use of a full-time librarian is one approach to making sure reading and research materials are available to students. Other approaches might involve distributing these duties among teachers, or working in partnership with public libraries, or even expanding access to digital materials. By dictating the use of the resource, the allocation asserts central authority and creates some level of uniformity across schools, thereby perpetuating the existing resource decisions.[10]

Another disadvantage of making resource allocation decisions primarily in staffing terms is that these decisions become profoundly disconnected from the actual dollar value of the different services provided in the school district. District leaders do not know whether the dollar allocations are distributed fairly. And they do not assess how much they spend on one service or another, whether those expenditures are appropriate for the service, or whether there is a lower-cost alternative for a comparable service. For instance, districts do not explore whether the costs of math instruction are rising or falling and how those costs compare with the current investment in music or foreign language instruction. They do not explore how much it costs to have students participate in basketball versus physical education class.

One additional by-product of the many constraints imposed by the multiple layers is a lack of budget transparency. Witness, for example, the recent debates over how much is spent per pupil in Newark, New Jersey, where estimates vary by the thousands of dollars, depending on what funding streams are counted.[11] Even comparing benefit rates or total staffing in districts or states requires months of researcher hours.[12] The result is a spending picture that lacks coherence and efficiency and is unsustainable and yet is unable to adapt to a rapidly changing context.

Conflict between Resource Allocation Patterns and District Goals

District expenditures are not coded by subject matter. This means that the district cannot compute the current investment in foreign language instruction or the basketball team. Nor, in most districts, does the leadership know whether it spends more per pupil at Riverside Elementary than at Meadowleaf School. In truth, existing school district financial systems make it extremely difficult to extract the per student costs of basic district services. And since districts allocate staff, not dollars, they are often in the dark as to the actual dollar cost of what is delivered.

Without this information, district leaders cannot know how their investments compare across key priorities. What is worse, in many of the districts where research has explored actual dollar costs, district leaders' instincts about how their investments compare across priorities were dead wrong.

Take for instance, the relationship between districts' allocations and districts' goals for disadvantaged students. Most large urban district leaders claim an emphasis on improving schooling for poor and minority students. Yet in one district after another, the strategy implicit in the distribution of dollars would suggest the opposite. As is now well documented, teachers in predominantly white and wealthier schools tend to be more senior and thus are paid more than those in high-minority and high-poverty schools in the same district.[13] When the actual salaries of the staff assigned to different schools are divided across their pupils, per pupil spending on classroom teachers in wealthier low-minority schools comes out ahead.[14]

At this point in presenting these uncomfortable data to the public, an audience member will undoubtedly point out that salaries are not indicative of teacher quality, so the spending differences ought to be considered irrelevant.[15] Whether

Table 3-1. *District Spending Patterns in Relation to Stated Objectives*

Objectives for student outcomes	Reality evident in school spending
Narrow the achievement gap between whites and minorities.	On average, districts employ less-expensive teachers to teach minority students than whites.
Give poor students a leg up.	Districts spend a greater share of unrestricted funds on nonpoor than on poor students.
Get students up to speed in core subjects.	Schools spend more per pupil in elective courses than in core subjects.
Divert resources to help lower performers.	Schools spend more per pupil on advanced placement and honors courses than on remedial and regular courses.
Prepare students for a changing economy.	Schools spend more per pupil for participation in ceramics and basketball than in math or science.

or not teacher quality varies substantially across school types, the truth is that the current compensation and teacher assignment policies persistently drive a larger share of public funds in a way that explicitly conflicts with district objectives. Teacher compensation systems are district policy choices, and thereby they become instruments of the district strategy, whether intended or not.

As it turns out, this example is not the only inconsistency inherent in the current allocation system. Researchers from the Center on Reinventing Public Education have investigated actual spending patterns within districts and uncovered numerous inconsistencies. Table 3-1 lays out typical conflicts that have been uncovered between district resource allocations and stated goals for students.[16]

The uneven spending patterns are also evident within schools, where differences in course costs might suggest a district strategy focused most heavily on electives. As figure 3-1 illustrates, in one district studied, higher salaries and lower class size in noncore subjects yielded higher price tags for noncore courses ($1,206 per student per course) than for core subjects ($950 per student per course).[17]

In other research, the team at the Center on Reinventing Public Education has found similar patterns that work against a district's goal of addressing gaps between high and low performers. In one district, spending across course types indicates more than double the per student spending on an honors or advanced placement course in comparison with a regular or remedial course.[18] Here again, lower spending happens when the lowest-salaried teachers land in overcrowded remedial and regular classrooms, while the highest-paid teachers are assigned to the advanced courses. Given that a typical accelerated student might take three

Figure 3-1. *Per Pupil Cost of Core versus Noncore Courses in One Large Urban District*[a]

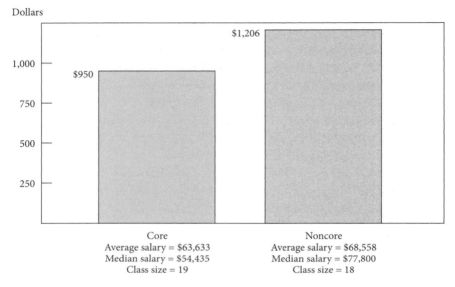

Dollars

Core
Average salary = $63,633
Median salary = $54,435
Class size = 19

Noncore
Average salary = $68,558
Median salary = $77,800
Class size = 18

Source: Paul Hill, Marguerite Roza, and James Harvey, *Facing the Future* (Seattle: Center on Reinventing Public Education, 2008).

a. Core subjects in this analysis include math, English, social studies, and science courses. Noncore subjects include art, music, physical education, and foreign language courses.

or four honors courses, whereas a struggling student might be in multiple regular or remedial courses, the uneven course costs get compounded in a way that directs much larger sums to educate the most advanced students than is spent on the lower achievers. Some might attribute it to a human capital problem, but it is a human capital problem manifested from resource decisions (many not even recognized as resource decisions), imposed by layers of influencers, such that the effect is to concentrate resources in ways that make spending patterns wholly disconnected from district objectives for students.

In another example, the recent push for improvements in math and science has not been accompanied by a comparable investment in teacher compensation for these subjects. A study of teacher pay in the state of Washington shows that most districts in the state pay math and science teachers less than they pay teachers of other subjects.[19] This is a deliberate wording choice intended to highlight the uneven effects, often dismissed, of a uniform pay scale. Sure enough, despite its "uniform" nature, the schedule does create some predictable pay differences across different types of teachers who are anything but uniform. For instance, even casual observers might agree that teachers with math and science degrees operate in a different labor market than do French teachers, or photography teachers, and

Figure 3-2. *Relative Earnings of STEM versus All Other Teachers*
in Washington State, by School District, 2009[a]

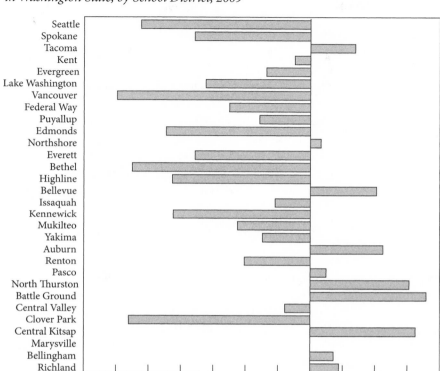

Percent

Source: Jim Simpkins, Marguerite Roza, and Cristina Sepe, "Washington State High Schools Pay Teachers Less for Math and Science Than for Other Subjects" (Seattle: Center on Reinventing Public Education, 2010).

a. Figure shows the percent difference in base salary between math and science teachers and other teachers in the thirty largest districts in Washington. Districts ranked by enrollment. STEM = science, technology, engineering, and math.

indeed math and science teachers appear less likely to stay in teaching for lengthy terms (perhaps being lured by nonteaching career opportunities). The result is that, because the system compensates largely on the basis of longevity and disregards labor market differences across different teacher types, math and science classes tend to be taught by lower-paid teachers. In an illustration of the trend, figure 3-2 shows the salary differential between math and science teachers in Washington state's thirty largest districts, arranged in order of district size (Seattle being the largest).[20]

One might assume that these patterns are unintended oddities that pop up now and again and are not related to the various governance structures that

influence finance. Yet the issue of pay for math and science teachers has been battled about in the Washington state house before. In fact, in 2007 the Washington
Education Association, the state's union affiliate, pushed hard to block what
would have been a $5,000 bonus for national board–certified teachers who teach
math and science at struggling schools and then later worked to oppose a 2008
bill to study subject-based pay scales in other states.[21]

The stark contrast between spending patterns and typical district objectives
makes it clear that current resource allocation systems are not effective in
directing funds in ways that support district goals. Although it is easy to write off
the spending patterns as artifacts of other unrelated policies that have no negative
consequences for the strategy at hand, doing so means giving up on the premise
that resources matter, and in accepting that notion, the governance system has
surrendered its ability to use resources strategically, effectively, and productively.

The Effect of Spending Practices on the Price of Services

There is a popular question among state lawmakers redesigning state-finance
formulas: How much does a high-quality education cost? In asking it, most are
assuming, first, that there is a singular process for schooling and, second, that we
need only to add up the price of the ingredients involved in that process to arrive
that the total cost. Both assumptions are flawed.

Regarding the first assumption, students can learn (albeit to different degrees)
in many different kinds of schooling processes. Although most do involve a
teacher and a student cohort, the rest of the processes are matters of policy.
Different choices about the processes determine the basic ingredients required.
For instance, the teacher might be paid a lot or a little or a different amount
depending on subject matter. The teacher might be supported by a counselor and
vice principal and other staff who have nonteaching roles. The vice principal
might double as a music teacher. Class sizes might average twenty-five (or more,
or less) or might vary depending on the subject. Since we do not yet have
replicable examples of districts where all students are achieving at acceptable
levels, and there are many processes we have not tried, there is no singularly
desirable and accepted schooling process.[22]

Yet various dimensions of policies that drive decisions around resources do
indeed assume a singular model of schooling. Take for instance, the silo effects
created by the multilayered funding structure. Funds for learning disabilities,
for instance, must be used to address the needs of disabled students who have
qualified for the program. Imagine a new approach to teaching reading that is so
successful that it dramatically reduces the rate at which elementary students are
referred to learning disability programs. Despite the benefit for students and the
potential savings for the learning disability program, most districts would assert

that funding restrictions would not permit use of learning disability funds for the new reading program. In the end, the costs of teaching students to read would be higher with the funding silos than under the alternate approach.

Also pertinent is the trend in states to fund a uniform set of services across all districts. Take, for example, the Georgia policy to put "graduation coaches" in its high schools to boost graduation rates, even though the schools have differing base-level graduation rates and differing contexts behind student dropout problems. Funding formulas that dictate one-size-fits-all staffing ratios or standardized service delivery ignore the many differences in students and context across dissimilar schools and communities, driving up spending without a corresponding return.

Also flawed is the notion that the current schooling inputs are paid for at a market price. In basic economic terms, *price* refers to the value agreed on by the sellers and buyers in a functioning market. Since public education works more like a monopoly, there is no useful market. Rather the decision about how much to spend on an input is more a function of available resources and policy than of market value.

That teacher salaries are the largest input serves as a prime example. Every few years the school board makes decisions on incremental cost-of-living adjustments through its labor negotiations, and though market forces may be a factor, labor unions also consider a district's available resources and the tolerance for granting raises into a multiyear contract. But cost-of-living adjustments tell only part of the compensation story. Also relevant to teacher wage levels are factors such as who stays in the system, how many new master's degrees are awarded, and whether the state continues to fund incentives such as bonuses for national board certification.

Take, for example, Jim Simpkins's analysis of Seattle's teacher pay since the inception of the recession.[23] As figure 3-3 indicates, over the four-year period from 2006 to 2010, continuing teachers earned 37 percent raises, which far outpaced the 13 percent growth in the local consumer price index for the same time period. The price of labor appears particularly disconnected from context during 2008–09, when teachers earned a 14 percent increase just after the onset of the economic downturn.

How did the district justify the ballooning 2008–09 salaries that appear so indicative of a misalignment between wages and market conditions? In casual conversation at a local reception, I asked the school board president what he thought of the 14 percent raise. He looked puzzled and then admitted that he had not realized teachers had earned such a pay increase. Indeed, that should have been no surprise to me, since the rising wages were not captured in any one budget document but were instead an artifact of numerous forces playing out at multiple levels. Pay had drifted up with low attrition amid step-and-column raises that

Figure 3-3. *Increases in Teacher Salary and Consumer Price Index, Seattle, 2006–10*

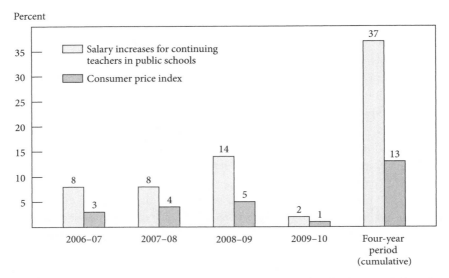

Source: Jim Simpkins, *Seattle Teacher Pay over the Last Five Years* (Seattle: Center on Reinventing Public Education, 2011).

drive up wages on the basis of longevity and degrees and was then augmented by the larger cost-of-living adjustments that had been approved five years and two superintendents earlier. Finally, many teachers took advantage of a state program to pay $5,000 and $10,000 bonuses for national board certification. All told, continuing teachers brought their pay from an average of $63,736 to $74,789 in a year when some private sector industries were doling out pay cuts.

Finance policies can work to damp prices as well, particularly in expanding economies, when public wage changes might lag those in other sectors. And, as was previously explained, policies can distort pricing for math and science teacher salaries. Here the teacher compensation system had the effect of inhibiting salaries in the high-demand math and science areas.

The fine print of state and federal allocations can also drive district prices. In their efforts to ensure that districts adhere to the intent of state and federal allocations, many grant allocations include terms that shape what gets purchased and at what price. For federal grants, for instance, schools can designate which staff member salaries are charged to the grant line and which are funded by district unrestricted funds. As often happens, districts charge their least-expensive staff to the grant, from which any remaining funds are still applied at the school.

In contrast, more-expensive staff are assigned to district fund accounts, which do not return savings associated with lower-cost staff. The result is that clever accounting practices intended to take advantage of differences in formulas work to yield lower staffing prices on federally funded programs and corresponding higher prices on nonfederal programs. It certainly seems harmless enough (even a bit entrepreneurial), but the downside is that such practices communicate different pricing depending on the revenue source.

Another example of distortion involves a state's transportation fund, which reimburses districts a set dollar amount for each bus rider, the number of riders being determined by a one-week count. To maximize its state reimbursement, one district's transportation director hustles parents to encourage attendance with a notice that reads as follows: "If you do not normally ride the bus, or do not ride the bus on a regular basis, it is very important that all [accelerated progress program] students ride during 'ridership' [week]. . . . If your student does not normally ride, it is like writing a check to the district for $3500 to support your classrooms just for riding this week."[24] Such practices imply that states' transportation-funding policies work to reimburse busing services for a particular student group, when, in fact, those same policies work to distort states' understanding of transportation usage and pricing.

Thus the questions policymakers pose to inform their finance formulas become circular. Finance policies manipulate the cost of inputs, yet policymakers try to factor the cost of inputs into their formulas. For policymakers at the state or federal levels wondering how much public education costs, at least a partial answer is that it depends on what those same policymakers choose to spend on their local districts.

Unsustainable Spending Structures

When it comes to education spending decisions, school boards are essentially the ultimate deciders. Perhaps because of the vast and unstable nature of this group, other parties have sought to impose policies and practices that have the effect of institutionalizing various spending decisions, the result being that decisions on district resource allocation remain steadfast even when school board members come and go, hire and fire superintendents, or make changes in priorities or strategies. The point of these efforts is to manipulate not only this year's spending patterns but also those for next year and subsequent years.

One result is that school budgets are filled with entitlement-like allocations that force spending escalation. School districts are labor-intensive operations, and changes to wages and benefits are the biggest driver in year-to-year spending changes. As noted above, most teacher compensation schedules include both steps for automatic yearly pay increases and column pay increases that are associated with degree attainment. Assuming continuation of the salary schedule, these pay increments are guaranteed, and in practical terms they work like an entitlement for teachers. Certainly, this is not to say that teachers should not be fairly and appropriately compensated; but by establishing a pay scale that does not involve much room for district modifications, the pay increments become essentially automatic.

Although such allocations do, indeed, create more predictability for staff, the flip side is that they continue to escalate even when revenues do not. Take, for instance the master's bump—a pay increase of some $2,000 to $10,000 a year awarded for any teacher who earns a master's degree. The workforce has indeed responded to this promise and is increasingly seeking degrees. In 2008, 52 percent of teachers had a master's, up from 49 percent in 2004.[25] Teacher pay for the master's bump is growing not because districts are doling out pay hikes but because teachers have been awarded more degrees.

Similarly, some states and cities (such as Seattle) promise bonuses to teachers who earn national board certification, and teachers have responded by seeking certification at rates that tripled in the first three years of the program. The cost for making good on Washington state's promise to award a bonus for national board certification, for example, skyrocketed from $10 million in 2008 to $45 million just four years later, creating pressures on an already constrained revenue structure.[26]

Pensions, too, create promises that can strain ongoing revenues. In many states, pension promises made during more robust economic climates are necessitating substantially greater investments now that returns on pension investments have stalled. The interdependencies between pensions and terminal salaries mean that any raise given to teachers near retirement creates an added drag on pension funds that promise a retirement pay pegged to wages at retirement. In other words, where the master's bump or national board bonuses drive up teacher pay before retirement, they also drive up long-term pension obligations.

Teacher health benefits can be another source of cost escalation when promises are made in terms of benefit levels (instead of dollar contributions) and those benefit levels correspond to increasing outlays from year to year. In states like Massachusetts, Washington, and Illinois, such benefit promises forced double digit percentage growth in expenditures in a single year (2007 to 2008).[27]

Just as projections of slow economic growth are being extended into the future, cost escalators are on the rise, so much so that cost escalation now exceeds likely revenue growth. With a slower economy, teacher attrition drops as teachers hold on to their jobs in response to fewer opportunities elsewhere in the labor market. Since steady attrition helps stabilize spending on salaries (as junior teachers replace more senior teachers), a dip in attrition has the effect of causing a corresponding

Figure 3-4. *Built-In Cost Escalators and Likely Revenues in U.S. Public Education, 2011–20*

Billions of dollars

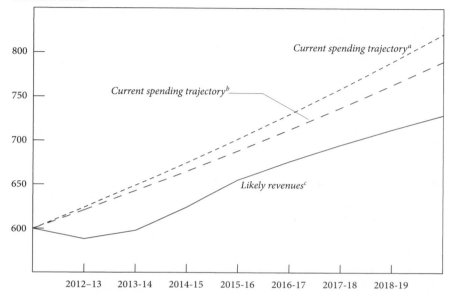

Source: Author's calculations. Forecast of GDP growth follows Congressional Budget Office figures at www.cbo.gov/doc.cfm?index=12316.

a. Assumes no incremental reforms, spending growth of 4 percent.

b. Assumes no incremental reforms, spending growth of 3.5 percent.

c. Pegged to Congressional Budget Office projections of GDP growth.

acceleration in teacher pay. And as the average age of the workforce climbs, so can the cost of health care benefits. Finally, increased teacher retention means a larger share of the workforce will tap the full pension benefits, creating a double whammy for pension funds already down from low investment returns. For pension funds, the two factors require increased contributions on the front end.

All told, the cost escalations can force an increase in spending of an estimated 3–4.5 percent a year.[28] How does that growth compare with likely changes in revenues? Assuming that revenues follow projected growth in the GDP, figure 3-4 maps total projected public education revenues (beginning in 2011–12 at $600 billion) and their effect on expenditures (absent any cuts).[29] As the figure shows, expenditures, modeled at both 3.5 and 4 percent a year, drift up faster than projected revenues, creating budget gaps that must be addressed year after year. If the projections hold, district leaders will be forced to address the gap with some solution of enhanced revenue or spending cuts. Funding new reforms will compete with demands to maintain compensation and pension promises. In any case, the effect of finance policies that project spending increases into future years is a system that is clearly unsustainable.

Effect of Finance Governance Structures on Adaptation and Innovation

Today's finance system is a product of a complicated web of governance that has produced many intertwined but unrelated policies and practices that, in combination, burden the very system they were designed to serve. In the many ways detailed above, the model does not optimize student learning but merely perpetuates the system at hand.

Part of the challenge is a by-product of multilayered revenues. Each governmental layer that has added funds has also slowly and gradually layered on restrictions. Couple that with the desire for stakeholder groups to add predictability to school district allocations through entitlement-like compensation structures, as well as a host of practices that dictate the duties of staff inside schools, and the result is a finance system that cannot free up money to try new things.

This reality is blatantly clear in a course sequence that this author and other professors teach to school leaders on entrepreneurship in education at Rice University. As part of the sequence, students and professors routinely toss up ideas for how schooling might work. Nearly always there is someone in the room who reminds us, "We can't do that because. . . ." District leaders see barriers within the system to just about everything they might try. As Michelle Davis reports, officials inside the system come up against those same barriers as they contemplate change.[30]

But the story of why school districts cannot adapt and innovate is as much a story of what states will not do as of what they do too much. Given that education is the largest single investment states make, it is no surprise that state lawmakers want some guarantees that taxpayer money is put to good use. Practically speaking, states have two options: they can dictate how districts use the funds, or they can clearly articulate desired outcomes and then withdraw funds (and apply them elsewhere) when districts use them poorly, yielding low returns for state funds. Given the unwillingness to do the latter, states stick with the former.

The pursuit of adaptation and innovation, however, assumes the latter—that funds in a system are moved to more productive uses as those uses emerge. It anticipates that money and employees can be shifted in support of the adaptation. It assumes that potential innovators in a system can use funds flexibly to develop new approaches. And it assumes that as district circumstances change, as they often do, practices will be adapted to meet the new conditions. If the district sees significant changes in enrollment types (for example, English-language learners, with rising immigration), practices will be changed to better meet the changing context.

The willingness to move money to more productive uses sets the stage for continuous improvement. No arrangement for delivering services is ever assumed to be sufficient; rather, each arrangement, even one that looks good at the present time, is subject to challenge and replacement when improved options come along or when the context changes.

Perhaps it is because of the school boards' perceived ownership over a set of students in a geographic area, but despite all their authority, the one thing states rarely do is withdraw funds from districts. In most locales, funds are not designed for portability across providers. Thus unproductive uses of funds are perpetuated, in most cases calcified in policies and practices throughout the system, ensuring that despite the deficiencies in current spending patterns, the system will continue to spend the public education dollars in almost exactly the same way next year.

Rather than continuous improvement, the current spending system prefers binary spending choices over relevant trade-offs. Take, for instance, a recent radio spot on the devastating cuts to one district's revenues, in which a journalist explored the consequences of cutting a critical after-school program for needy primary students. Coverage of the story included interviews with school staff, who agreed that the program was vital and that the most disadvantaged students would be much worse off now that the program had been scrapped. What the story did not cover was any information about what trade-offs were considered before eliminating the program and why this choice was made over other options. A quick glance at the district's website, however, yielded a photo of the district's golf team gearing up for another banner competition season. Was the after-school program for vulnerable elementary students scrapped in order to keep the golf team? Were the two ever considered side by side?

The truth is that district leaders do not regularly consider meaningful trade-offs in the context of their budget decisions, in large part because the current governance structure has imposed such a complex layering of constraints on various expenditures. Rather, since each expenditure comes with a different set of constraints, funding silos, and accounting rules, different spending decisions cannot be considered side by side. Decisions about investments are more likely to be binary, for example, should we invest in this new program or not, or should we cut summer school or not? Binary decisions like these prevent policymakers from making fair comparisons between alternative uses of funds.

Most of us are familiar with the concept of trade-offs in decisionmaking from personal financial choices. For instance, one might travel on vacation in a summer or buy a jet ski and spend summer leisure time at a local lake. Doing both would exceed the family budget, so one would have to choose between

Figure 3-5. *Spending Options for the Typical U.S. School District*

Reduce class sizes in grades four through twelve by two students	or	Pay the top contributing 15 percent of teachers $10,000 more

Allow benefits spending to increase by 10 percent	or	Add sixty minutes to the school day in the lowest-performing 25 percent of schools

Give all teachers annual step increases	or	Provide half-day prekindergarten for 50 percent of all students

Source: Karen Hawley Miles, "Can You Spare Some Change?" paper prepared for the annual PIE-Net Conference, Seattle, 2011.

them. Yet for districts, the budgets are so large and managed by so many different governmental layers that managing the hundreds or thousands of parts cannot be done intuitively; instead, informed consideration of trade-offs hinges on solid, reliable accounting systems that inform resource allocation decisions. Because of the diffuse governance system, no one policymaker owns all the decisions, and thus such decisions invite all parties to lobby for their favorite thing with no discussion of the opportunity costs.

Yet as Karen Hawley Miles has noted, district leaders should be considering highly relevant trade-offs that create important options for what schools can offer. Figure 3-5 illustrates three standard trade-offs that involve adding pre-kindergarten, raising teacher pay, and lengthening the school day—all priorities on many districts' reform agendas. First on her list for consideration is a cost-equivalent swap that would raise class sizes in the older grades in exchange for substantial ($10,000) bonuses for the top 15 percent of teachers. Such an exchange, if made, would enable a district to shift funds in a way that emphasized teacher quality over numbers of staff.

Some district officials will rightly point out that restrictions of some sort prevent district policymakers from making those trade-offs. A state's class size limits, for instance, might inhibit the first trade-off. State or labor contract rules that prevent measurement of teacher effectiveness might make identification of the top 15 percent of teachers untenable. More important than top-notch financial accounting systems is the flexibility needed to even consider the trade.

For those who believe that technology and information system will ultimately redefine schooling, such trades are critical. A school system will indeed need both the financial accounting data to clarify how much a school spends on key services, such as math instruction, and the flexibility to change the manner in which those services are delivered. For technology applications especially, trade-offs between investments in staff and other inputs may prove essential.

Education's Own Worst Enemy

The endemic failings of the existing governance of resource allocation for American schools renders it essentially ineffective against even the most basic expectations for an operation of this magnitude. The resource allocation system channels funds in ways that directly conflict with stated objectives for students. The structure of resources is focused on maintaining programs, ensuring mostly uniform spending choices, compensating staff, and regulating process, not on searching for the most productive way to educate students. We know we have not yet landed on the best way to educate students (indeed, there may be multiple best ways); yet the system acts as though we have and funds only processes in current use to the exclusion of all others. We know that the system needs to experiment with technologies and information-driven processes that might change the nature of staffing; yet the resource allocation system forces spending on a fixed set of processes, programs, and staffing arrangements. The system is not transparent, or coherent, and funds are not portable across schooling options. The allocations escalate in a way that makes the system unsustainable; yet that same system pushes back against adjustments that would work to contain costs. All told, the education finance structure inhibits the nation's ability to apply resources coherently, effectively, and productively. Sad to say, with so much built-in resilience we should anticipate that the same system will be in place next year and the year after that.

Notes

1. There are many more districts with smaller budgets, and these smaller districts collectively educate a smaller share of the students. Ranking all districts (ignoring enrollment), we find the median district budget is $10 million.

2. Christopher T. Cross and Marguerite Roza, "How the Federal Government Shapes and Distorts the Financing of K–12 Schools," SFRP Working Paper 1 (Seattle: School Finance Redesign Project, Center for Reinventing Public Education, 2007).

3. Melissa Junge and Sheara Krvaric, "Federal Compliance Works against Education Policy Goals" (Washington: American Enterprise Institute, 2011).

4. Michael Griffith, "Understanding State School Funding," *Progress of Education Reform* 13, no. 3 (2012): 1–6.

5. Marguerite Roza, *Educational Economics: Where Do School Funds Go?* (Washington: Urban Institute Press, 2010).

6. Dan Goldhaber and Jane Hannaway, eds., *Creating a New Teaching Profession* (Washington: Urban Institute Press, 2009).

7. Karen Hawley Miles, Kathleen Ware, and Marguerite Roza, "Leveling the Playing Field: Creating Funding Equity through Student-Based Budgeting," *Phi Delta Kappan* 85, no. 2 (2003): 114–19.

8. The New Teacher Project, "The Widget Effect," 2009 (http://widgeteffect.org/downloads/TheWidgetEffect.pdf).

9. Jon Fullerton, "Mounting Debt," *Education Next* 4, no. 1 (2004): 11–19.

10. Marguerite Roza, *Allocation Anatomy: How District Policies That Deploy Resources Can Support (or Undermine) District Reform Strategies* (Seattle: Center on Reinventing Public Education, 2008).

11. See, for example, New Jersey Spotlight, "The Newark Challenge: Solve for Per-Pupil Costs," October 6, 2010 (www.njspotlight.com/stories/10/1005/2133/).

12. Marguerite Roza, Chris Lozier, and Cristina Sepe, *K–12 Job Trends amidst Stimulus Funds: Early Findings* (Seattle: Center on Reinventing Public Education, 2010).

13. Some might argue that targeted categorical allocations more than make up for the differences in actual salaries, although it should be noted that categorical allocations are not intended to make up for inequities created in unrestricted funds. Rather, categoricals like Title I call for equitable distribution of unrestricted funds before additional targeted resources are allocated. For a discussion of the loophole that enables such salary inequities, see Marguerite Roza, *What If We Closed the Comparability Loophole?* (Washington: Center for American Progress, 2008).

14. EdTrust West, *California's Hidden Teacher Salary Gap* (Oakland, Calif., 2005).

15. For a discussion of the consequences for high-poverty schools of a system that continually sends them more junior teachers and fuels higher turnover rates among staff, see Roza, *What If We Closed the Comparability Loophole?*

16. Paul Hill, Marguerite Roza, and James Harvey, *Facing the Future* (Seattle: Center on Reinventing Public Education, 2008); Marguerite Roza, "Breaking Down School Budgets," *Education Next* 9, no. 3 (2009): 29–33.

17. The district is a large urban Eastern district that was granted anonymity as a condition of releasing full data needed for this study.

18. Marguerite Roza, "Now Is a Great Time to Consider the Per Unit Cost of Everything in Education," in *Stretching the School Dollar,* edited by Frederick M. Hess and Eric Osberg (Harvard Education Press, 2010).

19. Jim Simpkins, Marguerite Roza, and Cristina Sepe, "Washington State High Schools Pay Teachers Less for Math and Science Than for Other Subjects" (Seattle: Center on Reinventing Public Education, 2010).

20. Ibid.

21. Peter Callaghan, "Salaries Don't Reflect State's Commitment to Math, Science," *Tacoma Tribune,* August 17, 2010.

22. A point consistent with the findings in chapter 12 in this volume.

23. See Jim Simpkins, *Seattle Teacher Pay over the Last Five Years* (Seattle: Center on Reinventing Public Education, 2011).

24. Quoted in Seattle Public Schools Transportation Update for the school year 2010–11.

25. Data for 2003–04, U.S. Department of Education, "Schools and Staffing Survey," table 20 (http://nces.ed.gov/surveys/sass/tables/sass_2004_20.asp); data for 2007–08, U.S. Department of Education, *Digest of Education Statistics, 2011,* NCES 2012-001 (National

Center for Education Statistics, 2012-001), introduction and chapter 2; U.S. Department of Education, Schools and Staffing Survey, Teacher Data Files, National Center for Education Statistics, 2007–08.

26. Jim Simpkins, *What Does Washington State Get for Its Investments for Bonuses for Board Certified Teachers* (Seattle: Center on Reinventing Public Education, 2011).

27. Author's calculations from data reported in National Center for Education Statistics, Common Core of Data.

28. Author's estimates.

29. Author's calculations. Forecast of GDP growth follows Congressional Budget Office figures at "Budget and Economic Outlook," August 2011 (www.cbo.gov/doc.cfm?index=12316).

30. See chapter 4 in this volume.

MICHELLE R. DAVIS

4

Governance Challenges to Innovators within the System

The superintendent of the Prince George's County, Maryland, school district saw his proposal to invest scarce funding toward innovative programs blocked when interest groups lobbied the elected school board to instead shore up more-traditional programs and leave redundant jobs in place. In Oregon, a superintendent in the Springfield Public Schools had to cut technical programs for her high school students but could not get access to similar courses offered at a local community college, owing to a lack of coordination between K–12 and higher education in the state. And in Indianapolis, the mayor wanted to take responsibility for city schools that had consistently underperformed, saying that clear accountability was key to school improvement. At many school districts across the county, education leaders are often frustrated by challenges they have no power to control or systems that prompt responses which don't always take into account what's best for students.

Although the governance of school districts has often been viewed as a static factor to be worked around or challenged from within, recent vigorous debate and experimentation around alternative arrangements for the architecture of K–12 education has thrown the door wide open to those who can find the political will to challenge and update the status quo—everything from how schools are funded to who is ultimately accountable for both large-scale successes and failures in student progress. In some circumstances it is the systems themselves that must change; in others there may be ways to work around governance challenges within existing systems. "There are so many barriers that are just perceived," says Deborah Gist, Rhode Island's commissioner of education. "Barriers that people believe are real are so frequently the manifestation of people's interpretations of law and regulation and are things that can be changed."[1]

As scholars studying the shifts delve into the mechanics of these changes and their effect, it is important to talk directly to those in the field about how structural alterations are impacting students in the classroom. State education leaders, school superintendents, principals, and teachers can give us a realistic picture of what it is like to work within more traditional K–12 governance frameworks, as well as the true nature of how new governance structures play out in schools.

One factor prompting the urgency behind attempts by some governors and mayors to gain greater influence over their K–12 systems is the current collection of data that assesses how districts are doing and the sometimes poor outcomes for students in terms of achievement, graduation, and dropout rates. These data now, in many cases, must be disaggregated has changed the way both the public and political leaders view education, says Aimee Guidera, the executive director of the Washington-based Data Quality Campaign. And of course, the requirement by the federal No Child Left Behind Act that school and districts disaggregate their student testing data has made this information evident to communities as well. "Aggregation hides a whole lot of stuff under the rug," Guidera says. "All of a sudden we can no longer ignore the fact that we're failing a huge number of kids. It's in our face all of the time."[2]

At least thirty-six states now have all ten of the essential elements of a K–12 state data system that the Data Quality Campaign has identified as critical, including the ability to collect data on individual students as they progress through the K–12 system, demographic and enrollment information, student growth from year to year, and student-level graduation and dropout statistics.[3] Many other states are close behind, Guidera remarks.

With these data in hand, presented in a clear and organized fashion, both state and local education leaders and the public can identify school systems that are struggling or have repeatedly failed to improve, either as a whole or for a particular group of students. Guidera notes that the data are being used as leverage to prompt some changes in governmental structures related to K–12 education.

Some of the changes surrounding K–12 governance structures started years ago and are providing clues to states and districts currently considering alterations in their own K–12 governance arrangements. The details of newer system overhauls are still being hashed out, but they have the potential to set precedents for the future. Oregon's efforts to establish a birth-through-twenty education system; a bid by the mayor of Indianapolis to take over several struggling schools from the state; and an effort in Washington state to allow the governor more direct control of education policy are all being watched to see whether they will ultimately provide a template for other states and districts. "Many of these have been a long time coming," says Kathy Christie, the chief of staff at the Education Commission of the States, a nonpartisan research organization based in Denver. "Governors, mayors, and legislatures have definitely been trying to take a stronger hand in education."[4]

Case Study: Creating a Birth-to-Twenty Education System in Oregon

Nancy Golden, the superintendent of schools in Springfield, Oregon, says she has been frustrated for years by the lack of preparation she sees in some young children arriving in kindergarten. In Oregon there is no agreement about what preschoolers should be taught, so some kindergarteners are ready to learn while others start off with a deficit that is hard to shake. But K–12 districts have no say in how preschoolers should be equipped for kindergarten, Golden says.[5]

Golden has also struggled with the issue of technical programs. Budget cuts forced many districts across the state, including Springfield, to eliminate such programs. Although most local community colleges offer similar classes, a lack of coordination prevented high school students from accessing them. In addition, Golden says, her district was more focused on getting students to graduate—the incentive prioritized for K–12 schools by the state—than on preparing them for college or careers. Golden often saw school guidance counselors working toward that end rather than making sure students were ready for the next step in life. "Until now, there's been no coordination" along the continuum of the education process, Golden says. "Already I see the conversations changing."

That is because Oregon is now in the process of revamping its approach to education, creating a birth-through-twenty system that emphasizes continuity among all the branches of the education tree. In an effort to bring more accountability to education, state lawmakers have already abolished the position of elected state superintendent of public instruction in favor of an appointed version under the purview of Governor John Kitzhaber.[6] Although Oregon governors have often run campaigns that include promises regarding education, with an elected superintendent of public instruction the governor has had little opportunity to influence this area, other than through the budget process. In May 2012 Kitzhaber announced that he had chosen Rudy Crew, a former chief of public schools in New York City and Miami, as his chief education officer.

Kitzhaber is also focused on boosting the number of Oregon adults who earn degrees and credentials beyond high school.[7] The system will provide incentives to K–12 districts to push them toward this goal, including grants for innovative practices and increased flexibility for districts showing high performance. Districts that continue to stagnate will be subjected to mandatory requirements regarding how they educate students. The intent is a "tight-loose" arrangement in which the goals are firm but the way districts get there allows for wiggle room.[8] "What I really like about this is that it's based on a handshake between the state and us, that if we do well, there will be a commitment from them to find new ways to leverage resources, fewer barriers, and less paperwork and reporting," says Golden, who advises Kitzhaber on education issues.

While many of the details of Kitzhaber's plan to realign state education along a birth-through-twenty continuum are still being worked out by the newly created, twelve-member Education Investment Board, chaired by the governor and formed to oversee the reforms, some details have come to light. The underlying goal of the plan's strategies will work toward Kitzhaber's ambitious goal of 40-40-20: that is, by 2025, 40 percent of adults in the state should have earned a bachelor's degree or above; 40 percent should have an associate's degree or similar credential; and the remaining 20 percent should have a high school diploma or its equivalent.[9]

The plan requires a new data system to help track student achievement and a significant professional development initiative for teachers, says Duncan Wyse, president of the Oregon Business Council, who is also advising Kitzhaber on education issues. "We know there's a high correlation between education and earnings, and we want to create a robust, vibrant, and innovation-based economy," Wyse says. "Our goal is to raise incomes."[10]

Under Kitzhaber's reforms, K–12 funding will change drastically. Currently, funding in the state is based mainly on seat time for students, but under Kitzhaber's plan the focus will be on learning. Each district will work out an achievement compact with the state, showing how it plans to reach its markers toward the 40-40-20 goal.

Districts will receive base grants for operational funding. But they'll also be able to earn additional funds through outcome grants. For example, a district might receive extra money for each student who meets high school exit standards, whenever the student meets them—at age fifteen or age eighteen.

Sandy Husk, the superintendent of the 40,000-student Salem-Keizer Public Schools district, says she likes the idea of focusing on a student's progress rather than on mandates as to how and when they get there. She expressed an "enormous amount of frustration" with requirements of the federal No Child Left Behind Act, which define success mostly based on the standardized testing snapshots of students and not on individual students' growth.[11]

Husk supports the concept of financial incentives to move students along the pathway toward college and career readiness. For example, she says, the idea of providing extra funds for each student a district moves from English-language learning classes to the general education program could be significant. Currently, there is extra funding for those students only when they are designated as English-language learners and little incentive to ensure that they become proficient in English and move out of the program. "It would be motivating to give financial credit for [English-language learners] when they exit the program," Husk says.

Under the new reforms, Oregon districts could also receive funds from the state to take successful programs statewide or to provide training to other districts. One of the greatest financial concerns about the plan, however, is how to handle districts that continue to struggle. It seems counterproductive to provide those districts with less money, but it remains to be seen how the financial aspect of the tight-loose approach will work with districts and schools that continue to underperform. The intent of the plan is not, of course, to have the reforms become a punitive measure, particularly financially, for failing schools, but the details remain unclear. "I'd be glossing over the concerns if I said everybody was comfortable with that," Husk says.

Many educators in Oregon remain hopeful about these governance changes, but others—including some in states such as Idaho, Washington, and Indiana, where sweeping reforms are still being hashed out—are wary of the effect that reforms will have in the real world, at the school level. "There are many decisions to be made," says Jeff Rose, the superintendent of the 38,000-student Beaverton, Oregon, school district. "The actual impact is yet to be known."[12]

The core goal in this effort is to connect all the silos of education that currently exist and force them to consider what they are doing in relation to the next level of education along the continuum. Consistent standards and assessments play into that, but a united and aligned governance structure that looks at education from prekindergarten all the way through higher education is the key.

Case Study: State Takeover in Indianapolis

At Emmerich Manual High School in the Indianapolis, Indiana, school district, teachers and students have spent years watching reform efforts come and go. There was the failed plan, launched in 2005 and funded by the Bill & Melinda Gates Foundation, to split Manual into three smaller schools on the same campus. Adopting a program dubbed Project Lead the Way, the school committed to a focus on science, technology, engineering, and math. More recently, the long-time principal was replaced with a new leader. School hours were altered to start the day later, allowing students to get more sleep in the morning.

Although some in the district argue that the reforms have helped Manual's students make gains, the urban, inner-city school still had only a 44 percent graduation rate by 2008–09—though it had risen to 71 percent by 2010–11—and is considered one of the worst schools in the district.[13] In 2011 Manual High School, along with three other schools in the Indianapolis district, was taken over by the state.

The move was prompted by the state's Public Law 221.[14] Passed by lawmakers in 1999, before the 2001 federal No Child Left Behind Act, the law was Indiana's effort to incorporate more accountability into the public school system. The law gives the state of Indiana the option to take over schools that fail to hit specific progress targets after six years. The 2011 takeovers, which also included one school outside the Indianapolis district, marked the first time state leaders had actually used the provision, as schools finally began reaching and passing that six-year mark.

"In this situation we felt like the best thing we could do was act with a sense of urgency and really try to put every bit of resources the state has into revitalizing these schools," says Tony Bennett, the Indiana superintendent of public instruction. "These schools have failed to serve children, and we need to take whatever action is needed."[15]

The state department of education is trying to determine the best way to make a change in these schools, which have persistently resisted efforts to boost academic achievement, and state officials remain acutely aware that studies of similar takeovers in others states do not necessarily show success. At the same time, Gregory A. Ballard insists that as the mayor of Indianapolis, he is the right person to oversee this takeover—not the state.

Against this backdrop, the Indianapolis public school system is making significant changes, many of them prompted or accelerated by the state takeover. Although the city's school district no longer has responsibility for the four schools involved in the takeover, the proceedings continue to have consequences that reverberate within its boundaries. The takeover may ultimately affect Indianapolis schools in two separate ways—directly, through reform interventions laid out for the schools under state oversight, but also indirectly, by putting pressure on local officials and school leaders to be more assertive with reforms and the pace at which they are instituted. "We're going to take this crisis as an opportunity to transform and reinvent the district," says Eugene G. White, the district's superintendent. "We're not going to be passive. We're going to be aggressive and proactive. At the end of this process, we hope to take a crisis and turn it into a transformational opportunity to really compete in an education marketplace."[16]

Indianapolis already has a complex education landscape. In 1970 Mayor Richard Lugar began the process of consolidating city and county functions under the Unigov reforms. Because the governmental boundary of the city expanded countywide under Unigov, Indianapolis now features eleven different school districts.[17]

The 33,000-student Indianapolis school district is the largest district in the city, and more than three-quarters of its student body qualifies for free or reduced-price lunch. It is also racially diverse: 53 percent of students are black, 22 percent are white, 18 percent are Hispanic, and 5 percent are multiracial, according to district statistics.[18]

The city also plays host to charter schools, which are directly under the purview of the mayor's office, a feature unique to Indianapolis. No other mayor in the country has the authority to grant and oversee school charters. In 2001 lawmakers passed legislation allowing the Indianapolis mayor's office to charter its own schools and oversee them.[19] In 2011 the mayor's office oversaw twenty-three charter schools, setting education standards and hiring and monitoring the charter school operators. In the first four years of his term, the mayor's office received fifty applications for charter schools and approved four, and Ballard recently announced plans to double the number of charters in the city over the next five years.

Only traditional public schools, however, are subject to Indiana's Public Law 221. The law places every school each year into five categories, ranging from exemplary progress to academic probation, based on state testing. Schools on academic probation for six continuous years face the possibility of a state takeover. Last year, five schools in the state were chosen for state takeover. Four were in the Indianapolis public school system—Manual, Arlington, and Howe High Schools, and Emma Donnan Middle School—and one was in the Gary Community Schools system. "We believed we needed to do this to allow schools to start fresh," Superintendent Bennett explains.

Under the takeover model, the Indiana department of education chose two takeover operators to run the four Indianapolis schools. The companies, Charter Schools USA and EdPower, already operate charter schools overseen by the mayor's office in Indianapolis, though this would be their first experience with traditional schools in Indianapolis.

Bennett is keenly aware that state takeovers in other places—such as Pennsylvania and New Jersey—have not been declared successes, and his goal is to avoid some of the pitfalls experienced elsewhere. For example, Bennett considers the 2011–12 school year an "observation" year to allow the "turnaround school operators" to spend the year looking at how the schools function and devising a plan to reform them. The plan will not be implemented until the following school year. The observation year is critical to deliberate planning for the schools' futures and to avoid rushing forward with changes, he says.

In addition, Bennett notes that the state did not set up a new layer of bureaucracy to oversee the turnaround operators—another complication experienced with state takeovers in other states. The operators will be accountable to the state superintendent of public instruction and the state board of education. The state department of education also spelled out in contracts with the turnaround operators what each is accountable for and goals that must be met to retain their contracts.

For example, at various times in the process, the operators will be required to develop evaluation systems and strategies to ensure that teachers are highly effective and to create a school turnaround plan, including concrete performance goals, which must be approved by the Indiana department of education. If goals are not met, the contracts can be canceled.

Turnaround operators will have the freedom to replace each school's entire staff of teachers and administrators, to revamp the curriculum, and to make decisions about testing and extracurricular activities—all changes that were often difficult or impossible to make when the school was part of the Indianapolis district system, bound by union requirements, and where decisions for individual schools were often made at the district level or on a districtwide basis.

The state board of education is overseeing the initial transition phase. However, Mayor Ballard has signaled his intention to petition the state for oversight of the schools. In 2011 he convinced lawmakers to approve a provision allowing him to make his case for oversight to the state board of education, and Bennett has signaled that he would not object to the idea. Bennett says that if Ballard comes to the state board with a well-defined plan for oversight, he will be open to the suggestion. "I think local control is the best control," he says.

Ballard argues that his office already has experience overseeing the charter schools in his district, though he pledges that the four Indianapolis public schools taken over will not morph into charter schools and will ultimately transition back to local control. Ballard says the fact that his office has already worked directly with the charter operators is critical. "They know we're results based," he says. "We're the only ones in the state who have closed a school" for poor performance.

Some are suspicious of the mayor's true intent and point out that Ballard has provided few details about his plan for oversight or any indication of how the schools might one day be returned to the Indianapolis public school system. In addition, points out Ann Wilkins, the president of the Indianapolis Education Association, the turnaround operators have no experience running public schools with the types of challenges the four targeted schools face. "When you look at big, urban districts, the [charter school operators] think they can use the same methods as in smaller schools," she says. "The kids have to be the priority, not a money-making factor and not a test score factor."[20]

But David Dresslar, the executive director of the Center of Excellence in Leadership of Learning based at the University of Indianapolis, says the idea of moving oversight of failing schools to the mayor's office brings a more direct accountability to the reform process. School board members, Dresslar argues, can be fairly anonymous in a large school district: parents and community members often do not know their names or even vote in school board elections. "The idea of a mayor, who everyone knows and is familiar with, taking over brings an increased level of accountability simply because there is an increased level of knowledge as to who they are and what they're doing," he says.[21]

Joshua S. Smith, the director of the Center for Urban and Multicultural Education at Indiana University, says he remains concerned that the mayor's office "doesn't have the staff capability needed to weigh in, this hands-on in education."

A mayoral takeover does not come with added resources and adds a new layer of bureaucracy to the oversight, he argues. The mayor's current plan is short on details. "I question whether the goal is to ever return local control [with these schools] or to set up a new, semi-permanent structure," Smith says.

Whichever entity—the state department of education or the mayor's office— winds up with ultimate oversight of the four Indianapolis schools, it is clear that the entire procedure will have significant and lasting effects on the Indianapolis public school system as a whole.

In discussions with Bennett in 2010, district superintendent White stunned the community by admitting that at least 60 percent of teachers at the schools in question were ineffective.[22] White says that administrators in the district had not provided proper oversight of these teachers and that union rules prevented large-scale dismissals of these teachers.

Although the new turnaround operators have no ability to fire Indianapolis public school teachers from the system, they can dismiss them from the schools under state takeover. A teacher who wants to stay at Manual High School, for example, would have to go to work for Charter Schools USA, the company running the school, and leave the Indianapolis school district system.

Those teachers who leave the four schools under state takeover must be reassigned within the school district or effectively laid off. White says he has already put all teachers and administrators—not only at the four takeover schools but at every district secondary school—on notice that they will be evaluated during the first semester of the 2011–12 school year to determine who will be kept on staff. "We're going to keep the best teachers and get rid of the ones that do not pass," he says.

By losing the four schools, the Indianapolis district loses 3,800 students, which means there will be a need for a "reduction in force," White says. But even before that loss, he notes, the district was still operating, in terms of staffing, the same way it had when it served 10,000 students, and a realignment of resources in the district is sorely needed.

White became more empowered to take such steps after April 2011, when Indiana governor Mitch Daniels signed into law a provision that restricts teachers' collective bargaining ability. The law, White comments, frees him to make significant changes in staffing without worrying about seniority. "It's a whole new ball game," he says. "We think we're going to be the better for it."

The state takeover also prompted White to accelerate a strategic plan to redo the district organization itself. White reports that he is currently putting a strategy in place to create three categories of schools, each with its own level of district oversight. Successful schools will get more independence to make their own decisions on everything from budget matters to personnel and purchasing on a buildingwide basis. Schools that are not making progress will be put on probation and will get intensive support from the district through professional development and interventions. Those in a middle category will get additional training and aid to move to the more autonomous level, he hopes.

Although the state takeover took some of the district's most notorious schools out of the district's purview, the process continues to have a lasting impact. "We couldn't convey the sense of urgency to people like this action did," White says. "We've been trying to get people to see that it is later than they think, and now they know the time to act is yesterday." But White, who admits to a fractious relationship with both Bennett and Ballard, remains concerned about the lack of detail on plans for the state takeover schools and the lack of experience those two offices have in dealing with low-income, urban schools. He says he has no opinion about whether the mayor's office or the state department of education is better suited to oversee the turnaround process.

Hanno Becker, a chemistry teacher at Emma Donnan Middle School, thinks the state takeover could ultimately benefit the entire district. District leaders can weed out low-performing staff members and keep the best teachers and principals, putting them in positions where they can have the most impact. But he acknowledges that the district now will find itself in the most intense competition phase yet when it comes to keeping high-quality teachers. "The best teachers in the district are going to also be lured away by these takeover organizations as well as other school districts," Becker says. That is in addition to the existing charter schools and those planned for the future. White is intent on repositioning the district to compete at a high level in the new Indianapolis education scene for both students and staff. "We're going to compete for those students and aggressively get them to attend our secondary schools," he says.

It remains to be seen whether a new structure for oversight of these four struggling schools can bring about change when so many other measures have not. However, many of those other measures centered around policy, working within a more traditional K–12 governance structure. Supporters of the new reforms hope shifting governance responsibilities and arrangements will finally make the difference. But the marketplace of education in Indianapolis is shifting quickly and in ways that are new and unique. Education leaders around the country will surely be watching to see whether this will be a model that can be duplicated to help other failing schools find the recipe for improvement.

Case Study: Evolving Governance Structures in New Orleans

Sometimes it is not a political leader or even an education leader who prompts a governance change in education, even when that change has been sorely needed for decades. In the case of New Orleans, the devastation left by Hurricane Katrina in 2005 forced systemwide changes in the city's school system after the K–12 schools were effectively wiped out by the storm.

It had been clear before the storm that the New Orleans schools were not working for many of its students. Before the hurricane, the majority of students in the city attended schools in the Orleans Parish school system, overseen by the Orleans Parish School Board. The district was plagued by dismal test scores, theft, waste, and incompetence in many areas.[23] Students attending district schools were mostly minority and from low-income families, and enrollment numbers were falling every year. In 2005, before the storm, 60 percent of the district's schools had been rated unacceptable by a state performance system, and student achievement levels in New Orleans were significantly below the state average. In 2005, for example, 67 percent of Louisiana fourth graders received a Basic or higher score on state English tests, but only 43 percent of New Orleans students met that standard. Before Hurricane Katrina hit, the state had already formed a recovery school district and had taken over a few struggling schools, and there were a small number of charter schools in the Orleans Parish district, but neither option played a significant part in the city's educational offerings.

The public school landscape in New Orleans today looks nothing like it did before the hurricane. The district features schools overseen by three different entities: the state-run Recovery School District, which directly operates sixteen schools; the Louisiana Board of Elementary and Secondary Education, which has authorized more than fifty charter schools; and the Orleans Parish School Board, which runs six schools and has authorized eleven charter schools.[24] In addition, New Orleans now features citywide choice for students. Any public school in the city is open to any student living within the city limits.

That the majority of schools in New Orleans are now public charter schools is also a huge shift, says Laura Mogg, a research manager at the Scott S. Cowen Institute for Public Education Initiatives based at Tulane University in New Orleans. Nearly 71 percent of public school students in New Orleans attended a charter school during the 2010–11 school year. "Katrina allowed the change in governance to happen on a massive scale," Mogg says. "Otherwise, it would have been impossible."

In New Orleans, school performance is on its way up. Since 2007, the percentage of students performing at grade level on the state's high-stakes tests has increased by nearly 20 percentage points, compared with a state average growth of 6 percentage points, according to the Cowen Institute.[25]

Of course, not everyone has declared success. Concerns remain about a variety of issues, including whether some of the schools will ever be freed from state oversight and returned to local control. In addition, as there are at least three different entities overseeing various pieces of the New Orleans school offerings, a significant amount of overlap and replication is created, says Debra L. Vaughan, the Cowen Institute's assistant director over research. This governance issue surfaces in a variety of areas, including purchasing power, where schools lose out on economies of scale, from procurement to transportation. In some places, Vaughan says, buses from separate schools may be operating on the same route. In addition, because several small schools may be close to one another, each school on its own may not be able to offer as many advanced classes, electives, or even special-education services to students as they could if they were combined.[26]

"The verdict on whether this is the right thing forever is still out," she says. Many educators are also concerned that the governance changes do not always have the intended impact, says Cheryllyn Branche, the principal of Benjamin Banneker Elementary School, which is directly operated by the Recovery School District, and who was also the principal of the school before Hurricane Katrina.[27]

For example, schools directly run by the recovery district must provide transportation for students, even from far-flung areas of the city. Of 511 students at Banneker Elementary school in the 2011–12 academic year, only about ten live in the surrounding neighborhood, Branche says. "It's a burden on recovery schools," she says. "We have to use a large chunk of money [for transportation] that would have gone to the classroom."

Although she does have a bit more flexibility in choosing curriculum and educational materials for her students since Katrina, Branche says she often does not get the money to support those choices. In addition, while she believes in the concept of school choice, she says it has not played out the way it was meant to. Branche believes many schools cherry-pick the best students by saying they do not have room for lower-performing or special-education students. "We have thousands of parents saying their children are not getting to go where they want," she says.

There is plenty of anecdotal evidence to back up this allegation (though no existing studies of the issue), says Vaughan, but as of 2012, this problem was being addressed. The Recovery School District began accepting school applications and processing them in a central office, rather than having them done at the school level, which "takes away the power to have some type of informal or selective admissions process," Vaughan says. The difficulty in the old system was "that there was no incentive to serve those hard-to-serve populations."

And though test scores have been rising in other schools in New Orleans, Branche says that test scores at Banneker Elementary have gone up only about five percentage points compared with prehurricane scores, Branche says. When she looked closely at some of the factors involved, she realized that Banneker had a huge attrition rate. Data showed that each year the school was losing 30 percent of its student body and gaining a new 30 percent. "It's very, very tough here," she says. "I'm not saying the present structure is not a workable one, but you have to look at how things are functioning over time."

Case Study: Economy Prompts Idaho's Reform Package

In some ways, the economic crisis of today and the lack of funds for education has also created an opportunity for modifications in the structure of K–12 and a path to building public support for drastic alterations in the education governance setting. Tight fiscal times can be seen as an "opportunity by some to make major changes," says Christie, of the Education Commission of the States. "It just makes it more politically palatable to the public."

The fiscal crisis across the country necessitated state budget cuts in education that have prompted a search for new approaches that can generate improved fiscal efficiency as well as improved outcomes. A bleak financial atmosphere may, in some cases, make the public more receptive to drastic alterations in governance structures.

In Idaho, for example, the state was forced to funnel more than $200 million away from K–12 education, and Idaho superintendent of education Tom Luna says he had to get creative. "We're entering the third year of having to make significant cuts to our education system, and we were cannibalizing the system for no other reason than to preserve the system," Luna says. "We were not going to watch it be dismantled piece by piece. We chose instead to change the system."[28]

Luna introduced three highly controversial education reform measures passed by legislators in 2011 and signed into law.[29] The new laws covered a wide range of changes, from eliminating teacher tenure to instituting a pay-for-performance plan. In addition, lawmakers passed Luna's proposal to require students to take at least two online courses during their school careers, while at the same time instituting a significant change in the funding formula for Idaho schools.

That change divvies up the per student state funding each district receives to reflect how much of a student's education is provided directly by the district. Under the plan, if one of a student's six classes is taught by an online provider, two-thirds of funding for that class will go to the online provider for instruction and the district will keep one-third for providing space and support. Luna argued that in the past, the state was paying twice for online courses—to the district and then to a state-supported online provider.

For some districts, like the tiny Notus School District 135, the consequences of the funding change may have an unintended impact. The city of Notus sits amid acres of rich Idaho farmland, and its tiny main street features a gas station and a farm supply store. It does not see enough cars in a day to warrant a traffic light.

But the 330 students who attend schools there want access to the same level of education as their peers in the state capital of Boise, thirty-five miles southwest. They want to take Spanish and digital photography and have access to college-level courses, such as algebra and English, that earn them dual credits.

So during the 2008–09 school year, former superintendent Benjamin Merrill (who once served as the superintendent, the high school principal, and the football coach, all at the same time), decided to tap online classes to bring those resources to his tiny district, where many students did not have computers at home, let alone broadband access. He created Pirate Academy, a roster of online courses that students at Notus High School took as part of their regular school day, using a computer lab stocked with eighteen personal computers.

Merrill tapped into high-quality online courses created and offered by the state-sponsored Idaho Digital Learning Academy. The cost for each course was $50 per student. At the same time, Merrill was able to take advantage of Idaho's broadband program, which put high-speed fiber optic Internet access in every school district with a high school. "I could teach thousands of online courses for the cost of one teacher," Merrill says. "I leveraged the technology within our building to offer courses that were offered at the biggest schools in Idaho. We were matching their curriculum."

The program was successful. Students at Notus High School who took the digital courses had a 95 percent pass rate. But Merrill ran up against a problem. The school district received most of its funding from the state, based on average daily attendance of students for face-to-face instruction from 8:00 a.m. to 3:00 p.m. However, with Pirate Academy, Merrill was tapping online courses for part of the school day but still receiving the full amount of state funding. Some state officials began to grumble, accusing Merrill of "double dipping," as the district still received the same amount of per pupil funding and the state was also underwriting the cost of the online courses to keep their price low.

To head off the criticism and keep the program in place, Merrill began an annual trek to the state legislature and every year found himself "begging for forgiveness" to allow the program to continue. Merrill argued that a clause in the Idaho constitution required communities to provide an equal education for students in Idaho, regardless of location. With so few students, he says, "we were inherently not providing an equal education because we couldn't provide courses offered in big schools."

For the first few years, the legislature accepted Merrill's argument. But in the 2010–11 school year, his last year as superintendent in Notus, the budget crisis settled deeply in Idaho, and state lawmakers and the Idaho department of education, led by Luna, were looking for ways to make significant cuts. The state slashed funding for the Idaho Digital Learning Academy and essentially said that to continue operating it would have to start charging a market rate for its products. The goal was to create an equal playing field among online providers in the state.

All this was taking place against the backdrop of Luna's massive education reform proposal, which includes a change in the state per pupil funding formula.

The change, Merrill says, will siphon off some of district's $1,000 per student state funding for pupils. Since nearly every student in the high school takes an online course, some more than one, Merrill says the result will be the loss of thousands of dollars in the tiny district. The Idaho Digital Learning Academy was also forced to raise its per student, per course price from $50 to $75.

Now, says Merrill, "it is almost counter-productive to have kids in online courses in Idaho." Although Merrill procured grants to help defray some of the added expenses, it was only enough to keep Pirate Academy going for one more year. Merrill says if he were still superintendent, finances would most likely force him to shut the program down after the 2011–12 school year. "After that it would have been almost impossible."

The irony, says Merrill, is that at the time this was evolving, Luna was lobbying to require students to earn two online learning credits—not just the online "experiences" other states have mandated—to graduate from high school. In November, Idaho became the first in the nation to adopt this requirement.

Although Luna's efforts to alter the governance system in Idaho, particularly in terms of funding and emphasizing online courses, were made to create new approaches and a fiscally sound system in Idaho, the effects must be examined closely to determine whether they have had the intended outcome. The measures have been so controversial in the state that a referendum on the 2012 ballot asked voters whether they want to repeal the education laws.

Potential in a Variety of Models

Although budget cuts and fiscal crises may provide a rationale for revamping the structure of the K–12 system rather than continuing to reduce funding to an existing system, state and city leaders are also looking at revamping school governance structures as a way to improve state and local economies and lure new jobs and industries. Mayors are also looking at economics and the connections between a city's future prosperity and its schools. "Mayors . . . much more so than traditional school board members, often see the interconnectedness between the city's overall economic health and schools," says Francis X. Shen, a visiting assistant professor at Tulane Law School, who has studied the issue of mayoral control closely.[30] U.S. secretary of education Arne Duncan has pushed for more mayoral control of struggling urban school districts, saying in 2009, "At the end of my tenure, if only seven mayors are in control, I think I will have failed."[31]

The jury remains out on whether mayoral control of districts, as a structural system, is successful. Numerous studies have found mixed results in city districts in which mayors have fiscal control of schools and a high level of power to appoint those with direct oversight of schools. A 2010 study by the Institute on

Education Law and Policy at Rutgers University finds that cities with a high level of mayoral control show an increased public commitment to education and increased funding for schools but no conclusive evidence that governance changes necessarily increase student achievement.[32]

In addition, the public is not always clamoring for such structural changes, despite their dissatisfaction with school performance, says Shen. "There's a lot of resistance to these governance changes," he says. "Public opinion is split."

However, some arrangements have been successful. In 1991 the Massachusetts legislature gave the mayor of Boston the power to appoint all seven members of the Boston School Committee, which hires the superintendent of schools, who serves as a member of the mayor's cabinet. Although the Boston school district had once been plagued by low test scores and a high dropout rate, following the adoption of mayoral oversight the district slowly saw significant improvements. And by 2006 Boston Public Schools was awarded the Broad Prize for Urban Education for a range of outcomes, from increasing overall student achievement, to reducing the achievement gap between white and Hispanic students, showing a boost in math and reading among African American students, and increasing the number of minority students taking advanced placement tests.[33]

Carol R. Johnson, the superintendent of Boston Public Schools, says the current structure, particularly with an appointed school board, is working. "Elected boards have to run every other year and sometimes that can lead to some fragmentation of purpose as people operate with agendas," she says. Taking away that elected board allows the mayor-appointed panel to "be more aligned and develop a set of strategies around the work."[34]

It is clear, however, that the political clout of long-time Boston mayor Thomas M. Menino has made a difference in pushing the school district's agenda forward by influencing state lawmakers to pass innovative education legislation and provide the district with the ability to use creativity and flexibility within its schools. In 2010 lawmakers approved a sweeping education bill that enabled the city to transform low-performing schools into district charter schools without union approval. Menino lobbied hard for the legislation.

Menino's credibility and longevity in his position (he has been elected five times as mayor) has clearly "laid some great groundwork for being able to move forward and turn around underperforming schools, create charters within the district, and get some flexibility," Johnson says. "He's been able to use his influence and political capital."

That influence often comes in the form of providing cover for tough school district decisions, Johnson says. Since Menino and the district are so closely linked, he often fields the fallout from controversial measures and has the ability to deflect it. "You really do need some political support and political coverage to make tough decisions, like closing underperforming schools, moving school leaders or staff who have not proved to be successful," Johnson says. "It's not always favored by the community or the collective bargaining groups."

Governance structures too often allow politics to play an overwhelming role in education, sometimes blocking innovation, some educators say. In the 127,000-student Prince George's County, Maryland, schools, former superintendent William R. Hite Jr. says the school board evolved from an elected board to a governor-appointed board and then back to an elected board. Currently the board is made up of representatives from nine single-member districts. The arrangement sometimes thwarts his attempts to be inventive, he says. "The process by which you have to seek approval on things related to policy and budgets can become a roadblock to innovation," he says. The board members are "being lobbied by constituents and then we spend a lot more time . . . talking about things I consider noise, as opposed to addressing the real work."[35]

At budget time recently, lack of funds forced the district to propose positions and programs for cuts. Although Hite made his recommendations, lobbying efforts by individuals and groups continued many of the programs he sought to cut or pare back. "The money to continue those programs would have been better spent on investments in innovative approaches," he says.

Other types of governance structures appear to make changes to the education system easier. One reason she wanted the Rhode Island post as education commissioner, says Deborah Gist, was that "there are structures in place in our state that give us greater ability to do things that in other places would take much more effort." In particular she cites the fact that the Rhode Island Board of Regents, which oversees the state's elementary and secondary education system, has the power to set regulations that hold the force of law. Gist has simplified the system of pushing forward education reforms without having to navigate the politics of passing legislation. She notes that in November of 2011, the Board of Regents approved a new teacher evaluation system that determined that any teacher deemed ineffective on evaluations for five years in a row will automatically lose teacher certification.[36]

Gist says the new system, which took effect in January 2012, is linked to student achievement and effective teacher performance and that it is less bureaucratic than the state's previous system. Several other states have also pushed for reform of their teacher evaluation systems but had to do it as part of large legislative packages that often got mired in political battles. Rhode Island did not have to do that, Gist says. "Our Board of Regents passed a regulation on teacher evaluation . . . and we were done."[37]

Two factors that are often the impetus for increased mayoral control over urban school districts are a persistent lack of improvement in student achievement and financial inefficiency or waste without results (or both), Shen says. That was certainly the case in Washington, D.C., where the district had a history of below-average scores on standardized tests and one of the highest per pupil spending rates in the country.

The District of Columbia had had a form of mayoral control over the schools since 2000, when the mayor gained the power to appoint four of the nine members of the board of education. Over the years following, student achievement barely improved. In 2007 the city council voted to give Mayor Adrian Fenty the power to create a cabinet-level agency reporting to the mayor to oversee the schools and to replace the superintendent of schools with a chancellor reporting directly to the mayor. For the chancellor's position Fenty tapped Michelle Rhee, who had never overseen a school district but had experience as an education reformer.

Rhee says mayoral control was a huge factor in instituting many changes in the district, including new evaluations and revised retention and layoff policies. The success of mayoral control, however, can often be linked directly to the talents of the person in the leadership position, and that is a risk, says Rhee, now the founder of the advocacy organization StudentsFirst. Rhee credits her ability to make changes in Washington, in part, to Fenty's leadership and the positive working relationship that developed between them. But she cautions that not every scenario that includes mayoral control will have the same outcome. "Mayoral control of the schools . . . has tremendous potential," Rhee says. "But it does not mean that innovation and aggressive reform are guaranteed to happen. If you have a bad mayor, you're not going to have a great system."[38]

Although many initiatives that alter the governmental structure for K–12 are driven by charismatic, politically savvy leaders or pushed to the surface by a particular circumstance or environment, those conditions are not sustainable forever. Politicians leave office, replaced by new leaders who may or may not share the same ideas on education and economies and workforce issues ebb and flow. The challenge is to put sustainable policies and structures into place so the personalities involved in establishing new governmental structures are not needed to maintain them in the future.

Addendum

The November 2012 elections had important implications for some of the policies and leaders discussed in this chapter. In Indiana, Republican Tony Bennett was defeated in his bid for reelection as state superintendent of public instruction by Democratic challenger Glenda Ritz. Some called the defeat a referendum on Bennett's education proposals, and it remains to be seen whether Ritz will move forward with Bennett's plans for the four Indianapolis schools discussed earlier in the Indiana case study.

Also, in Idaho citizens voted to repeal all three controversial education laws discussed earlier that Superintendent of Education Tom Luna had proposed and the legislature and governor had incorporated into state law. They voted against a proposal to pay teachers bonuses based on student test scores, restrictions on teachers' unions, and against Luna's plan to give every Idaho high school student a laptop along with the graduation requirement of two online credits. On November 19, the state board of education voted to scrap the online course graduation requirement in deference to voters, and the board is likely to continue dismantling many of Luna's plans.

Notes

1. Telephone interview with author, September 29, 2011. Unless otherwise noted, all direct quotations come from the author's interviews.

2. Telephone interview with author, September 2011.

3. See Data Quality Campaign state analysis, "Data for Action," 2011 (www.dataquality campaign.org/stateanalysis/executive_summary/).

4. Telephone interview with author, fall 2011.

5. Telephone interview with author, November 14, 2011.

6. Kimberly Melton, "Support Is Growing for Appointing Oregon's School Superintendent," *The Oregonian*, February 16, 2011.

7. See State of Oregon, "Memorandum: Members, Oregon Education Investment Board," November 18, 2011 (www.oregon.gov/Gov/docs/11-18-11_GovernorGuidance Memo.pdf?ga=t).

8. Ibid.

9. Ibid.

10. Telephone interview with author, November 19, 2011.

11. Telephone interview with author, November 10, 2011.

12. Telephone interview with author, November 2011.

13. Indiana Department of Education, Compass, "Emmerich Manual High School: Graduates Overview," n.d. (compass.doe.in.gov/dashboard/graduates.aspx?type=school &id=5481).

14. Indiana Department of Education, "2011 Public Law 221" (www.doe.in.gov/ improvement/accountability/2011-public-law-221-pl-221).

15. Telephone interview with author, October 18, 2011.

16. Telephone interview with author, October 20, 2011.

17. *Indianapolis Star*, "Library Fact Files: Uni-Gov," 1984 (www.indystar.com/library/ factfiles/gov/unigov/unigov.html).

18. See Indiana Department of Education, Compass, "Indianapolis Public Schools: Overview," n.d. (http://compass.doe.in.gov/dashboard/overview.aspx?type=corp&id =5385).

19. See Indianapolis Office of Education Innovation, "Welcome," n.d. (www.indy.gov/ OEI/Pages/home.aspx).

20. Telephone interview with author, fall 2011.

21. Telephone interview with author, October 12, 2011.

22. Matthew Tully, "Years of Massive Failure Put 8 IPS Schools on the Brink," *Indianapolis Star,* March 28, 2010, p. A1.

23. Scott S. Cowen Institute for Public Education Initiatives, *The State of Public Education in New Orleans: Five Years after Hurricane Katrina* (New Orleans: Tulane University, 2010).

24. Scott S. Cowen Institute for Public Education Initiatives, "Governance Structure, 2011–2012 School Year," 2011 (www.coweninstitute.com/wp-content/uploads/2011/10/Governance-Chart-2011-121.pdf).

25. Cowen Institute, "Spotlight on Choice," n.d. (www.coweninstitute.com/our-work/applied-research/spotlight-on-choice).

26. Telephone interviews with author, November 16, 2011, and January 27, 2012.

27. Telephone interview with author, November 2011.

28. Telephone interview with author, September 30, 2011.

29. Jessie L. Bonner, "Governor Signs Final Idaho Education Reform Bill," Associated Press, April 8, 2011.

30. Telephone interview with author, November 17, 2011.

31. Quoted in Libby Quaid, "School Chief: Mayors Need Control of Urban Schools," Associated Press, March 31, 2009.

32. Ruth Moscovitch and others, *Governance and Urban School Improvement: Lessons for New Jersey from Nine Cities* (Newark, N.J.: Rutgers University, Institute on Education Law and Policy, 2010).

33. Broad Prize for Urban Education, "Boston: Overview of the District," Broad Foundation, 2006 (www.broadprize.org/asset/2006BostonPublicSchoolsOverview.pdf).

34. Telephone interview with author, October 14, 2011.

35. Telephone interview with author, November 22, 2011.

36. Gist, interview.

37. Ibid.

38. Telephone interview with author, September 30, 2011.

STEVEN F. WILSON

5

Governance Challenges to Innovators outside the System

Just north of Central Park in New York City, two schools share a building. Public School 149 is operated by the New York City Department of Education, and Harlem Success Academy, a "No Excuses" charter school, is run by the Success Charter Network. Both serve students from the surrounding community, which is overwhelmingly black and low income.[1] In 2010 Harlem Success third graders (the earliest grade tested by the state) scored in the top 1 percent of schools in the state (outperforming their peers from wealthy suburbs) on the state's English language arts exam, while P.S. 149 scored in the bottom 2 percent.[2]

Eva Moskowitz, who founded the Success Charter Network, is one of a growing number of education entrepreneurs who aim to post academic results starkly superior to those of traditional district-run schools. The long-standing governance arrangements of primary and secondary education, they contend, are inimical to fundamental change. Rather than attempt reform from within, they have chosen to work from outside. Taking advantage of hard-won legislative beachheads—charter school laws, supplemental educational services providers, alternative certification pathways, and more—they have formed new organizations delivering a wide range of services and products, all aimed at demonstrably boosting student achievement.

For years, James Comer and other prominent reformers have contended that barring wholesale social change, only modest improvements in urban student achievement can be expected. For instance, the Broader, Bolder Approach to Education calls for dramatic investment in health care services, early childhood education, after-school programs, and more.[3] Yet today, schools run by the Knowledge Is Power Program and other top No Excuses charter school networks are posting academic outcomes that bridge the racial and economic achievement gaps—and cost less to operate than district-run schools.[4] For decades, our primary and secondary schools, especially in our central cities, have been staffed by teachers who graduated from the bottom of their high school class and attended nonselective schools of education. This year, 18 percent of seniors at Harvard and other top colleges and universities vie for admission to Teach for America. Bypassing traditional teacher training, they will instead undergo an intensive summer preparation to teach in impoverished urban and rural communities. Since the days of the nineteenth-century common school, education has meant a teacher, students, and a classroom. Today, more than a million elementary and secondary students take at least one course online.[5]

The efflorescence of entrepreneurship in public education engages many components of schooling. For-profit companies and social entrepreneurs are building advanced information systems for integrating student and academic data, launching new programs for sourcing and preparing principals, devising electronic assessments, providing tutoring to children in failing schools, offering outsourced guidance counseling to high schools, establishing online banks of exemplary class lessons, and managing schools and districts under contract. How entrepreneurs in each sector engage—or avoid—the governance structure of K–12 education is well beyond the scope of this chapter. Most such initiatives will fade from view, either because they lack the capacity to transform public education or because the system proves impervious to their advances. But disruptive innovations in three sectors—charter schools (specifically, so-called No Excuses schools), teacher training, and digital learning—are likely to erode long-standing governance arrangements.

Entrepreneurial initiatives in these sectors are likely to demonstrate stronger achievement effects and lower costs than the long-standing practices they replace. The growing public attention they attract will add to the pressure on underperforming institutions—local school boards, unionized schools, state education agencies, and teachers colleges—and the governance structures that sustain them. If their claims withstand scrutiny, these initiatives will gradually erode the power of education interests, chiefly the teachers unions but also the array of other education lobbies that have long dominated state houses across the country. Central tenets of these interests—such as the salutary effects of unions on schools, maximum student-to-teacher ratios, and barriers to the teaching profession—will be undercut. Governors and state legislators will be emboldened to challenge these institutions and their lobbies through legislation, regulatory reform, and the appointment of outspoken reformers to key rule-making positions—as has already begun in some places.

The vulnerability of the K–12 system heightens the three sectors' disruptive potential. Already, the United States has a smaller percentage of twenty-five- to thirty-four-year-olds with a college degree than eleven other countries.[6] Our schools place twenty-sixth in the 2012 World Economic Forum's global rank of education systems.[7] Many Americans fear that their children will not be equipped to compete with their peers from an ascendant East. As an anxious public confronts grim evidence of the slack performance of American schools, few politicians of either party rise to their defense. A weak system of primary and secondary education is seen as a threat to American prosperity—and with that comes a new willingness to challenge the governance structures that sustain and protect that system.

Change will come incrementally to the governance of American education, spreading across state jurisdictions over a period of many years. But as entrepreneurial initiatives benefit from seemingly modest governance reforms and gather momentum, a broad transformation of primary and secondary education may be unleashed.

Governance Obstacles to Reform from Within

Laws in every state authorize local education agencies to establish and operate public schools at taxpayer expense. In the nation's more than 15,000 school districts, there are typically a school board or committee, a superintendent, and a district office. Most states also have a board of education or the like, a state education officer (variously titled), and an education bureaucracy, all of which enjoy specific powers to regulate the local school districts.

Yet the most powerful actor in the governance of public schools is none of these parties. Collective bargaining laws in forty-three states permit teachers to vote to form a union and bargain collectively with their district employer. Upon a majority vote, all teachers must accept the union as their exclusive representative, and the district must negotiate exclusively with the union.[8] (In large districts, most every other school worker, from custodians to lunch workers—and, until recently, principals—also bargained collectively.) Over time, teacher contracts have swollen to cover not only compensation but virtually every aspect of employment, including the assignment and layoff of teachers based on seniority and the maximum ratio of students to teachers. Dismissing even the most manifestly incompetent teacher in many urban districts can take two years and exceed $200,000 in legal costs. Understandably, few principals try. One study finds that of 95,000 tenured teachers in Illinois, only two were dismissed for poor performance over an eighteen-year period.[9] District school governance has established an adversarial system in which the union's role is to protect teachers from administrators who are assumed to be their opponents. In turn, in the largest urban school systems, a culture of chronic distrust, inflexibility, and grievance has taken hold that has proved incompatible with nearly every effort to dramatically increase school quality.

Teachers unions are the most influential lobby in state legislatures, where legislators are hesitant to take positions opposed to the lobby for fear of losing their support for reelection. Unions routinely oppose statutory, regulatory, and contractual reforms that streamline tenure; strengthen the power of the school's executive over teacher evaluations, assignments, and duties; or increase teacher accountability for the academic gains made by their students as measured by standardized tests. Voter turnout at school board elections is frequently so poor that union-run candidates are assured of prevailing. At the bargaining table, board-appointed superintendents have over the past fifty years surrendered their power to lead. Regaining it is a practical impossibility.

Beginning in the early 1990s, a growing number of reformers concluded that, absent fundamental change to this governance structure, the nation's largest school systems were unfixable. The operating system of district schools—elected school boards, 300-page teacher contracts, sclerotic district offices, and notoriously weak teacher education programs—was irretrievably broken.

Charter Schools and No Excuses

In 1991 Minnesota became the first state to enact charter school legislation. The innovation quickly spread to other states and was to prove the most radical governance reform in K–12 education in decades. Charter schools in effect proposed a new definition of "public school": Charter schools are public schools open to, paid for by, and held accountable to the public. The idea struck a deep chord with educators, school reform activists, and politicians long frustrated with the public education system and skeptical that it could ever be reformed from within. Today, more than 5,600 charter schools enroll more than 2 million students in forty-one states and the District of Columbia. While this represents only 3.7 percent of public school students nationally, charter enrollment is growing rapidly.[10] In six districts, 30 percent or more of public school students are today enrolled in charters; in New Orleans, that figure is 70 percent.[11]

Although the legal framework of charters varies widely from state to state, the underlying mechanism is the same. Each statute authorizes at least one state body—the state board of education, a newly formed charter authority at the state level, one or more public universities—to review charter proposals and authorize new schools. Generally, local school districts are also authorized to charter. The governing board of a new school enters into an agreement with the authorizer for a certain period, typically five years, under which the school is eligible to receive public funds in proportion to the number of enrolled students. The schools generally enjoy a high level of autonomy; they are free from district school board policies and many state and local education regulations (though not special education laws or safety codes), although they must adhere to state education standards and participate in state testing regimens. Parents choose the charter school for their children; students are not assigned on the basis of geography, as in most districts.

Although details vary, charter laws require that the schools be open to all students within the district or a specific region and that, if there are more applicants than seats, the school conduct a lottery for admission. Teachers, too, work in the school by choice and generally are not governed by the union contracts of the district in which the school is located, though they may unionize if they choose. If at any time the school fails to meet the terms of its charter, the authorizing agency may revoke the charter. At the end of the agreement's term, if the academic results have been unsatisfactory, the authorizer may decline to renew the charter. In either instance, the school closes.

In principle, authorizers hold schools accountable for meeting the academic outcomes set out in their charter applications. In actuality, the new laws spawned many schools not better and at times worse than district schools; and authorizers, like district school boards, have proved reluctant to close academically underperforming schools and face angry parents. In the early years of the charter school movement, few schools were closed for poor academic performance. Lax authorizer oversight has been a primary contributor to the mixed performance of the schools

As charter legislation swept the states in the late 1990s, charter enthusiasts seemed to forget that their hard-won laws were merely a vehicle for creating strong schools, not a guarantee. Advocates expected that the governance advantages of charters—the new bargain extended to founders of authority and autonomy in exchange for accountability; the shared purpose that would result from faculty and students who were there by choice; and the freedom from tenure and union contracts—would by themselves fuel sharply better outcomes than district schools. But these privileges alone did not unleash a new generation of dramatically superior schools, as many charter proponents had hoped.

Especially in the early years of the charter movement, many schools were long on aspiration and short on results. Charter school founders often proposed school designs that adhered to the progressivist orthodoxies of the schools of education and set out for the central cities, where they identified the greatest need. There, they watched in dismay as their utopian models proved no match for the harsh realities of urban poverty and chronic underachievement. Courtney Sale Ross, the widow of Steve Ross, the former chief executive officer of Time Warner, founded the successful Ross School in East Hampton, New York, as an alternative to homeschooling for her daughter. With a progressive curriculum, lavish facility, and an annual tuition of $30,700 for the middle grades, the private school educates the children of the elite.[12] In 2006 she founded a charter school to bring the Ross model to New York City. The school promised to teach the history of civilization across cultures, with instruction in yoga and organic eating. In 2011 the New York City Department of Education closed the school; 75 percent of its primarily black and Hispanic students had failed the state's English test, making it the lowest-performing charter school in the city.[13] Children with every advantage require little to prosper, but children from poverty, who must overcome years of social and intellectual deprivation, thrive when they are first afforded abundant structure and explicit teaching.

As a whole, charter schools have posted equivocal results. The most comprehensive recent evaluation of charter schools nationally, conducted by the Center for Research on Education Outcomes at Stanford University, examined the longitudinal gains in reading and math of more than 70 percent of charter school students nationally. The 2009 study compares their performance with that of their peers in "twin" traditional public schools matched by students' demographics. Almost half of the subject charter schools posted results no different from their district twins, and more than one-third had academic outcomes that were worse. Only 17 percent delivered academic results superior to their district counterparts.[14] Looking deeper, however, the researchers also find that students from poverty fared better than in district schools. "Charter schools that are organized around a mission to teach the most economically disadvantaged students in particular seem to have developed expertise in serving these communities."[15] In fact, a subsequent study by the Stanford center completed in 2010 finds that students in New York City charter schools learned more than their peers in district schools in both reading and math, and the effects were most pronounced for black and Hispanic students.[16] A growing body of evidence suggests that suburban charter schools perform no better, on average, than their district counterparts, but that urban charters do—especially as they mature.[17]

If charters were intended to foster experimentation in schooling, then it is unsurprising that results were on average undistinguished and that it would take time for effective models to emerge and be replicated. Twenty years into the movement, a growing number of urban and rural charter schools have posted arresting results, with their low-income students, primarily African American and Hispanic, outperforming students statewide—and in some cases, their white peers from affluent suburban districts.[18]

Among this smattering of gap-closing schools, one broad approach, frequently called No Excuses schooling, dominates. Under the No Excuses approach, teachers adopt high expectations for their pupils and stoutly reject explanations for low achievement from any quarter, whether from a child for failing to complete an assignment or from a district apologist's appeal to demographic destiny.[19]

The No Excuses model combines elements that are all but impossible to adopt within the constraints of a district school: long school days and school years, rigorous teacher-led instruction, frequent assessment, explicit efforts to shape values and attitudes, a relentless drive to high achievement, and teacher accountability for results. The Knowledge Is Power Program (KIPP) network of charter schools is the exemplar, but the approach is proliferating in other networks, including Achievement First and Uncommon Schools, and in stand-alone schools, many of which plan to replicate themselves in the coming years.

The Knowledge Is Power Program now has 125 schools nationally serving more than 39,000 students in twenty states and the District of Columbia.[20] A 2010 study by Mathematica Policy Research of twenty-two KIPP middle schools finds "educationally substantial" impacts on state scores from the program. Three years after entering KIPP schools, many students are experiencing achievement effects that are approximately equivalent to an additional year of instruction, enough to substantially reduce race- and income-based achievement gaps.[21] While the Mathematica study offers the most rigorous examination of the No Excuses model, other charter management organizations (CMOs) employing the No Excuses approach also cite evidence of closing the achievement gap. Uncommon Schools has thirty-two affiliated schools in New York and New Jersey. In 2011, on average across the network's fifteen New York schools, 84 percent of test takers in grades three through eight (98 percent of whom were black or Hispanic) scored Proficient or Advanced on state tests in math, compared with 73 percent of white students statewide.[22] Achievement First, which manages twenty-two schools in New York and Connecticut, has posted similar results at its New York schools: 61 percent of fourth graders scored Proficient or Advanced in English language arts and math, compared with 40 percent in the local districts.[23]

These outcomes are unlikely to be the result of the selection effect of motivated parents, as evidence from Massachusetts bears out. The second state to pass a charter school law, Massachusetts has benefited from one of the best of these laws, many years of high-quality charter school authorizing, and a strong supply of education entrepreneurs coming out of Boston's many universities. A Harvard-MIT research study of Boston's charter schools compares the performance of students in four No Excuses middle schools and two high schools with students who entered the enrollment lottery but were not admitted. With an experimental design eliminating selection effects and establishing a true control group, this study finds "strong evidence that the charter model has generated substantial test score gains" for students in the No Excuses schools in comparison with students who remained in the Boston Public Schools.[24] The reverse selection effect, from the attrition of low-performing students, could also distort No Excuses outcomes. Yet a 2011 study by Mathematica, following up on its study of twenty-two KIPP schools (which reported substantial educational impacts from the program), finds attrition rates were on average no higher at the KIPP schools than at a comparison group of local district schools. Nonetheless, given that students who stayed in the program were likely to be doing better than those who left, researchers eliminated the possibility of bias by continuing to count students who withdrew as part of the study's treatment group.[25]

Of seventeen charters in Boston in 2009, seven posted striking results on the state's highly regarded Massachusetts Comprehensive Assessment System test: 75 percent or more of students in their final year at the schools scored Proficient in math and English language arts (averaged across the two subjects).[26] All seven dramatically outperformed the Boston Public Schools in English and math, where proficiency levels range from 33 to 50 percent, depending on the grade and subject. In the three highest exit grades—seven, eight, and ten—all seven schools also outperformed the statewide average (students of all income levels) in the three tested subjects of English, math, and science, except for tenth-grade English language arts and eighth-grade science. Furthermore, four of the schools outperformed students in the neighboring affluent Public Schools of Brookline, where only 12 percent of students are from low-income families.[27] All but one of the seven high-performing schools hew to the No Excuses model. With a citywide cap on Boston charters recently lifted, at least four of the seven schools are being replicated, backed by the NewSchools Venture Fund.[28]

A 2011 study of Massachusetts charter schools by the MIT researchers Joshua D. Angrist, Parag A. Pathak, and Christopher R. Walters finds that students enrolled in urban charter schools in the state are typical of the urban student population, yet their schools boost achievement well beyond noncharter levels. The effectiveness of these schools, the researchers conclude, "can be explained by adherence to a No Excuses approach to urban education that emphasizes instruction time [and] comportment, and focuses on traditional math and reading skills."[29] Seventy-one percent of the urban charter-school administrators identified somewhat or fully with the No Excuses model, while none of the nonurban charters identified with this approach.[30]

Governance Obstacles

Education entrepreneurs who seek to open and replicate No Excuses schools are constrained by the complex web of governing institutions that exists at state and local levels, the K–12 regulatory regimen that this web establishes and to which charters remain subject, and defects in the charter school governance model. First, charter laws vary widely, and even those that are most accommodating to charters subject them to regulations that thwart the creation and growth of effective schools. Charter school reforms were predicated on autonomy from the accretion of rules made over decades by state and federal agencies, union contracts, and the courts, but many such rules remain in place. In twenty-two states, district and state laws and regulations are automatically or broadly waived; six other states waive only certain provisions, and in the remaining fourteen states with charter laws each school must petition the state education agency for exemptions.[31] In nine states, teacher tenure laws still apply, depriving operators of agility in responding to underperforming teachers, and yet perhaps the most essential privilege for charter operators is the freedom to hire, compensate, promote, and terminate school personnel. Many charter schools remain subject to district collective bargaining agreements. Beginning in the 2005–06 school year, the No Child Left Behind Act requirement for "highly qualified teachers" in every classroom where a core academic subject is taught forced charter schools to adhere to each state's licensure and credential policies, which are promulgated by state legislatures, state boards of education, and in some cases, teacher licensing boards.[32]

Teachers unions are generally antagonistic toward charter schools. In states with the most powerful public sector unions, state education agencies may be staffed by administrators hostile to charters, who use their discretion to impose debilitating constraints. The New Jersey Department of Education, for instance, ruled that instructional coaches provided by a charter school management organization could not be counted toward the agency's requirement that 70 percent of school spending be instructional. In New York, charter founders whose schools had been chartered after an eighteen-month vetting process by city and state officials were then required by the state department of education to submit elaborate needs assessments as part of their application for federal charter school start-up funds—and the applications were often declined. When applications were approved, the department imposed elaborate and arbitrary rules on how the funds could be spent.[33]

The recent appointment of charter school entrepreneurs (including Teach for America alumni) to top regulatory positions in key charter jurisdictions, however, is certain to diminish such regulatory hostility. Christopher Cerf, former president of Edison Schools, is now the commissioner of education for New Jersey; New York State commissioner of education John King cofounded Roxbury Preparatory Charter School in Boston and was the managing director at Uncommon Schools; and John White, Teach for America alumnus and veteran of the New York City school district's school turnaround and Innovation Zone efforts, is now superintendent of the New Orleans Recovery School District.

Second, the charter laws themselves impose important constraints on schools. Some 90 percent of the present 600 authorizers nationwide are school districts, which are often reluctant to approve schools that will compete for their students and funding.[34] Effective authorizing requires access to a broad range of expertise, including education leadership; curriculum, instruction, and assessment; special education; performance management and accountability; law; finance; facilities; and nonprofit governance and management.[35] Many authorizers, lacking the resources or skills to perform their duties effectively, approve poor school plans, provide lax oversight, or fail to close chronically underperforming schools. School districts have generally not made effective authorizers. By contrast, states with a small number of authorizers serving a large number of schools have fared well, owing to an uncompromised agenda and a scale that affords expert staff and sophisticated oversight of portfolio schools.[36]

Charter school laws were forged in often fierce state house battles. A common compromise involved caps, imposed by twenty-six states, on the number of charter schools in the state (and sometimes in specific cities) or on the number of charters that can be granted each year (as in North Carolina).[37] For example, Massachusetts's original 1993 legislation limited the number of charter schools statewide to 25. When lawmakers subsequently raised caps in Massachusetts and elsewhere, the price was often changes to the law that undermined school autonomy. For instance, in 2010 New York raised its cap on the number of schools permitted statewide from 200 to 460. The original law required a school that enrolled 250 or more students in its first year to adopt all the collective-bargaining agreements of the district in which the school is located; the new law extended this period to two years.[38] Most CMOs regard work rules and other features of district contracts as incompatible with their programs and policies.

Other states limit the percentage of a district's spending that can be diverted to charters—or reimburse districts for their loss of funds when students leave for charters, resulting in taxpayer expense for two schools for a single student while also insulating districts from competitive pressures that might spur reform. Most states offer charters significantly less money than regular schools; the disparity ranges from 5 percent in New Mexico to 40 percent in South Carolina.[39] By one estimate, charter schools receive on average 21 percent less in public funds than district schools.[40]

Still more important to charter school operators is that little provision is made in charter laws for facilities. Unlike district schools, which generally occupy school buildings paid for by state or municipal bond issues, charter schools have had to lease privately owned facilities and pay rent out of operating funds, reducing the funds available for instruction by 20 percent or more. Three states— Florida, Minnesota, and California—complement their per pupil operating grant with a per pupil facility allocation. By 2004, twenty-four states and the District of Columbia provided some form of facility assistance to charter schools, but these arrangements, whether in the form of loans, grants, bond issues, or tax breaks, are nearly always inadequate.[41] Charter schools, barred from securing public debt to build schools, tried turning to private capital markets. But limited operating histories, weak balance sheets, and the requirement for periodic renewal of the charter were all underwriting obstacles. In 2002 the U.S. Department of Education devised a credit enhancement program to spur private lending to charter schools, but federal grants to community development financial institutions that issued the partial guarantees were limited; with the economic recession, they have nearly stopped.

Regulations regarding governance at the school level make replication of effective schools, including high-performing No Excuses schools, needlessly difficult. In nearly every state, each charter school must have its own independent governing board, whose authority cannot be delegated. To build a network of schools, school entrepreneurs have had to establish management organizations that enter into multiyear contracts to provide a broad range of education and operational services to each board, to which they are ultimately accountable.

Most authorizers initially approached replication with hostility—replications were disparaged as cookie-cutter schools. The 200-year tradition of localism in primary and secondary education contained two expectations that were at odds with centrally managed networks of similar schools: local control and differentiation. Charter school laws, authorizers and state education agencies often contended, were intended to spawn community-based schools—each with its own lay board, each tailored to the unique needs of its students, and each a laboratory for an innovative model—not to foster a system of schools that implemented a common design and was operated by an out-of-state corporation. The responses of for-profit education management organizations to these expectations in the late 1990s approached the disingenuous; they assembled boards to meet these requirements. Not-for-profit CMOs have approached the requirement of individual boards earnestly, but the structure remains cumbersome and inefficient.

School entrepreneurs must recruit accomplished volunteer board members for each school in the network; the authorizer's reception of the application depends on the skill and capacity of the members. But the members' loyalty to the management organization is also essential, both to protect the organization's investment in starting the school and to ensure that the school remains faithful to the network's mission and education design. Founders quickly exhaust their network of such individuals. As CMOs grow, managing increasing numbers of boards and ensuring their sustained commitment to the centralized model become increasingly unwieldy.

Not only do such governance requirements waste effort, they also interfere with sound management practice. Maintaining legally separate entities for each school and the charter management organization weakens the chain of command and makes precise implementation of the school's academic, cultural, and operational practices less likely. Authorizers and local education agencies have interpreted such statutes as prohibiting the board from delegating authority to hire and fire the school's chief executive (the principal) to the CMO and requiring all school staff to report to that principal. This introduces organizational tensions between the CMO and the schools, as the CMO, the school's board, and the principal vie for control over the school, and it raises irresolvable questions about the level of discretion schools are afforded and where compliance with central policies of the CMO is required.

The governance structure also radically increases the complexity of doing business. Each school in the network has to maintain separate books and accounts, obtain its own tax-exempt status, conduct its own audits, apply for separate grants, and comply with elaborate reporting requirements. A major impediment to securing and developing facilities—always the greatest challenge facing charters—is the inability to pool the schools' assets; the balance sheets and operating histories of established schools cannot aid new schools in securing credit.

Finally, the governance structure prevents schools in the network from combining efforts to serve students with special needs, such as those requiring highly restricted settings, or from feeding middle school students into a single high school. Charter management organizations have to create a jury-rigged system in which each feeder middle school operates high school grades at a co-located facility where teachers are employed by multiple entities. For example, KIPP NYC College Prep educates high school students who formally remain students of four separate middle schools: KIPP Academy, KIPP STAR, KIPP AMP, and KIPP Infinity.[42]

Governance Reforms

Effective governance of charters will promote the formation of educationally successful, rather than unique, schools by fostering charter management organizations and other networks of schools. Charter experimentation and differentiation will occur between charter networks rather than within them. As news of the success of KIPP and other No Excuses school networks spreads, authorizers are newly focused on easing replication. At least one leading authorizer, the Charter Schools Institute of the State University of New York, along with the New York City Charter School Center, has interpreted recent amendments to the New York charter law as permitting charter schools to merge, resulting in a single surviving governing board. The center has decried the requirement that a CMO enter into a management contract with each school in its network: "It is hard to estimate precisely," its executive director writes, "the number of wasted hours and money that result from inefficiencies; it is clear that they are significant and avoidable."[43] Although merged schools can now be governed by a single board, they are still accountable for fulfilling the commitments of their individual charters. If this governance initiative proves practicable and survives legal scrutiny, it will dramatically simplify the tasks of expanding No Excuses networks, including securing school facilities, maintaining fidelity to the education model, and complying with regulatory and reporting requirements.

Parental choice, charter renewal requirements, and accountability to state education agencies for academic outcomes are strong mechanisms for ensuring both school quality and responsiveness to the needs of parents. The local advisory board could serve as a formal mechanism for community and parent voice.

Human Capital Providers

To improve the performance of America's schools, we must have better teachers. Teacher effectiveness has a greater effect on a student's achievement than any other school characteristic, including class size, race, poverty, and parent's education.[44] Cohorts of students with comparable abilities and initial achievement levels post dramatically different academic outcomes as a result of the teachers to whom they are assigned. In one well-known study, William L. Sanders and June C. Rivers classify teachers in quintiles of effectiveness based on the gains their students made in reading and math over one year and then compare the performance of students exposed to sequences of these teachers of varying quality. Students taught for three successive years by teachers in the top quintile performed on average 50 percentage points higher than students taught by the teachers from the lowest quintile on the Tennessee Comprehensive Assessment Program Achievement Test in math.[45]

It is widely known that America's education system sources its teachers from among its least successful students. The problem has worsened over the past few decades: in the period from 1964 to 1971, 20 to 25 percent of female teachers scored in the top decile of high school achievement tests; by 2000, less than 13 percent did.[46] The top-performing education systems in the world attract top students to the teaching profession. Countries, such as Finland, South Korea, Singapore, and Hong Kong, that consistently score at the top of the two respected international assessments, Trends in International Mathematics and Science Study and the Programme for International Student Assessment, draw their teachers not from the bottom third of their high school classes, as in the United States, but from the top 5 to 30 percent, depending on the country.[47]

It is not an accident that our schools are staffed by teachers who themselves were poor students. Together, states and teachers unions govern who is allowed to teach and how teachers are recruited and trained. Other human capital policies, including statutes, regulations, and union contracts, govern how teachers are assigned, promoted, and terminated. To receive a license to teach, teachers in forty-five states must complete a teacher preparation program approved by the state and run by a school of education. Seventy percent of the nation's teachers attended as undergraduates one of the country's 1,400 schools of education, which, supported by teachers unions, lobby state higher education boards and accreditation bodies to maintain their exclusive franchise and to oppose genuinely alternative paths to certification that bypass their institutions.[48] The quality of education schools has been much criticized; standards of admission are low, the curriculum is lacking in rigor and of questionable usefulness, and requirements for graduation are lax. The SAT and Graduate Record Examination (GRE) scores of education school students who go on to become elementary school teachers are very low; GRE scores are 100 points below the national average.[49] Education school coursework centers on theories of learning and the sociology of education rather than on developing teaching techniques and honing teachers' skills.[50] Faculties, curriculum, and research are disconnected from practitioners and schools; for example, aspiring teachers are rarely videotaped and critiqued. Research by faculty members is widely regarded as lacking in academic rigor by their peers in other university programs.[51] School principals are overwhelmingly prepared by the same institutions; 95 percent of principals rise from the ranks of teachers.[52]

In the past two decades, social entrepreneurs have sought to devise new institutions for recruiting and training teachers and school leaders. Most such programs aim to draw prospective teachers and principals from varied education and professional backgrounds. New Leaders for New Schools, Building Excellent Schools, the New Teacher Project, Troops for Teachers, and the American Board for the Certification of Teacher Excellence Program are among the best known of these.

The largest such program, Teach for America, founded in 1990, prepares recent graduates of selective colleges and universities to teach for a minimum of two years in urban and rural schools across the country. The program is highly selective; in 2010, 4,500 corps members were selected from 50,000 applicants. Corps members do not attend a school of education but rather are prepared in the program's six-week summer training program. Independent research finds that in their first year of teaching, they perform as well as or better than other beginning teachers and are as effective as veteran teachers.[53]

Teach for America's less obvious impact, however, is in developing education leaders. A study of the work history of the management teams of the forty-nine most influential entrepreneurial education organizations has found that Teach for America spawned more members of the organization's top management teams than any other teacher training program. The organization that appears second most frequently in the team members' histories is KIPP, which itself was founded by two Teach for America alumni, Mike Feinberg and David Levin.[54] Other alumni include Sarah Usdin, who launched New Schools for New Orleans, and Michelle Rhee, a former schools chancellor for the District of Columbia and the founder of the New Teacher Project.

But even Teach for America has not entirely bypassed the lock of the schools of education on teacher licensure. During their teaching commitment, corps members must complete pedagogical coursework—in most states, through a school of education, and in a few states, through a school district. Only rarely can Teach for America or another nonprofit organization provide such training.[55] After exceptionally long days, corps members must attend night courses on education theory at a significant cost.[56] Furthermore, teacher compensation policy is governed by school districts, and unions have succeeded broadly in conditioning pay promotions on the acquisition of course credits and advanced degrees—largely from schools of education. Corps members have no choice but to enroll in a master's program to be eligible for increased pay.

Frustration with conventional teacher preparation led to the founding of Teacher U, an alternative master's degree program at Hunter College. Now an independent, degree-granting institution known as Relay Graduate School of Education, the school focuses on mastery of specific teaching techniques known to work. The program claims to be the first to require that aspiring teachers demonstrate proficiency and achievement, as measured by student test scores, to earn the degree.[57] Unions have strongly opposed certification, recertification, and tenure eligibility policies that consider a teacher's efficacy as measured by the gains made on standardized tests. Unsurprisingly, then, Relay's application to the New York State Board of Regents for degree-granting authority was opposed by many colleges and universities in New York City canvassed by the board.[58]

Relay's radical emphasis on technique and practice is based on the work of the school's founders, Norman Atkins and Doug Lemov, of Uncommon Schools. Lemov observed the highest-performing teachers at Uncommon's own schools and other high-achieving schools. He developed a taxonomy of their teaching techniques, discrete classroom management and instructional skills that, strangely, are neglected by teacher training programs. Instructional techniques include the effective use of cold calling (teachers call on students without waiting for a raised hand), "right is right" (teachers break the ubiquitous habit, when calling on students, of endorsing incorrect answers) and "stretch it" (teachers reward "right" answers by asking follow-up questions that extend student knowledge). Each of these skills can be taught and practiced; together, Lemov argues, they can lift a classroom from mediocrity to excellence.

> Teaching is a performance profession, and in any other performance profession, be it the arts, or athletics, or surgery, the thing that people do before the performance is they practice. . . . You would never have the temerity to walk on center court of the U.S. Open without practicing ten thousand backhands. We are socializing teachers to practice in schools, beginning with simple techniques in front of their peers.[59]

In 2010 Lemov published the forty-nine techniques, along with video clips on the techniques in action. The book has become the heart of professional development at nearly all No Excuses schools and charter management organizations. In these schools, the Lemov taxonomy and its pithy labels have become the language of teacher observations, the diagnosis of classroom problems, and the feedback to teachers on how to overcome them.

The excitement over Lemov's techniques-based teacher training has not been limited to charter schools or high-poverty schools; erasing ideological divides, teachers from schools of every sector and community have embraced his ideas, and principals from districts large and small have reached out to Lemov. But education schools, with few exceptions, have been silent. "The difference in response has been striking between the operating and training sectors," Lemov says. "There have been precious few inquiries."[60]

But change may come quickly. Beginning in 2013, New York State, like Relay Graduate School of Education, will hold all graduate students in education accountable for what students learn in their classrooms. A complete redesign of teacher and principal certification will focus on the practice of teaching and involve performance assessments, value-added standards, and video analysis. Twenty-two states, including New York, are testing accountability standards under a pilot program out of Stanford University. Along with other states, New York is piloting a program backed by the National Council for Accreditation of Teacher Education that reshapes teacher education around not academic study but teacher practice.[61]

Digital Learning

The revolution in information technology that is sweeping the globe is only beginning to penetrate our schools, but there its impact will be no less transformative. In time, students will be able to access the finest teachers and most effective instruction anytime and anywhere. The cost of education will decline, while quality and access improve. The governance structures of public education can thwart digital learning's progress, but they cannot stop it. The right actions by government can speed it along.

Already, online learning, which takes place partially or entirely over the Internet, is well established in higher education. By 2010, the number of students taking at least one online course was 5.6 million (30 percent of the total), an increase of 21 percent over the previous year.[62] Digital learning has been slower to take hold in primary and secondary education, but its use is accelerating. The International Association for K–12 Online Learning estimates that more than 1.5 million K–12 students were engaged in online and blended learning in the 2009–10 school year.[63] That number is expected to grow by more than 40 percent a year.[64] Online schooling takes several forms. In 2010–11 virtual charter schools were operating in twenty-seven states and the District of Columbia and enrolled 217,000 students, who took some or all of their classes online.[65] Many such schools are run by for-profit companies, including K[12], Connections Academy, and Advanced Academics. The Pennsylvania Cyber Charter School, opened in 2000, enrolls more than 10,000 students.[66] By 2009, thirty-nine states had established state-level online schools or learning initiatives.[67] The largest, Florida Virtual School, served more than 122,000 students in 2010–11.[68] Michigan and Alabama require all high school students to take at least one course online to graduate. Florida requires all schools to make online courses available to students.[69]

Hybrid schools combine traditional bricks-and-mortar schooling with online components. One leading hybrid operator, Rocketship Education, aims to eliminate the achievement gap in its charter elementary schools. By engaging students for a portion of the day in online learning, with less adult supervision, Rocketship is able to pay its teachers more. In 2011 its flagship school, Mateo Sheedy Elementary, ranked first in Santa Clara County, California, among low-income elementary schools.[70]

Metastudies of the efficacy of online learning find that it is as effective as face-to-face traditional instruction, but the conclusion is fragile because studies do not account for other differences, such as the amount of learning time.[71] The efficacy of online learning is likely to sharply increase in coming years, with improvements in content, technological tools, and connection bandwidth.

As digital learning develops, costs are likely to fall, with increasing amounts of content available free of charge. Khan Academy, a nonprofit corporation, has posted online some 2,400 video lessons on topics ranging from addition to differential equations that have been watched more than 75 million times by students around the world. Salman Khan, founder of Khan Academy, presents concepts explicitly with extraordinary clarity using a simple white board and audio format; adaptive testing gauges student mastery. Khan, who recorded all the lessons himself, aims to help educate billions of students around the world.[72] At Stanford University, two renowned computer scientists inspired by Khan's work offered an online course on artificial intelligence free of charge during fall 2011. Word of the course spread virally, and by August that year, 58,000 students from 175 countries had signed on to take the course—more than four times the size of the student body of the university. Testing allowed for automatic grading, and students voted on questions to be answered by the professors online.[73]

Governance Obstacles

To realize the full promise of online learning will require broad changes to the governance structure of K–12 education. The current regulatory regime of bricks-and-mortar schools has impeded the long-awaited substitution of capital for labor and, in turn, educational improvement.[74] Other governance obstacles include the heterogeneity of states' learning standards and assessments;

funding rules; caps on the number of students who may enroll in online class or attend virtual schools, including virtual charter schools; teacher licensure requirements; student-teacher ratios and interaction rules; portability of student credits; obsolete accreditation standards; and access to federal funding for high-bandwidth connections.[75]

The adoption by state education agencies of the Common Core standards and the development of corresponding assessments by two state consortiums will radically simplify the development of online content and courses and lower the cost of operation for online providers. (K^{12}, the largest provider of online curriculums, was saddled with high development costs because curriculum and assessment had to be adapted for each state.)[76] Historically, schools have been funded on the basis of seat time; each school receives an appropriation for educating a certain number of children over the course of a year—regardless of academic outcomes. In principle, when all instruction was delivered by a teacher in a classroom and students had to progress at the same pace, seat time worked as a basis for organizing and funding education. Today, online learning and assessments enable student competency to be measured; this, rather than seat time, should serve as the basis for funding, industry advocates contend. Individual rates of progress are essential to the model; students need to be able to progress at their own pace to ensure that all are successful.[77] Applied to virtual schools, this fee structure raises thorny questions. For one, should virtual schools receive the same amount per pupil as a traditional school, if they produce the same or better outcomes but their costs are lower? Should a school district receive the full allocation for a pupil who is enrolled for one or more courses at the state's virtual school? Should local school districts lose money to virtual charter schools located hundreds of miles away? Such questions have been hotly contested in both legislatures and the courts. Each state has arrived at its own tentative resolution. In some states, virtual charter schools receive significantly less money than regular charters. Funding follows the student to some state virtual schools; in other cases, the schools are funded by separate appropriation, which avoids any impingement on school district revenues but also limits enrollment and stymies innovation. Florida Virtual School is now funded on the basis of course completion (students must receive at least a D for the school to receive any funding), and other states have followed suit. Paying for outcomes is more efficient than paying for seat time, but it could create incentives for teachers to lower standards to maintain the institution's financial health. Externally proctored exams might be a solution, but they are operationally challenging and costly.[78]

Teacher licensure systems are particularly ill suited to online education. Unions have insisted that teachers in virtual schools be state certified, but limitations in teacher licensure reciprocity often prevent teachers licensed in one state from teaching a virtual course to students in another. Moreover, university professors and other manifestly competent teachers who have not attended education schools should not be prohibited from teaching online courses. Other rules mandate the ratio of online teachers to students or the minimum number of interactions between teachers and students over a period of time. Such constraints do little or nothing to ensure education quality while they thwart innovation and prevent the power of digital learning from being realized.

Governance Reforms

As governments at all levels continue to grapple with the challenges and opportunities digital learning creates, they should bear in mind some basic principles:

All students should have access to online learning. To ensure unfettered access, states should not cap enrollment in statewide online schools, limit enrollment in virtual or blended charter schools to students who live outside a region, or prohibit schools from establishing multiple campuses.

Providers must be free to devise new efficiencies, especially in how teachers are deployed. States should not attempt to prescribe how online schools are staffed and organized. Rules that mandate the minimum ratio of teachers to students or prescribe the amount of interaction between teachers and students should be eliminated. Current teacher licensure systems do nothing to ensure quality and restrict access to qualified teachers; until they can be comprehensively reformed, states should at a minimum ensure full licensing reciprocity.

Learning should be measured by outcomes and funded accordingly. Current funding and accountability systems presume same-age cohorts of students proceeding in lockstep. If a student fails a grade, he or she must repeat the full year. As Tom Vander Ark and Susan Patrick argue, students should be encouraged to learn as rapidly as they can, and schools should be rewarded for accelerating student progress. States should experiment in their online schools, credit recovery programs, and blended schools with student competency–based funding, where funding follows the student and schools are paid for learning outcomes, as at Florida Virtual School.[79]

What will K–12 education look like once digital learning is pervasive? Increasingly, online learning will lead to the unbundling of school services, as Patrick and Vander Ark and Frederick Hess have noted. Students will seek out the best choice for each area of study, enrolling in courses from a number of different providers, taught by far-flung teachers employed by remote entities. The student's transcript will reflect this assemblage of coursework. Instead of compensating schools for teaching students in all courses of study for one year, providers will be paid on a fractional basis, as is presently the case in Florida, Minnesota, and Utah.[80] A primary provider could be selected for managing students' transcripts, granting credits, providing guidance, and compensating other providers.[81]

Implications for School Governance

Never more than a platform for change, charter legislation initially spawned many schools that were barely better—and sometimes worse—than district schools. Yet after a decade of experimentation, a model for educating children from poverty emerged: the No Excuses model of schooling, which is now at the core of most charter schools that are bridging the achievement gap. New initiatives for sourcing and preparing teachers that focus on rapidly equipping well-educated and highly motivated new teachers with teaching techniques, rather than pedagogical theories, are challenging schools of education and their lock on who gets to teach in public schools. Teach for America and Relay Graduate School of Education together look remarkably like the system for sourcing, training, and credentialing teachers in top-performing Finland, where teachers are selected from the top of their high school class and training focuses on intensive practice in developing and deploying lessons.[82] Moreover, the potential of digital learning to deliver low-cost, effective, and engaging instruction to students anywhere anytime is beginning to be realized—as a new generation of children arrives to school wedded to their digital devices.

As word spreads of these disruptive innovations and the educational opportunities they create, especially for disadvantaged families, public support for the powerful alliance of interest groups that maintains the governance status quo is beginning to erode. Political actors, such as Democrats for Education Reform and big-city mayors traditionally loyal to the teachers unions, are adopting an increasingly jaundiced view of their aims.[83] These trends are likely to continue, bolstered by two major governance reforms of the past two decades: First, state and federal accountability systems, which the move to the Common Core standards and corresponding assessments will sharpen, starkly reveal what is working and what is not.[84] Second, choice—of what school to attend, or where to teach, or what online course to take—diverts talent and public and private funds out of mainstream institutions and into entrepreneurial initiatives. Existing institutions, shackled by institutional inertia and dysfunctional governance, will be hard pressed to compete successfully in the new currency of academic outcomes. The operating system of district schools—the rules by which they are governed and operate—is hopelessly obsolete and must be rewritten.

Change will take time. Incremental governance reforms will be enacted in one jurisdiction and gradually spread to others. To give steam to the three disruptive innovations, the states and the federal government should consider taking several short-term actions.

To encourage the proliferation of highly effective urban charter schools, states should limit authorizing to a small number of large-scale statewide authorizers. Each would be subject to caps that increase automatically as a function of the academic performance of their portfolio's schools as compared with demographically comparable schools. Charter schools that make up a network of schools should be permitted to merge under a single governing board. To boost private lending for charter school facilities, the federal government should dramatically expand its credit enhancement program for charter school facilities.

To build a new generation of capable teachers, states should authorize new teacher training institutions that focus on technique and practice and also reform state licensure systems. The door should be open to teachers who have not attended education schools but can demonstrate content knowledge and have shown value-added gains for their students.

To realize the potential of online learning, states should lift arbitrary caps on enrollment in virtual state and charter schools; fund schools based on fractional payments for mastery of each course, using external proctored exams; ensure state reciprocity in teacher licensure; and cease prescribing class size and teacher interaction frequencies.

Each such change will enhance the reach and impact of the three initiatives and in turn build the case for deeper reforms to the nation's antiquated system of school governance. At the same time, education entrepreneurs in each of the three sectors will need to attend to apparent weaknesses in their own plans, weaknesses that threaten their impact and, in turn, the reform of school governance. The No Excuses charter school model relies on a small pool of teachers from top undergraduate institutions, and management organizations often make unsustainable work demands on them; both components limit the model's capacity to scale.[85] For their part, teacher training providers need to confront the limits of the "teacher as hero" premise; teachers, no matter how motivated or well prepared, parachuting into broadly dysfunctional urban schools cannot by themselves regularly produce gap-closing results. Finally, digital learning entrepreneurs risk squandering a decade to faulty education designs, as did the charter movement. As a U.S. Department of Education study of digital learning programs has found, expository approaches post the greatest achievement effects.[86] Repudiating the Partnership for 21st Century Learning Skills (an organ of large technology companies), digital learning entrepreneurs should resist seductive pedagogical fads and focus instead on what is known to work—lucid, explicit, and engaging instruction in the liberal curriculum.

Ultimately, reforming the governance of K–12 education requires breaking the exclusive franchises of school districts and schools of education. No longer should these institutions dictate where children may go to school and who may teach them. Cities and towns, after contributing within their means to the financing of public schools statewide, could elect to operate their own schools, as today, or contract with one or more school operators. Funding would newly be a function of enrollment, with supplements for children with special needs. Operators not under district control, including virtual schools, could be chartered by one of several statewide authorizers and compete for students. Many schools, both district operated and charter, would elect to hire fewer teachers at higher pay, to tap digital learning technologies to increase educational productivity, and even to manage the enrollment of their students in online courses delivered by third parties. Beyond the minimum of a college degree and demonstrated knowledge of subject matter, schools would be free to hire teachers who hold the credentials they deem important; schools of education would educate and train teachers in the capacities operators find most valuable. All schools would be accountable for academic outcomes to the state education agency, which would assess performance using nationally recognized and validated assessments.

Notes

1. Seventy percent of students at P.S. 149 qualify for free or reduced-price lunch, 13 percent have limited English proficiency, 75 percent are black, and 22 percent are Hispanic. At Harlem Success Academy, 76 percent of students qualify for free or reduced-price lunch, 2 percent have limited English proficiency, 79 percent are black, and 15 percent are Hispanic. For demographic information, see New York State Education Department, "2009–10 Report Cards," 2011 (https://reportcards.nysed.gov/view.php?county=yes&year=2010).

2. Jenny Sedlis, "Getting the Numbers Right on Harlem Schools," *Reuters* blog, August 31, 2011 (http://blogs.reuters.com/great-debate/2011/08/31/getting-the-numbers-right-on-harlem-schools/).

3. See James P. Comer, *Waiting for a Miracle: Why Schools Can't Solve Our Problems—and How We Can* (New York: Penguin, 1997). For the Bigger, Bolder Approach, see www.boldapproach.org.

4. On the whole, charter schools have not performed better than district schools, as discussed later in this chapter. Knowledge Is Power Program, "KIPP: 2010 Report Card," 2011 (www.kipp.org/reportcard/2010). For a comparison of funding in charter and district public schools, see National Alliance for Public Charter Schools, "Charter School Funding: 2009–2010, National," 2011 (http://dashboard.publiccharters.org/dashboard/policy/page/funding/year/2010).

5. Anthony Picciano and Jeff Seaman, *K–12 Online Learning: A 2008 Follow-Up of the Survey of U.S. School District Administrators* (New York: Graduate Center and Hunter College, City University of New York, 2009), p. 1.

6. John Michael Lee Jr. and Anita Rawls, *The College Completion Agenda: 2010 Progress Report* (Reston, Va.: College Board, Advocacy and Policy Center, 2010), p. 8.

7. Klaus Schwab, *The Global Competitiveness Report, 2011–2012* (Geneva: World Economic Forum, 2011), p. 363.

8. Terry M. Moe, *Special Interest: Teachers Unions and America's Public Schools* (Brookings Press, 2011), p. 277.

9. Scott Reader, "The Hidden Costs of Tenure," 2005 (www.thehiddencostsoftenure.com).

10. National Alliance for Public Charter Schools, "Students Overview: 2010–2011, National," 2011 (http://dashboard.publiccharters.org/dashboard/students/page/overview/year/2011).

11. National Alliance for Public Charter Schools, *A Growing Movement: America's Largest Charter School Communities,* 6th ed. (Washington, 2011), p. 1.

12. Ross School, "Tuition and Fees," 2011 (www.ross.org/admissions/tuition).

13. David W. Chen, "Charter School Loses Bid to Stay Open," *New York Times,* January 21, 2011. For academic performance and demographic information, see New York State Education Department, "The New York State Report Card: Accountability and Overview Report 2009–10: Ross Global Academy Charter School" (https://reportcards.nysed.gov/files/2009-10/AOR-2010-310200860905.pdf).

14. Center for Research on Education Outcomes, *Multiple Choice: Charter School Performance in 16 States* (Palo Alto, Calif.: Stanford University, 2009).

15. Ibid., p. 7.

16. Center for Research on Education Outcomes, *Charter School Performance in New York City* (Palo Alto, Calif.: Stanford University, 2010).

17. Center for Research on Education Outcomes, *Multiple Choice,* p. 6. A third study by the center examining the performance of charter schools in New Orleans finds that more than half of the schools are posting gains significantly greater than those of district schools, and 23 percent are making gains at about the same rate as district schools.

18. Steven F. Wilson, *Success at Scale in Charter Schooling* (Washington: American Enterprise Institute, 2008). Samuel C. Carter, *No Excuses: Lessons from 21 High-Performing, High-Poverty Schools* (Washington: Heritage Foundation, 2000).

19. David Whitman calls schools like these "paternalistic." See David Whitman, *Sweating the Small Stuff: Inner City Schools and the New Paternalism* (Washington: Thomas B. Fordham Institute, 2008).

20. Knowledge Is Power Program, "KIPP: About KIPP," 2012 (www.kipp.org/about-kipp).

21. Christina Clark Tuttle and others, *Student Characteristics and Achievement in 22 KIPP Middle Schools: Final Report* (Princeton, N.J.: Mathematica Policy Research, 2010).

22. Uncommon Schools, "State Test Results," 2011 (www.uncommonschools.org/results).

23. Achievement First, "Achievement First Results in New York," 2011 (www.achievementfirst.org/results/in-new-york).

24. Atila Abdulkadiroglu and others, *Informing the Debate: Comparing Boston's Charter, Pilot, and Traditional Schools* (Boston: Boston Foundation, 2009), p. 39. A strength of the study is also a limitation: comparing the performance of students who are admitted to a charter school in an admissions lottery against those who applied but were not admitted eliminates the selection effect of parent motivation, but it also limits the universe of schools to those where there are more applicants than seats. These popular schools may also be the academically strongest schools.

25. Ira Nichols-Barrer and others, "Student Selection, Attrition, and Replacement in KIPP Middle Schools," Working Paper (Princeton, N.J.: Mathematica Policy Research, April 8, 2011).

26. The schools are the Academy of the Pacific Rim Charter Public School in Hyde Park, Edward Brooke Charter School in Roslindale, Boston Collegiate Charter School in

Dorchester, Excel Academy Charter School in East Boston, Boston Preparatory Charter Public School in Hyde Park, the Media and Technology Charter High School in Kenmore Square, and the Roxbury Preparatory Charter School in Roxbury.

27. See Massachusetts Department of Elementary and Secondary Education, "2008 MCAS Report (District) for Grade 10: All Students," 2008 (http://profiles.doe.mass.edu/state_report/mcas.aspx). See also Massachusetts Department of Elementary and Secondary Education, "Selected Populations (2008–09)," 2009 (http://profiles.doe.mass.edu/profiles/student.aspx?orgcode=00460505&orgtypecode=6&leftNavId=305&&fycode=2009).

28. NewSchools Venture Fund, "NewSchools Announces $3 Million in Grants for Expansion of Four High-Performing Boston Charter Schools," 2011 (www.newschools.org/news/boston-charters).

29. Joshua D. Angrist, Parag A. Pathak, and Christopher R. Walters, "Explaining Charter School Effectiveness," Working Paper 17332 (Cambridge, Mass.: National Bureau of Economic Research, 2011), p. 3.

30. Ibid., p. 5.

31. Bryan C. Hassel, *Studying Achievement in Charter Schools: What Do We Know?* (Washington: Public Impact for the National Alliance for Public Charter Schools, January 2005).

32. Center for Education Reform, *Charter School Laws across the States: Rankings and Scorecards,* 12th ed. (Washington, 2010).

33. New York State Education Department, "Federal Charter Schools Program Planning and Implementation Grant Application: Request for Proposal," March 2010.

34. Karen Girolami Callam and Alex Medler, *The State of Charter School Authorizing, 2010* (Chicago: National Association of Charter School Authorizers, 2010).

35. Alex Medler, William Haft, and Margaret Lin, *Principles and Standards for Quality Charter School Authorizing* (Washington: National Association of Charter School Authorizers, 2010), p. 11.

36. Louann Bierlein Palmer and Rebecca Gau, *Charter School Authorizers: Are States Making the Grade?* (Washington: Thomas B. Fordham Institute, 2003), p. 1.

37. Andrew J. Rotherham, *Smart Charter School Caps* (Washington: Education Sector, 2007).

38. See New York City Charter School Center, "New York State Charter Schools Act of 1998 (as Amended)," 2011 (www.nyccharterschools.org/learn/about-new-law).

39. Chester E. Finn Jr. and Eric Osberg, *Charter School Funding: Inequity's Next Frontier* (Washington: Thomas B. Fordham Institute, 2005).

40. Shaka Mitchell and Jeanne Allen, *Solving the Charter School Funding Gap* (Washington: Center for Education Reform, 2005).

41. Kim Smith and James Wilcox, "A Building Need," *Education Next* 4 (Spring 2004): 44–51.

42. Knowledge Is Power Program, "KIPP NYC College Prep," 2011 (www.kipp.org/school-content/kipp-nyc-college-prep).

43. New York State Education Department and others, memorandum from New York Charter School Center to Sally Bachofer, April 18, 2011, p. 2.

44. Kevin Carey, "The Real Value of Teachers: Using New Information about Teacher Effectiveness to Close the Achievement Gap," *Thinking K–16* 8 (Winter 2004): 4.

45. William L. Sanders and June C. Rivers, *Cumulative and Residual Effects of Teachers on Future Student Academic Achievement* (University of Tennessee, Value-Added Research and Assessment Center, 1996).

46. Sean Corcoran, William Evans, and Robert Schwab, "Changing Labor Market Opportunities for Women and the Quality of Teachers, 1957–2000," *American Economic Review* 94 (May 2004): 230–35.

47. Programme for International Student Assessment, *Assessing Scientific, Reading, and Mathematical Literacy: A Framework for PISA 2006* (Paris: Organization for Economic Cooperation and Development, 2006). Programme for International Student Assessment, *PISA 2009 Results: What Students Know and Can Do – Student Performance in Reading, Mathematics and Science,* vol. 1 (Paris: Organization for Economic Cooperation and Development, 2010).

48. David Steiner, "Skewed Perspective," *Education Next* 5 (Winter 2005): 54–59.

49. Arthur Levine, *Educating School Teachers* (Washington: Education Schools Project, 2006).

50. Steiner, "Skewed Perspective."

51. Ibid.

52. Susan Gates and others, *Who Is Leading Our Schools? An Overview of School Administrators and the Careers* (Arlington, Va.: Rand Education, 2001).

53. Zeyu Xu, Jane Hannaway, and Colin Taylor, "Making a Difference? The Effects of Teach for America in High School" (Washington: National Center for Analysis of Longitudinal Data in Education Research, 2009). "Teach for America Evaluation Report" (Charlotte, N.C.: Center for Research and Evaluation Office of Accountability, Charlotte-Mecklenburg Schools, 2009); "Teach for America National Principal Survey" (Washington: Policy Studies Associates, 2009); George H. Noell and Kristin A. Gansle, "Teach for America Teachers' Contribution to Student Achievement in Louisiana in Grades 4–9: 2004–2005 to 2006–2007" (Louisiana State University, 2009).

54. Monica Higgins and others, "Creating a Corps of Change Agents," *Education Next* 11 (Summer 2011): 19–25.

55. Teach for America, "Why Teach for America?" 2011 (www.teachforamerica.org/why-teach-for-america/training-and-support/teacher-certification).

56. Kate Walsh and Sandi Jacobs, *Alternative Certification Isn't Alternative* (Washington: Thomas B. Fordham Institute and National Council on Teacher Quality, 2007), p. 8.

57. Sarah Otterman, "Ed Schools' Pedagogical Puzzle," *New York Times*, July 21, 2011.

58. New York State Education Department, memorandum to Higher Education Committee from Joseph P. Frey, 2011 (www.regents.nysed.gov/meetings/2011Meetings/February2011/211hea2.pdf).

59. Doug Lemov, telephone interview with author, April 13, 2011.

60. Ibid.

61. Rick Hess, "Straight Up Conversation: Former New York Commissioner David Steiner," *Education Week* blog, August 15, 2011 (http://blogs.edweek.org/edweek/rick_hess_straight_up/2011/08/straight_up_conversation_former_new_york_commissioner_david_steiner.html).

62. I. Elaine Allen and Jeff Seaman, *Class Differences: Online Education in the United States, 2010* (Wellesley, Mass.: Babson Survey Research Group and the Sloan Consortium, 2010).

63. International Association for K–12 Online Learning, "Fast Facts about Online Learning," Washington, February 2012 (www.inacol.org/press/docs/nacol_fast_facts.pdf).

64. Susan Patrick and Tom Vander Ark, "Authorizing Online Learning" (Chicago: National Association of Charter School Authorizers, 2011), p. 1 (www.qualitycharters. org/images/stories/publications/Viewpoints/Vander_Ark-Patrick_Cyber_Learning_View point_August_2011.pdf).

65. Ambient Insight, "2011 Learning Technology Research Taxonomy: Research Methodology, Buyer Segmentation, Product Definitions, and Licensing Model" (Monroe, Wash., June 2011) (www.ambientinsight.com/Resources/Documents/AmbientInsight_ Learning_Technology_Taxonomy.pdf).

66. Pennsylvania Cyber Charter School, "PA Cyber and Midland," 2011 (www.pacyber. org/about.jsp?pageId=2161392240601291297846033).

67. John Watson and others, *Keeping Pace with K–12 Online Learning: An Annual Review of Policy and Practice* (Durango, Colo.: Evergreen Education Group, 2010).

68. Florida Virtual School, "Quick Facts," 2011 (www.flvs.net/areas/aboutus/Pages/ QuickFactsaboutFLVS.aspx).

69. Moe, *Special Interest*, p. 277.

70. Rocketship Education, "Mateo Sheedy Elementary," 2011 (http://rsed.org/index. php?page=mateo-sheedy-elementary).

71. Barbara Means and others, *Evaluation of Evidence-Based Practices in Online Learning: A Meta-Analysis and Review of Online Learning Studies* (U.S. Department of Education, September 2010).

72. Khan Academy, "Frequently Asked Questions," 2011 (www.khan academy.org/ about/faq).

73. John Markoff, "Virtual and Artificial, but 58,000 Want Course," *New York Times,* August 15, 2011.

74. Paul E. Peterson, *Saving Schools: From Horace Mann to Virtual Learning* (Belknap Press of Harvard University Press, 2010), p. 256.

75. Meris Stansbury, "Virtual Schools in a Fight for Adequate Funding," *eSchool News,* October 14, 2010 (www.eschoolnews.com/2010/10/14/virtual-schools-in-a-fight-for-adequate-funding/); Becky Vevea, "Virtual School Advocates Call for Removal of Enrollment Cap," *Milwaukee Journal Sentinel* blog, December 2, 2010; Terry Stoops, *Virtually Irrelevant: How Certification Rules Impede the Growth of Virtual School* (Raleigh, N.C.: John Locke Foundation, 2011); John Watson, *The State of Online Learning in California: A Look at Current K–12 Policies and Practices* (University of California College Prep, 2006); Ray Parker, "Online Students Find Problems with Credit Transfer Policy," *Arizona Republic,* October 16, 2009; Gene Glass and Kevin Welner, *Online K–12 Schooling in the U.S.: Uncertain Private Ventures in Need of Public Regulation* (Boulder, Colo.: National Education Policy Center, 2011), p. 9.

76. Chester E. Finn Jr., "Lessons Learned: Technology, Reform, and Replication," in *What Next? Educational Innovation and Philadelphia's School of the Future*, edited by Mary Cullinane and Frederick M. Hess (Harvard Education Press, 2010), p. 201.

77. Susan Patrick, letter in response to a public letter released by the Federal Communications Commission on November 3, 2009 (Washington: International Association for K–12 Online Learning, 2009) (www.inacol.org/research/docs/FCC_Filing_ 121109.pdf).

78. Peterson, *Saving Schools*, p. 257.

79. Patrick and Vander Ark, "Authorizing Online Learning."

80. Ibid., p. 3; Frederick M. Hess, *Quality Control in K–12 Digital Learning: Three (Imperfect) Approaches* (Washington: Thomas B. Fordham Institute, July 2011).

81. Hess, "Straight Up Conversation."

82. Finland Ministry of Education, *Attracting, Developing, and Retaining Effective Teachers: Country Background Report for Finland* (Helsinki: Finland Ministry of Education, 2003).

83. Moe, *Special Interest*, pp. 379–83.

84. The adoption by the states in the next five years of the Common Core standards and corresponding assessments now being developed by state consortiums will make outcome data generated by state accountability systems much more meaningful than they are today.

85. Wilson, *Success at Scale*; Education Sector, *Growing Pains: Scaling Up the Best Charter Schools in the Nation* (Washington: Education Sector, 2009), p. 8; Robin Lake and others, *The National Study of Charter Management Organization Effectiveness: Report on Interim Findings* (Seattle: Center on Reinventing Public Education, 2010).

86. Means and others, *Evaluation of Evidence-Based Practices in Online Learning*, pp. 28–29.

PART II

TRADITIONAL INSTITUTIONS IN FLUX

FREDERICK M. HESS *and* OLIVIA M. MEEKS

6

Rethinking District Governance

The nation's nearly 14,000 school boards are charged with providing the leadership, policy direction, and oversight necessary to promote excellent schooling. As the vehicle for parents and voters to shape school decisions, school boards have long been defended as bastions of democratic government and local control. In his 2010 book *School Boards in America: A Flawed Exercise in Democracy*, Gene Maeroff notes, "The idea of governing from the grass roots adds to the appeal that local school boards have with the public. Too many Americans would consider any other arrangement as undemocratic, however inaccurate this notion of democracy may be."[1] School boards have also been hailed as a channel for representation and empowerment among underrepresented communities.[2]

But boards have faced fierce criticism in recent decades, as student achievement has stagnated and reforms have floundered. The Center for American Progress's Matt Miller has counseled that a crucial step in school improvement is to "first, kill all the school boards."[3] In a 2008 *Atlantic Monthly* article, Miller argues that local control "essentially surrenders over the schools to the teachers' unions" and that "in an ideal world, we would scrap [school boards]—especially in big cities, where most poor children live." The Fordham Institute's Chester E. Finn Jr. has similarly declared, "School boards are an aberration, an anachronism, an educational sinkhole. . . . Put this dysfunctional arrangement out of its misery."[4] Even U.S. Secretary of Education Arne Duncan, a former superintendent of Chicago Public Schools who served under mayoral control, has suggested that mayoral control is superior to board governance, stating, "I absolutely, fundamentally believe that mayoral control is extraordinarily important."[5]

The most damning critiques of school board failings come from school board members themselves. In a 2010 *Education Week* piece describing his new experience as a school board member, Matt Winkle laments, "Almost anyone will, in time, become conditioned by the blunt force of his head hitting a brick wall. It was apparent to me that the other board members had traveled the same road I was on, and had run into the same brick wall often enough to eventually accept the premise that some things are so institutionalized they cannot be changed, or simply are not worth the effort."[6] Such diagnoses have convinced many observers that boards need to be radically altered or replaced.

These critiques have unfolded within a changing policy environment that has posed new challenges for district governance. In the past decade, the No Child Left Behind Act, new state accountability systems, and a relentless focus on student achievement have brought district governance into a new era. The heightened visibility of the past decade has given new urgency to the question of whether, after decades of largely ineffectual reform efforts, school districts and their boards are equal to the challenge. Unfortunately, to date, skirmishes over district governance have focused on the shape of the governing entity (for example, the board) while turning a blind eye to the nature of the school district itself. We have focused on the merits of altering or replacing school boards while paying little attention to whether these proposals are likely to address the deeper challenges of district-based governance.

Today's problems with board governance are largely the legacy of a poorly conceived and incoherently executed reform agenda advanced a century ago, and they remain with us as the penalties for slapdash efforts to remake political structures that are large and enduring. It would be a cruel irony if efforts to replace school boards with mayoral control were to repeat those earlier missteps. Yet the critiques voiced by those ready to abolish or overhaul boards seem to imply tacit approval of the antiquated, geographically configured school district itself. Instead of addressing the fact that the ship itself is taking on water, those pursuing governance reforms have focused on who should be at the helm. Although a good captain is undoubtedly preferred over a bad captain, reformers serious about righting the ship must be ready to address the bigger challenges.

School Boards Today

Before wading too deeply into the contemporary debate about whether to eliminate elected school boards, it is useful to spend a moment considering the reality of school boards as they exist today. In 2010 the authors wrote a study based on a national survey of school board members conducted in partnership with the National School Boards Association and the Fordham Institute.[7] The 900 respondents shared their views on issues ranging from membership demographics and school board elections to board behaviors and their own views on school reform.

Several findings stood out. First, school board elections are rarely competitive. When asked about how they came to be board members, respondents reported a smooth path to election. Nearly half of elected members reported that their most recent election was very easy, while just 6 percent found theirs very difficult. Nearly three-fourths reported that they had spent less than $1,000 in their most recent race; just 3 percent spent more than $25,000. Moreover, the most common campaign funding sources were board members' personal funds (59 percent) or contributions from family and friends (38 percent). Only a minority of board members reported raising funds from anyone besides friends and family: 19 percent of members reported receiving funds from the business community, 12 percent from the teachers unions, and 8 percent from parent groups. In short, board elections are typically nonpartisan and rarely contested. This makes them rather sleepy and fairly staid affairs that provide little opportunity for serious, sustained, or engaged debate about the performance and direction of the school system.[8]

Second, once elected, board members voice concerns about student performance, but they remain skeptical of disruptive reform proposals. Two-thirds of board members reported that the current state of student achievement is unacceptable. However, 40 percent thought that recruiting nontraditional teachers offered little or no promise of promoting school improvement, more than 50 percent felt that way about within-district school choice, more than 60 percent about year-round schooling, and more than 80 percent about the creation of new charter schools.

Third, when asked which reforms they deemed most likely to improve student learning, board members typically cited genteel measures while steering clear of more disruptive proposals. For example, 86 percent of members considered professional development extremely or very important, and three-fourths said the same of boosting the quality of school leadership. Board members also reported that they tend to take their lead from their local superintendent for most decisions. Fifty-six percent reported that they almost always rely on the superintendent for information to make decisions, and 89 percent do so either often or almost always.

In short, most school boards today feature limited electoral accountability, are populated by members skeptical of systemic change, and are heavily reliant on superintendents for information and direction. Without much in the way of electoral accountability, and absent faith in systemic reform, board members have little cause to push for transformative change—despite their concerns about achievement. The chances that such institutions will be the bearers of revolutionary change in governance are, therefore, slim, at best.

Exploring Mayoral Control

Given this reality, critics have understandably suggested that districts require more accountability and leadership than elected boards can provide. The most popular alternative is replacing elected boards with some form of mayoral control, a model of district governance that replaces an elected school board's authority with that of the mayor.

Today, mayoral control models have blossomed in cities nationwide, ranging from high-profile districts such as New York, Boston, Chicago, and the District of Columbia to less visible locales such as Harrisburg, Akron, St. Louis, and Trenton. As Kenneth Wong has noted, "In the past 15 years, a new breed of education mayor has emerged to challenge the traditional governance model of school districts insulated from the rest of municipal service delivery. Unwilling to sit on the sidelines as their cities' schools continue to fail, these mayors have set an example."[9]

Although mayoral control generally gives mayors much more control over decisions such as the district budget and the selection of the superintendent, there are many flavors of mayoral control. In *Mayoral Leadership and Involvement in Education*, the U.S. Conference of Mayors sketches four models of mayoral control. Under total control, school board members and the superintendent are appointed by the mayor. Under partial control, some or all school board members are appointed by the mayor; the school board then selects the superintendent. In a partnership relationship, superintendents and the mayor collaborate on reform initiatives. And with medium involvement, the mayor has some authority, in concert with other stakeholders.[10]

Regardless of the model, these trends in governance reflect what Columbia University's Jeffrey Henig calls "the end of educational exceptionalism," that is, the reabsorption of the once fiercely local issue of education back into the fold of general policy topics.[11] Understanding why advocates are seeking this shift is critical to understanding the mayoral control debate.

The Case for Mayoral Control

Support for mayoral control is premised on what the education scholar Michael Kirst has deemed "an implicit policy assumption . . . that mayors are better equipped than school boards to highlight school problems and mobilize the personnel and resources to solve them."[12] That mayoral control is preferable to elected boards is generally argued on four counts: it will increase electoral accountability, reduce the influence of special interests, foster continuity of leadership, and encourage professional leadership. These arguments are all, to greater or lesser degrees, legacies of the Progressive Era effort to separate education governance from politics. Indeed, most calls for mayoral control suppose that school governance is hampered not by too much politics but by the wrong kind of politics or by undisciplined leadership.

Electoral Accountability

Although elected school boards are regarded as testaments to grassroots democracy, their largely inaccessible and unnoticed election cycles threaten the electoral power of local voters. Across the nation, turnout in school elections is extraordinarily low. For example, New Jersey's average school board election turnout in the past few years has hovered around 15 percent,[13] while Iowa's average turnout in 2007 was 6 percent.[14] In truth, it is hard to count on elections to keep public officials in line when the public does not know who is in office. Public Agenda has reported that 63 percent of adults and 50 percent of parents say that they cannot name their local superintendent; similar percentages (62 and 48 percent, respectively) could not name one member of the local school board.[15] This is all made more confusing by nonpartisan elections, which mean voters cannot rely on party affiliation to guide their selections. As Public Agenda explains, "Most people, for whatever reason, are simply not active in or mindful of school affairs on a routine basis."[16]

Chester E. Finn Jr. and Lisa Graham Keegan have keenly observed that "the romantic notion that local school boards are elected by local citizens has been replaced with the reality that these elections are essentially rigged. They are held at odd times, when practically nobody votes except those with a special reason to do so."[17] The public's disengagement with school elections does not have to be taken as a given. By coupling school decisions with more visible elections and candidates, like those in mayoral races, a mayoral control model can increase the electoral accountability facing district leadership.

Influence of Special Interests

Critics of elected school boards argue that this pervasive electoral apathy has allowed mobilized constituencies, especially public employee unions (for example, teachers unions), to exert disproportionate influence on board elections and decisions. As the philanthropist Eli Broad has observed, "I look across America and I see 14,000 to 15,000 school boards frankly made up of political wannabes, well-meaning parents, people representing labor organizations—many of whom think they're in the business of giving jobs away rather than educating kids."[18]

Stanford University professor Terry Moe documents union success in electing favored candidates in California. In one 2000–03 study, he finds that school board candidates endorsed by the union won 76 percent of the time, but candidates not favored by the union won just 31 percent of the time. Even among incumbents, who enjoy advantages that might counter union influence, those backed by the union won 92 percent of the time, and others just 49 percent of the time.[19] Moe concludes that boards have largely become venues for union influence and that "wherever teachers unions engage in collective bargaining—and in many places where they don't—they should [be expected to] have advantages over other groups; and these advantages show up in electoral outcomes and in the types of people who win office and exercise local authority over the schools."[20] To wit, as Moe relates in his 2011 book, *Special Interest: Teachers Unions and America's Public Schools*, the Michigan Education Association has provided local union leaders with a forty-page guidebook called "Electing Your Own Employer: It's as Easy as 1, 2, 3."[21]

Because school boards govern districts and oversee contract negotiations, teachers unions are effectively helping to select their ostensible bosses. This has been blamed for lethargic district leadership, a failure to challenge union prerogatives, and problematic personnel practices. Mayoral control promises to dilute the influence of teachers unions by forcing them to compete alongside all other parties in shaping policy, contracts, and spending. Rather than being free to dominate their own isolated, local education sphere, education interests are brought into the larger give-and-take of municipal governance, where they will have to vie for political influence alongside transportation, health services, environmental management, business development, and a number of other advocacy groups.

Continuity of Leadership

Elected boards have been charged with contributing to a lack of coherence and continuity in district leadership. Shifting membership, concern with public perception, and the desire to placate restive communities by showing rapid improvement mean that superintendents are, as Tony Wagner, the director of Harvard's Change Leadership Group, notes, "under tremendous pressure to produce short-term results" and "feel they must undertake everything all at once."[22] When such quick-fix efforts inevitably fall short, superintendents pay the price with their jobs, resulting in constant changes in direction and inattention to implementation.[23]

Even when superintendents manage to meet their goals, the culture of school boards can still seal their departure. National reformers saw this play out in 2008 when Miami-Dade's board ousted the superintendent and acclaimed former New York City chancellor Rudy Crew even though the district had been named a finalist for the Broad Prize.[24] On the other hand, there is at least anecdotal evidence—from cities such as New York, Boston, and Chicago—that mayors are more inclined and more able to retain superintendents for extended periods.

For a case study of the stark differences in stability between elected school boards and mayoral control, consider Cleveland.[25] During the twenty-year period from 1978 to 1998, the city had twelve superintendents, six during 1990–98 alone. Conversely, since the city moved to mayoral control thirteen years ago, it has had just three. Given that mayors can and often do serve multiple consecutive four-year terms, it is easy to see why mayoral control appeals as a strategy for providing stability in systems plagued by superintendent turnover.

Professionalism of Leadership

School boards have been faulted for a lack of discipline, a tendency to micromanage, and an inability to handle the essential tasks of governance. Indeed, nearly two-thirds (63 percent) of superintendents surveyed in 2009 agreed that "there are times when the school board's role and the superintendent's role are confused."[26] As director of the Center for Reform of School Systems, Don McAdams observed such chaos; he notes that "more often than not, school board members are not certain what they are supposed to do—reflect or shape public opinion, micromanage, or act as a rubber stamp."[27]

Poor management can result in much worse than confusion. Indeed, control of purse strings by school boards without much in the way of oversight or attention has led to outright corruption. A number of boards in Florida, for example, have recently come under criminal investigation for their dealings: some of Broward County's school board members were arrested for wasting billions over the past ten years on unnecessary school building projects that benefited a select group of contractors, and mismanagement and suspected malfeasance by the Palm Beach County's school board earned it an ethics investigation.[28] Unsurprisingly, mayors, and the district leaders they appoint, often bring a higher level of project management skill and professionalism to their work than does the average school board member. Although they are not immune from the pitfalls encountered by elected boards, these leaders are often more experienced and more thoroughly vetted before taking on the complex responsibilities of school district management.

Cautions Regarding Mayoral Control

In their fervor, many school board critics have pushed ahead without taking much time to ponder the potential costs of mayoral control. Four particular concerns deserve consideration: challenges to transparency, reduced opportunities for minority representation, accommodation of special interests, and politicization of education governance.

Decreased Transparency

Critics of mayoral control have raised serious concerns about the loss of transparency once decisionmaking is limited to private meetings and backdoor dealings. Malfeasance in recent years at private sector firms such as Enron and Tyco, as well as the irresponsible actions of the country's largest investment banks, has shown how an overly familiar board and governance culture can enable management to take shortcuts, cook the books, or adopt practices that do not effectively serve the interests of clients, customers, or shareholders.[29] Doing away with elected boards could make it easier for politically self-conscious mayors and superintendents to control data, limit accountability, and reduce opportunities for citizen input.

One need not look far for an example of how this could play out at the district level. In 2009 the New York Civil Liberties Union lambasted Mayor Bloomberg's failure to comply with a civil rights investigation. As the future of New York City's mayoral control arrangement was being considered that year, the union's policy director, Udi Ofer, argued, "Whatever system state policy makers adopt . . . it must be a system that includes greater transparency and accountability than the system that currently exists."[30] Board members or officials appointed by a mayor may be reluctant to ask uncomfortable questions or raise unpleasant issues on behalf of all of their constituencies. The risk is that this deference may come at the expense of necessary oversight.

Marginalized Minorities

Many proponents of the elected school board model warn that some voices are likely to be silenced or marginalized under an appointed board or mayor-controlled system. One can note, without excusing the pettiness and ineptitude of much board governance today, that many personal conflicts or accusations of micromanagement often reflect tensions over resource allocation or real disagreement about the school system's direction. Appointed officials, buffered from political and constituent considerations, are more likely to leave significant distributional or value-laden issues unaddressed.

Stefani Chambers's 2006 analysis of mayoral control in Chicago and Cleveland, for instance, reports fewer opportunities for participation by minority parents and citizens in the mayor-controlled school system. In the case of Detroit, this anomie led to a popular vote to terminate mayoral control in 2005.[31]

Intriguingly, studies have also suggested that elected boards, by offering more opportunities for minority representation and engagement, may benefit black or Latino students. For instance, Kenneth Meier and Robert England, in their analysis of district data on resource allocation, staffing, and other policy concerns in eighty-two large urban districts, find that black membership on boards was correlated with policies that were more equitable for black students and staff.[32]

Succumbing to Pressure

Many critics of mayoral control have noted the risk that appointed boards would work well initially only to later "go native," reverting to practices of the elected board. As in other regulated industries, mayoral-appointed regulators may tend, over time, to become dominated by those they are supposed to regulate. The concern is that mayoral control might settle into a quiet arrangement focused on rewarding friends and placating powerful interests. Politically savvy mayors and their appointed boards may eventually reach comfortable accommodations with teachers unions, other school employee unions, and major service providers.

A telling example is the case of Baltimore City Public Schools, which operated under mayoral control for a century, from 1898 to 1997. Baltimore's mayors used their power over city bureaucracies and the public school system as a source of patronage for the local black community. This arrangement was identified as a significant cause of the city's education challenges, but the electoral support provided by those in the patronage system made it hard for anyone to champion serious reform.[33] As the University of Washington's Ashley Watson and Paul Hill note, "When the mayor's office assumes control with the support of a reform coalition . . . positive change can be expected. However, when the mayor's electoral support is dependent upon the very people who have a stake in the status quo, change will be unlikely, if not impossible."[34] In the end, mayors are subject to the same interest group pressures as elected school boards. The open question is whether they will be more immune.

Increased Politicization

Even mayoral control advocates must admit that mayors, like boards, can be self-serving. The New York University professor Joseph Viteritti has cautioned that mayors "are not beyond the reach of the same organized interests that have retarded reform on local school boards."[35] Mayors, too, can be susceptible to the influence of teachers unions and aggrieved neighborhoods. Indeed, though their broader constituency may dilute the impact of narrow interests, it is also the case that mayors' acute political antennas and professional ambitions may render some of them more sensitive to the concerns of such groups. Michael Usdan, a veteran observer of board governance, has noted, "Although the evidence so far suggests that mayoral involvement in education has largely been a positive experience for cities . . . less enlightened mayors may exacerbate problems through their involvement or seek to politicize public schools in self-serving ways."[36]

Mayors also have a more visible platform from which to politicize and leverage education issues for their own purposes. The temptation to make education policy decisions based on their effects on a mayor's political portfolio might leave district policies even more vulnerable to shifts, depending on the political winds of the day. As the Manhattan Institute's Sol Stern notes, New York City's Bloomberg administration was a victim of the politicization of mayoral control. After unveiling a major funding reform initiative that penalized schools with veteran staff, Bloomberg encountered fierce resistance from the United Federation of

Teachers, which organized massive rallies at City Hall to oppose the measure. One day later, Bloomberg met American Federation of Teachers president Randi Weingarten for breakfast and subsequently removed the provision from his strategy. Stern opines, "A big fight with the teachers would have damaged his reputation as the 'education mayor' and threatened his potential White House run."[37]

Mixed Results for Mayoral Control

Ultimately, there is no "best" model of school governance. Appointed boards can provide coherence, focus, and a degree of removal from factional politics; elected urban boards are typically chosen in low-turnout elections in which particular interests wield great control. However, such rules are neither hard nor fast. Some elected boards can provide coherent leadership, and some mayors may prove susceptible to short-term, self-interested pressures. The incentives to avoid a fight with vocal constituencies is not exclusive to elected boards; mayors and their appointed boards also face pressure from special interest groups that will help decide their fate in the next election. Table 6-1 summarizes the advantages and disadvantages of each model.

If a mayor's appointees are insulated from the demands of interest groups or teachers unions—as was arguably the case in the District of Columbia Public Schools (DCPS) under Chancellor Michelle Rhee—these groups only need to wait until the next election to make their influence known. The DCPS experience is an example of the dangers of romanticizing mayoral control or ignoring its limitations. Before election day, the lines were well drawn. Sixty-eight percent of white voters cited Mayor Adrian Fenty's support for Rhee as their reason to support him, and 54 percent of African American voters cited Rhee as their reason to oppose him.[38] Because Rhee's efforts were integral to Fenty's legacy, he was held accountable for the largely unpopular reforms that occurred under Rhee, and the challenger who unseated him had particular incentive to alter the course in a visible way. Ultimately, rather than Fenty's political muscle providing ballast to Rhee, it turned out that Rhee's ambitious, frequently jarring reform agenda helped allow city council chairman Vincent Gray to unseat Fenty in the Democratic primary.

Furthermore, the evidence that mayoral control leads to more effective governance and higher performance is mixed. In 2005 Wong and Francis Shen conducted another analysis, examining how mayoral control affected finances and staffing in the nation's 100 largest urban school districts during the period 1992–2001. They find that "mayoral takeover did not bring with it the increased financial stability it promised" and that it had little impact on district staffing, with a "lack of a consistent, significant relationship between mayoral takeover and [a] host of management and staffing outcome measures."[39] The authors con-

Table 6-1. *Advantages and Disadvantages of Elected versus Appointed Boards*

Model	Advantages	Disadvantages
Elected school board	Community engagement: gives community opportunity to engage on school district issues	Special interest influence: biases community input toward established and engaged interest groups
	Transparent governance: provides more accessible information on decisionmaking	
		Inconsistent policy leadership: suffers from high turnover of superintendents and school leadership initiatives
	Diverse representation: allows for greater minority participation in district leadership	
	Electoral accountability: holds members directly accountable in frequent elections	Weak management: draws on talent pool without experience in public administration and management
Appointed board with mayoral control	Reduced influence of special interests: offers leaders greater autonomy from influential interest groups	Decreased transparency: grants more executive powers for concealment of information and processes
	Continuity of leadership: provides longer-term and more-stable leadership	Marginalized minorities: deprives underrepresented groups of a voice in district leadership
	Professional management: employs leaders with experience in public administration and management	Regulatory capture: allows for leaders to be influenced by interest groups and lose regulatory objectivity
	Political clout: leverages relationships with other citywide stakeholders for collaborative efforts	Increased politicization: creates opportunity for politicizing education

clude that "no general consensus is emerging about the overall effectiveness of mayoral takeover" and that "although there certainly are anecdotal examples of positive change—our analysis suggests that when aggregated across districts at the national level, takeover has not yet changed fundamental district operations."[40] In a later analysis, Wong and Shen find that mayor-led school systems experience higher student performance, more efficient management, greater financial stability, and increased public confidence, but they caution that the "research also suggests that successful governance will require mayors to partner with state and local officials, as well as community organizations, employees' unions, and civic organizations."[41]

The Tensions of Public Governance

These underwhelming results are not exclusive to school systems; in a variety of cases, skeptics can reasonably question whether appointing public sector service providers leads to better outcomes. For decades scholars have researched the impact of electing rather than appointing public utility commissioners. Studies have found few differences between the two approaches when it came to setting household rates for regulated utilities.[42] In an influential and exhaustive study of the electricity rates produced by various regulatory commissions, however, Timothy Besley and Stephen Coate examine forty states over a thirty-seven-year period and find that "elected regulators are more pro-consumer" and that "residential prices are significantly lower in states that elect their regulators."[43] As Besley and Coate note, "When regulators are appointed, regulatory policy becomes bundled with other policy issues the appointing politicians are responsible for. [On the other hand,] because voters have only one vote to cast and regulatory issues are not salient for most voters, there are electoral incentives [for appointed officials] to respond to stakeholder interests."[44] Thus elected governance officials, whether in electricity utilities or in school governance, are more likely to have laserlike focus on specific consumer demands than are the jack-of-all-trades appointed officials.

Other research has found that elected officials are more likely to keep telephone rates down, that their pro-consumer policies have a negative effect on the bond ratings of electric utilities, that centralized officials are more likely to be lobbied, and that they tend to favor consumers over life insurance companies. Such behaviors are appealing but are not obvious signals that elected boards are better—only that they are more responsive to the population of consumers (that is, voters). The costs of this behavior appear to include a lesser degree of financial discipline on the part of elected boards, as scholars have reported that elected public utility commissioners have a strong negative effect on utility bond ratings.[45]

Overall, weighing the relative benefits and costs of elected boards and appointed officials requires a fine-tuned understanding of the responsibilities at hand. In their work on provision of public goods, Alberto Alesina and Guido Tabellini have found that elected officials and appointed bureaucrats are each best suited for particular sectors. Alesina and Tabellini argue, "Politicians are preferable if ability is less important than effort or if there is little uncertainty about whether the policymaker has the required abilities; bureaucrats are preferable in the opposite case."[46] In other words, there is no optimal solution.

Deeper Problems with the Progressive Legacy

After trying to weigh the pros and cons of the debate for replacing school boards and considering the broader research on the merits of elected boards, we are basically back where we started. It is hard to argue, based on either theory or evidence, that school boards will drive school improvement—but it is also tough to be confident that mayoral control will provide dramatically better results in most communities over the long haul. This seeming dead end points to a larger truth: Perhaps the problem with today's school systems is not the hands on the tiller so much as the design of the ship itself.

Fights about district governance could more fruitfully start by asking whether the familiar district governance model is suited to the challenges of twenty-first century urban education; whether schools and systems should continue to be staffed by public employees governed by complex contractual and statutory rules; whether the Progressive Era model of a hierarchical system governed by the dictates of 1920s-style "scientific management" is suited to seizing today's opportunities. Mayoral control may indeed be a useful step but only if pursued with an eye to these larger questions and as a catalyst to abandon an organizational model that has lived past its expiration date.

In their efforts to squash mere politics and professionalize schooling, early twentieth-century Progressives successfully championed reforms that made school board elections nonpartisan and moved the elections off cycle. The hope in shifting these races so that they were no longer held at the same time as major state or national elections was, in the words of scholar Joseph Viteritti, to "insulate schools from [partisan] politics."[47] In a time of patronage-driven politics and flagrant corruption, such ambitions were sensible enough. Progressives achieved their dream of shielding board members from political accountability and of separating school governance from municipal power centers, though they unknowingly did so by imposing arrangements that would eventually produce board factionalism, incoherence, and an absence of accountability. During ensuing decades, districts would undergo a massive consolidation, with the number of districts slashed by more than 75 percent between 1930 and 1970. As Martin West and Christopher Berry have noted, this process led to the centralization of regulatory power and the reduction of school board discretion.[48] The result today is a network of 14,000 insular, bureaucratic districts.

Promoting "nonpolitical" control and rigid management routines as the proper and "scientific" way to improve education, Progressives happily sacrificed flexibility in favor of uniformity. Those twin legacies, the putatively nonpolitical governance of school systems and the rigidity of school operations, have been with us for most of the past century. It is indeed a useful step to recognize that school districts are inevitably political entities and that governance must address that reality. However, equally crippling is the legacy of rigidity and uniformity that infuses management, staffing, compensation, and the broader education enterprise. Those deeper, thornier problems are left unaddressed by the shift to mayoral control. If pursued as an alternative to tackling these challenges, mayoral control may serve primarily as a distraction.

Aggravating Inequities

Although their size has grown, districts have consistently played an organizing role in the provision of American schooling. As Chief Justice Warren Burger wrote for the U.S. Supreme Court in the 1974 case *Milliken* v. *Bradley*, in which the court ruled that suburban Michigan districts could not be required to engage in busing with the Detroit schools, "School district lines may not be casually ignored or treated as a mere administrative convenience."[49] The inviolability of district autonomy and the ongoing push toward consolidation had the unfortunate effect of aggravating socioeconomic stratification, as districts became a barrier to more economically and racially diverse schooling. Whereas the rich and poor tended to live closer to one another in the nineteenth century, when cities were smaller, transport became a bigger concern with the post–World War II rise of commuter suburbs and the new living conditions increasingly led to economically segregated communities.[50]

With the twentieth-century emergence of wealthier suburban communities surrounding the urban core, the district model wound up inadvertently aggravating and accelerating divisions. Schooling organized by districts reinforces the self-perpetuating cycle between community affluence and school quality, as the affluent drive up home prices in communities with good schools, making those communities more exclusive and less accessible to low-income families. As Harvard University professor of government Jennifer Hochschild explains, "Racial and economic separation across geographically based local school districts . . . exacerbate[s] unequal outcomes of schooling."[51]

Outdated Model

Despite seemingly good cause for taking another look at the school district, we have clung reflexively to the notion of district governance. But why? School districts were institutionalized in the early twentieth century, a time when the travel and communication technologies that we take for granted did not yet exist. In 1837, the same year that Horace Mann became president of the Massachusetts School Board, President Andrew Jackson's trip from Washington, D.C., back to the Hermitage in Nashville, Tennessee, took eighteen days. In 1849, during Mann's last year in office, traveling from Washington to California was still a six-month ordeal.

Although districts have grown through consolidation since then, their shapes, norms, and roles are the products of an era when coordinating and overseeing teaching and learning from a distance of even fifty miles would have been costly and difficult and when there was no sensible alternative to geographically compact school systems. School leaders at the turn of the century were hamstrung by the day's travel and communication conditions, which made anything other than geographic monopolies prohibitive in terms of cost, logistics, and coordination.

The contemporary school district faces a ridiculously daunting set of demands. Districts are asked to find an effective way to meet every educational need of every student who happens to live in a catchment area. Moreover, they are asked to do this by more or less hiring all of the education professionals who happen to live in that same physical community. This makes specialization impossible and demands that each of the nation's school districts be adept at meeting every need of every student with special needs, of every gifted child, and of every one of their peers. If and when one district finds a way to meet one need or serve one population, the typical response is for other systems to fly in their staff for two-day dog-and-pony shows in which they are determined to learn the secrets behind the success. We ought hardly be surprised that most districts have not excelled when confronted with this monumental challenge.

Having all-purpose operations focus on serving a given geographic community was common in the early twentieth century and hardly unique to schooling. In fact, it was pretty much the state of the art up until a few decades ago, when it was thought natural for a given store to meet all your shopping needs—stocking washers and shoes and dresses and tires. A glance at catalogues from the early years of the twentieth century shows the one-stop-shop business mentality of the era. The Sears, Roebuck catalog, for instance, features firearms, baby carriages, jewelry, saddles, and even eyeglasses with a self-test for "old sight, near sight, and astigmatism."[52]

Looking Past Geography

The centralized, Sears approach is no longer the way providers in most sectors are organized. A more sensible configuration would allow providers to deliver their services directly to a growing population of students or across a range of schools and geographies. Today we push thousands of districts to embrace and implement unwanted programs. If the private sector operated in this fashion, Amazon.com would have restricted its clientele to residents of Washington state, while would-be imitators from across the country flocked in to learn its secrets and then return home to emulate them. These best-practice imitators would frequently have fumbled the execution of the business, and a cottage industry of consultants would pad their pockets claiming to explain Amazon's secrets. We would regard the whole experience as another failed effort to leverage technology or take a boutique provider to scale. Instead of encouraging school districts to emulate the KIPP academies model, for instance, policymakers and reformers might focus on enabling and encouraging KIPP to open schools more readily to satisfy local demand. The provider would be focused on serving its target population with staff it has selected and trained rather than hoping that districts will faithfully deliver its model—without the personal commitment, hand-picked staff, or specialized expertise.

Rather than school boards enjoying a local monopoly, multiple boards might operate in any given locale—with some presumably operating across a wealth of locales. Competing boards could vie to serve, support, and monitor its schools, providing them with a variety of potential partners. Such an arrangement could allow "districts" to focus on serving a particular swath of students or schools, enabling an expertise, focus, and coherence that is so often lacking in all-purpose bureaucracies.[53] Similarly, Paul Hill suggests that boards can be placed under competitive pressure by district chief executive officers and New Orleans–style recovery school district institutions, both of which will assert power if boards fail to act or fail to serve.[54]

Another option is to empower nonprofit or for-profit networks that might contract directly with a state. Alongside existing districts, states might contract directly with a network that would provide schooling and would be held accountable in accord with agreed-on criteria (for example, something very much like what strong statewide charter school boards do in some states today, except they would be dealing with more than individual schools).

A third approach is to do away with districts altogether. One could imagine states turning every school into a charter school. States might put every school on a performance contract and then permit schools to engage in any number of potential arrangements and combinations to secure support and central services. Monitoring with regard to special education or Title I might be handled entirely by the state education agency or perhaps by one or more contractors or independent agencies.

Today, every school district is asked to devise ways to meet every need of every single child in a given area. Since they cannot tailor their service to focus on certain student needs, districts are forced to try to build expertise in a vast number of specialties and services. This arrangement demands that districts juggle a vast array of demands and requires them to become the employers of nearly all educators in a given community.

These suggestions are intended not as a call for some headlong rush to disband geographic districts but to spell out the benefits of no longer assuming the district as an inviolable fact. With a clearer understanding of the new possibilities for district governance that technology presents, we can begin to explore alternative ways to coordinate, manage, and deliver services.

Bridging Distances and Reshaping Geography

Today, the world is dotted with providers that specialize in doing a few things—or just one thing—well. Organizing schooling around a sea-to-sea chain of local monopolies made good sense when the cost of travel and communication was high and communities were composed of residents who routinely lived in one place for decades or even a lifetime. Advances in communications, transportation, and data management technology now make it possible, though, for one provider to oversee outlets in thousands of locations—and to offer the same specialized service in each of them. Yet school districts are not permitted to operate in this fashion. Delivering a new reading program or replacing a problematic human resources department requires sending a handful of administrators to visit an acclaimed district for a few days and then asking them to mimic it locally with existing staff and some consulting support.

Districts thus inadvertently become chokepoints in the delivery of new services and an important reason why promising models seem so incredibly hard to duplicate successfully. Once a provider has developed a way to serve a population effectively or solve a problem, why wouldn't we opt for arrangements that allow them to do so in more and more locales? Why do we continue to imagine that a better course is to have thousands of districts and tens of thousands of schools scrambling to adopt someone else's new "best practices"? Why does a district's governing body have to consist of only those people who happen to live within the school district's reach?

It is tempting to conclude that technology can be a significant force bringing about transformative change in local governance and that deconstructing the role of school boards is less a product of policy than the expression of a logical next step given new technological conditions. But a rush to judge local districts as toothless is hazardous. Space may be becoming less relevant, but place—as a repository for social relationships and a privileged node of formal political power—is not. A nongeographically configured district structure would also make it enormously difficult to selectively hire educators who agree on mission, focus, or pedagogy, and the resulting grab-bag of faculty and leaders must then strive to forge coherent cultures. This is a needlessly exhausting strategy and one unlikely to lead to wide-scale excellence. Transforming any sprawling, underachieving organization is enormously challenging under even the best circumstances; it may well be impossible under such conditions.

That said, technology is an undeniable force for change in school governance as it lessens the significance of geography and physical space. Scholars including John Chubb, Terry Moe, Clayton Christensen, and Paul Peterson have suggested that technology is rendering traditional schooling and school governance obsolete. As

Terry Moe and John Chubb assert, technology makes it possible for elected officials to overcome the information barriers that bar them from fully understanding what goes on in the schoolhouse. Moe and Chubb argue that school board members can improve oversight through technology "by collecting accurate, comprehensive information about the organization and performance of the public schools, compiling and storing the information in data warehouses—and using it to hold the schools accountable for boosting student achievement."[55] In the same way, many tasks central to school governance, such as strategizing policy, reviewing school reports, and discussing potential hires, might be pursued more powerfully (and certainly more cost-effectively, more conveniently, and in a more customized fashion) through web-based technologies. Technology also allows districts to expand their talent search for school board members beyond those that happen to reside nearby, allowing boards to pipe in the best candidates and improve their work.

The pertinent question is not whether online or tech-focused education is good or bad; what matters for governance is whether these tools are employed in a fashion that enables leaders to boost performance, cost-effectiveness, and customization. An increasing number of transactions that once depended on face-to-face relationships with local professionals can be completed online, even as the reality of modern air travel can allow a data maven to sit down with educators in Baltimore, Boston, and Buffalo in the space of a single day. It would be unfortunate if these revolutionary developments, which have triggered seismic shifts in finance, trade, industry, and culture, continued to make little headway in an education system locked into arrangements that continue to be defined by geography.

New Challenges for a New Era

If one accepts that district governance is a balky vestige of a centuries-old system, and that localized decisionmaking is embedded in the American system, redesigning the organizing principles of school governance will require tackling at least three often overlooked challenges.

First, how do we think about regulatory and governance apparatuses for providers educating a million kids in forty communities in ten states? This is not a futurist fantasy; we can see the first glimmerings of this challenge now, with providers like K^{12}, Edison, or KIPP. While the challenge is coming into focus, public debate has tended to embrace one or another oversimplification, either declaring this a panacea or touting it as a dangerous threat. The result is inattention to constructing a framework for accountability, negotiation, and regulatory oversight that creates a dynamic, quality-conscious landscape for providers.

Absent such reform, two suboptimal options loom. One is that providers are forced to negotiate an array of local, distinctive governance arrangements (for instance, there are TEAM schools rather than KIPP schools in New Jersey, even though TEAM schools actually are KIPP schools and in the KIPP network, because New Jersey state law stipulates that if a private entity establishes a charter the "name of the charter school shall not include the name or identification of the private entity"). The alternative is that venue shopping and loopholes mean that providers are essentially off the grid (as with commercial tutoring firms). This can prove problematic both politically and substantively when we note that providers will be collecting public funds and serving public ends, all under the auspices of a weak public procurement system where charlatans and shoddy products will abound.

This is quite similar to the challenge that changing technology has posed in transportation or banking—as people or capital become more mobile, they start to seep past old regulations. Either regulatory structures adjust to that, or they stifle some kinds of provision while encouraging providers to seek loopholes— rewarding those who play fast and loose. We either encourage that kind of dysfunctional search for limitations and vulnerabilities in the old arrangements, or we seek ways to retool oversight, transparency, and quality control so as to render it more agile and better suited to new conditions and needs.

Second, what might it mean to organize governance arrangements based on networks or communities that are organized around some dimension other than geography? We have historically organized communities spatially, but that is not inevitable. In fact, private groups such as the Masons or the Catholic Church have formed communities, chosen officials, and governed themselves across great distances and formal lines of governance. It is true that organizations like these have tended to form their own geographic units, such as a local parish or community lodge. This is equally evident in the case of school communities, as Margaret Goertz has pointed out, as geographically bound districts have created local communities around schools that include not only students, teachers, and their families but also taxpayers who live nearby and contribute to school resources.[56] However, it may be that this type of proximity is not essential or that some similar accommodation is possible in schooling. It is also true that self-selection into networks and communities risks segregating and fractionalizing outcomes that are threatening to social cohesion and important concerns about equity. That identifies a critical factor to consider in structuring governance, but it is a challenging aspect of place-based governance arrangements, as well.

Tapping into the power of these new opportunities, and doing so in a way that is responsible and shows attention to quality and equitable provision, requires new ways to govern and organize schooling that reflect the shape of a changing world. That may be one of the pressing challenges of twenty-first-century schooling, yet it is one that we have thus far barely deigned to acknowledge.

Third, how can policymakers or parents go about holding multiple providers accountable for student learning? One reason the familiar system of governance remains largely intact is that it is a comfortable fit for conventional models of accountability and financial oversight. Geographic districts are responsible for the familiar schools within their bounds and for all the students in those schools. Performance can be readily tracked when tallied by school or district, while resources can be counted and tracked similarly. This offers a straightforward approach to monitoring performance, even if it impedes efforts to employ new technologies, tap new talent, or rethink how best to provide instruction.

As one seeks to tap such opportunities by rethinking familiar models of teaching and schooling, one starts to combine services in ways that do not lend themselves to the same kind of place-based tracking. Online courses mean that some instruction is being provided by teachers who reside outside the district. Hybrid school models mean that students are no longer solely the charges of a single classroom teacher. Such developments call for new models of accountability and oversight, in which we gauge the performance of multiple providers who all help instruct a single student. The push for Common Core state standards and other assessment alignment can move us in the right direction, but the political and logistical hurdles ahead suggest that we are still far from achieving this goal. The challenge is big enough when it is just a matter of metrics and accountability; but the governance challenge is equally severe. After all, it is not clear who can or should be responsible for policing the quality of providers operating in thousands of districts, and it seems unlikely that having local districts do so will prove effective or efficient. But what smarter governance solutions would look like, or how we transition toward them, are questions we have barely broached.

Conclusion

Given the widespread dissatisfaction with school board governance today, many have turned to alternative governance models such as mayoral control for more effective leadership. However, a quick look at the cases for and against this reform do not offer much hope that either side has the key to building a more promising, effective model. Gene Maeroff may reasonably argue that school board members need more professional development, a tighter application process, and greater consolidation among boards; however, none of these will do much to transform the current system into a governance structure for the twenty-first century. Proposals to do away with elected boards in favor of mayoral control make some legitimate points but ultimately leave the problematic superstructure of school districts largely untouched.

The trouble with such suggestions is that they fixate on boards instead of recognizing that boards themselves are only one symptom of a dysfunctional and outdated Progressive approach to schooling. Mayoral control may be a promising alternative in poor-performing districts where corrupt and inept board leadership has led to failing schools, but since it does not address the fundamentally flawed governance design, it falls short of offering a meaningful departure from ineffectual school board governance.

For reformers seeking to transform school governance, the very first step is questioning the underlying assumptions of school districts and asking how we might redesign them to take advantage of new providers and new technologies. In the twenty-first century, that requires thinking about how we might organize schooling around function rather than geography. It would be sad indeed if well-intentioned advocacy around mayoral control amounted to little more than a shift change at the helm of a foundering ship.

Notes

1. Gene Maeroff, *School Boards in America: A Flawed Exercise in Democracy* (Washington: Palgrave Macmillan, 2010).

2. Kenneth Meier and Robert England, "Black Representation and Educational Policy: Are They Related?" *American Political Science Review* 78 (June 1984): 392–403.

3. Matthew Miller, "First, Kill All the School Boards," *The Atlantic*, January–February 2008.

4. Jane Elizabeth, "School Boards' Worth in Doubt: Some Think Members Are In over Their Heads due to Complex Duties," *Pittsburgh Post-Gazette*, November 30, 2006.

5. Quoted in Carl Campanile, "BAM Backs Mike School Rule: Ed. Czar's Message to Albany," *New York Post*, March 30, 2009.

6. Matt Winkle, "'That's Not the Way It Works in Education' (What Not to Tell a New School Board Member)," *Education Week*, September 27, 2010.

7. Frederick M. Hess and Olivia Meeks, *School Boards Circa 2010: Governance in the Accountability Era* (Washington: National School Boards Association, 2010).

8. For more information on the tendencies toward upholding status quo policies in "down ballot" elections such as school boards, see Ned Augenblick and Scott Nicholson, "Ballot Position, Choice Fatigue, and Voter Behavior," University of California, July 2011 (http://faculty.haas.berkeley.edu/ned/Choice_Fatigue.pdf).

9. Kenneth Wong and Francis Shen, "Mayors Can Be 'Prime Movers' of Urban School Improvement," *Education Week*, October 12, 2009.

10. United States Conference of Mayors, *Mayoral Leadership and Involvement in Education: An Action Guide for Success* (Washington, 2010), pp. 14–15.

11. See chapter 9 in this volume.

12. Michael Kirst, "Mayoral Control of Schools: Concepts, Tradeoffs, and Outcomes," Working Paper (New York: Commission on School Governance, 2007), p. 2.

13. "N.J. School Elections Voter Turnout Is More Important than Ever," editorial, *Times of Trenton*, April 27, 2011.

14. Lisa Bartusek, *School Board Elections: Voter Turnout Needs Your Help* (Des Moines: Iowa Association of School Boards, 2007).

15. Steve Farkas, Patrick Foley, and Ann Duffett, *Just Waiting to Be Asked: A Fresh Look at Attitudes on Public Engagement* (Washington: Public Agenda, 2001).

16. Ibid.

17. Chester E. Finn Jr. and Lisa Graham Keegan, "Lost at Sea," *Education Next* 4 (Summer 2004): 15–17.

18. Quoted in Carl Campanile and Yoav Gonen, "Ambitious Course: City Plans for 100,000 Charter Kids," *New York Post*, April 10, 2009.

19. Terry M. Moe, "Teachers Unions and School Board Elections," in *Besieged: School Boards and the Future of Education Politics*, edited by William Howell (Brookings Press, 2005), pp. 254–87.

20. Terry M. Moe, *Special Interest: Teacher Unions and America's Public Schools* (Brookings Press, 2011), p. 153.

21. Ibid., p. 113.

22. Tony Wagner, *How Schools Change: Lessons from Three Communities Revisited* (New York: Beacon Press, 2004), p. 79.

23. Frederick M. Hess, *Spinning Wheels: The Politics of Urban School Reform* (Brookings Press, 1998).

24. Damien Cave and Yolanne Almanzar, "Miami Schools Chief to Leave amid Discord," *New York Times,* September 8, 2008.

25. Patrick O'Donnell, "Mayoral Control of the Cleveland City Schools Has Brought Stability, but Other Improvements Hard to Measure," *Cleveland Plain Dealer,* August 21, 2011.

26. Albert Nylander, "National Teacher Survey 2009" (Cleveland, Miss.: Delta State University, 2011), (www.oldham.kyschools.us/files/reports/National_Surveys/National%20Teacher%20Survey%20on%20School%20Boards%202009%20Final%20Results.pdf).

27. Don McAdams, *What School Boards Can Do: Reform Governance for Urban Schools* (Teachers College Press, 2006), p. 65.

28. John Rehill, "Under Budget Microscope, Florida School Boards Find Mismanagement," *Bradenton (Fla.) Times*, July 8, 2011.

29. Christopher Small, "Do Independence and Financial Expertise of the Board Matter for Risk Taking and Performance?" Harvard Law School Forum on Corporate Governance and Financial Regulation, 2011 (http://blogs.law.harvard.edu/corpgov/2011/06/27/do-independence-and-financial-expertise-of-the-board-matter-for-risk-taking-and-performance/).

30. Quoted in Philissa Cramer, "NYCLU: Lawmakers Should Stop DOE from Being So Secretive," *Gotham Schools Blog,* May 14, 2009 (http://gothamschools.org/2009/05/14/nyclu-lawmakers-should-stop-doe-from-being-so-secretive/).

31. Joseph Viteritti, *When Mayors Take Charge: School Governance in the City* (Brookings Press, 2009), p. 8.

32. Meier and England, "Black Representation and Educational Policy."

33. James Cibulka, "Old Wine, New Bottles," *Education Next* 1 (Winter 2001): 28–35; Marion Orr, *Black Social Capital: The Politics of School Reform in Baltimore* (University Press of Kansas, 1999).

34. Ashley E. Watson and Paul T. Hill, *Mayoral Intervention: Right for Seattle's Schools?* (University of Washington, Center on Reinventing Public Education, 2008), p. 23.

35. Joseph Viteritti, "The End of Local Politics?" in *Besieged,* edited by Howell, pp. 308–23, 321.

36. Michael Usdan, "Mayors and Public Education: The Case for Greater Involvement," *Harvard Educational Review* 76 (Summer 2006): 147–52, 150.

37. Sol Stern, "Grading Mayoral Control," *City Journal* 17 (Summer, 2007) (www.city-journal.org/html/17_3_mayoral_control.html).

38. Nikita Stewart and Jon Cohen, "Poll Shows D.C. Mayor Fenty Getting More Credit Than Support in Primary Race against Gray," *Washington Post*, August 28, 2010.

39. Kenneth Wong and Francis Shen, "When Mayors Lead Urban Schools: Toward Developing a Framework to Assess the Effects of Mayoral Takeover of Urban Districts," in *Besieged*, edited by Howell, pp. 81–101, 95, 99.

40. Ibid., pp. 86, 99.

41. Kenneth Wong and Francis Shen, "Mayors Can Be 'Prime Movers' of Urban School Development," *Education Week*, October 12, 2009.

42. William Boyes and John McDowell, "The Selection of Public Utility Commissioners: A Reexamination of the Importance of Institutional Setting," *Public Choice* 61 (April 1989): 1–13; Walter Primeaux and Patrick Mann, "Regulator Selection Methods and Electricity Prices," *Land Economics* 62 (February 1986): 1–13.

43. Timothy Besley and Stephen Coate, "Elected versus Appointed Regulators: Theory and Evidence," *Journal of the European Economic Association* 1 (September 2003): 1176–78.

44. Ibid., p. 1177.

45. John Formby, Banamber Mishra, and Paul Thistle, "Public Utility Regulation and Bond Ratings," *Public Choice* 84 (1995): 119–36.

46. Alberto Alesina and Guido Tabellini, "Bureaucrats or Politicians? Part I: A Single Policy Task," *American Economic Review* 97 (March 2007): 169–79, 177.

47. Viteritti, *When Mayors Take Charge*, p. 2.

48. Christopher Berry and Martin West, "Growing Pains: The School Consolidation Movement and Student Outcomes," Working Paper Series 07.03 (University of Chicago, Harris School of Public Policy, 2010), pp. 3, 6.

49. *Milliken* v. *Bradley,* 418 U.S. 717 (1974).

50. Jennifer Hochschild, "What School Boards Can and Cannot (or Will Not) Accomplish," in *Besieged*, edited by Howell, pp. 324–38, 330.

51. Ibid.

52. "History of the Sears Catalog," *Sears Archives,* n.d. (www.searsarchives.com/catalogs/history.htm).

53. Paul Hill, "Change the Rules," *Blueprint Magazine,* April 15, 2003 (www.dlc.org/ndol_ci099b.html?kaid=110&subid=181&contentid=251499).

54. See chapter 15 in this volume.

55. Terry M. Moe and John E. Chubb, *Liberating Learning: Technology, Politics, and the Future of American Education* (San Francisco: John Wiley and Sons, 2009), p. 101.

56. Margaret Goertz, remarks at the conference, Rethinking Education Governance in the Twenty-First Century, Thomas B. Fordham Institute and the Center for American Progress, Washington, December 1, 2011.

KATHRYN A. MCDERMOTT

7

Interstate Governance of Standards and Testing

Compared with many other industrialized countries, the U.S. education governance system remains highly decentralized. In much of Europe and Asia, nationally administered student examinations are an entirely unremarkable feature of public education. By contrast, in the United States, even voluntary national standards have aroused intense controversy.[1] Standards-based reform, one of the dominant education policy ideas since the 1980s, began in the states. Even after the No Child Left Behind Act of 2001 required states to have particular kinds of standards, testing, and accountability policies as a condition for continued receipt of federal compensatory education funds, the actual setting of the standards remained in the states' hands. Although many policy analysts viewed the diversity of state-level standards as a key weakness in the U.S. system, federally mandated standards remained both politically and constitutionally untenable.

Since 2009, an interstate network has worked around these barriers to develop standards that are national in scope, through a state-led process. The Common Core State Standards Initiative (CCSSI) is an effort to overcome the fragmentation that many analysts have criticized in the U.S. education system. Forty-five states have adopted the Common Core State Standards. The CCSSI has the potential to enhance the ability to compare states' performance with one another and with international benchmarks. The Common Core State Standards may also help states' assessment budgets go further. States that participated in a much smaller state consortium, the New England Common Assessment Program, found that by collaborating on assessments they could get a higher-quality test for the same or less money than they had spent on their own assessments. The New England experience shows both the potential and the challenge of interstate standards and testing. If the CCSSI and the two interstate assessments that are being designed to measure students' attainment of the standards succeed, they will represent a new type of education federalism, shifting the system's balance

Figure 7-1. *Multistate Common Standards*[a]

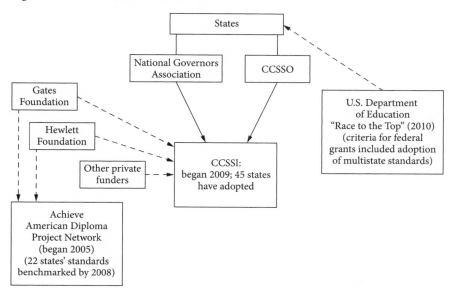

a. Dashed lines indicate funding.

between centralized and decentralized governance in the interests of improving standards and accountability policy.

A Brief Introduction to the Standards and Assessment Consortiums

The Common Core State Standards Initiative, created in 2009, is a collaboration between the National Governors Association and the Council of Chief State School Officers. Figure 7-1 identifies the participants and their relationships. As of January 2012, forty-five of the states (all except Alaska, Minnesota, Nebraska, Texas, and Virginia) and the District of Columbia have committed to using the Common Core standards for mathematics and English language arts. Minnesota has adopted the standards for English language arts but not for mathematics. The CCSSI is privately funded, with grants from the Bill & Melinda Gates Foundation, the Hewlett Foundation, and other foundations. Both Gates and Hewlett previously funded the American Diploma Project Network undertaken by Achieve in 2005, which involved states in benchmarking their standards. State leaders endorsed common standards because they wanted to make interstate and international benchmarking easier and to achieve economies of scale in education reform. Later, the federal government's Race to the Top grant competition provided a strong incentive for states to adopt the standards. To earn all possible

Figure 7-2. *Multistate Assessment Consortiums*[a]

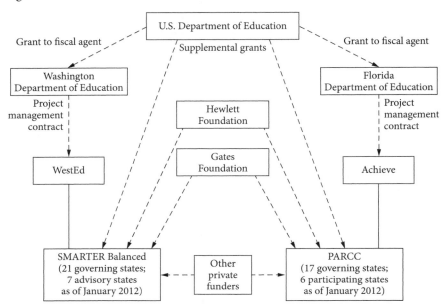

a. Dashed lines indicate funding. Both SMARTER Balanced and PARCC are assessments of Common Core state standards.

points in the Race to the Top competition, states needed to document their "participation in a consortium of States that is working toward jointly developing and adopting a common set of standards" and that "includes a significant number of States."[2] The Race to the Top did not explicitly require that states participate in the CCSSI, but the initiative was and remains the only consortium that fits this description.[3]

The U.S. Department of Education also set aside $350 million of economic stimulus funds for grants to interstate consortiums to develop assessments tied to internationally benchmarked common standards for college and career readiness. Figure 7-2 maps out the participants in these consortiums and their connections. The Partnership for the Assessment of Readiness for College and Careers (PARCC) and the SMARTER Balanced Assessment Consortium (SBAC) won the federal funding and are developing assessments that are scheduled to be officially administered for the first time in 2014–15.[4] The fiscal agent for PARCC's federal grant is the Florida Department of Education, which contracts with Achieve for project management. The fiscal agent for the SBAC is the Washington State Department of Education, which contracts with WestEd for project management. In addition to their federal funding, both PARCC and the SBAC have received financial support from Gates, Hewlett, and other foundations.

Both assessment consortiums include "governing" states, which have pledged to use the assessment and which share in making decisions about it. Other member states have not yet committed to using the assessment. The SBAC calls these "advisory" states, and PARCC calls them "participating" states. As of September 2012, PARCC has eighteen governing states, plus Washington, D.C., and four participating states.[5] The SBAC has twenty-one governing states and four advisory states.[6] Three states are nongoverning members of both consortiums and will eventually choose to participate in one or the other.[7] Wyoming is a nongoverning member of the SBAC only; Kentucky is a nongoverning member of PARCC only. Minnesota and the states that did not adopt the Common Core standards are not members of either assessment consortium.

Standards-Based Reform in Education Policy and Governance

The standards-based reform model has been one of the dominant ideas in education policy and governance since it was first articulated in the 1980s. The core assumption of the model is that, rather than regulate education inputs and processes, government should instead identify what students should learn in school, require students to take tests on this material, and evaluate schools and districts on the basis of how well their students do on the tests. The entire education system, including preparation and professional development for teachers, should be organized around the same academic standards as the student assessments. As standards-based reform caught on, tests became a more important policy instrument. States that enacted policies based on the model also took on larger roles in school and district accountability.[8]

Advocates of standards-based reform believe that education policy should be organized around ways to support students to reach challenging academic standards (now described in terms of college and career readiness) and reducing gaps in achievement among demographic groups of students. One of the classic explanations of the model, by Marshall Smith and Jennifer O'Day, circulated widely among standards-based reform advocates in the 1980s and was published in 1991. Smith and O'Day make the case for state-level standards and also recommend that states create "coherent system[s] of instructional guidance."[9] In practice, however, sanctions and accountability have been a larger part of standards-based reform than has the development of improved training and professional development, better teaching materials, and other elements of the kind of support system that Smith and O'Day envisioned.

Standards-based reform fits well with the states' historic role in the U.S. public education governance system. The constitutions of all fifty states include language guaranteeing all resident children an education at public expense. The U.S. Constitution does not mention education as one of the areas over which

Congress has authority, so education has generally been understood to be a state power. To various degrees, the states delegate the funding and control of public schools to local school districts. In most of the country, school districts are legally separate from other local governing institutions, with their own taxing authority. Currently, states provide about 48 percent of funds for public education, localities provide about 44 percent, and the federal share is about 8 percent.[10]

It is hard to generalize about the state role in public education governance because its scope varies greatly among the states. For example, the share of all public education revenue that is provided by state governments ranges from about 31 percent (in Nevada) to more than 80 percent (in Hawaii, where the whole state comprises a single school district).[11] Some states, most notably California and Texas, specify which textbooks may be purchased with state funds, but most do not. Roughly half of the states require that students pass standardized tests to earn a regular diploma. Some states have extensive course requirements for high school graduation, while others leave this decision to school districts.

One valid generalization that can be made about the states is that the standards-based reform movement has led to more-centralized education governance and accountability. By 1994, forty-two states had developed or were developing content standards in academic subjects, and thirty had developed or were developing student performance standards based on those content standards.[12] These standards and tests were an especially dramatic break with previous policy and governance in the generally more locally controlled states of the Northeast and Midwest.

As a result of changes to the Elementary and Secondary Education Act (ESEA) in 1988 and 1994, the federal and state roles in standards, testing, and accountability became intertwined. The federal government's post-1994 expansion of its role in education performance accountability "borrows strength" from the states.[13] The 1994 reauthorization of the ESEA as the Improving America's Schools Act required that states have standards for core academic subjects and test students on the material in those standards at least once during elementary school, once in middle school, and once in high school. Under the new act, states also had to identify schools that were failing to make "adequate yearly progress" in student performance and to intervene in schools that persistently failed to improve. In practice, however, the Improving America's Schools Act did not influence state policies as much as its designers had hoped. In part, this was because the law itself permitted a great deal of flexibility. More significant, though, the new reauthorization and its companion program, Goals 2000, inspired an intense backlash against a larger federal role in education. In this hostile political climate, the U.S. Department of Education moved cautiously in implementing the laws.[14] The idea of voluntary national standards and tests was also discredited by conservative attacks on federally funded history standards for suggesting that understandings of history could change over time and for not emphasizing the roles of canonical historical figures as much as traditionalists thought they should.[15]

President George W. Bush broke with the Republican Party's usual resistance to a large federal role in education. Bush's first domestic policy initiative was the 2001 reauthorization of the ESEA, which he signed into law as the No Child Left Behind Act (NCLB) early in 2002. No Child Left Behind kept the basic standards and accountability framework of the Improving America's Schools Act but made it more prescriptive. To receive Title I funds, states had to test students annually on mathematics and English language arts in grades three through eight and once in high school. The NCLB defined adequate yearly progress as proficiency scores on state tests for all students by 2014 and left states less discretion over how to intervene in schools that did not make adequate yearly progress. In response, many state policymakers criticized the federal government for having overstepped its bounds (especially the law that prohibits the Department of Education from determining public school curriculums). Connecticut even sued the department, although a federal court ruled against the state in 2008. The NCLB was due for reauthorization in 2007, but Congress did not bring a bill to the floor during the remainder of the Bush administration.

By 2009, the beginning of the Obama administration, most federal and state policymakers remained committed to the general ideas of standards-based reform and performance accountability. However, even supporters of standards-based reform saw fundamental flaws in the NCLB. Although the law was quite prescriptive about the frequency of testing and the progression of accountability sanctions, it left the actual standard setting to the states. Several analyses indicated that these standards varied widely, so that a student whose mathematics performance was rated as Needs Improvement in one state might have been considered Advanced in another. Because states that set higher standards were likely to have larger proportions of schools identified for sanctions, the system created a perverse incentive to lower standards and cut scores.

In terms of governance and institutional design, by the 2007 deadline for reauthorization of the NCLB, the U.S. system of education accountability had become a simplified caricature of the standards-based reform model as it had been laid out in the 1980s. Instead of providing extensive systems of instructional guidance and professional development, states generally could only pressure schools and districts to improve by threatening sanctions for low test scores. The states did not offer many tools that districts and schools could use to improve their performance. State departments of education were doubly disadvantaged in efforts to improve schools, because many local educators resented the pressure they faced and because the states did not have much support to offer.[16]

The limits of state-level testing programs were also becoming clear. States' performance standards for proficiency varied greatly, and some were quite low.

The system came with a high price tag, since the vast majority of the states were contracting individually with testing companies to produce their assessments. Because of high assessment costs, states generally eschewed test questions that would require students to write or to demonstrate their knowledge in other ways than answering relatively inexpensive multiple-choice test questions. A great deal of test development effort was also being duplicated across states. From the perspective of the testing companies, the increased revenue the contracts generated came with a work volume that stretched their capacity to its limits.[17] Finally, policymakers and advocates who were interested in internationally benchmarked standards pointed out that few other industrialized countries had such decentralized education systems. For all these reasons, but primarily the latter, some education policy experts remained interested in setting national standards, or at least shared state standards, for U.S. public schools.

Moving toward Common Standards, 2002–12

Nearly simultaneously with the federal implementation of the NCLB, work began outside the federal government on benchmarking state standards. This work was the forerunner of the current Common Core State Standards Initiative. The Hewlett Foundation made a $2.4 million grant to Achieve, the Education Trust, the Fordham Institute, and the National Alliance of Business to work with five states on the American Diploma Project. The goal of the project was to identify gaps between the states' expectations for high school graduates, embodied in their exit tests and course requirements, and the expectations of higher education and the workplace. The participating states (Indiana, Kentucky, Massachusetts, Nevada, and Texas) pledged to revise their standards and tests, agree on common graduation benchmarks, and encourage other states to adopt the benchmarks.[18] A series of reports issued in 2004 by the American Diploma Project Network identified the specific English and mathematics skills needed by high school graduates to succeed in college or the workplace and found a gap between the content of high school graduation tests and the skills students need for college and the workplace. Additionally, the project surveyed states' high school graduation requirements and concluded that no state's course-taking requirements qualified as a "college- and work-preparatory curriculum."[19]

In the fall of 2004 the National Governors Association also began to focus on high school requirements. Virginia governor Mark Warner, who became the chair of the organization that year, announced that high school reform would be his main priority.[20] The governors held a high school reform summit in February 2005, after which thirteen states joined the American Diploma Project Network.[21] By the end of 2008, the network had twenty-two state members. According to Achieve's president, Michael Cohen, it was clear that if the member states' standards were all aligned with the project's benchmarks, then logically the standards must all be fairly close to one another. In essence, the states were converging on something like national standards.[22]

By 2006 the idea of national (but not necessarily federal) standards had clearly reemerged on the national policy agenda. A 2006 report by the Thomas B. Fordham Institute surveyed four possible models for national standards and recommended a system in which the federal government would develop national standards and tests, which the states could choose to use.[23] Later that year, the new executive director of the Council of Chief State School Officers, Gene Wilhoit, announced that common state standards would be his priority. At his first meeting as executive director, Wilhoit stated that "shared standards aren't simply an option, but a mandatory conversation,"[24] given the need to improve performance in U.S. schools.

The current Common Core State Standards Initiative began in 2008–09. The International Benchmarking Advisory Group, convened by Achieve, the National Governors Association, and the Council of Chief State School Officers, released a report in 2008 called *Benchmarking for Success*, which argued that the U.S. was falling behind other nations in terms of student knowledge and education attainment and recommended that the states adopt "a common core of internationally benchmarked standards in math and language arts for grades K–12."[25] For supporters of common state standards, the key governance characteristic of these standards was that states, not any part of the federal government, were in charge of the process. The American Diploma Project's report, *Out of Many, One*, also released in 2008, analyzed "college- and career-ready" standards in mathematics and English and concluded that the states with such standards had "arrived at a common core . . . as a byproduct of their deliberate, voluntary efforts to align their high school standards with the demands of college and careers."[26]

The National Governors Association endorsed the idea of common standards for "college and career readiness" at its 2009 winter meeting, cosponsored by the Council of Chief State School Officers. The CCSSI was formally launched in 2009 at a meeting in Chicago.[27] All of the states except for Alaska and Texas signed memorandums of understanding committing themselves to working on the standards, though not necessarily to adopting them once they were complete. Participants in and supporters of the CCSSI continually point out that it is a truly state-led effort and that they would not have wanted it to be led by the federal government. As Michael Cohen of Achieve, who also was assistant U.S. secretary of education in the Clinton administration, put it, "I've tried and failed more than anyone in American history to create national standards. One thing I was sure of was the federal government was not the way to get it done. The federal government would not help."[28] For the governors and chief state school officers involved in the CCSSI, it was crucial that the initiative originate in the states and continue to be led by them.

Although the originators of the CCSSI did not expect (or in many cases even want) federal support, the U.S. Department of Education has also backed the idea of common state standards. After the CCSSI began, the American Recovery and Reinvestment Act of 2009 (better known as the economic stimulus bill) set aside funds for the secretary of education to distribute as incentive grants to states that made "significant progress" in implementing reforms that included "adopting internationally benchmarked standards and assessments that prepare students for success in college and the workplace."[29] These grants were distributed through the Race to the Top competition. To win full points, a state had to provide evidence that it was participating in an interstate standards consortium comprising a "significant number of states." The Common Core state standards were, and are, the only such interstate standards. In 2011 Secretary of Education Arne Duncan announced criteria for NCLB waivers that echoed those for Race to the Top. To earn a waiver, a state must document that it has adopted "college and career ready standards" that are either "common to a significant number of states" or approved by a state network of higher education institutions.[30] Thus it is true both that the CCSSI is a state-led effort, in which many states were participating even before Race to the Top, and that federal policies have encouraged adoption of the standards.

The two Common Core assessments being developed by the SBAC and PARCC share several common characteristics. Both assessments will be at least partially computer administered, and the consortiums are conducting a shared survey of districts' technological capacity to do this.[31] Both consortiums are also producing curriculum resources and instructional materials in an effort to respond to the capacity issues that have frequently hindered standards-based reform.[32] With the sharing of states' knowledge and funds to develop, or to identify, curriculum materials and professional development, the initiative could potentially look more like the system of instructional guidance that standards-based reform advocates like Smith and O'Day envisioned in the 1980s and less like the simplified "tests generate pressure for improvement" version that has frequently frustrated educators and policymakers. Funding for administration of the assessments may be a future challenge; the federal grants from Race to the Top funds cover only development. To administer the tests, the states will probably use their own assessment budgets, or federal funds, assuming that the NCLB or a reauthorized ESEA continues to provide the states with financial assistance for administering assessments.

Challenges in Consortium Governance

Forging new relationships among existing institutions, determining how those relationships will work, and ensuring that the relationships actually serve the public interest pose several governance challenges. For the CCSSI and the assessment consortiums, one large challenge is the intense politics around the governance of public education in the U.S. federal system. A second challenge, a consequence of the first, is that because the common standards are not meant to be federally governed, some other governance structure (or structures) will be required. A third is that because the institutions include both public and private actors, accountability is complicated.

The United States has experienced national movements for various kinds of education reform,[33] and it is not particularly controversial to say that the nation as a whole has an interest in effective schools and equal education opportunity. However, the idea that the federal government should be in charge of reforming education arouses intense opposition. The result is a dilemma for advocates of national standards, even in the form of common standards agreed on and adopted by a group of states. The federal government's Race to the Top program presented states with an incentive to adopt the standards and provided major start-up support to two interstate assessment consortiums. This funding has contributed to the common standards project. However, opponents of the CCSSI have cited that same federal involvement as evidence that the whole collaborative project is really a federal power grab in disguise or that though it began as a state-led initiative it has been taken over by the federal government. State-level Tea Party groups have taken up the common standards as yet another example of federal overreach.[34] Because people from across the political spectrum have long criticized the NCLB as an unfunded or otherwise inappropriate federal mandate, this critique probably lands on fertile ground.

As Chris Minnich of the Council of Chief State School Officers says, "The rhetoric about federalism has been hard," even though it is clear from the history of the American Diploma Project Network and the CCSSI that state leaders were working together on common standards well before the federal government got involved.[35] Conservative organizations have attacked the CCSSI in ways that recall earlier rounds of controversy over the creation of the U.S. Department of Education and the enactment of national education goals in 1994. For example, a Backgrounder paper from the Heritage Foundation categorizes the CCSSI as "national standards" and warns that "this renewed push for common national standards and assessments should be resisted," just as conservatives resisted the Clinton administration's testing initiatives.[36]

Since nobody seems to want the U.S. Department of Education more involved than it already is, the second set of governance challenges has to do with setting up new institutions for making decisions about the consortiums. For the CCSSI and the assessment consortiums, this alternative structure is taking the form of networks of states, mediated by private sector organizations. In the case of the CCSSI, these mediating organizations are the National Governors Association and the Council of Chief State School Officers, which are themselves membership organizations for state officials. The SBAC and PARCC both contract with non-profits (WestEd and Achieve, respectively) for project management, and committees representing their member states are making decisions about the assessments.

The CCSSI and the two assessment consortiums are all still in the institution-building stage. None of the three has independent organizational existence, such as 501(c)(3) status; they are simply projects being undertaken by their host institutions. Neither the CCSSI nor the consortiums necessarily needs to become an independent organization, but at some point they have to decide on their long-term structure and also determine how they will handle future revisions to the standards and management and administration of the assessments. Until recently, getting the work under way has been a higher priority than resolving longer-term governance questions, though all three projects are now taking on these issues. Regarding the CCSSI, Dane Linn, of the National Governors Association, says, "We want all facets of this work moving forward to continue to be led by the states. But that's why its so important for us to get some resolution on what the structure looks like."[37]

Stephen Goldsmith and William Eggers identify the challenges of governing by network as "aligning goals, providing oversight, averting communications meltdown, coordinating multiple partners, managing the tension between competition and collaboration, and overcoming data deficits and capacity shortages."[38] The stability of any collaboration involving state government is threatened by turnover of officeholders. Most visibly, a new governor or a change in legislative leadership may lead to an abrupt shift in state policy and threaten collaboration. Complicating these networks still further, the state governments themselves are not unitary actors. Executive and legislative powers are separate and are often controlled by competing parties. Indeed, for the forty-nine states with bicameral legislatures, party control of the legislature itself can also be split. Tensions could conceivably arise within a state government's executive branch (for example, between the governor's office and the state department of education), within the legislature, or between the legislature and the executive. One part of a government may see advantages in participating in a network or collaboration that another part of the same government does not favor. As Paul Manna has pointed out, the role of legislatures can be problematic when a network unites states' executive agencies. If legislators feel like they have been cut out of the loop, they may respond by attacking the collaborative project.[39]

When states can secede from a collaboration without penalty, the stability of the collaborative project is threatened. Many collaborations depend on the work of less-visible civil servants in state government, who continue to network with their peers in other states. If a particularly important member of this network retires or changes jobs, or if the position that person occupies is eliminated, the network is weakened even if the state does not officially stop collaborating. Even without federal government involvement in an interstate collaboration, federal policy is a key component of the environment within which collaboration takes place. Barry Rabe notes that the Regional Greenhouse Gas Initiative has been challenged by its "political and legal frailty in the absence of a common mission with the federal government."[40] Alternatively, if federal policy creates incentives for states to work together, it may enhance the durability of interstate collaboration.

Even if the CCSSI and the assessment consortiums do not turn into new 501(c)(3) organizations, they will still bring together public and private organizations. In the CCSSI, the distinctions between public and private are somewhat blurry. Although the initiative itself is clearly a public-private partnership, Achieve, one of the private partners, was formed in part by governors. The state assessment consortiums involve private entities, but in something more like the traditional contracting relationship than a public-private network with shared authority and discretion. Both consortiums contract with nonprofits for project management, and ultimately both will have contracts with assessment companies. These relationships challenge conventional understandings of public sector accountability.[41]

These arrangements do not fit neatly into existing mechanisms for bureaucratic accountability, such as state laws meant to ensure honest awarding and evaluation of government contracts with the private sector. State procurement policies generally include barriers to sole-source contracts, to prevent sweetheart deals between public officials and favored private providers. Somehow, these policies will need to be adjusted to fit the situation in which the state is not purchasing a service from one vendor among many but rather is paying for the product of a collaborative planning process in which it participated.

The larger challenge for the interstate consortiums will be the ways in which voters might hold their state officials accountable for these collaborative decisions or evaluate whether or not their states ought to continue in the consortiums. Even with respect to a single state, using one's vote to hold public agencies accountable is a blunt instrument. For example, a citizen who approves of his or her state governor's record on environmental policy, but thinks the administration's education policy is misguided, cannot send both signals with a single vote. Political accountability in interstate collaborations is still trickier. Political instability within states (shifts in the party or ideology that prevails in the executive or legislative branch, or both) threatens interstate collaboration. The political process may send mixed signals, and officials in different parts of government may claim electoral mandates for conflicting policy agendas. However messy they are, though, such shifts are how political accountability happens.

One obstacle to electoral accountability for many interstate collaborations is that it can be hard for citizens to know that such collaborations exist and to follow what they do.[42] For example, there is no easy way for the public to get a full picture of how the CCSSI and the assessment consortiums are funded. The federal funding of the assessment consortiums is easy to track through the Department of Education website[43] because the Obama administration has insisted on a high degree of transparency for spending that is funded by the economic stimulus package. However, the assessment consortiums have also received foundation grants, and the CCSSI relies on foundation support. Information about private funding is harder to locate than federal spending information. The foundations supporting the CCSSI and the assessment consortiums provide information about their grants in press releases, annual reports, and their online databases. However, to know where to look, it is necessary to know which foundations are involved, since the interstate projects do not provide comprehensive lists of their funders. One person involved with the CCSSI says that overall budget information is "not generally something we share because we don't find it to be too pertinent to the conversation."[44]

One reason for participants' reticence may be a fear that any budget information they make public will be turned against them. The CCSSI's Gates funding and its organizational base in a group, such as Achieve, that draws board members from large corporations make it easy for people who already think corporations are taking over public education to see the standards as just the latest manifestation of a corporate agenda. Indeed, late in 2011 protesters connected with Occupy Wall Street disrupted a meeting of New York City's Panel on Education Policy, chanting, "The Core is out of touch."[45] Although foundations and for-profit corporations are legally separate, some critics of the Common Core initiative suggest that nonprofits like the Bill & Melinda Gates Foundation or the Pearson Foundation are involved simply so that Microsoft or Pearson can make money by selling Common Core–related products. A quick Google search on "Common Core" or a scan of current advertisements in *Education Week* makes it clear that many businesses are indeed marketing products and services that they claim are aligned with the Common Core state standards or otherwise designed to help teachers implement them. Obviously, the existence of these products and marketing strategies does not prove that the Common Core initiative is intended to boost corporate profits, but even inaccurate political messages can be quite potent.

The people and organizations at the center of the CCSSI and the assessment consortiums face the task of building new governance institutions in a fluid, and sometimes conflictual, political environment. These governing institutions need to be strong enough to get their work done but not so centralized that they seem to be usurping the states' constitutional role in public education. They also must be transparent enough to show that they are working in the public interest.

A Multistate Consortium in Action:
The New England Common Assessment Program

One clear precedent for the current interstate collaborations is the New England Common Assessment Program (NECAP), a set of standardized tests currently administered by Maine, New Hampshire, Rhode Island, and Vermont. The program has no separate organizational home; it exists as a professional network among the state education departments' staff. Rather than formal written policies and memorandums of understanding, a great deal is done through "gentlepersons' agreements." The four states contract with the National Center for Improvement of Educational Assessment to manage the consortium by coordinating decisionmaking and communications, scheduling meetings, and making travel arrangements.[46] Throughout its history, the NECAP decision rule has been consensus. In theory, in the absence of consensus the states would take a vote, each state weighted equally, but in practice a vote has never been necessary. States have individual, though identical, contracts with Measured Progress for the assessment program. Understanding the history of NECAP, how four states with long histories of local control have been able to implement an interstate test with only minimal controversy, and the governance of the assessment provides some insight into what may lie ahead for the nationwide consortiums.

The NECAP examinations were first administered in 2004. Following enactment of the No Child Left Behind Act, the four small New England states struggled to meet the federal requirement that they test all students annually in grades three through eight.[47] Vermont's and New Hampshire's state assessment systems included open-response components that were relatively expensive to administer, and the states did not want to replace these with less-expensive multiple-choice questions. Rhode Island and Vermont were already administering the New Standards Reference Examination, so the idea of interstate collaboration was familiar to them. Charles DePascale, who has been deeply involved with NECAP since its beginning, characterizes the choice the states faced as "multiple choice or collaboration."[48] They chose collaboration. The two New England states with the largest enrollments, Connecticut and Massachusetts, chose not to participate. They did not face the same financial constraints as the smaller states because they had larger student populations over which to spread the fixed costs of test development. Also, their state assessment programs were more established. The Massachusetts Comprehensive Assessment System had been administered since 1998, and the Connecticut Mastery Test program had been in existence since the mid-1980s. Both tests were (and are) highly regarded nationally.

Maine initially participated in the discussions but then decided not to join the testing consortium. Maine had some philosophical differences from the other states and also did not want to test students in the fall rather than in the spring.

Moreover, Maine was in the process of revising its own academic standards and did not want to shift to common standards. Maine rejoined the NECAP consortium after discovering that it needed to reduce its assessment costs by $1 million.

The general cost-sharing agreement among the states asks that each state pay the same share of the fixed costs of the assessment (such as developing items and ensuring statistical validity and reliability), with the variable costs (such as printing test booklets and scoring tests) spread proportionately according to the number of students in each state. The state test coordinators agree that this arrangement permits them to have a higher-quality assessment than they could have produced alone, for the same or perhaps a lower cost.

The NECAP examination materials are the same across the four states and are administered during the same fall "testing window," following the same procedures, and using the same standard accommodations. Psychometric analyses for item calibration, scaling, equating, and standard setting are done with the data from all four states,[49] so the results are statistically comparable. Rhode Island has made a point of reporting results from the other NECAP states along with its own because its state leaders have seen the comparison as a way to spur improvement. The other states report only their own scores. The states have retained their own individual websites for assessment information rather than creating a common NECAP assessment website. Having a common assessment means that the states also share academic standards. Administration of NECAP began with the assumption that the content of the standards would be reviewed and perhaps revised, but because the exam will no longer be administered after the nationwide consortiums' assessments begin, this revision work will not be done.

Despite the common standards and assessments, the states maintain separate accountability policies based on the assessment results. Following federal law, each state has a different starting point for measuring adequate yearly progress under the NCLB. The states have also made different decisions about the minimum size of student subgroups that will be included in determining adequate yearly progress under the NCLB. Conceivably, then, two identical schools with identical NECAP results, located in different states, could have different accountability statuses under the NCLB simply because of the states' different decisions about subgroup size. When NECAP began, none of the participating states used it as a high-stakes test for students, but that changed when Rhode Island incorporated NECAP scores into its high school graduation requirements. The cutoff for the Rhode Island graduation requirement is a score of Partially Proficient, lower than the NCLB threshold of proficiency. Students who do not meet this requirement the first time they take the test have the opportunity to try again. The retakes produce extra costs for the NECAP consortium, which must develop a larger bank of test items for the high school assessment. Rhode Island is bearing these extra costs itself.[50]

Given the strength of New Englanders' attachment to local control, NECAP has been surprisingly noncontroversial. In New Hampshire, the cost savings appealed to some conservatives who might otherwise have seen a multistate test as a violation of the principle of local control. Outreach to educators has also helped. Like state-level assessment programs, NECAP has involved teachers in item review and scoring. According to Peter McWalters, who was Rhode Island's commissioner of education when NECAP began, Measured Progress oversaw an eighteen-month process in which teachers from Rhode Island, Vermont, and New Hampshire reviewed student work to identify what different levels of performance would mean.[51] The testing directors attribute the development of a generally high level of support in the field to the continued involvement of teachers, even though the multistate assessment means fewer teachers from a single state can be involved at a given time. State assessment directors involved in NECAP say that educators support the test, and school administrators worry less that the state's test might be idiosyncratic, because of the multistate test development process.

Interviewees also said that the multistate nature of NECAP provided "political cover" for state officials, who could explain decisions about the assessment as having been a consensus among states rather than just the opinion of whoever happened to be in charge at one state department of education. For example, students in Rhode Island, Vermont, and New Hampshire scored low on the first administration of the high school NECAP. The states met and agreed that they had set appropriate cut scores for the test. They presented their states' unsatisfactory results to the public as part of a general problem shared among several states rather than a single state's failing. In Rhode Island, this logic seems to have underpinned the state's decision to report Vermont's and New Hampshire's scores along with its own. McWalters anticipated that Rhode Island students' scores would be the lowest, given the state's higher levels of urban poverty and otherwise more difficult demographics. He saw the interstate comparison as a way of introducing the reality of the state's low performance and focusing on reform.[52]

The New England consortium has faced some of the governance challenges identified in the previous section of this chapter. Although the state testing directors are quite pleased with the program, they also say that collaboration has proved more difficult than they initially expected. One of the original assumptions behind NECAP was that a common assessment would permit the states to divide work among staff in their state departments of education and thereby realize economies of scale. The reality has been different. The state-level content specialists wanted to make sure that they had each reviewed every test item. They felt a responsibility for making sure the assessments would work for their states' teachers, and they knew that they would have to explain and defend consortium decisions to teachers in the field. Very recently, the state content specialists have become more comfortable dividing their work among the states by grade level.

The states' testing directors have been able to share the administrative tasks related to the assessment system. According to one of them, they "fell into" their division of labor in creating administration manuals, making accommodations decisions, and shaping policy, depending on their individual expertise and interests.[53] All the state interviewees praised their assessment contractor, Measured Progress, for its flexibility in revising plans without raising the costs of the assessment and also appreciated the coordination by the National Center for Improvement of Educational Assessment. Although they are not formally related, Measured Progress and the center are both located in Dover, New Hampshire, a fact that presumably facilitates their ability to work together.

The main challenge of collaboration that the assessment directors identified was the length of time it takes to make a collective decision. Crucially, according to NECAP state-level interviewees, the states decided early on that it was better to take the extra time and make decisions they all actually supported rather than compromise core principles or settle for less-than-optimal solutions. New Hampshire's assessment director, Tim Kurtz, estimates that he now spends more time meeting with Measured Progress than he spent with the state's assessment contractor when it had its own assessment program.[54] Several interviewees identified the question of whether students could use calculators on NECAP as an issue that had posed an early challenge and set a precedent about collective decisionmaking. Before NECAP, Rhode Island and Vermont had used the New Standards Reference Examination, which permitted students to use calculators on the mathematics assessment. New Hampshire, whose testing director is a former math teacher with strong opinions on the issue, had not. The testing directors worked out a compromise that banned calculator use for the part of the mathematics assessment that specifically measures students' ability to do basic computations accurately but permitted it for other parts of the assessment. Vermont testing director Michael Hock characterizes this decision as "emblematic of the way NECAP has worked."[55]

At times, the participants have also agreed on ways to meet one state's specific needs without locking others into the same course of action. The compromise over Rhode Island's use of the high school NECAP as part of its graduation requirement is one example; another is whether test results should be aggregated at the school level by testing year (for example, all of the fourth graders at a particular school who took the math test) or by teaching year (all of the fourth graders who were taught math together the prior year). Vermont wanted to be able to do both, and Rhode Island did not, but Rhode Island agreed to collect data in a way that would make teaching-year analysis possible.[56]

Although collaboration has been challenging, interviewees also identified the interstate collaboration as the chief strength of NECAP. In addition to the financial advantage of sharing development costs, they all agreed that involving more people led to better decisions than would have been made at the individual-state level, even though they spent more time making the decisions. When I asked the state testing directors participating in NECAP whether they thought their experiences could provide any lessons for the nationwide standards and assessment consortiums, several referred to what they had learned about consensus building. Because they saw the decisions as high-quality ones, they were better able to stand by those decisions when controversies arose. As McWalters notes, "Collaboration provides an opportunity to go into discovery mode with enough cover to stumble."

The New England program's approach to accountability has emphasized reliance on state agency professionals to act in the states' interests. Bureaucratic accountability initially posed a challenge for NECAP because it presented barriers to the three original states' entering into a single contract with Measured Progress. The states worked around that challenge by each issuing a separate request for proposals for the assessment, following the particular requirements of their state procurement laws. Bidders then submitted the same response to each of the states separately. The states reviewed the proposals individually, then convened to agree on which one to accept, negotiated the details collectively with the contractor, and issued identical but separate contracts.[57] The states' solution to the contracting challenge highlights the importance of collegiality and professional accountability for NECAP. The NECAP interviewees all emphasized the importance of trust among representatives of the participating states. This trust grew out of professional respect and ongoing relationships, nurtured through many face-to-face meetings.

Political accountability has not been a major formal concern for NECAP, as the states' boards of education readily agreed to participate and none needed to get legislative approval. Although the states' boards of education had to approve the assessments and the standards, this happened with a minimum of controversy. The potential existed for backlash against such centralized decisionmaking, but this did not happen. McWalters says it was helpful that the three original NECAP states' commissioners all had good relationships with their state boards and that none required the governor's approval to participate in the consortium. As such, the commissioners were able to develop the consortium "under the radar" politically. None of the directors interviewed thus far recalls major difficulties with their state legislators over NECAP. According to Charles DePascale, who coordinates the NECAP states' work, the need to comply with the NCLB and the expense of single-state assessments limited possible opposition to NECAP.[58]

Had NECAP lasted longer, issues like revision of the standards might have attracted more public attention and become political matters.

It is worth noting that both the beginning and end of NECAP were the result of shifting incentives at the federal level. When the NCLB required annual testing in grades three though eight, the states embraced collaboration as a means of producing better assessments than they could afford on their own. The end came with the states' decisions to join the larger consortiums, which will replace NECAP. Vermont, New Hampshire, and Maine joined the SBAC, and Rhode Island joined PARCC.

The NECAP participants identify several lessons for the new, larger state consortiums. They all emphasize the importance of compromise, so long as no state has to compromise one of its core principles. McWalters notes that one of the positive effects of the entire performance-accountability movement has been that, when all states have disappointing test scores, no state can claim to have all the answers. Thus state leaders are open to sharing problems and learning from one another. He also cautions participants in the new consortiums to bear in mind that "we are trying to create something that doesn't exist" and warns that the federal incentive system needs to keep goals clear. DePascale underscores the importance of making sure that the standards drive the assessments, rather than the other way around, and of ensuring that interpretations of the standards do not diverge as multiple organizations get involved in developing supporting materials.[59]

The NECAP consortium provides a sort of "proof of concept" for multistate standards and assessments. It is possible to maintain such a system, albeit at a very small scale, in a context of mutual trust and goodwill, with stable federal policy incentives. As Chris Minnich, of the Council of Chief State School Officers, says, "The NECAP really gave states hope that this was possible . . . that a group of states can write a high-quality assessment or share standards . . . and that it would work, that you wouldn't have to give up your state's uniqueness in order to be part of a group."[60]

The state-level interviewees, particularly McWalters, say that the multistate nature of the standards and assessment provides more leverage for school improvement than a state-level test would. Involvement in the assessment development process also served as powerful professional development for teachers in the participating states. However, McWalters also attributes a great deal of Rhode Island's improved writing scores to a teacher-led professional development program that was unrelated to NECAP. Even with a high-quality assessment, the link between assessment results and school improvement depends on the extent to which the entire education system builds its capacity to improve.

Prospects for the Nationwide Consortiums and Educational Improvement

Although the New England Common Assessment Program provides an encouraging example, people who are involved in the SBAC, PARCC, and the CCSSI recognize that they have taken on a far larger and more complicated task. The scale of the new assessment consortiums dwarfs NECAP both in the number of states involved and the geographic distances between them (the SBAC includes Hawaii and thus spans five time zones). The states in PARCC and the SBAC are more diverse in their approaches to accountability than were Maine, Vermont, New Hampshire, and Rhode Island at the beginning of NECAP. Given this diversity of political cultures and prior histories, it may be difficult for the consortiums to make the kind of generally acceptable decisions that have been so important for NECAP. Both of the larger consortiums strive for unanimity but reserve the option of voting if they cannot reach consensus. States that get consistently outvoted may shift consortiums (which would not threaten the viability of the larger common-assessment project) or simply opt to go it alone (which might threaten the common approach if many states chose to do so).

The overall sustainability of the common standards and tests has three layers: national organizations' commitment to the standards project, federal policy that affects incentives for states to participate, and states' own politics and policy. The national organizations' continued participation seems the easiest to predict; the Council of Chief State School Officers and the National Governors Association remain committed to common standards, even though the 2010 elections produced large turnover among both governors and state education chiefs. The direction of federal and state policy and politics is harder to predict, particularly given the potential for intragovernmental conflict between executive and legislative branches. Recently, the combination of Race to the Top (with funding decisions under the control of the U.S. Department of Education) and deadlock on reauthorizing the Elementary and Secondary Education Act meant that the executive branch had the field to itself at the federal level.[61] In late 2011 Secretary Duncan's willingness to grant NCLB waivers seemed to galvanize Congress into action on ESEA reauthorization, as both the House and Senate education committees approved reauthorization bills. However, progress was short lived, and neither bill came up for a floor vote before the 112th Congress adjourned.

States' decisions about continued consortium membership will be influenced at least somewhat by evolving public opinion about the core standards and common assessments. Polls sponsored by Achieve have found that teachers' awareness of and support for the Common Core is increasing. The general public remains mostly unaware of the Common Core, though respondents tend to support the idea when they hear more about it.[62] Although we should not read too much into two surveys, we can probably assume that public attitudes about the standards are still forming and that what people hear about the standards will shape their opinion of them.

Americans remain generally resistant to the idea of greater federal authority over public education. If conservative organizations and elected officials dominate discussion of the CCSSI with their claims that it has been taken over by the federal government, public opinion could easily turn against the common standards. People who do not identify with the conservative movement might be receptive to a different critical claim: that private corporations are using the Common Core standards to increase their power over public education. However, voters could also hear more positive messages. For parents of children in public school, a great deal of what they hear will come from their children's teachers, who according to Achieve's surveys are becoming more supportive of the Common Core standards.[63]

If the Common Core standards and assessments survive political uncertainty, will this change in education governance lead to educational improvement? With the combination of multistate standards and assessments and less-prescriptive federal accountability requirements (through either NCLB waivers or a less prescriptive new ESEA), most states will be using the same academic standards and one of two common assessments, to which they will attach accountability policies determined at the state level within a much looser set of federal conditions. For performance accountability to lead to school improvement, states, districts, and schools need to respond effectively to poor performance. Several decades into standards-based reform, researchers and policymakers remain far from a consensus about how to turn around (and whether simply to close) persistently underperforming schools. A situation in which most states are working from common standards and assessments, with different accountability policies, could well provide a better opportunity for states to learn from one another's experience than does the current system. The NECAP states' assessment directors all agree that a combination of multistate standards and assessments with state-determined accountability policies worked well for them. The Common Core standards are intended to be more demanding than most states' current standards, and greater state-level flexibility about accountability and sanctions is likely to facilitate the maintenance of higher standards. Part of the "race to the bottom" problem with the NCLB was that states had more flexibility with their standards than with the accountability sanctions attached to them. With greater room to vary their accountability policies, states may be more willing to keep standards high.

States' other education policies will be a key factor in determining whether schools do a better job under the multistate standards and assessments than they are doing at present. Frequently, state policies and programs related to standards-based reform have emphasized the standard-setting and sanctions parts of standards-based reform while underdeveloping the system of instructional guidance that is at the core of Smith and O'Day's model. From the perspective of schools and teachers, the result was a great deal of pressure to improve without much help in doing so. Studies of states' capacity to guide education reform conducted before the introduction of Common Core standards generally concluded that most state education departments lack the resources and capabilities needed to support instructional improvement.[64] States are currently attempting to rectify this problem as they implement the Common Core standards. A recent survey of state education departments' progress in implementing those standards concludes that a great deal of planning work is under way, but only seven states have comprehensive implementation plans that address professional development, curriculum guides and other materials, and teacher evaluation.[65]

In addition to supportive state policies, districts, schools, and teachers need high-quality instructional materials. The designs of both PARCC and the SBAC are closer to a full instructional guidance system than are most existing state tests, since the consortiums' assessments will include interim and diagnostic measures. Both consortiums have received additional federal funds to be used in designing optional curriculum and instructional materials to accompany the assessments. Many vendors are also marketing products and services related to the Common Core. It is reasonable to expect that some of these will be well done and others will be pedagogical snake oil. To help educators decide what to use, it might make sense for some entity—perhaps the CCSSI or the assessment consortiums—to vet them and award something like a Good Housekeeping Seal of Approval to the ones that are of high quality and are well aligned with the standards. However, there is an obvious political dilemma here. In addition to helping educators spend their money effectively, a Common Core Seal of Approval would probably also reinforce the suspicion that the whole enterprise is just a thinly disguised power grab.

This tension between national-scale goals and a decentralized governance system is one of the oldest challenges facing U.S. policymakers. The CCSSI and its small-scale predecessor NECAP are both efforts to resolve this tension through state collaboration. The Common Core State Standards Initiative and the two multistate assessment consortiums have the potential to reduce fragmentation of governance without displacing states from their leading role in education policy. However, the entire enterprise remains vulnerable to political volatility. Interstate collaboration on standards and tests began outside the federal government, but federal incentives have facilitated its growth. If dramatic change in federal education policy takes place, state governments may prefer to move in different directions. Renewed fragmentation remains a distinct possibility.

Notes

1. *Why National Standards and Tests? Politics and the Quest for Better Schools* (Thousand Oaks, Calif.: Sage Publications, 1998); Gary B. Nash, Charlotte Crabtree, and Ross E. Dunn, *History on Trial: Culture Wars and the Teaching of the Past* (New York: Knopf, 1997).

2. "Overview Information for Race to the Top Fund," *Federal Register*, November 18, 2009, pp. 59836, 59843.

3. Sean Cavanagh, "New Standards Draft Offers More Details," *Education Week*, September 30, 2009; Michele McNeil, "Rules Set for $4B 'Race to Top' Contest," *Education Week*, November 11, 2009.

4. The SBAC was formed through a merger of the SMARTER (Summative Multi-State Assessment Resources for Teachers and Educational Researchers) consortium, the Balanced Assessment Consortium, and the Mosaic consortium. See "Frequently Asked Questions," Balanced Assessment Consortium, 2011 (www.k12.wa.us/SMARTER/FAQ.aspx).

5. Governing states in PARCC are Arizona, Arkansas, Colorado, Florida, Georgia, Illinois, Indiana, Louisiana, Maryland, Massachusetts, Mississippi, New Jersey, New Mexico, New York, Ohio, Oklahoma, Rhode Island, and Tennessee, plus the District of Columbia.

6. The SBAC's governing states are California, Connecticut, Delaware, Hawaii, Idaho, Iowa, Kansas, Maine, Michigan, Missouri, Montana, Nevada, New Hampshire, North Carolina, Oregon, South Carolina, South Dakota, Vermont, Washington, West Virginia, and Wisconsin.

7. Nongoverning members of both consortiums are Alabama, North Dakota, and Pennsylvania.

8. Kathryn A. McDermott, *High-Stakes Reform: The Politics of Educational Accountability* (Georgetown University Press, 2011).

9. Marshall S. Smith and Jennifer O'Day, "Systemic School Reform," in *The Politics of Curriculum and Testing: The 1990 Yearbook of the Politics of Education Association*, edited by Susan H. Fuhrman and Betty Malen, pp. 233–67 (New York: Falmer, 1991), p. 247.

10. National Center for Education Statistics, *Digest of Education Statistics, 2010* (U.S. Department of Education, 2011), table 180 (http://nces.ed.gov/programs/digest/d10/tables/dt10_180.asp?referrer=list).

11. Ibid., table 181 (http://nces.ed.gov/programs/digest/d10/tables/dt10_181.asp?referrer=list).

12. John F. Jennings, *Why National Standards and Tests? Politics and the Quest for Better Schools* (Thousand Oaks, Calif.: Sage Publications, 1998), p. 8.

13. Paul Manna, *School's In: Federalism and the National Education Agenda* (Georgetown University Press, 2006).

14. Jennings, *Why National Standards and Tests?*; Elizabeth H. DeBray, *Politics, Ideology, and Education: Federal Policy during the Clinton and Bush Administrations* (Teachers College Press, 2006).

15. Maris A. Vinovskis, *From A Nation at Risk to No Child Left Behind: National Education Goals and the Creation of Federal Education Policy* (Teachers College Press, 2009)

p. 126; Gary B. Nash, Charlotte Crabtree, and Ross E. Dunn, *History on Trial: Culture Wars and the Teaching of the Past* (New York: Knopf, 1997).

16. Angela Minnici and Deanna D. Hill, *Educational Architects: Do State Education Agencies Have the Tools Necessary to Implement NCLB?* (Washington: Center on Education Policy, 2007); Kathryn A. McDermott, "Trust and Capacity in Policy Implementation: Evidence from Massachusetts Education Reform," *Journal of Public Administration Research and Theory* 16 (January 2006): 25–45.

17. Thomas Toch and Peg Tyre, "How Will the Common Core Initiative Affect the Testing Industry?" paper prepared for the conference, Common Education Standards: Tackling the Long-Term Questions, Thomas B. Fordham Foundation, Washington, 2010.

18. Lynn Olson, "Two New Projects to Examine Quality, Impact of Exit Exams," *Education Week*, January 9, 2002.

19. Achieve Inc., *The Expectations Gap: A 50-State Review of High School Graduation Requirements* (Washington, 2004), p. 3.

20. Michelle R. Davis and Alan Richard, "Bush Test Proposal for High Schoolers Joins Wider Trend," *Education Week*, September 15, 2004.

21. Lynn Olson, "Summit Fuels Push to Improve High Schools," *Education Week*, March 9, 2005.

22. Michael Cohen, Achieve president and former assistant U.S. secretary of education, telephone interview with author, October 28, 2011.

23. Chester E. Finn Jr., Liam Julian, and Michael Petrilli, *To Dream the Impossible Dream: Four Approaches to National Standards and Tests for America's Schools* (Washington: Thomas B. Fordham Institute, 2006).

24. Jessica L. Tonn, "State Education Leaders Debate National Standards," *Education Week*, December 6, 2006.

25. National Governors Association, Council of Chief State School Officers, and Achieve Inc., *Benchmarking for Success: Ensuring U.S. Students Receive a World-Class Education* (Washington: National Governors Association, 2008), p. 6.

26. Achieve Inc., *Out of Many, One: Toward Rigorous Common Core Standards from the Ground Up* (Washington, 2008), p. 2.

27. Michele McNeil, "Standards to Receive Fresh Push," *Education Week*, April 22, 2009.

28. Cohen, interview.

29. P.L. 111-5, Sec. 14006, *Federal Register*, November 18, 2009, p. 59688.

30. U.S. Department of Education, *ESEA Flexibility* (n.d.), p. 7 (www.ed.gov/esea/flexibility/documents/esea-flexibility.doc).

31. Catherine Gewertz, "Common Assessments a Test for Schools' Technology," *Education Week*, April 27, 2011.

32. Catherine Gewertz, "Common-Assessment Consortiums Add Resources to Plans," *Education Week*, February 23, 2011.

33. Carl F. Kaestle, "Federal Education Policy and the Changing National Polity for Education, 1957–2007," in *To Educate a Nation: Federal and National Strategies for School Reform*, edited by Carl F. Kaestle and Alyssa E. Lodewick (University Press of Kansas, 2007), pp. 17–40.

34. See, for example, "The Great State Acquiescence in Education?" *Tea Party Bus Tour*, June 12, 2011 (www.teapartybustour.com/2011/the-great-state-acquiescence-in-education/).

35. Chris Minnich, Council of Chief State School Officers senior membership director, interview with author, October 21, 2011.

36. Lindsey M. Burke and Jennifer A. Marshall, *Why National Standards Won't Fix American Education: Misalignment of Power and Incentives* (Washington: Heritage Foundation, 2010), p. 2.

37. Dane Linn, National Governors Association, interview with author, November 2, 2011.

38. Stephen Goldsmith and William D. Eggers, *Governing by Network: The New Shape of the Public Sector* (Brookings Press, 2004), p. 52.

39. Paul Manna, "Networked Governance in Three Policy Areas with Implications for the Common Core State Standards Initiative" (Washington: Thomas B. Fordham Institute, 2010).

40. Rabe, "Regionalism and Global Climate Change Policy," p. 178.

41. Barbara S. Romzek and Melvin J. Dubnick provide a typology of bureaucratic, professional, legal, and political accountability in their article, "Accountability in the Public Sector: Lessons from the *Challenger* Tragedy," *Public Administration Review* 47 (May–June 1987): 227–38.

42. Zimmerman, *Interstate Cooperation*, p. 164.

43. See U.S. Department of Education, "Race to the Top Assessment Program," 2011 (www2.ed.gov/programs/racetothetop-assessment/awards.html).

44. CCSSI participant, interview with author, October 21, 2011.

45. Joy Resmovits, "Protesters Affiliated with Occupy Wall Street Disrupt Department of Education Meeting," *Huffington Post*, October 25, 2011 (www.huffingtonpost.com/2011/10/25/occupy-wall-street-department-of-education_n_1031812.html).

46. Charles DePascale, *The New England Common Assessment Program: Notes on the Collaboration among Four New England States* (Dover, N.H.: National Center for the Improvement of Educational Assessment, 2009).

47. Pasquale J. DeVito, "The Oversight of State Standards and Assessment Programs: Perspectives from a Former State Assessment Director" (Washington: Thomas B. Fordham Institute, 2010), p. 4.

48. DePascale, *The New England Common Assessment Program*, p. 2.

49. DeVito, "The Oversight of State Standards and Assessment Programs," p. 7.

50. Charles DePascale, e-mail to author, November 13, 2011.

51. Peter McWalters, chair of the Council of Chief State School Officers and a former Rhode Island commissioner of education, interview with author, October 19, 2011.

52. Ibid.

53. Michael Hock, Vermont Department of Education, testing director, telephone interview with author, October 17, 2011.

54. Tim Kurtz, New Hampshire Department of Education, assessment director, interview with author, October 7, 2011.

55. Hock, interview.

56. Ibid.

57. Ibid.

58. Charles DePascale, e-mail to author, November 10, 2011.

59. DePascale, e-mail, November 13, 2011.

60. Minnich, interview.

61. Lorraine M. McDonnell and M. Stephen Weatherford, "Crafting an Education Reform Agenda through Economic Stimulus Policy," *Peabody Journal of Education* 86, no. 3 (2011): 304–18.

62. Achieve Inc., *Strong Support, Low Awareness: Public Perception of the Common Core State Standards* (Washington: Achieve Inc., 2011), p. 1; "Growing Awareness, Growing Support: Teacher and Voter Understanding of the Common Core State Standards and Assessments," June 2012 (www.achieve.org/files/GrowingAwarenessGrowingSupport reportFINAL72012.pdf), p. 1.

63. Ibid.

64. Minnici and Hill, *Educational Architects*; McDermott, "Trust and Capacity in Policy Implementation."

65. Education First and Editorial Projects in Education Research Center, *Preparing for Change: A National Perspective on Common Core State Standards Implementation Planning* (Washington: Education First and Editorial Projects in Education Research Center, 2012).

KENNETH K. WONG

8

Education Governance
in Performance-Based Federalism

In his last public policy speech of his two-term presidency, George W. Bush chose to highlight his accomplishments in education reform at the General Philip Kearny School in Philadelphia. Seven years after the passage of the No Child Left Behind Act (NCLB), the president claimed that "fewer students are falling behind" and "more students are achieving high standards."[1] Addressing the concern that testing is punitive, the president commented, "How can you possibly determine whether a child can read at grade level if you don't test? To me, measurement is the gateway to true reform."[2] This debate over the benefits and limitations of the federal act continues as the Barack Obama administration works on the reauthorization of that legislation. President Obama supports the federal role to strengthen accountability, including annual student testing. At the same time, he sees the need to provide additional resources to schools so they can improve teacher quality and improve student readiness for postsecondary opportunities. The administration also encourages competitive applications from states and districts to implement new strategies to raise student achievement, as prominently featured in the Race to the Top competition.

From an institutional perspective, federal assertiveness as embodied in the NCLB and Race to the Top is a significant departure from a long-held tradition of federal permissiveness. The federal government has been mindful that states have constitutional authority over public education and that the American public adheres to the ethos of local control over public schools. The United States, in essence, maintains a decentralized education system. With the enactment of the NCLB, however, a more activist federal government seems to have emerged. To be sure, it is clearly not nationalization of education, since there is no national examination and states continue to design their own academic standards and decide how to intervene in persistently underperforming schools.[3] Even the current efforts toward Common Core and assessment standards rely on state voluntary participation. Nonetheless, the federal law requires all states to apply federal criteria in holding schools accountable. A central feature is the requirement that students in selected grade levels be tested annually in reading and mathematics and that the results be used as evidence to meet the academic proficiency targets as established by the adequate-yearly-progress (AYP) standards to avoid federally defined interventions. Similarly, the federal Race to the Top application requires states and districts to meet several policy assurances, such as the building of a longitudinal student performance–tracking system, to be eligible for the competition.

Three Phases of Educational Federalism

Table 8-1 proposes a conceptual framework that illuminates the key features in the evolving federal role in public education since the 1960s. It is important to underscore the "layering" effects of the federal role with the passage of time. Each wave of new federal activities did not replace entirely the preceding set of policy practices and governing arrangements. Instead, the new federal objectives and practices have tended to add to the existing policy system. In other words, the federal government continues to manage the policy system that has been in place for decades while also finding ways to resolve implementation and governance problems that arise from the new initiatives. The intergovernmental system, as a result, has become enormously complex. These policy realities—managing the existing system and creating new initiatives—define the governing challenges for each phase of education federalism. In setting a new vision in education policy, the federal government multiplies the governing and administrative arrangements not only in the short run but also for decades to come.

To understand the expanding federal role in public education since the 1960s, I propose three phases for analytical purposes (see table 8-1). Each of the phases signaled a major policy goal that reshaped and expanded the existing governing arrangements through new funding and administrative mechanisms. The first phase started with Lyndon Johnson's Great Society program and the passage of the first major federal comprehensive public education legislation, the Elementary and Secondary Education Act of 1965 that provided Title I funding to schools in low-income neighborhoods. I characterize this first phase as *categorical federalism* because of the federal government's extensive use of single-purpose, formula-based programs to support socially redistributive objectives, especially reversing poverty.

The second phase started with the passage of the No Child Left Behind Act of 2001, which marked the beginning of an assertive federal role in directing state and local practices to meet student performance standards. Unlike the first phase's focus on distributing resources to the targeted populations, the second phase

Table 8-1. *Changing Federal Role in Public Education*

Category	Categorical federalism (1960s–present)	Performance-based federalism (2001–present)	Innovative federalism (2009–present)
Federal objective	Redistributive	Redistributive Outcome-based accountability	Redistributive Outcome-based accountability Institutional innovation
Institutional boundary for service delivery	Confined within the public sector	Boundary opens to diverse service providers	Boundary opens to diverse service providers
Funding mechanism	Formula-based categorical (Title I, Integrated Disability Education and Awareness program)	Formula-based categorical (Title I, Integrated Disability Education and Awareness program)	Formula-based categorical Competitive grants (Race to the Top, Investment in Innovation)
Tension in intergovernmental process	Administrative compliance, for example, supplement not supplant	Local and state resistance to federal direction (for example, annual testing and adequate-yearly-progress evaluation) Local and state lawsuits filed for more federal funds Achievement gap for various subgroups Mixed support for diverse provider model and school choice	Local and state resistance to drastic restructuring Limited capacity to track student performance longitudinally Achievement gap for various subgroups Mixed support for diverse provider model and school choice
Actors who gain in decisionmaking power	Policy professionals at different levels	Diverse service providers	Governors, state chiefs, mayors, unions, networks

began to sharpen the federal focus on student performance as measured by annual yearly performance standards. Although they continue to exercise substantial authority over their academic proficiency standards and teacher certification, under No Child Left Behind states are required to meet federal expectations on annual testing and reporting on subgroup performance. I characterize this second phase as the emergence of *performance-based federalism.*

I label the third phase *innovative federalism,* characterized by the broadening of performance-based federalism with President Obama's launching of the Race to the Top initiative. This initiative started a new wave of competitive funding allocation in that eligibility was closely connected to state and local systemic reform efforts. These new federally directed reform standards were designed to reshape the institutional practices in delivering public education. This third phase is distinguished from the second by its focus on institutional innovation and competition as well as its strong push to restructure the persistently low-achieving schools. In the third phase, unlike the second, funding is no longer a matter of formula-based categorical allocation to support federal policy objectives. Instead, the Obama administration has promoted competitive grants at the state and local levels, such as Race to the Top and the Investment in Innovation grant program.

The Rise and Growth of Categorical Federalism

Historically, the U.S. federal government has taken a permissive role in education that is consistent with what the political scientist Morton Grodzins characterized as "layer cake" federalism.[4] Public education was primarily an obligation internal to the state. Federal involvement in education sharply increased during the Great Society era of the 1960s and the 1970s. Several events converged to shift the federal role from permissiveness to engagement. During the immediate post–World War II period, Congress enacted the G.I. Bill to enable veterans to receive a college education of their choice. The Cold War competition saw the passage of the National Defense Education Act in 1958 shortly after the Soviet Union's satellite, Sputnik, successfully orbited the earth. At the same time, the 1954 landmark Supreme Court ruling on *Brown* v. *Board of Education* and the congressional enactment of the 1964 Civil Rights Act sharpened federal attention to the needs of disadvantaged students. Consequently, the federal government adopted a major antipoverty education program in 1965: Title I of the 1965 Elementary and Secondary Education Act.

The passage of the education act and other federal grants-in-aid programs marked the creation of a complex intergovernmental policy system. To avoid centralization of administrative power at the national level, Congress increased its intergovernmental transfers to finance state and local activities. During the

Table 8-2. *Per Pupil Spending in Public Schools, by Source of Revenue,*
1962–2009
Constant 2011 dollars

Year	Per pupil expenditure	Percent increase over previous period	Source of revenue[a] Federal	State	Local
1961–62	3,139	...	4.3	38.7	56.9
1971–72	5,358	71.0	8.9	38.3	52.8
1981–82	6,391	19.3	7.4	47.6	45.0
1991–92	8,471	32.5	6.6	46.4	47.0
2001–02	10,973	29.5	7.9	49.2	42.9
2008–09	12,253	11.7	9.6	46.7	43.7

Source: U.S. Department of Education, National Center for Education Statistics, *Statistics of State School Systems, 1961–62* (1964); *Revenues and Expenditures for Public Elementary and Secondary Education, School Year 1971–72* (1974); *Revenues and Expenditures for Public Elementary and Secondary Education, School Year 1981–82* (1984); *Common Core of Data, National Public Education Financial Survey 1991–92* (1994); *National Public Education Financial Survey 2001–02* (2004); *National Public Education Financial Survey 2008–09* (2011).

a. Percent of total.

presidency of Lyndon B. Johnson, the number of categorical (or single-purpose) programs, including Title I, grew from 160 to 380. By the end of the Jimmy Carter administration in 1980, there were approximately 500 federally funded categorical programs. Particularly important was the redistributive focus of many of the programs that were designed to promote racial desegregation, protect the educational rights of the learning disabled, assist English-language learners, and provide supplemental resources to children from at-risk backgrounds. Despite several revisions and extension of the Elementary and Secondary Education Act, its Title I continues to adhere to its original intent "to provide financial assistance . . . to local educational agencies serving areas with concentrations of children from low-income families to expand and improve their educational programs . . . which contribute particularly to meeting the special-educational needs of educationally deprived children."[5]

Federal engagement in redistributive policy is reflected in its spending priorities. As suggested in table 8-2, federal contributions accounted for 9.6 percent of the total revenues for public elementary and secondary education during 2008–09, a noticeable increase from 4.3 percent in 1961–62, when the federal role was clearly more limited. The enactment in the 1960s of the Elementary and Secondary Education Act as well as other Great Society programs contributed to a significant growth in federal funding for schools. From 1962 to 1972, per pupil spending jumped 71 percent in real-dollar terms, and the federal contribution climbed to almost 9 percent. Beginning in the 1980s, state education revenue has, on average, exceeded the local contribution, while per pupil spending between 1962 and 2009 rose from $3,139 to $12,253 in real-dollar terms. During the first two years of the Obama administration, stimulus funds further increased federal spending on public education.

More important, growth in federal aid continues to be associated with the policy focus on disadvantaged populations. As suggested in table 8-3, federal aid to programs for special-needs students showed persistent growth overall in real-dollar terms. Between 1996 and 2005, these programs amounted to more than 60 percent of total federal spending in elementary and secondary schools. The Title I program for the education of the disadvantaged increased from $8.9 billion to $14.6 billion in 2005 constant dollars. Federal aid in special education more than doubled, the school lunch program increased its funding from $9.8 billion to $12.2 billion, and Head Start jumped by 50 percent in real-dollar terms during this period. This trend of growing federal involvement in programs for the disadvantaged continues in the Obama administration. Congress appropriated $98.2 billion dollars to support education in the American Recovery and Reinvestment Act in 2009. The act provided additional funds to several major categorical programs for a two-year period, including $10 billion for Title I, $12.2 billion for the Integrated Disability Education and Awareness program, $650 million for technology, and $100 million in impact aid construction grants.

Redistributive federal grants, such as Title I, have taken on several institutional characteristics. First, under the grants-in-aid arrangement, the federal government provides the funds and sets the programmatic direction, but the delivery of services is up to state and local agencies.[6] Second, categorical grants focus on well-defined eligible students, and only they receive the services. Third, federal funds are meant to supplement, not supplant, state and local spending.[7] Federal guidelines on nonsupplanting and maintenance of fiscal efforts ensure that federal resources are not diverted away from the eligible beneficiaries. Fourth, federal intergovernmental transfers have become a key revenue source to support the administrative capacity of state education agencies. In providing matching funds and enacting their own redistributive initiatives, state agencies further complicate the intergovernmental categorical system by creating underfunded programs and unfunded mandates.[8] Fifth, the regulatory "stick" has gained acceptance at the state and local level along with the funding "carrot." Because categorical grants are widely distributed through formulas to schools and districts across many congressional districts, bipartisan political support remains strong for these programs.

As public schools showed mixed performance, policymakers became increasingly concerned about the effectiveness of federal grants. During the first term of the Ronald Reagan administration, the publication of the federal report *A Nation at Risk* expressed a clear need to raise student performance in an increasingly

Table 8-3. *Federal Expenditures on Special-Needs Programs as Share of Elementary and Secondary Education Expenditures, 1996–2005*
Millions of 2005 dollars

	1996	1997	1998	1999	2000	2001	2002	2003	2004	2005
Federal spending for elementary and secondary education										
Total	43,818.4	43,171.5	44,914.5	46,818.0	49,685.8	53,842.0	57,270.0	62,914.4	64,775.9	67,959.2
Percent change over previous period	. . .	−1.5	4.0	4.2	6.1	8.4	6.4	9.9	3.0	4.9
Special-needs programs										
Education for the disadvantaged	8,853.9	8,763.1	9,367.0	7,839.4	9,673.1	9,541.2	10,039.3	11,944.1	12,909.3	14,638.2
Special education	4,010.8	4,022.2	4,383.4	5,209.7	5,612.9	6,416.0	7,599.3	9,012.1	10,079.7	10,226.5
Head Start	4,443.7	4,843.6	5,208.9	5,460.4	5,973.6	6,841.0	7,096.6	7,076.2	7,003.9	6,843.2
Child nutrition programs	9,802.3	10,099.6	10,262.1	10,407.3	10,835.6	10,528.0	11,131.7	11,493.3	11,586.1	12,163.9
Bilingual education	229.7	220.6	247.9	634.9	563.0	494.4	n.a.	n.a.	n.a.	n.a.
Native American education	96.3	68.1	63.1	76.0	74.1	93.2	112.8	123.1	118.3	129.9
Subtotal	27,436.7	28,017.2	29,532.4	29,627.7	32,732.3	33,913.8	35,979.7	39,648.8	41,697.3	44,001.7
Percent change over previous period	. . .	2.1	5.4	0.3	10.5	3.6	6.1	10.2	5.2	5.5
As percent of federal spending	62.6	64.9	65.8	62.7	65.9	63.1	62.8	63.0	64.4	64.8

Source: U.S. Department of Education, National Center for Education Statistics, *Digest of Education Statistics, 2005*, table 358 (2006) (www.nces.ed.gov); *Digest of Education Statistics, 2004*, table 366 (2005) (www.nces.ed.gov).

global marketplace. The passage of the Improving America's Schools Act in 1994, during the Bill Clinton administration, signaled the beginning of federal efforts to improve program coordination and to allow for public school choice and competition. Among the most important features in the act was a provision that encouraged state and local education agencies to coordinate resources in schools with a high percentage of children who fell below the poverty line. This Title I schoolwide reform was designed to phase out local practices that isolated low-income students from their peers in order to comply with the federal auditing requirement on the "supplement not supplant" guideline. Furthermore, the Improving America's Schools Act enabled public school competition with the allocation of federal charter school start-up planning grants.

The Improving America's Schools Act also aimed at monitoring Title I schools that persistently failed to meet state proficiency standards. However, the legislation did not specify the consequences when Title I schools repeatedly fell short of the federal expectations. It required states to adopt standards aligned with state assessments but allowed states full autonomy to make instructional, governance, and fiscal policy decisions to support their academic performance standards. The political reality was that holding schools and districts accountable to high-stakes mandates was not feasible under the act. There was little enforcement of its provisions, even when Title I schools performed poorly, and few states made substantial progress in meeting its requirements. The limited federal involvement occurred within a broader institutional context in which efforts to improve low performance were seen more as a program priority than an agency-wide mission. The program-oriented mentality was further reinforced by the categorical funding stream and program eligibility that perpetuated an administrative silo culture.

In short, categorical federalism focused primarily on the level of resources, regulatory safeguards, and other inputs to meet the learning challenges of special-needs students. In providing supplemental funding to state and local government, the federal government did not press for accountability in student achievement. However, with the No Child Left Behind Act of 2001, the federal government aimed at combining an input-based framework with outcome-based accountability. In this regard, the NCLB constitutes the next phase in our intergovernmental education system.

The Challenge of Performance-Based Federalism

The passage of the 2001 No Child Left Behind Act marks the beginning of a serious effort toward performance-based federalism. To some analysts, the NCLB so changed the terms of federal-state relations as to signal a regime change. In his historical review of the federal role, Patrick McGuinn sees the NCLB as a transformative moment in that well-entrenched political interests began to depart from their traditional policy positions.[9] Conservatives were ready to set aside their long-standing belief in local control and to endorse a visibly stronger federal presence in education. Liberals moved to support a fairly comprehensive set of accountability measures, including annual testing of students in core subject areas and consequences for poor performance. The de-alignment of traditional political relationships, as enactment of the NCLB might be characterized, embodies a fundamentally different set of ideas, interests, and institutions. Federal direction on student achievement now applies to all students, schools, and districts, regardless of whether they receive federal Title I funds. The federal government has placed education performance at the center stage of the nation's policy agenda.

With the NCLB, the federal government holds states, districts, and schools accountable for a comprehensive set of standards, including annual academic progress, teacher quality, and achievement gaps. To determine whether a school meets adequate yearly progress requirements as mandated in the NCLB, student achievement is disaggregated by grade and by subject area for each school. All students in grades three through eight and one additional grade in high school are tested annually in mathematics, reading and English language arts, and science. The school-level report includes the percentage of students proficient in each of the core content areas, student participation in testing, attendance rates, graduation rates, and dropout rates. Equally important, depending on their socioeconomic characteristics, schools are required to report the academic proficiency of students in the following subgroups: economically disadvantaged students, students from major racial and ethnic groups, students with disabilities, and students with limited English proficiency. In this regard, the NCLB has made the achievement gap within a school more transparent for accountability purposes.

The emergence of performance-based federal policy has created tension in the intergovernmental policy system. As Paul Manna puts it, there is a significant gap between the theory of accountability based on the federal intent and the practice of accountability at the state and local levels.[10] The federal government has relied primarily on state and local capacity to implement the policy. Manna argues that "borrowing strength" from state governments can facilitate federal capacity in the education policy arena, where the social license is historically weak.[11] At the same time, tensions arise when many state and local systems have limited capacity in analyzing large-scale data on student performance on an ongoing basis, in providing alternative instructional services in failing schools, and in making achievement and other schooling information more transparent to parents in a timely manner. These new expectations are largely incongruent with the existing categorical practices, which focus primarily on regulatory compliance.

Implementation of the NCLB illustrates several governing challenges.[12] First, federalism is not designed to support accountability uniformly across states. According to a fifty-state report card on the first anniversary of the NCLB legislation, only five states received federal approval on their accountability plan.[13] Furthermore, only half of the states were prepared to monitor performance of various subgroups and to undertake corrective actions in failing schools. More than 80 percent of the states were not ready to meet the federal expectation on placing highly qualified teachers in the classroom. Not until four years after implementation of the NCLB were all the states' accountability plans approved by the federal government. More recently, in a 2011 study conducted by the Center for American Progress, state commissioners pointed out that strong accountability and innovative practices are the exception and not the routine in state education agencies.[14]

In response to the NCLB, states were ready to exert their power to define the pace of meeting AYP requirements. States' accountability plans suggested three broad patterns to ensure that students reach proficiency: equal yearly goals, the steady stair-step, and the accelerating curve.[15] For example, Arizona, Arkansas, Hawaii, and South Carolina, among others, settled with relatively low starting points compared with Colorado, Georgia, and Tennessee. The former would have to make much greater progress on their standards to meet the 100 percent proficiency target by 2014. The steep climb in meeting the rising proficiency bar is indicated by the growing number of schools that did not reach the AYP goals. According to a six-year-trend study conducted by the Center for Education Policy, the number of schools that failed their state-specified AYP standards jumped from 29 to 48 percent of all the schools in the nation between 2006 and 2011.[16]

The extent to which a district or a school meets AYP requirements is affected by the number and size of the subgroups. In their analysis of this issue in California, James Kim and Gail Sunderman find that the percentage of schools meeting AYP performance levels declined as the number of subgroups in these schools rose.[17] Whereas 78 percent of the schools with only one subgroup met the reading AYP standard in 2003, only 25 percent of the schools with six subgroups were able to do so. Moreover, they find that in Virginia 85 percent of the schools that met both the state and federal proficiency standards had two or fewer subgroups. Only 15 percent of the proficiency schools had three or more subgroups.

Faced with state power and differences in the socioeconomic characteristics of student enrollment across states, the federal government loosened the standards for adequate yearly progress by allowing a "safe harbor" provision. Under this guideline, a subgroup is deemed to have achieved AYP if the percentage of students performing below basic proficiency is reduced by 10 percent from the previous year. In Philadelphia, a large urban school district with 266 schools, for example, 37 percent of the 158 schools that met AYP proficiency standards in 2010 did so by achieving the safe harbor target.

Second, during this phase of performance-based federalism, the federal government continued to rely on formula-based categorical funding allocation to support its new policy objectives. The federal government clearly faced the challenge of aligning its limited resources with its ambitious goal of intervening in persistently low-achieving schools. A key federal strategy was to reallocate existing Title I funds roughly proportional to the problems of student achievement. More specifically, the NCLB calls for a set of progressively intensive "corrective actions" when districts and schools fail to make adequate yearly progress for consecutive years. These sanctions require low-performing districts and schools to use their Title I funds differently. The sanctions begin with the relatively modest requirement for a school improvement plan, transfer options for families in schools that have not made adequate yearly progress, and the implementation of Title I–funded supplemental educational or tutorial services after school. In other words, sanctions in the first years of academic failure are not designed to change the structure or governance of the low-performing school. Following four consecutive years of failure, the NCLB requires the more intensive sanctions. These include state-driven interventions that alter school governance and hiring decisions, such as school or district takeovers and replacement of personnel in poorly performing schools. Only in the most drastic restructuring are federal resources integrated with local and state funding to support the federal objectives.

Third, the new performance-based accountability system places tremendous pressure on state and local capacity in gathering, analyzing, and reporting student achievement on an annual basis. The annual testing requirement, a core concept in the new accountability system, faced major resistance during the initial years of the NCLB.[18] Several states registered their opposition with legislative actions. In 2004 the Virginia House passed a resolution calling on Congress to exempt states such as Virginia, which had a well-developed accountability plan in place, from the NCLB requirements. The resolution called the NCLB "the most sweeping federal intrusion into state and local control of education in the history of the United States, which egregiously violates the time-honored American principles of balanced federalism and respect for state and local prerogatives."[19] The resolution passed ninety-eight to one, the lone dissenter being a Democrat. Furthermore, after extensive lobbying by the Bush administration, the Republican-controlled Utah House modified a law that would have prohibited the state from participating in the NCLB. The law was amended to prohibit the state and local districts from implementing the NCLB in the absence of adequate federal funding.[20] Other states, including Connecticut, Hawaii, New Hampshire, North Dakota, Oklahoma, and Vermont, passed similar resolutions. In March 2004 the chief state school officers from fifteen states sent Secretary of Education Rod Paige a letter asking for more flexibility in determining which schools were making adequate yearly progress.

State and local opposition also took legal action against the federal government. The first legal challenge came from a coalition of districts in Michigan, Texas, and Vermont and the National Education Association, the nation's largest teachers union. The plaintiffs argued that the NCLB imposed federal mandates without adequate financial support. In November 2004 a federal judge in the U.S. District Court for the Eastern District of Michigan rejected the challenge, ruling that Congress had the authority to specify policy conditions on states.[21] Subsequent rounds of appellate court decisions led to the U.S. Supreme Court, which decided in 2010 not to interfere with the earlier district court decision.

Another suit was filed by Connecticut against the U.S. Department of Education. The state sought full financial reimbursement from the federal government for the $41 million state funds it spent to implement the NCLB between 2002 and 2008.[22] The state also claimed that the federal agency had acted in an "arbitrary and capricious manner" in deciding on state requests for waivers and exemption.[23] Connecticut cited, as one example, the Department of Education's rejection of the state's request that students be tested every other year instead of annually. The U.S. Court of Appeals dismissed the suit in July 2010 because the federal government had not taken any action against Connecticut on NCLB implementation. The three-judge panel, however, stipulated that Connecticut could take administrative action against the federal government.

Finally, performance-based federalism opened up the delivery of educational services to a broader set of providers, including for-profit organizations. Local districts were generally protective of their control over supplemental education services and were slow to support parents who wished to transfer their children from low-performing schools. For example, in his study of California, Julian Betts observes that school choice, as stipulated by the NCLB, was largely underused throughout the state.[24] Reasons for limited local implementation included the delay in making data available to parents, failure of districts to clearly communicate the choice program to parents, an inadequate number of seats in better-performing schools, and lack of parental interest in moving children to schools outside their neighborhood.

The California case also shows that participation rates in supplemental education services were low, though not nearly as low as for the transfer option. Barriers cited by state personnel to implementing these services included a general lack of information from the state about state-approved providers, tardiness of districts in providing parents with information about supplemental education services, and the refusal by some districts to allow nondistrict providers to work on district property. Districts also had a considerable number of complaints about service providers. Finally, like school choice, one of the greatest impediments to participation in supplemental education services was the substance and form of communications sent by districts to parents.

The extent to which local political power has reshaped the federal effort to redraw the boundary in service delivery is seen in large urban districts. An example is Chicago's success in gaining federal approval to continue to provide supplemental services to students in schools that failed to make adequate progress. Under the NCLB, districts that did not meet the AYP criteria, including most large urban districts, were prohibited from providing after-school supplemental instructional services to their students. The U.S. Department of Education required that Chicago replace its own services with outside vendors in January 2005. Mayor Daley stepped in and put his political capital behind the district chief executive officer's decision to continue the district services. In a series of private meetings between the mayor and Margaret Spellings, the U.S. secretary of education, compromise was reached. In return for the district's continuation of its supplemental services, the city agreed to reduce barriers for private vendors' provision of tutorial services. When the compromise was formally announced by Secretary Spellings in early September in Chicago, Mayor Daley hailed the efforts as the "beginning of a new era of cooperation" across levels of government in education.[25] Similar waivers were subsequently granted in such cities as New York and Boston. Clearly, intergovernmental politics is far from absent from performance-based federalism.

In short, performance-based federalism shifts the policy focus from inputs to outcomes, opens service delivery to diverse providers, and requires local and state agencies to publicly report on student performance. This phase of federalism has created new governing tensions. There are, to be sure, pronounced examples of intergovernmental conflict, including local constitutional challenges on annual testing and state and local charges of unfunded federal mandates. Notwithstanding governmental conflicts, performance-based federalism has created the supportive conditions for greater visibility on key challenges such as achievement gaps, for greater transparency on school performance data, and for broader involvement among stakeholders and service providers to find ways to improve teaching and learning. Clearly, the compliance-driven paradigm of categorical federalism has been modified as a result of performance-based federalism.

Innovative Federalism in the Obama Era

Performance-based federalism turned into innovative federalism during the Obama presidency. The Obama administration extended NCLB accountability by creating new competitive funding streams to promote institutional innovation at state and local levels. Under federal direction, states and districts competed in Race to the Top, Investment in Innovation grants, and other federal funding sources to transform their current policy and practices in educator accountability, charter schools, and the treatment of low-performing schools. These innovative initiatives sought support from key state and local actors—including governors, state commissioners, mayors, unions, and networks of diverse providers, among others.

Building on the NCLB framework of corrective actions, the Obama administration has continued the push for more direct district intervention in persistently low performing schools. In his proposal to reauthorize the federal law in elementary and secondary education, Secretary Arne Duncan argued for four strategies to "turn around" the nation's lowest-performing 5 percent of the schools (approximately 5,000 schools). The federal government committed $5 billion during 2010–12 to support these efforts. The four strategies tightened the approaches that were established under the NCLB, allowing for fewer district options. Duncan's strategies are as follows:

—Turn around the school under a new principal who can recruit at least half of the teachers from the outside.

—Transform the school by strengthening professional support, teacher evaluation, and capacity building.

—Restart the school, reopening it either as a charter school or under management by organizations outside of the district.

—Close the school, moving all the students to other, higher-performing schools.

In making its first school improvement grants to support school turnarounds, the Obama administration allocated a $3 billion federal fund to more than 730 schools in forty-four states in December 2010. Of these schools, an overwhelming number (71 percent) had chosen the transformation option, whereas very few decided to use either restart (5 percent) or school closure (3 percent). The remaining 21 percent opted for the turnaround option, whereby the principal and a majority of the teaching staff were replaced.[26] Equally important, only 17 percent of the students in all the schools receiving school improvement grants were white, as compared with 44 percent African American and 34 percent Hispanic. The choices made by the grant recipients seem to suggest a leaning toward a more incremental approach to school improvement. This tension between the federal push for innovation and local realities is likely to persist. In anticipation of local inertia and the preference for incremental organizational changes, the Obama administration created the Office of School Turnaround in late 2011 to monitor and support local efforts to bring about measurable school improvement.

Innovative federalism provides stronger guidance and expectations on local and state institutional reform. The Obama administration has strengthened the NCLB-like accountability system by making new federal investment in public education. In return, the federal government requires state and local government to meet a set of new expectations on reforming public education. The American Recovery and Reinvestment Act of 2009 and Race to the Top provide examples.

The American Recovery and Reinvestment Act of 2009, for a targeted period of time, substantially expanded federal funding in several categorical program areas, including education for disadvantaged children (the Title I program), the Integrated Disability Education and Awareness program for special-education students, and financial assistance for eligible college students. Moreover, in return for federal stabilization support to prevent teacher layoffs, states were expected to meet several reform conditions: more equitable distribution of well-trained, well-qualified teachers to address students with greater needs; ongoing monitoring of student progress with a data system that links prekindergarten to college and career development; development and implementation of college- and career-ready standards; and effective actions to turn around the persistently lowest performing schools.

More important, the Obama administration invited states to submit their best ideas on system transformation and school innovation for the national competition for the Race to the Top program. Delaware and Tennessee were selected as winners of the first round of the competition in April 2010. The second round of competition resulted in awards to ten states and the District of Columbia.

The winning applications submitted by Delaware and Tennessee shared several features in their approach to transforming public education. First, teacher accountability was prominent. Student achievement would become a cornerstone of a new teacher-assessment system, according to the Tennessee education commissioner. Delaware proposed to use the annual evaluation results to remove teachers who were rated as ineffective for some number of consecutive years. Second, a system of support was proposed to enhance professional capacity. Delaware planned to hire thirty-five data coaches to train teachers in the use of data for instructional improvement. The state also planned to hire fifteen development coaches to support principals and teachers in schools with the highest need. Third, external partners, such as the Mass Insight Education and Research Institute, were brought in. Fourth, the two states were successful in gaining approval from key stakeholders on the reform agenda in the long term.

Phil Bredesen, Tennessee's sitting governor at the time, was able to gain the endorsement on the application from all Tennessee's gubernatorial candidates. To ensure institutional commitment, the two states set up administrative offices to oversee program implementation. Tennessee opened an achievement school district office, and Delaware set up a project-management division to monitor fulfillment of the reform initiatives. Finally, the two states showed their support for expanding innovation. Tennessee recently passed legislation that increased the number of charter schools and broadened student eligibility in school choice.

The Race to the Top competition seemed to have leveraged significant efforts to redesign the state policy system.

Innovative federalism facilitates a climate of systemic reform that tends to reshape the institutional boundaries between the public and nonpublic sectors. A prime example is the involvement of charter management organizations and other networks of diverse service providers to improve school performance. The federal government has continued to increase its funding support for development of networks of charter schools. During 2009–10, about 1.67 million students were enrolled in 4,903 charter schools. About a third of the charter enrollment was black, and almost a quarter Hispanic. Of these schools, 492 were managed by education management organizations (both for-profit and nonprofit organizations), and 573 were managed by charter management organizations.[27] The diverse-provider approach was further enhanced by urban governance, especially in those districts that were under the control of the mayor or the governor (or both). Chicago, New York, and Philadelphia provide prominent examples of portfolio management or diverse service-provider models.[28]

With the widening use of corrective actions under the NCLB, the issue of holding schools and teachers accountable has gained public support. In several states, governors and state legislatures are beginning to experiment with differential compensation for educators. Florida and Texas, for example, provide individual cash bonuses to teachers whose students show improved results on standardized tests. Arizona, Minnesota, and North Carolina connect part of teacher salaries to student achievement. In Minneapolis and Denver, union leadership actively participated in negotiating with management to redesign the teacher compensation package. Denver's ProComp Agreement did not eliminate collective bargaining. Instead, it gained voters' approval for new taxes to pay for the expanded salary schedule that takes into account knowledge and skills, professional evaluation, market incentives, and student growth. In response to state and local interest in compensation reform, the federal government has expanded its investment in support of alternative compensation initiatives. Consequently, the federal Teacher Incentive Fund has grown from $99 million to $443 million between FY2006 and FY2010.[29] The policy conditions created by the new federal initiatives have aimed to align with state and local innovation.

Consistent with the expectations of innovative federalism, the Obama administration invites state applications for waivers in meeting the NCLB goals. In the first cycle of application in November 2011, eleven states formally sought alternative ways to implement their accountability system in exchange for fulfilling a new set of federal assurances. By August 2012 thirty-two states and the District of Columbia were granted waivers by the U.S. Department of Education. Among the new federal expectations are the establishment of high-quality content standards that support career- and college-ready expectations; differentiated accountability for low-performing schools; adoption of student academic growth and other measures to hold educators accountable; and elimination of duplicative administrative rules. An analysis of the first group of applications suggests that these states tend to adopt Common Core standards, use multiple indicators to measure annual student progress, use differentiated actions to intervene in low-performing schools, and avoid using school choice or supplemental education service as a key strategy to raise student performance.[30]

As innovative federalism allows for variation in states' strategic approaches, including their departure from the NCLB accountability system, there is an urgent need to build a reliable data-tracking system. Innovative federalism signals a strong push for longitudinal, reliable data on student achievement. State and local agencies face a capacity gap in systems to manage and track data. Meeting this federal expectation will require a major shift in governance and management of state and local systems. With a more comprehensive, longitudinal data system in place, states and local districts can move toward a decisionmaking process that is grounded in reliable data.

To be sure, the data capacity in our federalism is uneven. State and local agencies continue to be governed by a silo-oriented culture.[31] The Data Quality Campaign, a nongovernmental organization, focuses on the necessary elements in creating a "robust longitudinal data system" in which each state would gather data on a student while that student is in school. The student data are matched with other data files, such as teacher records and instructional support programs. A robust statewide data system, according to the Data Quality Campaign, features ten elements.[32] These include a unique statewide student identifier that matches individual student achievement with other information, a unique teacher identifier that links teachers to their students, and individual student data that are collected from public school through college.

Based on a 2009 survey on the adoption of these ten key elements on individual student performance, the Data Quality Campaign finds that twelve states have instituted all ten elements, and another thirty-four states have eight or more.[33] Although all fifty states reported that their data systems have statewide student identifiers for tracking academic performance (including graduation and dropout), only twenty-four states have adopted a statewide teacher identifier that matches students to teachers. In these states with more robust systems, the governor's office has played a critical role. In Delaware, two-term Democratic governor Thomas Carper successfully pushed through a comprehensive education accountability plan between 1993 and 2000. A key feature of Governor Carper's reform was to link individual students' test scores to their teachers. The 2000 reform plan enabled a professional standards board to use students' test achievement as the basis for "at least 20 percent of the performance reviews given to teachers, administrators, and other instructional staff members."[34] Governor Carper's successor, Ruth Ann Minner, continued to advocate for using student achievement to hold teachers accountable.[35]

Seeing the need to implement the data system, the Data Quality Campaign started surveying the states on their policies and practices on using data to improve student achievement in 2009. The first survey, published in January 2010, focuses on ten actions that link statewide data across all grades, prekindergarten through college as well as the workforce, expanded data access to key stakeholders, and ensured professional capacity to use data for instructional practices.[36] The survey finds that only eight states were tracking individual students from prekindergarten through college and across workforce sectors, an assurance required for second-phase state fiscal-stabilization funds. Although ten states reported strategies in sharing individual student-progress data with educators, fewer than half of the states provided aggregated data reports to key stakeholders. Clearly, state leadership is much needed to meet the data challenges in performance-based, innovative federalism.

Future Prospects for Innovative Federalism

Federal assertiveness on education accountability is now at a crossroads as President Obama broadens his own education agenda. On one hand, the Obama administration has shown its strong support for performance-based accountability. Both the president and his secretary of education, for example, take the position that student performance matters in educator employment and compensation. Recent public opinion polls indicate a clear majority supportive of teacher accountability. On the other hand, the sustainability of the new performance-based policy paradigm meets governing challenges and managing uncertainties in the decentralized system; and there have been legal challenges to the annual testing requirements and other federal provisions. In Congress, federal education reform has shown partisan polarization. The recovery stimulus package, which included almost $100 billion In federal dollars in school aid, won congressional passage without a single Republican vote in the House and only three Republican votes in the Senate. There remains political concern about federal infringement on state and local control in education.

Clearly, the 2012 election will shape the overall governing conditions under which performance-based federalism operates. Drawing on the findings of this chapter, several scenarios in governing public education in our federalism can be expected. First, partisanship may not have a substantial effect on the redistributive focus of the federal intergovernmental grants system. Over the years, the federal redistributive aid system faced and survived significant challenges, notably during the first years of the Reagan administration and the start of the

Table 8-4. *The Future of the Federal Role in Governing Public Education: Implications of the November 2012 Election*

	Presidency	
Control over Congress	Obama's second term	Romney's first term
Democratic	Federally driven institutional innovation	State-driven innovation and accountability
Republican	Institutional innovation under fiscal constraints	Parental choice and federal deregulation

Newt Gingrich's term as House Speaker. Despite the growing Tea Party influence within the Republican Party, a clear majority in Congress realizes the electoral importance of having federal categorical funding that is widely distributed to virtually every congressional district. My analysis on federal spending, as indicated in this chapter, suggests that Republican presidents did not slow down federal support for redistributive programs. The federal government has consistently allocated about 60 percent of its K–12 funding for socially redistributive programs. The redistributive focus of federal programs may not be altered substantially following the 2012 election.

Institutional innovation has been a key focus of the Obama administration. As suggested in table 8-4, federally driven systemic innovation is likely to be intensified with President Obama's reelection in November 2012. Even though the Republican Party maintained its majority in the House, Obama's second term will see a greater effort toward state and local implementation of the policy assurances as defined in the Race to the Top competition as well as other reform initiatives—educator accountability, college-readiness support systems, and longitudinal tracking of individual student achievement, among others. The Obama administration will sharpen its focus on turning around the lowest-performing schools by leveraging systemic reform initiatives in the proper governing context, such as mayoral control in urban districts, Promise Neighborhoods that integrate various service sectors, and portfolio management systems with diverse providers.[37] In this regard, mayors, unions, state commissioners, governors, networks of diverse providers, and community organizations will continue to gain power in education policymaking.

The pace and scope of the Obama administration's effort to carry out institutional innovation will be shaped by the balance of power in Congress. Divided governance, with Republican control over Congress, is likely to constrain federal direction on accountability and limit spending to protect teachers' jobs and to support school construction. An example of the Republican policy preference was indicated by an amendment to a bipartisan senate bill on the reauthorization of the Elementary and Secondary Education Act in the Senate Health, Education, Labor, and Pensions Committee during October 2011. Republican senator Lamar Alexander of Tennessee succeeded in gaining the senate committee's vote to allow state flexibility in determining how to intervene in low-performing schools.[38] Republican senator Rand Paul of Kentucky went one step further to register his opposition to the federal requirement on annual testing.[39] At the same time, given the House Republicans' strong opposition to the education stimulus package, new federal initiatives on institutional innovation during a second Obama term are likely to be subject to fiscal discipline and congressional efforts to reduce federal regulations in divided governance. In contrast, if Congress turns over to Democratic control after the 2012 election, there is likely to be an expansion of several of the competitive grants to turn around low-performing schools and districts as well as to build the capacity of the state systems.

Because of a full agenda in pushing for institutional reform, Obama's second term is less likely to devote much attention to the governing challenges of the layering of federal regulations and policy directions. Each administration inherits the policy decisions, regulations, and rules of its predecessors without much opportunity to revisit or reprioritize them. Nonetheless, Republican Mitt Romney, as the new president, would be likely to garner the political support to change the priorities of the many existing regulatory layers. Again, the pace and scope of this effort will be shaped by the power distribution of the new Congress. The reprioritizing effort will be constrained by a Democratic Congress. Under this divided governance, the federal government may rely more on the states to direct institutional innovation. State-led systems of performance-based accountability will most likely emerge. In contrast, if Romney gains unified governance after the 2012 election, there will be a strong tendency to shift the power of decisionmaking in education to consumers. Parental choice will be prominently promoted, and federal dollars will be used to encourage parental demands for schooling opportunities, thereby substantially reducing federal regulations.

From an institutional perspective, it remains to be seen how the performance-based framework will be fully functional in our intergovernmental policy system. After all, categorical management remains the standard in the way government operates at all three levels. The culture of regulatory compliance is not likely to be entirely replaced by performance-based accountability in the immediate future. Nonetheless, the federal government is now well positioned to push for institutional changes in two areas. First, data transparency on student performance will inform the debate on the future of governance in public education at all levels of the federal system. Second, a culture of innovation will foster a broader range of strategies to turn around low-performing schools and districts. Given public concerns on school performance and the proliferation of innovative practices across a growing number of states and districts, there is likely to be growing public support for federal leadership in leveraging systemic reform.

Notes

1. Quoted in Dan Eggen and Maria Glod, "President Praises Results of 'No Child' Law," *Washington Post*, January 9, 2009.

2. Ibid.

3. Governance arrangements in England, New Zealand, and several other countries are examined in chapters 10 and 12 in this volume.

4. Morton Grodzins, *The American System*, edited by Daniel Elazar (Chicago: Rand McNally, 1966).

5. Elementary and Secondary Education Act of 1965, Pub. L. 89-10, 20 U.S.C. 70 (1965).

6. Paul E. Peterson, Barry G. Rabe, and Kenneth K. Wong, *When Federalism Works* (Brookings Press, 1986).

7. Ibid.

8. Bryan Shelly, *Money, Mandates, and Local Control in American Public Education* (University of Michigan Press, 2011).

9. Patrick J. McGuinn, *No Child Left Behind and the Transformation of Federal Education Policy, 1965–2005* (University Press of Kansas, 2006).

10. Paul Manna, *Collision Course: Federal Education Policy Meets State and Local Realities* (Washington: CQ Press, 2011).

11. Paul Manna, *School's In: Federalism and the National Education Agenda* (Georgetown University Press, 2006), p. 33.

12. On the implementation and design of the NCLB, see Frederick M. Hess and Michael J. Petrilli, *No Child Left Behind: A Primer* (New York: Peter Lang, 2006); Gail Sunderman, James Kim, and Gary Orfield, *NCLB Meets School Realities* (Thousand Oaks, Calif.: Corwin Press, 2005); Frederick M. Hess and Chester E. Finn Jr., eds., *No Remedy Left Behind: Lessons from a Half-Decade of NCLB* (Washington: AEI Press, 2007); and David K. Cohen and Susan L. Moffitt, *The Ordeal of Equality: Did Federal Regulation Fix the Schools?* (Harvard University Press, 2009).

13. Kenneth Wong and Anna Nicotera, *Successful Schools and Educational Accountability* (Boston: Pearson Education, 2007).

14. Cynthia Brown and others, *State Education Agencies as Agents of Change* (Washington: Center for American Progress, 2011).

15. Wong and Nicotera, *Successful Schools and Educational Accountability*.

16. Alexandra Usher, *AYP Results for 2010–11* (Washington: Center on Education Policy, 2011).

17. James S. Kim and Gail L. Sunderman, "Measuring Academic Proficiency under the No Child Left Behind Act: Implications for Educational Equity," *Educational Researcher* 34 (November 2005): 3–13.

18. Kenneth Wong and Gail Sunderman, "Education Accountability as a Presidential Priority: No Child Left Behind and the Bush Presidency," *Publius: The Journal of Federalism* 37 (Summer 2007): 333–50.

19. Virginia House of Delegates, House Joint Resolution 192, passed January 23, 2004.

20. Utah House of Representatives, House Bill 43 1st Sub., passed February 10, 2004.

21. Michael Janofsky, "Judge Rejects Challenge to Bush Education Law," *New York Times,* November 24, 2005.

22. Mark Walsh, "Court Upholds Dismissal of Conn.'s NCLB Suit," *Education Week, School Law Blog,* July 14, 2010 (http://blogs.edweek.org/edweek/school_law/2010/07/ a_federal_appeals_court_has_4.html).

23. Janofsky, "Judge Rejects Challenge."

24. Julian Betts, "California: Does the Golden State Deserve a Gold Star?" in *No Remedy Left Behind,* edited by Hess and Finn, pp. 121–52.

25. Sam Dillion, "Education Law is Loosened for Failing Chicago Schools," *New York Times,* September 2, 2005, A11.

26. Alyson Klein, "Turnaround-Program Data Seen as Promising though Preliminary," *Education Week,* January 11, 2011.

27. National Alliance for Public Charter Schools, various reports, especially *CMO and EMO Public Charter Schools: A Growing Phenomenon in the Charter School Sector; Public Charter Schools Dashboard Data from 2007–08, 2008–09, and 2009–10 (2011).*

28. Kenneth Wong, "Redesigning Urban Districts in the USA: Mayoral Accountability and the Diverse Provider Model," *Education Management, Administration, and Leadership* 39 (July 2011): 486–500.

29. U.S. Department of Education, "Teacher Incentive Fund," n.d. (www2.ed.gov/ programs/teacherincentive/awards.html).

30. Wayne Riddle, *Major Accountability Themes of Initial State Applications for NCLB Waivers* (Washington: Center on Education Policy, 2011).

31. Brown and others, *State Education Agencies as Agents of Change.*

32. See Data Quality Campaign, n.d. (www.dataqualitycampaign.org).

33. Data Quality Campaign, *DQC 2009–10 Survey Results Compendium: 10 Elements* (Washington, 2010).

34. Joetta Sack, "Del. Ties School Job Reviews to Student Tests," *Education Week,* May 3, 2000.

35. Robert Johnston, "Math Specialists Sought for Del. Middle Schools," *Education Week,* February 2, 2005.

36. Data Quality Campaign, *Inaugural Overview of States' Actions to Leverage Data to Improve Student Success* (Washington, 2010).

37. Wong, "Redesigning Urban Districts"; Katrina Bulkley, Jeffrey Henig, and Henry Levin, eds., *Between Public and Private: Politics, Governance, and the New Portfolio Models for Urban School Reform* (Harvard Education Press, 2010).

38. Alyson Klein, "Obama Administration Concerned with Harkin-Enzi Accountability," *Education Week, Politics K–12 Blog,* October 21, 2011 (http://blogs.edweek.org/ed week/campaign-k-12/2011/10/obama_administration_unhappy_w.html).

39. Alyson Klein, "ESEA Bill Gets Day in Sun in Senate Hearing," *Education Week, Politics K–12 Blog,* November 8, 2011 (http://blogs.edweek.org/edweek/campaign-k-12/2011/11/teacher_evaluation_and_the_bes.html).

JEFFREY R. HENIG

9

The Rise of Education Executives in the White House, State House, and Mayor's Office

In an array of settings and at all levels of our federal system, elected executives are increasing their formal power and political engagement with issues relating to education and school reform. In some cases they are leading the demand for a stronger role; in some cases they are responding to such a demand voiced by others.

On the contemporary scene, it is mayoral control of schools that has received the most attention, with proponents arguing that it catalyzes reform and opponents complaining that it marginalizes parent and community groups. But the shift of formal power from school boards to mayors needs to be understood in conjunction with similar expansions of executive involvement at the state and national level. Indeed, the emergence of so-called education governors and education presidents predates the movement toward mayoral control.[1]

What accounts for the growing role of elected executives in education? Popular accounts frequently zero in on the personal characteristics of strong leaders: their insight into the critical role of education in a global economy, their ability to reframe issues in the public arena and build supporting coalitions where none existed before, their determination to improve educational performance, and their willingness to be held responsible if they fail. Scholars, who typically recognize that leadership represents more than an act of will or assertion of charisma, nonetheless have tended to examine a narrow slice of the phenomenon. Focusing separately on either governors or presidents or mayors, they treat the three movements as distinct, as if each can be accounted for by elements specific to the level of government in which they operate. Both perspectives understate the importance of the broader political institutional landscape and the ways in which shifts in the views and power of other interests help determine whether and when executive muscle could be effectively exercised.

A review of the emergence of the new education executives can identify patterns in timing, place, and political dynamics. These patterns suggest that this is a broader phenomenon than conventionally portrayed, that it extends beyond tinkering with formal governance structures to include a range of informal political factors relating to power and shifting agendas, and that the growing involvement is not limited to one branch of government.

Compared with most other important areas of domestic policy—for example, the ways in which we make decisions about the economy, welfare and income support, family policy, civil rights, crime and punishment, and most questions relating to environment, transportation, and health care—decisions about public schools historically have been highly localized, consigned to special single-purpose governance structures, and dominated by a small array of highly focused interest groups. This special status of education decisionmaking has been eroding, and we are now witnessing the gradual reabsorption of educational decisionmaking into multilevel, general-purpose government and politics. The broad changes under way constitute the end of educational exceptionalism in the United States.

An extensive literature about American exceptionalism focuses on the ways in which institutions, norms, and political practices in the United States differ from those in other nations.[2] While the U.S. system of education governance is indeed unusual when compared with that of other developed nations, here I focus less on the differences between the United States and other countries than on the differences between the handling of education and the institutions, norms, and practices characterizing the handling of other major domestic policies. Education policy in the United States has traditionally been seen—and treated—as different and distinct, a thing apart.

The expanded assertion of leadership by mayors, governors, and presidents is part of a broader governance shift that is increasingly placing key education decisions in the hands of public officials who have other issues in their portfolio as well. Compared with school-specific decisionmakers, general-purpose governance institutions and the officials who operate within them face more cross-cutting demands, deal with a broader range of interest groups, and are familiar with a wider array of policy tools. Education, in other words, is becoming more like other domestic policy arenas. This means that policy ideas and instruments that have been more common in those other arenas—things like contracting out, vouchers, and reliance on for-profit and nonprofit providers—face a more receptive (or at least more informed) audience now than when school-specific institutions dominated. And it has implications for how politicians, parties, interest groups, and citizens should act if they hope to shape effective and sustainable efforts to improve education. In particular, as decisions about schools and their budgets migrate into general-purpose arenas where they no longer have favored status, it may be more important for education advocates to form coalitions with multipurpose organizations and to reframe their arguments to better attract support from those who are not personally connected to public schools.

Education Governors

Among education executives, first out of the gate were the so-called education governors. During the 1970s a handful of mostly Southern governors began to take a more proactive stance in engaging with K–12 public education, framing school improvement as a critical component in their efforts to attract and hold jobs. Among the standouts were Lamar Alexander (R-Tenn., took office in 1979), Bill Clinton (D-Ark., 1979), Bob Graham (D-Fla., 1979), James Hunt (D-N.C., 1977), Thomas Kean (R-N.J., 1982), Richard Riley (D-S.C., 1979), and William Winter (D-Miss., 1980).[3]

To the extent that there is such a thing, the standard explanation of the expanding role of governors focuses on the catalytic role played by these early governors as policy entrepreneurs. The concept of policy entrepreneurship in the public sector builds on the image of the private market entrepreneur who spots a latent demand, mobilizes investment to create the product to fill that demand, and realizes profit in return for acumen and the assumption of risk. Policy entrepreneurs, analogously, detect an unmet societal need, unrepresented constituency, or untried policy and carry it onto the policy agenda, reaping political support and influence as the reward.[4]

Left ambiguous in the standard accounts is whether these early education governors were unusually astute—spotting needs and possibilities their predecessors had overlooked—or were responding to changing conditions that made education either more important to the states' well-being or more politically appealing to ambitious politicians. Several factors argue against viewing this as a simple assertion of outstanding leadership. First, the near simultaneity of the emergence of this cohort of education governors across a range of states suggests that something beyond individual perspicacity was involved. The global economy and increasing mobility of capital were creating new competitive pressures; and the increasing attention governors gave to education was more an extension of their traditional responsibility for economic development than a sudden shift in priorities. Second, this initial wave of governors' acting individually quickly evolved into a more collective phenomenon. In the 1980s and 1990s, the National Governors Association became a prominent voice in reformers' efforts to push education higher on the national agenda and place greater emphasis on standards and accountability.[5] Finally, the expanding role of governors was not simply a case of aggressive leaders' challenging powers that had been long present, though latent, in the office. The assertion of leadership on the education issue was accompanied by formal changes in governors' authority over education, and these formal changes in how state boards of education and state superintendents were selected often preceded the emergence of recognized education governors and were not limited to the states where these high-profile education policy entrepreneurs emerged.

Although the popular lore about education governors focuses on the personalities and strategies of individual leaders, scholars who study governors more typically zero in on how state laws either do or do not give governors the formal power to make and shape policies. Political scientists who study governors measure their power by looking at formal authority along several dimensions, the most commonly included being tenure potential (length of terms and term limits); appointment power (ability to appoint heads of key agencies and the degree to which this requires approval by other bodies); budgetary power (exclusive or shared with others); and veto power (line-item veto power and how hard it is for legislatures to override).[6] Reviewing the empirical literature, Charles Barrilleaux and Michael Berkman conclude that "overall, state governors are stronger than ever before."[7]

But a governor's overall power may or may not translate into the realm of public education. The standard way to measure the role of governors in education policy is to examine their formal role in selecting chief state school officers and state boards of education. When boards are elected, governors must pitch and pursue their education agendas in competition with board members who have their own priorities, political ambitions, constituencies, and claims to electoral mandates. When chief state school officers are either directly elected or appointed by elected state boards of education, executive oversight of education is divided, with governors less able to act authoritatively, dependent for implementing their policies on agencies whose loyalties may lie elsewhere, and facing a rival who can use the reality and reputation for having greater education expertise as tools for developing their own bases of support. Beginning some time in the late 1940s, there was a steady shift away from direct election of the chief officers to selection by the state board of education. From 1945 to 1967 the number of states electing the chief state school officers dropped from thirty-three to twenty-two, while the number giving the state board authority to appoint the officers increased from eight to twenty-four. Direct appointment by governors was rare and declined slowly throughout the first two-thirds of the twentieth century; at the turn of that century nine governors had that power, and in 1967 only four did. But the second shift, unfolding over the past forty years, has seen a substantial increase in the governor's appointment power. The sharpest period of change was between 1980 and 2005, with the number of states allowing governors to appoint chief state school officers increasing from five to fourteen.[8]

Even when they do not directly appoint chief state school officers, governors have had indirect formal power through their role in selecting the members of the state boards of education. Governors have always played a role in the majority of states, and the number of states with fully elected boards has been relatively stable for more than fifty years. Between 1954 and 1972 there was a sharp increase in the number of states that empowered governors to select all of the board members; even before this, though, governors in most states had the power to appoint at least some. As of 2010, governors had total appointment power (in thirty states) or partial appointment power (in seven states) in three-quarters of the states, with direct election of the board in ten states.[9]

Formal power is like a shovel in the woodshed. Its availability makes it more likely that a hole will be dug, but for that to happen someone has to pick it up and have the will and skill to use it. Recently, governors such as Scott Walker in Wisconsin, John Kasich in Ohio, and Chris Christie in New Jersey have instigated high-profile challenges to teachers unions on a number of fronts: challenging collective bargaining, replacing strict salary schedules with merit pay, and introducing value-added measures into decisions about salaries and tenure. But these were not dependent on an injection of new formal authority. Have increases in the formal appointment authority of governors coincided with increases in their inclination to make education an important part of their policy priorities and public identity?

To develop a rough measure of gubernatorial leadership on education issues across all fifty states and throughout their political history as states, I turned to an online database of more than 2,300 governor biographies compiled by the National Governors Association.[10] To identify education governors, my research assistant, Elizabeth Chu, and I first searched the database for all governors whose biographies included the keyword "education," "school," or "schools." We then skimmed each of these selected biographies and determined whether the biography included a substantive reference to K–12 education policy.

Figure 9-1 summarizes the percentage of governors, over time, who qualify as education governors based on the indication that they made K–12 education a prominent element in their agenda.[11] As with governors' formal appointment power, this measure of governors' informal involvement with education shows a growing role, especially over the past fifteen years. This does not appear to be an artifact of growing media coverage; the overall length of the governor biographies did not change overtime, so the increase reflects a greater relative attention to education. Education governors were no more or less likely to come from large, or urban, or older states, but their prevalence was higher in Southern states (37 percent) than in the rest of the country (22 percent).[12] Reinforcing the fact that formal power does not automatically translate into action, there is no correlation between this measure and the extent to which governors are legally

Figure 9-1. *Education Governors, 1775–2009*[a]

Percent

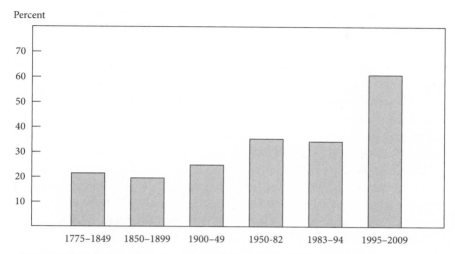

Source: Author's analysis of data from National Governors Association database.

a. Graph displays percentage of governors whose biographies mention substantive interest in K–12 education.

empowered to appoint state boards and superintendents. North Carolina, whose four-term governor James Hunt is often cited as the prototype education governor, also has had the highest percentage of governors who qualify as education governors on this index, yet measured on a scale of formal gubernatorial appointment power it is among the weaker states.

Education Presidents

Just as there were governors who dealt with education before the contemporary era of education governors emerged, so, too, at the national level there have been presidents who seriously attended to education before the term *education president* came to anyone's tongue. Maurice Berube labels Thomas Jefferson the nation's "first education president" but admits that Jefferson's claim to such a title depends mostly on his writing and actions "outside the presidential office," and he characterizes the role of the presidents in education policy as "periodic" until Lyndon Johnson took office.[13] Lawrence McAndrews labels Johnson the "first self-proclaimed" education president.[14]

Despite the ambiguity in timing, the transition from Ronald Reagan to George H. W. Bush provides something like a continental divide and gives the mid- to late-1980s the most credible claim to the onset of an era of education presidents. Reagan came into office in some ways as the antithesis of an education entrepreneur. He conceived of education as properly the province of states and localities, and his primary objectives at the national level were to dismantle the Department of Education that had been created under President Jimmy Carter and to institute education vouchers as a way to reduce the government role more generally in favor of an education marketplace driven by supply and demand. Despite his inclination to disengage the White House from education policy, Reagan ended up having considerable influence. Chester Finn goes so far as to call him the "original education president," not missing the irony that "Reagan's legacy includes a larger role for the federal government itself in education than he could have imagined, perhaps larger than he would have liked."[15]

If Reagan was a reluctant education president, Bush was eager to wear that mantle, making a national leadership role in education reform a central defining characteristic of his 1988 presidential campaign. In office, Bush assembled a group of governors in Charlottesville, Virginia, for an "education summit" that helped launch a partnership to establish national education goals.[16] Bush had no substantial legislative achievements on the education front, but by working directly with the nation's governors he was able to combine a cheerleader role with traditional Republican deference to states' rights. In exploring common ground on issues of standards and accountability, presidents and governors played a role in defusing the hot politics that had pitted the national government's desegregation efforts against states' rights and helped set the stage for collaboration between White House and state house that has continued in subsequent administrations.

In emphasizing education, George H. W. Bush was responding to a changing set of public expectations for presidential leadership in this area. From the 1960 election, which pitted John F. Kennedy against Richard Nixon, through the 1984 election between Walter Mondale and Reagan, education had never ranked among the top ten issues considered most important to the American public. When Bush ran against Michael Dukakis in 1988, education issues ranked eighth out of twenty-six in the months leading up to the election; in 1992, when he ran against Clinton, they ranked fifth.[17]

Figure 9-2 shows the relative emphasis presidents have put on education in their State of the Union speeches between 1948 and 2005. The data are drawn from the Policy Agendas Project and summarize the percentage of speeches that deal with education relative to other policy areas.[18] Bush senior placed about 75 percent more emphasis on education than did Reagan; Bill Clinton was by far the overall leader, more than one in ten of his policy references being to education. Gerald Ford, in his abbreviated presidency, gave only one brief address, and it included no substantive mention of education. Overall, the three presidents who were first elected after *A Nation at Risk* (Bush, Clinton, Bush) gave more than two and one-half times the relative attention to education that the seven who preceded did.

Figure 9-2. *Education Presidents, 1945–2005*[a]

Percent

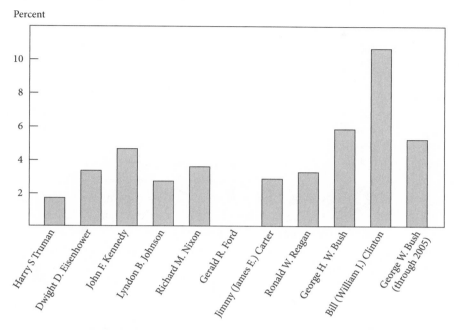

Source: Author's analysis of data compiled by Policy Agendas Project (www.policyagendas.org).
a. Graph displays percentage of State of the Union addresses that make reference to education policy.

Although the Policy Agendas Project data run only though 2005, *Smart Politics,* a political analysis blog hosted by the University of Minnesota's Humphrey School of Public Affairs, did a similar content analysis of President Obama's annual addresses to Congress for 2009–11. In a 2009 address to Congress, education was second only to his attention to budget issues relating to deficit, debt, and spending. Education dropped in attention during his 2010 State of the Union, when the economy and budget issues dominated, but rebounded to take up a greater part of his 2011 speech than any other of more than twenty-six issues.[19]

As important as the increased volume of messages about education is the change in the degree to which presidential involvement in education has shifted from marginal and deferential to assertive and core. As president, George W. Bush did not talk about education as much as Bill Clinton had, but No Child Left Behind (NCLB) was, by almost anyone's calibration, a major escalation in the federal government's reach into the day-to-day practices of schools.[20] Clinton's pursuit of national standards and accountability was moderated by Republicans' suspicions of a White House–led encroachment on states' rights, but because Bush was a Republican—"one of them"—in a classic twist on the "Nixon goes to

China" phenomenon, he was able to push the federal role further than any of his Democratic predecessors.

Obama and his aggressive secretary of education, Arne Duncan, pledged to keep up the pressure begun under the NCLB. But what really ratcheted up the visibility and muscle of the president's impact was Race to the Top. Race to the Top began somewhat as a ride-along on the American Recovery and Reinvestment Act, the administration's effort to stimulate the economy after the huge financial collapse it confronted in its first months in office. The act provided $100 billion in education funds. "While the vast majority of [American Recovery and Reinvestment Act] money went to preserve teachers' jobs and fund existing programs, a smaller pot of $4.35 billion was set aside for 'state incentive grants.'"[21] By attaching strong conditions and a weighting system that penalized applications that failed to include program elements it favored, the Department of Education was able to entice many states to make commitments (for example, raising caps on the number of charter schools) that they were not otherwise inclined to make. Largely because of this policy leverage, Frederick Hess concludes that Race to the Top has "arguably become the most visible and celebrated school reform effort in American history."[22]

Although it was tied to new funding, this expansion of the White House governance role masked to some extent the redistribution of authority that potentially eroded the leverage and autonomy of other institutions. School districts were visible losers in some senses, as the NCLB put them under much closer scrutiny and control, but the act also gave districts more resources and license to strengthen their oversight of schools. Similarly, the NCLB both constrained states and empowered them to assert stronger leadership vis-à-vis failing districts; and as long as states retained the right to calibrate the proficiency levels that were the key trigger embedded in the law, the constraints were less rigid than they initially seemed to be. That Race to the Top was a competitive grant, not a mandate, meant that states had the option not to play if they found the federal criteria too confining. But the zero-sum aspects of the governance changes came into sharper relief as money tightened, and as the Obama-Duncan team sought to expand the use of NCLB waivers to further advance its priorities. The administration threw down the gauntlet to Congress, which heretofore had considered itself more or less an equal partner in an expanded national role but now became more inclined to fret that it was being forced into the back seat.

Presidents "see scant political reward for spending time on education," Chester Finn wrote in 1977.[23] Some thirty-five years later, it appears that this observation has been turned on its head. Although much of the first two years of his administration was spent wrestling with the economy and health care, in his 2001 address to Congress, Obama had a lot to say about education, and he underscored its centrality, linking public investment in education and research to innovation and pulling out the old trope of global competitiveness to declare, "This is our generation's Sputnik moment."

Mayoral Control

The erosion of traditional education-specific policy institutions has been more evident at the local level than in the White House or governors' mansions.[24] That is not because the local level is where the role of general-purpose government and politics is most prevalent—to the contrary. But it is at the local level that education-specific institutions historically have held sway. In the early twentieth century, public education in large cities often was housed in an agency that reported to a mayor, much as was the case with law enforcement or public works. During the Progressive Era, many communities removed oversight of schools from the mayor's responsibility in the belief that this would lead to a more professional approach and one less responsive to partisan politics and the temptation to use school jobs and school building contracts as forms of patronage. Some urban districts, such as New Haven, Connecticut; Jackson, Mississippi; and Yonkers, New York, never took schools out of the mayor's portfolio of control. In that sense, mayoral control of schools is less a new idea than a reengagement of an old one.

It is the sharpness of the shift, from long-dominant school boards to newly mobilized mayors, that has made mayoral control the most talked about manifestation of the end of educational exceptionalism. Since Boston adopted mayoral control in 1992, a series of large urban school systems have followed suit, including Chicago (in 1995); Cleveland (1998); Harrisburg, Pennsylvania (2000); New York City (2002); Providence, Rhode Island (2003); and the District of Columbia (2000; 2007). Although the details of the arrangement differ, each city formally strengthened the mayor's role to include greater power in selecting superintendents and school boards, authorizing charter schools, determining the budget, or all of the above.[25] Although the rate at which large districts are adopting the model seems to have slowed for the moment, the possibility of moving in that direction remains under discussion in a number of other places, including Milwaukee, Newark, Los Angeles, Sacramento, Rochester, and Rockport, Illinois. Detroit, which had mayoral control from 1999 to 2004, is talking about it once again.

As with governors, giving formal authority to mayors—to appoint school boards, to hire superintendents, to set school budgets—does not ensure that they will take up the cause of school reform with wisdom or even energy. In theory, mayors are better situated than school boards or superintendents to mobilize a broad constituency for education investment and improvement and to find and develop positive spillovers between schools and the work of other municipal agencies that host programs that can help families and youth.[26] But theory and practice do not always align. In Baltimore, for example—where the mayors long held power to appoint the school board and, through their power on the city's board of estimates, to tightly control spending—even strong and dynamic mayors like William Donald Schaeffer traditionally preferred to play a minimal role.[27] This was also the case in Chicago, where from 1947 to 1980, though the mayor formally controlled both the board and budget, "most mayors avoided public school debates and disavowed any responsibility for their problems."[28]

Nor does lack of formal authority preclude strong mayoral leadership in the education arena. Michael Kirst and Fritz Edelstein highlight Long Beach, California, as a "prime example of how mayoral involvement in education need not rely on formal changes to governance." There, Mayor Beverly O'Neill has worked closely with the superintendent's office in a partnership that appears to have provided much of the multiagency coordination and public support that proponents of mayoral control talk about. Long Beach won the Broad Prize for Urban Education in 2003.[29] Francis Shlay, the mayor of St. Louis, made up for a lack of appointment power by backing a slate of reform-oriented school board candidates and helping them all get elected. Kenneth Wong and others cite Douglas Wilder, mayor of Richmond, Virginia, as an example of a politically skillful mayor who has used his informal power and authority to hold the superintendent accountable to him even when there was no formal line of authority to call on.[30]

Probably the strongest formal version of mayoral control is the one instituted in New York City beginning in 2002. For most of its history New York City school governance included a major role for the mayor, but reforms in 1969 weakened the mayor's role by decentralizing some functions to thirty-two separate school districts and by strengthening a citywide board of education (of which the mayor appointed two of the seven members) that hired the chancellor and ran high schools.[31] At the request of the newly elected mayor, Michael Bloomberg, the state legislature greatly strengthened the mayor's authority. Among the formal changes were empowering the mayor to appoint the chancellor (that is, the superintendent) of the system and eight of the thirteen members of the city's board of education (which Bloomberg renamed the Panel for Educational Policy). Some grants of formal appointment authority are more checked and limited than others. Consider the U.S. president's authority to appoint a Supreme Court justice, which is limited at the front end by the requirement that the Senate provide its "advice and consent" and at the back end by the fact that the appointment, once made, cannot be rescinded. In the New York City case, Mayor Bloomberg was given the power to select an appointee without the need for subsequent approval and with the unchecked power to revoke such appointment should the mayor so choose.[32]

Although the legislation was strong, what has made the New York City form of mayoral control extreme has had as much to do with the aggressive use of the delegated authority by Bloomberg and his first chancellor, Joel Klein. For example, a mayor's formal power to appoint school board members can in practice be a mild form of control or a strong one. The formal power is mild if the mayor relies heavily on the judgment of others in identifying candidates, heavily weighs the views of education experts, seeks consensus candidates, avoids second-guessing and challenging appointees once they are in office, and accommodates the decisions by the board even when they might differ from the mayor's preferences. The same formal power can be strong if the mayor aggressively manages the process of identifying and selecting nominees, puts allegiance to the mayor's agenda and priorities above education expertise as a selection criterion, and uses the formal power to remove board members as a means of enforcing loyalty to that agenda and priorities after the board member is in office. Midway in Michael Bloomberg's first term in office, when a few members of the Panel for Educational Policy expressed doubts about approving the chancellor's plan to end social promotion for the city's third graders, Bloomberg, as reported in the *New York Times*, simply "fired them, had three new members appointed and rammed his policy home—in one workday."[33]

The New York City case provides a useful illustration of an additional aspect of mayoral control. Although the movement from elected school boards toward more active mayors takes place at the local level, its unfolding often involves states and sometimes even national actors. Initiating mayoral control in all states requires at minimum the consent of the state legislature; indeed, sometimes the impetus has come largely from the state level, when governors or legislatures became frustrated by what they considered to be recalcitrant districts. In New York, though, the legislature was something of a reluctant partner. Rudolph Giuliani, Bloomberg's predecessor, had tried and failed to get such power while he was mayor. Some legislators argued against extending the authority to Bloomberg, and in reflection of such hesitation, the legislature included a sunset provision ending the arrangement on June 30, 2009, unless affirmatively renewed before that time. Mayoral control was renewed, but not without a lengthy battle and some modest concessions to parent and community groups that had strongly objected to what they considered to be the administration's authoritative and nonresponsive regime.[34]

The role of the national government in reinforcing mayoral control for the most part has been more indirect. Arguably, the accountability pressures exerted by the NCLB have added to the sense of dissatisfaction with school boards and districts, making the soil more fertile for proposals for governance reform. However, during the debate surrounding the extension of mayoral control in New York City, the Obama administration took an even more forceful stand. At the height of the debate, and despite criticisms by some parents' groups that were concerned that New York–style mayoral control was far too centralized, the U.S. education secretary, Arne Duncan, told a local newspaper, "I absolutely, fundamentally believe that mayoral control is extraordinarily important. I'm absolutely a proponent."[35] White House support for mayoral control also became a central focus of controversy in Milwaukee, where the governor and other supporters of an effort to institute mayoral control openly argued that failure to do so would put the state's effort to win a federal Race to the Top grant in jeopardy.[36]

Beyond the Executive Branch

The growing prominence of mayors, governors, and presidents makes it clear that important changes in education governance are under way. But are these changes specific to the executive branch? Or are they better understood as one current in a broader reassertion of general-purpose governance?

Changes in the tasks of governance, in popular conceptions of governance, and the impact of media may be giving elected executives a more powerful platform for engagement and making it more feasible for them to expand their reach into areas they previously left to legislatures, courts, or their agency heads. As government grows—in personnel, in professionalism, in scope of responsibility, and in regulatory reach, management, and administration—the challenging task of riding herd on the governmental apparatus becomes more important in actuality and in people's minds. That, arguably, creates an environment in which the executive branch stands to gain in stature relative to the legislature and judiciary. New data systems that give agencies informational advantages also may add to the musculature of the executive branch.

What these explanations fail to account for, though, is that the courts and legislatures have not been passive bystanders as presidents, governors, and mayors maneuvered onto center stage. This is a distinction that could make a large difference. Proponents of stronger executive leadership hold out the prospect that this could lead to more coherent policies, tighter linkage between policy and implementation, and less of the policy "churn" that substitutes shallow and ephemeral change for sustained change in core education functions.[37] If general-purpose institutions are being activated more broadly, courts and legislatures might pursue crosscutting agendas, and checks and balances might generate a new form of education policy gridlock. Critics of strong mayors, governors, and presidents have fretted about an overcentralization of authority that they see as promoting a narrowness of vision and coming at the expense of traditional mechanisms for asserting democratic control. If these general-purpose institutions are, in fact, being activated, there may be prospects for a more pluralist approach to agenda setting, one in which courts and legislatures bring to the fore rights, values, and contrasting ideas that currently are marginalized. Of course, with so many cooks in the kitchen, this extra dash of pluralism could come at the cost of greater incoherence.

The Courts

Although reluctantly, and against the grain of their normal deference to precedent and wariness of proactive policymaking, courts have featured prominently as catalysts for the emergence of stronger executive leadership. They have done this by challenging and diminishing the traditional role of local school boards, by helping to push education decisionmaking up the ladder of federalism to the state and national level, where school-specific institutions were never as strong as local ones, and, somewhat paradoxically, by making the minefields of race and class politics somewhat less treacherous for risk-averse politicians.

In taking on school segregation, the judiciary, a general-purpose institution, came head-to-head with school districts. Local responses varied—from tooth-and-nail resistance through resigned accommodation to constructive and willing embrace—but districts' legitimacy and power were dented overall.[38] In the extreme cases, the courts literally displaced them, directly issuing orders or appointing special masters to gather information, shape remedies, and oversee implementation.[39] Even when they did not get quite so directly involved themselves, the effect of the courts' efforts was to push decisions further up the ladder of federalism and into general-purpose arenas such as state legislatures or Congress: "As courts assert their legal authority in this fashion to leverage desegregation, they centralize the power to make decisions about equal educational opportunity in institutions that are sometimes geographically and institutionally distant from local levels where this change is to occur."[40]

On issues of fiscal equity and adequacy, the courts' encroachment on the turf of local school districts was less dramatic; there were no televised images of children being escorted into previously segregated school buildings by police or National Guard. But when it comes to the relationship between general-purpose institutions and special-purpose ones, the story line was similar to that with race and segregation. When courts found that their states' school funding systems violated state constitutions, they typically opted, at least at first, to defer to the legislatures to create and implement the remedies. This in and of itself pushed decisionmaking up the ladder of federalism, both because it was in state constitutions—not local law—that the courts found the violations and because the fiscal capacity to remedy the situation demanded state leadership.[41] As with desegregation, though, iterative efforts to force compliance on the part of reluctant legislatures and districts also drew the courts deeper into the weeds of education practice.[42] Court rulings in school finance cases "have traditionally issued vague orders or guidelines to state legislatures," but a handful have "issued sets of rather precise orders about how to restructure funding across local districts," and over the past two decades several courts have moved beyond issues of funding to consider "precise types of resources that additional funding can buy, such as qualified teachers and staff, school supplies, facilities repairs, and lower student-teacher ratios."[43] Although some judges restrict themselves to doing nothing more than kicking the problem to legislatures, increasingly judges find they must work with legislatures, executives, and even broad swathes of civic leadership if their remedies are to take hold.[44]

The catalyzing action of the courts most immediately and directly came from their demanding action on the part of the other branches, but there is a second, less direct role the courts may have played in opening the gates to greater involvement by general-purpose institutions and actors. Presidents, governors, and mayors had incentives to take positions on education even before the contemporary reform era, but these were met and usually checked by the powerful disincentive to take on the political hot potatoes of race, class, religion, and local control that often swirl around schools. Race in particular was a deterrent. Even when they wanted to, when elected executives ventured into school quality issues, their actions were invariably interpreted within the polarizing context of desegregation and states' rights. McAndrews notes that at a May 26, 1976, news conference in Columbus, Ohio, President Gerald Ford "found himself having to respond to a reporter's implication that 'quality education' were code words for 'segregation.'"[45]

Judicial intervention could hardly be said to have "solved" the tough issues of race and equity, but by bringing them into the open and by absorbing some of the body blows associated with impinging on local school board control, they arguably made it safer for both elected executives and legislatures to brave the waters of school reform. That elected politicians—both executives and legislatures—are venturing more confidently into the territory of education policy is not only because they have new reasons to do so but also because the courts have eliminated some of the long-standing obstacles to their doing so.

Legislatures

President Lyndon Johnson may have been the first to say that he wanted to be known as the education president, but count him also among those who realized that the national government's ramped-up responsibility extended beyond the White House.[46] In praising Congress for passing the Higher Education Facilities Bill, Johnson called it the "education Congress" on December 10, 1963.[47]

In examining national policy initiatives in education, two events stand out: the initial passage of the Elementary and Secondary Education Act and its later reauthorization as No Child Left Behind. The dominating narrative in both cases focuses on executive leadership, and clearly both Johnson and George W. Bush were important actors in publicly framing the issues, giving them high priority, and helping to leverage the necessary votes. In both cases, however, there is a counternarrative in which legislatures loom large.

Johnson and the White House made the passage of the Elementary and Secondary Education Act their highest priority following the 1964 election. White House strategists deliberately framed the education bill as an extension of the War on Poverty, pushing into the background the hot potato issues that had bedeviled federal education policy efforts previously: states' rights as tied to race and desegregation and funding for schools as it intersected with the question of religion and separation of church and state.[48] And the president's legendary phone calls, featuring sweet-talking and arm-twisting, clearly were important. But also important was the fact that the 1964 election had given Johnson better than a two-thirds majority to work with in both the Senate and House. Nor did White House strategizing and arm-twisting bowl over a passive and accommodating Congress; some of the specific components, including the shape of the allocation formula—which spread the funding broadly rather than concentrating it where the need was the greatest—and the general lack of specificity about how the funding should be used were crafted precisely to win sectors of congressional support.

Congress was at least as critical to the crafting of the NCLB. The original George Bush proposal was not a fleshed-out bill but a thirty-page blueprint that pulled together various previous proposals that were known to have some built-in support. The administration was anxious to garner broad bipartisan support, and to get that it relied on bargaining on Capitol Hill to shape key provisions. To bring in Democrats such as Senator Edward Kennedy, for example, it was necessary to raise the envisioned amount of federal spending and drop the initial plan for vouchers. Congress found ways to work through these issues, such as trading off vouchers for supplemental income. Although the NCLB came to be seen as a "Bush law . . . the reality is that the final bill's 681 finely printed pages were filled with a tangled assemblage of Bush administration proposals, New Democrat proposals drawn from reforms crafted during the Clinton administration, liberal ideas put forth by leading democrats like Kennedy and [Democratic congressman George] Miller and proposals and cautions introduced by countless other constituencies."[49] Whether the legislative horse-trading diluted or strengthened the policy that emerged, there is little question that Congress's fingerprints were all over the final product.

Earlier, I presented evidence of growing involvement of presidents and governors based on the extent to which education was emphasized in State of the Union speeches. Figure 9-3 adds a comparable measure of congressional attention to education drawn from the same Policy Agendas Project data. The project's database has coded more than 65,500 congressional hearings over the period

Figure 9-3. *Attention to Education by Congresses and Presidents, 1946–2005*[a]

Percent

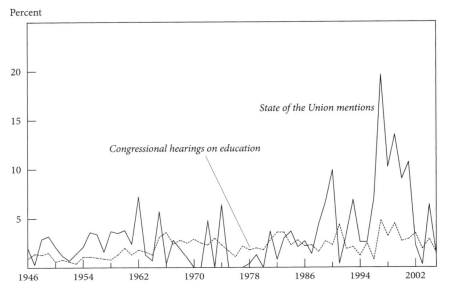

Source: Author's analysis of data from Policy Agendas Project (www.policyagendas.org).

a. Graph displays percentage of congressional hearings and of State of the Union addresses that mention the issue of education.

1946–2008, of which 1,549 dealt with some dimension of education as their major topic.

Several observations are warranted. First, as with the presidents, Congress shows increased attention to education as a percentage of its agenda. From 1946 through 1979, among congressional hearings, 1.64 percent dealt with education; from 1980 through 2005, that portion rose to 2.6 percent. Second, Congress overall has been steadier than the executive branch and less erratic in its allocation of attention to education. Talk is cheap, so it is perhaps not surprising that presidential mentions of education can fluctuate more wildly and spike on occasion, as they did in 1981 and in 1997–2001. A president who decides to emphasize an education issue can use a lot of sentences to do so, and some presidents accommodate this just by talking at greater length. Organizing a hearing is a more substantial undertaking, which makes it less likely that Congress will careen about from issue to issue. Also, both the House and the Senate have committees for which education is a major part of their responsibility. Because these committees have other responsibilities besides public education, they are free to devote their time and attention elsewhere, but institutionally they represent what might be considered a more hospitable venue for education enthusiasms to take root. From 1946 to 2005, 71.7 percent of the hearings dealing with education were held by either of the two primary education-focused committees: the House Committee on Education and the Workforce and the Senate Committee on Health, Education, Labor, and Pensions.[50] The other 28.3 percent were spread among forty-four committees.

Third, Congress is not just the tail on the dog. The late 1990s spike in presidential emphasis on education is probably the most prominent feature in figure 9-3, but in many years Congress has devoted proportionally more attention to education than has the president. There are three rather distinct periods in terms of the relative primacy given to education by the two institutions. Presidents gave greater emphasis to education in sixteen of the seventeen years from 1946 to 1962. From 1963 to 1987, however, the relative emphasis shifted, with Congress giving a higher proportional emphasis to education in eighteen of the twenty-five years. After 1987, the scales tipped back to the president, who placed a higher agenda priority on education in fourteen of those eighteen years. Congressional and presidential attention most likely interact, feeding and responding directly to each other and also indirectly through the media, which may pick up and amplify their activities.

State legislatures have been active, as well. To get a broader sense of legislative activity regarding education, I compiled a data set of bills and resolutions dealing with prekindergarten through high school education and enacted from 1994 to 2009 in all fifty states.[51] Results appear in figure 9-4. Some of the more active states examined are larger, more urban ones like California and Illinois, but others (for example, Arkansas and Louisiana) are more active than would be predicted by their size alone, and some large states (Pennsylvania and Massachusetts) anchor the low end of the legislative activity scale.[52] Simple activity, of course, is not necessarily an indicator of serious engagement; a single well-crafted, far-reaching piece of legislation could have more influence than a scattershot of minor bills. As at the national level, though, this is indicative of the fact that it is not just the executive branch that is actively involved. The allocation of state legislative attention across sixteen categories, as shown in figure 9-4, indicates that a little more than one-third of all bills related to contemporary reform areas such as curriculum and teaching, accountability, and school choice.

Since 1975, fourteen states have increased the governor's role in appointing either or both the chief state school officer and state board of education; preliminary analysis shows that legislative activity was higher in these states, suggesting that gubernatorial and legislative involvement may work in tandem rather than as competing institutions, with activity by one prompted by or inducing passivity in the other. Another indication that we are witnessing an expansion of the role of general-purpose institutions, rather than a redistribution of a fixed pie of power among them, is that legislative activity at the state level is associated with what is happening nationally; before enactment of the NCLB (that is, from

Figure 9-4. *State Legislation Related to Prekindergarten through High School Education, 1994–2009*

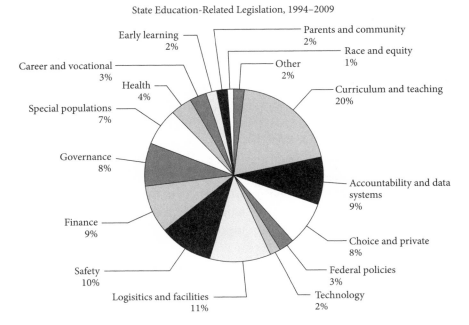

State Education-Related Legislation, 1994–2009

Source: Author's analysis of data from Education Commission of the States.

1994 to 2001), states averaged 10.2 bills a year, whereas afterward (2002–08), that number more than doubled, to 21.6.

The End of Exceptionalism: Implications for the Future

The growing role of education executives has implications for how education is governed, which, in the coming years, will alter the configuration of interests, issues, and policies that influence the nation's schools. This is especially true if, as I suggest here, the new leadership by elected executives is just a more visible feature of a broader reabsorption of education policy into general-purpose arenas.

The education policy subsystem that matured through most of the twentieth century was specifically organized around public education and provided favored access to a limited set of interest groups with intense interest in public schools and a commitment to maintaining and expanding public investment in education. The tight dominance of the education-specific groups, such as the teachers unions, was most prominent at the local level but extended all the way to Washington, D.C. Hyperlocalization meant that schools were often seen as extensions of dominant community norms and that investment in good schools would accrue as appreciation in local property values. Buffered from the broader interplay of party politics, frequently funded by dedicated revenue streams, and with leadership selected in off-cycle low-turnout elections dominated by parent and teacher organizations, it was a somewhat closed and protected system, and designed to be so.

These attributes were a source of genuine strength but also developed into problems and tensions that fueled a potent backlash. The strengths included a prominent place for professional expertise and a stability of funding and support that was less vulnerable than other domestic policies to competing demands, shifting public priorities, changing political regimes, and the vicissitudes of fiscal pressure. When changing demographics brought new minorities into local communities, however, the closed nature of the systems contributed to frustrations on the part of newcomers, who felt they had limited access to jobs and limited influence on policies. When the nation's economic and political dominance on the world stage weakened, the view that America's schools were falling behind bruised their image and opened the education profession to criticism from which it had been largely spared. The public K–12 school system controlled huge amounts of resources: jobs, dollars, and contracts. Those outside the systems—general-purpose politicians looking for ways to build power and influence; private companies looking for a piece of the action akin to that they had obtained through contracting arrangements for providing other public services—had long been held at bay, intimidated by the iron triangle that protected the status quo and also, too, perhaps by the treacherous currents of race, religion, and family values that threatened to flare up when local equilibrium was disrupted. The single-purpose, buffered, and protected status of American education in some ways was always an anomaly, and in that sense the reassertion of general-purpose politics and government once its vulnerabilities emerged was less a surprise than the fact that it had taken so long.

In her analysis of the changing politics of federal education policy, Elizabeth Debray-Pelot identifies seven interest groups as "formerly influential" in setting federal education policy. Each of them is education specific in focus (the American Association of School Administrators, the American Federation of Teachers, the Council of Chief State School Officers, the Council of Great City Schools, the National Association of State Title I Directors, the National Education Association, and the National School Boards Association). In contrast, five of the eight groups she identifies as "newly influential" are multi-issue organizations (the Business Roundtable, the EXPECT Coalition, the Heritage Foundation, the National Governors Association, and the Progressive Policy Institute), and none of the newly influential education-focused groups (the Education Trust, the Education Leadership Council, and the Thomas B. Fordham Foundation) is a constituency-based group with members tied to the traditional education sector.[53]

That education policies are shaped and implemented today by a more all-purpose arena of governance means that unconventional ideas for delivering education are more likely to get a hearing. This is partly because the mix of interest groups that has access to general-purpose venues is broader than that of school-specific arenas. Policy entrepreneurs who lack traditional education credentials—who have not been teachers or principals; whose academic training is in management, or law, or science and technology—are better able to make the case that their different kinds of expertise are relevant and should be taken into account. Greater openness to new ideas is also likely to be the result of the different backgrounds and experiences of the general-purpose officials themselves. Although schools systems have a fair amount of experience contracting with private parties for auxiliary services such as janitorial and food services, providing core aspects of the education enterprise in this way is a new and somewhat alien and threatening concept for those accustomed to the traditional public school model. But contracting out has been a major and somewhat routine experience for mayors, governors, and their associated legislative bodies for many years in areas such as road and highway construction, parking enforcement, day care provision, and the like.

For those frustrated with what they consider to be complacency, lack of imagination, or self-serving bureaucracy, the changes in the institutional landscape have been welcome. There are bitter and still unresolved debates about whether the new reform elements—and the initiatives they have launched in charter schooling; test-based accountability for students, teachers, and schools; portfolio management districts; new education technologies; alternative certification; and the like—are leading to better education or worse, or if they are narrowing achievement gaps or exacerbating inequalities.[54] But there are few who would deny that a system with a reputation for stasis has been opened to disruption and change.

There are many uncertainties about how the shifting sands of education governance, characterized by a greater role played by general-purpose leaders and groups, will play out in the long term: But there is at least one potentially critical cost and at least one potentially damaging risk. It is reasonable to be suspicious of the notion that the only expertise worth valuing is that steeped in the particularities of education, detailed in its understanding of curriculum and instruction, delivered through traditional institutions for training professional educators, and leavened by years in the trenches of classroom experience. Yet it is totally unreasonable to assume that these traditionally recognized forms of expertise are not important. David Cohen and Susan Moffit make a compelling case that much of the energies and resources burned in the contemporary efforts to reform education have come to naught precisely because they were disconnected from knowledge about the aims, instruments, capabilities, and environment that shape education practice and determine its consequences.[55] And the reform models that seek to work around the traditional model of professionalism—charter schools that depend on waves of young teachers willing to work longer days, weeks, and years with fewer job protections and benefits; education technology solutions that envision teachers able to handle large classrooms while students spend increasing amounts of their time doing self-paced learning—are largely untested in terms of their sustainability and scalability.

The risk is that investment in public education will not fare well in the broader arena of general-purpose politics. The initial expansion of executive involvement and the growing role of general-purpose institutions rode in on a wave of broad enthusiasm for the importance of education as a way to leverage economic competitiveness and narrow the inequalities associated with race, ethnicity, and socioeconomic class. It benefited as well from a relatively expansive economy, through many of the key years, and strong philanthropic support that, after years of some frustration with the slowness of change in the traditional public school sector, found working with mayors and governors and the White House more appealing. To the extent that public education can deliver on these fronts, its contribution to social well-being is objectively important. But there is no guarantee that objective importance will drive the politics and policy agenda of the future. Having played a major role in the previous four presidential elections, education was not a prominent feature in the 2008 campaign or the lead-up so far to 2012, displaced, at least for the time being, by concerns over the economy, deficits, and federal health care reform. Within general-purpose governance arenas, calls to invest in public education must compete head-to-head with other demands on governmental attention as well as the arguments for the alternative strategy of cutting spending and taxes and relying more on private incentives and market forces to generate and allocate the education the public wants and needs. Research on governmental agenda setting establishes both the somewhat fickle nature of public attention and the ways in which objective measures of need compete with politics, ideology, symbolism, biased perceptions about beneficiaries, external events, and serendipity as determinants of what government chooses to focus on.[56] Advocates for public education may need to find new ways of framing their issues to attract and maintain allies among groups that, though not specifically focused on schools, share some of their aspirations but are also competing for public and philanthropic support.

Even if general-purpose institutions keep education high on the policy agenda, there is no guarantee that they will deliver effective policies. Enthusiasts for stronger executive involvement portray it as a step toward more rational, comprehensive, and decisive decisionmaking. This vision may prove naïve if, as I have suggested, the governance changes under way may include more active legislatures and courts. Each branch of general-purpose governance has its own history of dysfunction, and the clashes among them could just result in new forms of policy churn or gridlock.[57]

As a necessity and at the least, education advocates will need to find more and better ways to work in multi-issue coalitions to compete within these general-purpose arenas. Their ability to do so will depend on both the political resources they bring to the table and their ability to make the case to potential allies that investment in education will generate benefits even for those who do not work directly within the sector or do not have children currently enrolled in public schools. Americans historically have shown allegiance to the idea that schools are a public good—what Terry Moe refers to as the "public school ideology"—but in the emerging arenas of general-purpose politics they are likely to have to build a stronger evidentiary case.[58]

Although the political challenges of operating in a broader, multi-issue arena make it likely that the initial posture of traditional education interests will be defensive, one potentially salutary outcome of the increasing importance of education executives and general-purpose governance could be the erosion of bureaucratic and political barriers that have pitted proponents of school reform against those who adopt a broader vision of education and seek to integrate education policy with other social policy efforts to address concentrated poverty, income inequality, housing, and public health. When schools do what they are supposed to do, payoffs are not limited to school performance; they include an array of human- and social-capital outcomes, and the causal arrow runs in the other direction as well. The new politics of education governance makes it more likely, as I have argued elsewhere, that the false choice between pursuing school-based and non-school-based policies can be bridged. "Trade-offs and spillovers across policy domains are more visible in these general-purpose arenas, and the levers for addressing them more readily in reach."[59]

In conclusion, let me add some disclaimers. I believe that the structural shifts I discuss are real and important, but I do not claim or believe that they are sharp, dramatic, or inexorable. The changes I highlight are like the shifting of tectonic plates, not the earthquake to end all earthquakes. Core institutions take root and last because they are resistant to change, and once in place they develop defending mechanisms (that may be different from the originating rationale and the groups that initially pushed for the changes). Dominating structures sometimes do suddenly dissipate. I do not project that special-purpose governance arrangements, institutions and venues that specialize in education, and single-purpose interest groups are destined for obsolescence. I expect them to be resilient, to use power and argument to resist some of the end of educational exceptionalism, to adjust tactics and settle into somewhat new patterns of interaction, but still to be around for many years to come.

Just as the early development and long domination of local school districts did not make general-purpose governance and politics irrelevant for education decisionmaking, so too the muscling up of the general-purpose venues we are witnessing now will most likely stop short of displacing or even marginalizing local school districts and education-specific agencies, committees, and interest groups. The game is changing, but given the many special and political forces that enforce incrementalism, many of the familiar rules, familiar groups, familiar tactics, and familiar outcomes will stay on the scene. The effect, as others have written about institutional change, is more like layering than replacement.[60] The result is a complex field of play, where groups' dexterity and slack resources become critical as shopping for the most hospitable venue becomes an increasingly important tactical tool.[61] The layered and overlapping decisionmaking venues potentially open more avenues for influence by different groups with differing ideas and interests, but to the degree that public education is undermined by the lack of coherent management and clear lines of accountability (as many argue), this more complex field of play has the potential also to make things worse.[62]

Notes

1. Some of the discussion in this chapter borrows and builds on arguments I first offered in Jeffrey R. Henig, "Mayors, Governors, and Presidents: The New Education Executives and the End of Educational Exceptionalism," *Peabody Journal of Education* 84, no. 3: 283–99, and are developed much more fully in *The End of Exceptionalism in American Education: The Changing Politics of School Reform,* a forthcoming book, to be published by Harvard Education Press, that considers the dynamics and implications of the reabsorption of education decisionmaking into general-purpose government an politics.

2. Godrey Hodgson, *The Myth of American Exceptionalism* (Yale University Press, 2010); Seymour Martin Lipset, *American Exceptionalism: A Double-Edged Sword* (New York: W. W. Norton, 1997).

3. Maris A. Vinovskis, "Gubernatorial Leadership and American K–12 Educational Reform," in *A Legacy of Innovation: Governors and Public Policy,* edited by Ethan G. Sribnick (University of Pennsylvania Press, 2008),

4. John W. Kingdon, *Agendas, Alternatives, and Public Policies,* 2nd ed. (Boston: Little, Brown, 1995); Michael Mintrom, *Policy Entrepreneurs and School Choice* (Georgetown University Press, 2000).

5. Gareth Davies, *See Government Grow: Education Politics from Johnson to Reagan* (University Press of Kansas, 2007); Paul Manna, *School's In: Federalism and the National Education Agenda* (Georgetown University Press, 2006); Vinovskis, "Gubernatorial Leadership."

6. On the measurement issue, see N. C. Dometrius, "Measuring Gubernatorial Power," *Journal of Politics* 41, no. 2 (1979): 589–610; J. A. Schlesinger, "The Politics of the

Executive," in *Politics in the American States,* edited by H. Jacob and K. N. Vines (Boston: Little, Brown, 1965): 207–38. A classic application is T. R. Dye, "Executive Power and Public Policy in the States," *Western Political Quarterly* 22, no. 4 (1969): 926–39. For a comprehensive set of contemporary and historical measures and their definitions, see Thad Beyle, "Gubernatorial Power: The Institutional Power Ratings for the 50 Governors of the United States," 2008 (www.unc.edu/~beyle/gubnewpwr.html).

7. Charles Barrilleaux and Michael Berkman, "Do Governors Matter? Budgeting Rules and the Politics of State Policymaking," *Political Research Quarterly* 56 (December 2003): 409–17, 409.

8. F. F. Beach and R. F. Will, *The State and Education: The Structure and Control of Public Education at the State Level* (U.S. Government Printing Office, 1955); Ward W. Keesecker, *State Boards of Education and Chief State School Officers: Their Status and Legal Powers* (Federal Security Agency, Office of Education, 1950); Martha M. McCarthy and others, *State Education Governance Structures* (Denver, Colo.: Education Commission of the States, 1993).

9. For up-to-date information on state governance models, see Education Commission of the States, "ECS Policy Analysis Topics: Governance," 2012 (www.ecs.org/html/educationIssues/ECSStateNotes.asp?nIssueID=68).

10. This database is searchable by many criteria, including state, governor's name, time in office, number of terms, and keyword. In writing the biographies, the National Governors Association staff draws on a variety of sources, including state archives, state history museums, and online databases, such as the Political Graveyard. Since these biographies are designed to be overviews, they do not provide definitive information as to which governors prioritized education. The advantages of having near universal coverage of governors from all states throughout their history makes even this imperfect source valuable, however, as an additional window into the phenomenon of governors' involvement with education. Further details regarding coding are available from the author.

11. The first three time periods depicted are relatively arbitrary efforts to capture half-century spans. The years 1983 (*Nation at Risk*) and 1994 (Improving America's Schools Act) provided substantively meaningful benchmarks for dividing the contemporary era.

12. The p value for the difference in averages is less than .001.

13. Maurice R. Berube, *American Presidents and Education* (Westport, Conn.: Greenwood Press, 1991), p. 17.

14. Lawrence J. McAndrews, *The Era of Education: The Presidents and the Schools, 1965–2001* (University of Illinois Press, 2006), p. 133. Backing up that claim was the fact that Johnson—who had graduated from a teachers college, taught school, and even served a brief stint as a principal—had signed more than sixty education bills during his presidency, including the path-breaking Elementary and Secondary Education Act and the bill creating Head Start. See Humanities Texas, "LBJ the Teacher," 2007 (www.humanities texas.org/newsroom/spotlights/lbjteacher/index.php).

15. Chester R. Finn Jr., "The Original Education President: Reagan's ABCs," *National Review,* June 9, 2004 (www.nationalreview.com/articles/211015/original-education-president/chester-e-finn-jr#). Finn's assessment of the Reagan administration's education accomplishments might be buoyed by the fact that he served as assistant secretary of education during Reagan's second term in office.

16. Manna, *School's In*, pp. 80–81.

17. Patrick J. McGuinn, *No Child Left Behind and the Transformation of Federal Education Policy, 1965–2005* (University Press of Kansas, 2006), p. 149. See also Manna, *School's In*, pp. 50–66.

18. The Policy Agendas Project uses "quasi sentences," to account for the fact that a single sentence sometimes includes more than one policy idea. The analysis further distinguishes offhand or ritualistic mentions of education from those with "policy content." The length of a speech is not necessarily a determination of how much policy content was present. The presidents with the highest percentage of speeches devoted to statements with education policy content are Jimmy Carter (95.2 percent) and Dwight D. Eisenhower (90.2 percent). Author's analysis of data from Policy Agendas Project (www.policyagendas.org).

19. For more, see University of Minnesota, Humphrey School of Public Affairs, *Smart Politics* (blog), "A Content Analysis of Barack Obama's 2011 State of the Union Address," 2011 (http://blog.lib.umn.edu/cspg/smartpolitics/2011/01/a_content_analysis_of_barack_o.php).

20. The ongoing pressures of responding to 9/11, terrorism, the invasion of Iraq, and similar foreign policy events quite likely led Bush to talk less about the NCLB and education in general as a president than he had as a governor or presidential candidate.

21. Patrick McGuinn, *Creating Cover and Constructing Capacity: Assessing the Origins, Evolution, and Impact of Race to the Top* (Washington: American Enterprise Institute, 2010), p. 2.

22. Frederick Hess, foreword to McGuinn, *Creating Cover.*

23. Chester E. Finn Jr., *Education and the Presidency* (Lexington Mass.: Lexington Books, 1977), p. 104.

24. Parts of this section draw on some of my earlier writing about mayoral control. See, for example, Jeffrey R. Henig, "Mayoral Control: What We Can and Cannot Learn from Other Cities," in *When Mayors Take Charge: School Governance in the City*, edited by Joseph P. Viteritti (Brookings Press, 2009), pp. 19–45; Jeffrey R. Henig and Wilbur C. Rich, eds., *Mayors in the Middle: Politics, Race, and Mayoral Control of Urban Schools* (Princeton University Press, 2004).

25. The District of Columbia gave its mayor partial control in 2000 and adopted a stronger form of mayoral control in 2007. Some districts (for example, Detroit; Oakland, California; and Prince George's County, Maryland) adopted (or had imposed on them) mayoral control but then reverted to elected school boards during this same time period.

26. Kenneth J. Meier, "Structure, Politics, and Policy: The Logic of Mayoral Control," in *Mayors in the Middle*, edited by Henig and Rich, pp. 221–31.

27. Marion Orr, "Baltimore: The Limits of Mayoral Control," in *Mayors in the Middle*, edited by Henig and Rich, pp. 27–58.

28. Dorothy Shipps, "Chicago: The National 'Model' Reexamined," in *Mayors in the Middle*, edited by Henig and Rich, pp. 59–97.

29. Michael W. Kirst and Fritz Edelstein, "The Maturing Mayoral Role in Education," *Harvard Educational Review* 76 (Summer 2006): 152–64.

30. Kenneth Wong and others, *The Education Mayor: Improving America's Schools* (Georgetown University Press, 2007).

31. Diane Ravitch, "A History of Public School Governance in New York City," in *When Mayors Take Charge*, edited by Viteritti, pp. 171–86.

32. State law did set some formal limits by stipulating that school superintendents must meet certain certification requirements relating to their education background, training, and teaching or leadership experience. Mayor Bloomberg twice chose to appoint candidates with almost no background in education, which required a waiver from the requirement by the New York State commissioner of education. In both cases, this waiver was granted.

33. Michael Winerip, "Fired for Disagreeing, Ex-Panelist Fears the Mayor Is Discouraging Advice He Needs to Hear," *New York Times*, March 24, 2004.

34. Eva Gold and others, *Bringing a Public Voice to the School Governance Debate: The Campaign for Better Schools and Mayoral Control in New York City (Year One Report)* (Philadelphia: Research for Action, 2010).

35. Carl Campanile, "BAM Backs Mike School Rule," *New York Post*, March 30, 2009.

36. Erin Richards, "Race to the Top Program Extended; Mayoral Control Won't Determine Winners, Duncan says," *Milwaukee Journal Sentinel*, January 19, 2010.

37. Frederick M. Hess, *Spinning Wheels: The Politics of Urban School Reform* (Brookings Press, 1998).

38. Robert L. Crain, *The Politics of School Desegregation* (Garden City, N.Y.: Anchor Books, 1969).

39. For example, see the story of Judge Arthur Garrity's involvement in the Boston case, in J. Anthony Lukas, *Common Ground: A Turbulent Decade in the Lives of Three American Families* (New York: Vintage Books, 1985).

40. Benjamin Michael Superfine, "Court-Driven Reform and Educational Opportunity: Centralization, Decentralization, and the Shifting Judicial Role," *Review of Educational Research* 80 (March 2010): 108–37, 114.

41. On the dynamics of legislative recalcitrance and the way in which it forced the courts to become more prescriptive, see Richard Lehne, *The Quest for Justice: The Politics of School Finance Reform* (New York: Longman, 1978). On the empirical literature demonstrating the centralization consequence, see Henry Levin and William S. Koski, "Twenty-Five Years after Rodriguez: What Have We Learned?" *Teachers College Record* 102 (June 2000): 480–513.

42. On legislative and local resistance, see Katherine McDermott, *Controlling Public Education: Localism versus Equity* (University Press of Kansas, 1999), and Douglas S. Reed, *On Equal Terms: The Constitutional Politics of Educational Opportunity* (Princeton University Press, 2003).

43. Superfine, "Court-Driven Reform."

44. James S. Liebman and Charles F. Sabel, "Changing Schools: A Public Laboratory Dewey Barely Imagined: The Emerging Model of School Governance and Legal Reform," *NYU Review of Law and Social Change* 28, no. 2 (2003): 183–304.

45. McAndrews, *The Era of Education*, p. 979.

46. McAndrews, *The Era of Education*.

47. Lyndon Baines Johnson Library and Museum, "LBJ for Kids!: Education Timeline for 1963–1968," 2012 (www.lbjlib.utexas.edu/johnson/lbjforkids/edu_timeline.shtml).

48. Davies, *See Government Grow*, chap. 2.

49. Frederick M. Hess and Michael J. Petrilli, *No Child Left Behind: A Primer* (New York: Peter Lang, 2006). See also Andrew Rudalevige, "The Politics of No Child Left Behind," *Education Next* 3 (Fall 2003): 62–69.

50. The dominant role of these committees did not diminish over time; despite fluctuations from year to year, overall the two major committees accounted for exactly the same proportion of the education hearings before 1980 as they have since.

51. I started with a spreadsheet provided to Elizabeth Rigby, from George Washington University, by the Education Commission of the States (thanks to Professor Rigby for sharing this spreadsheet). The data include 30,327 education-related bills organized into 435 topic categories and information on their title, status, and a brief summary. Through an iterative process, Elizabeth Chu and I aggregated and recoded the topics, referencing titles and summaries for additional information in cases in which the original topic code was insufficiently clear. We use 16 categories, including a category, "other," of uncodable bills, which make up less than 1 percent of the total. For the analysis presented here, we restrict the sample to bills that focus on prekindergarten through twelfth grade and that have been signed into law ($n = 12,443$).

52. Massachusetts's lower level of activity may reflect the fact that it had passed a comprehensive education reform bill in 1993, just before this data series commenced.

53. Elizabeth Debray-Pelot, "Dismantling Education's 'Iron Triangle': Institutional Relationships in the Formation of Federal Education Policy between 1998 and 2001," in *To Educate a Nation: Federal and National Strategies of School Reform*, edited by Carl F. Kaestle and Alyssa E. Lodewick (University Press of Kansas, 2007), pp. 64–89. On the changing constellation of interest groups at the national level, see also Elizabeth DeBray-Pelot and Patrick McGuinn, "The New Politics of Education: Analyzing the Federal Education Policy Landscape in the Post-NCLB Era," *Educational Policy* 23 (January 2009): 15–42, and Carl F. Kaestle, "Federal Education Policy and the Changing National Polity for Education, 1957–2007," in *To Educate a Nation*, edited by Kaestle and Lodewick, pp. 17–40.

54. For a full-bore critique of the new reformers, see Diane Ravitch, *The Death and Life of the Great American School System: How Testing and Choice are Undermining Education* (New York: Basic Books, 2010).

55. David K. Cohen and Susan L. Moffitt, *The Ordeal of Equality: Did Federal Regulation Fix the Schools?* (Harvard University Press, 2009).

56. For example, Anthony Downs, "Up and Down with the Ecology: The Issue Attention Cycle," *Public Interest* 28 (Summer 1972): 28–50; Frank R. Baumgartner and Brian D. Jones, *Agendas and Instability in American Politics* (University of Chicago Press, 1993); David A. Rochefort and Roger W. Cobb, eds., *The Politics of Problem Definition: Shaping the Policy Agenda* (University Press of Kansas, 1994); and Anne Schneider and Helen Ingram, "Social Construction of Target Populations: Implications for Politics and Policy," *American Political Science Review* 87 (June 1993): 334–47.

57. On the institutional strengths and limitations of Congress to engage in education reform leadership, see Charles Barone and Elizabeth DeBray, "Education Policy in Congress," in *Carrots, Sticks, and the Bully Pulpit: Lessons from a Half-Century of Federal Efforts to Improve America's Schools*, edited by Frederick M. Hess and Andrew Kelly (Harvard Education Press, 2012), pp. 61–82.

58. Terry M. Moe, *Schools, Vouchers, and the American Public* (Brookings Press, 2001), pp. 86–91.

59. Jeffrey R. Henig and S. Paul Reville, "Outside-In School Reform: Why Attention Will Return to Non-School Factors," *Education Week*, May 25, 2011.

60. Kathleen Thelen, "How Institutions Evolve: Insights from Comparative Historical Analysis," in *Comparative Historical Analysis in the Social Sciences*, edited by James Mahoney and Dietrich Rueschemeyer (Cambridge University Press, 2003), pp. 208–40.

61. Baumgartner and Jones, *Agendas and Instability.*

62. Thanks to Paul Manna for suggesting this point.

PART III

LESSONS FROM OTHER NATIONS AND SECTORS

MICHAEL BARBER

10

English Perspectives on Education Governance and Delivery

In today's world higher standards are demanded than were required yesterday and there are simply fewer jobs for people without skill.

—PRIME MINISTER JAMES CALLAGHAN, 1976

The perspectives I bring to bear in this chapter are based on a number of different experiences during my career. The first was as an official for the National Union of Teachers between 1985 and 1993, during which time the Conservative governments of the era introduced a series of radical changes to the education system in England. The second was as a professor of education at the universities of Keele and London in the mid-1990s, when my research agenda combined history with school and system improvement and involved me, for the first time, in looking outside the United Kingdom. The third was my eight years of experience (1997–2005) in the Blair administration, during which time I first led the implementation of the school reforms and then, from 10 Downing Street, oversaw the implementation of all the prime minister's domestic policy priorities. Finally, from 2005 to 2011, as a partner at McKinsey, I set up and led the Global Education Practice, which, among other things, published a number of influential reports, cited in the notes to this chapter, on school system reform around the world.

One of the lessons of this experience, drawn on repeatedly during my time in the Blair administration, is that only a strong central government has the power to ensure radical devolution of resources and management influence to schools. Since that time successive governments have sought, with varying degrees of success, to define that role for local authorities and to establish a sustainable model of governance for the education system.

209

A Brief History of Education Governance in England

In the summer of 1944, a few weeks after the Normandy landings, the 1944 Education Act completed its passage through Parliament. It envisaged a world in which the local authorities (some 300 or so at the time) built and managed the postwar school system. Local authorities were elected, multipurpose institutions responsible for housing and transport, among other things, as well as education. The education system at the local level would be overseen by the education committee of the local authority with political leadership vested in the chairman of that committee and executive leadership in the chief education officer.

Central government, through the education minister and the U.K. Department for Education, would play a significant but limited role, the most important part of which was to provide around half of all the necessary funding, the rest to be raised locally through a property tax. Issues of national importance—most significantly teachers' pay—would be solved through tripartite negotiating bodies representing the local authorities, the national government, and teachers unions. Almost everything else was left to local determination, including the curriculum; this, after all, was an era when national curriculums were seen as the sort of thing fascists and communists imposed, not democrats.

The intention was that these new arrangements would ensure, for the first time, universal primary and secondary education and enable the system to expand to meet the demands for improved quality and quantity, which, as the war continued, grew ever stronger. The privations of wartime, it was believed, would give way to a new Jerusalem.

The 1944 arrangements stood the test of time, unquestioned until the 1970s and in place until the 1980s, when, like other institutional arrangements that have overstayed their welcome, they unraveled in a storm of controversy. The implicit assumption of the postwar settlement was that, at a local level, there were few, if any, issues that could not be resolved behind closed doors in a dialogue between union leaders and the chief education officer. Similarly, at the national level, for the minister for education, local authority leaders, and union leaders, a quiet word or a timely phone call would do the trick. This was quite different from continental Europe, especially France and Germany, where since the nineteenth century, the provision of public education had been firmly established as a central-state responsibility.

The measure of success was not performance, which was barely measured at all; it was numbers: numbers of children into schools, numbers of teachers recruited and trained, numbers of schools built and maintained—and on these measures, until the economic crises of the 1970s, the education system was doing well. Symbolically, in 1972, the year before the first Organization of Petroleum Exporting Countries–induced oil shock and its resulting economic crisis, the government published a business-as-usual white paper titled "A Framework for Expansion."[1] With hindsight we can see that the prediction in the title proved wholly false but did no harm to the minister for education at the time, a middle-ranking Conservative whom few expected to rise much further, by the name of Margaret Thatcher.

What went wrong? First, the failures of the postwar British economy, pitilessly exposed by the 1970s oil shocks, put pressure on government expenditure. Britain could no longer afford "expansion." Second, the postwar baby boom had passed through the schools by the mid-1970s, so the case for expansion lost plausibility. Third, the lack of accountability in the system had been revealed in a small number of scandalous cases that made front-page copy. The most celebrated of all was the case of William Tyndale Primary School in north London, where the teachers' attachment to progressive teaching methods had been taken too far and the parents who complained were accused by the principal of being "fascists."[2] Fourth, leading politicians heard a steady and growing drumbeat of complaints from leading employers that the young people emerging from the expanded postwar school system did not have the skills required for the late twentieth-century economy. In 1976 Labour prime minister James Callaghan caused a sensation by making a speech on education—prime ministers back then did not do that kind of thing—in which he argued,

> In today's world higher standards are demanded than were required yesterday and there are simply fewer jobs for people without skill. Therefore we demand more from our schools than did our grandparents. . . . There is a challenge to us all in these days and a challenge in education is to examine its priorities and to secure as high efficiency as possible by the skilful use of existing resources.[3]

Callaghan's government was swept away not long afterward, buried by its failure to tackle either the economic plight of the country or the unions, which were perceived to be a major cause of the problems. Margaret Thatcher became prime minister and, having spent her first few years in office on macroeconomics and bringing the unions to heel, turned her mind to education. In 1985 her government published the "Better Schools" white paper and a year later passed legislation that required each school to have a governing body that would include elected parent representatives.[4] The real revolution, however, came two years later with the 1988 Education Reform Act, which introduced a national curriculum, a national assessment system, devolution of budgets to schools, open enrollment, the possibility for schools to opt out of the local authority and receive funding direct from central government, and the break-up of the huge Inner London Education Authority. Meanwhile, in parallel legislation, the negotiating committees, in which local government, central government, and unions had settled teachers' pay and conditions, were abolished and replaced by a government-appointed independent review body. Almost at a stroke, the postwar settlement had been swept away.

The new arrangements took several years, and significant trial and error, to implement, but the key features to emerge were as follows. First, schools received devolved budgets on a formula basis, with student numbers determining at least 80 percent of the formula. Second, open enrollment increased choice, and the money followed the student. Third, the school's governing body became responsible for allocation of the budget, including appointment of the principal, who, in turn, appointed the staff. The school principals thus became much more powerful. Fourth, the central government became more powerful, too, imposing a national curriculum and national tests and setting out the terms of the devolution of budgets. In time (from the mid-1990s), the national government also strengthened the central grip on teacher preparation and school inspection. It also required that the results of national tests be published. Meanwhile, in a wider reform of local government finance, central government became by far the largest funder (around 80 percent) of local government services and, as we know, he who pays the piper calls the tune. Fifth, and finally, this left local government, which had been the leading influence in the postwar system, wondering what part it had to play in governing education. The U.K. Audit Commission captured this beautifully by choosing, as a title for its report on the subject, a phrase more widely applicable to postwar British history: *Losing an Empire.*[5]

If England and the United States provide an instructive contrast, it is because they have both sufficient similarity and illuminating differences of governance. The respective arrangements for education of the second half of the twentieth century were similar, after all: expand, leave it to the local district, focus on quantity, and do not prescribe curriculums. In the 1970s similar concerns arose: the need to control costs as the economy suffered, growing anxiety about performance, especially in relation to race in the United States, and a fear that the education system was failing to meet the needs of the future of the economy, captured symbolically in the warning in *A Nation at Risk* of "a rising tide of mediocrity,"[6] just two years before Thatcher's government published its similar report (with its less hyperbolic, more prosaic British title), "Better Schools."

The U.S. response, however, was very different from Margaret Thatcher's. The ideas were similar; indeed, it was in the 1980s that intensive exchange of ideas on education across the Atlantic began. The difference was in constitution and governance. Restricted by its Constitution, the U.S. federal government was far less powerful than its British equivalent. The states had confined themselves to a passive regulatory and funding role. Real power lay within the school districts, which were many in number, mostly small and, crucially, directly elected, not part of a wider local government arrangement, and often captured or heavily influenced by teachers unions, which in the United States had more influence than their English counterparts for several reasons. First, in any given jurisdiction there was only one union, whereas in England all six unions competed in every school building. (In fact this competition for members was the only pure market in English education at the time.) Second, the American teachers unions, partly because they were monopolies in each jurisdiction, charged much higher dues. Third, unions used that money to fund political campaigns both at state and at district level.

Thus while in England a powerful central government was able to recast the entire system in response to the crises of the 1970s and 1980s, in the United States this proved impossible. Instead, governance, like everything else, was locally contested, experiments came and went and, while some were very radical (vouchers in Milwaukee, for example), the impact of these experiments on the whole system was less.

This is not necessarily to say that England overall did a better job than the United States; the English approach created the possibility for central government to make huge mistakes (such as the first version of the national curriculum and national testing in 1989–92), and it also created a sense in the system that whenever a problem arose, instead of addressing it, everyone in the system should wait for central government to solve it. (As Margaret Thatcher's mentor Keith Joseph is reported to have said, "The first words a baby learns in this country are, 'What's the government going to do about it?'") Meanwhile, the American system depended on the courage and skill of local or state leaders for change, people such as Joel Klein, Michelle Rhee, and Paul Pastorek in recent times and Carl Cohn, Tom Payzant, and Governor James Hunt in the previous decade.

Three Paradigms

Against this historical backdrop, the Blair administration developed what Americans would call a theory of action about managing the major public services, especially health and education. Three paradigms of reform can be distinguished: quasi markets, devolution and transparency, and command and control, as figure 10-1 illustrates.

The most obvious approach to reforming public services is in figure 10-1 is command and control. Command and control involves the top-down implementation of a change the government wants to bring about. Examples in the Blair years include the approaches to literacy and numeracy in primary schools, between 1997 and 2001, and efforts to reduce waiting times in the National Health Service, from 2000 to 2004. It has become fashionable to criticize command and

Figure 10-1. *Making Sense of Large-Scale System Reform*

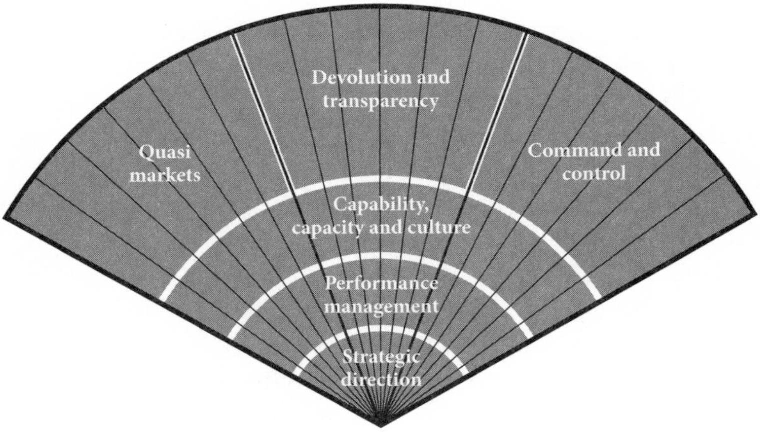

Source: Michael Barber, *Instruction to Deliver* (London: Methuen, 2007).

control, both because it is not popular with professionals, who, generally speaking, do not warm to being told what to do to by governments, and because, it is argued, it is unsustainable.

In fact, in some circumstances, command and control is the right approach to take—for example, where a service is failing or seriously underperforming, or where there is a high priority that is urgent. If a government chooses to adopt the approach in these circumstances, then crucially it is obliged to execute it excellently. It should go without saying that command and control done badly is disastrous. As it happens, in the cases of both literacy and numeracy and National Health Service wait times, the services were poor, the priority high, and—admittedly, with mistakes on the way—government did a very good job. As a result, in both cases, the services improved significantly in a short space of time. In fact, in the 2001 Progress in International Reading Literacy Study, England was ranked third in the world in literacy, and the 2007 Trends in International Mathematics and Science Study showed British ten-year-olds to be the most improved in the world over the previous decade or so.[7]

Although the approach is indeed unsustainable because of the energy and attention it requires at all levels in a service, the results it delivers can be and, in both examples quoted, have been, broadly sustained. As I argue elsewhere, command and control done well can rapidly shift a service from awful to adequate.[8] This is a major achievement, but not enough, because the public is not satisfied with adequate; the public wants "good" or "great."[9] But command and control cannot deliver good or great, for, as Joel Klein, the former chancellor of the New York City school system, puts it, "You cannot mandate greatness; it has to be unleashed."[10]

In seeking to do exactly that, Tony Blair, especially in relation to health and education, turned to the second paradigm, quasi markets. One could argue, in fact, that the command-and-control phase, while controversial, helped create the conditions for the introduction of the quasi-market phase. The argument for introducing marketlike pressures into public services is clear: people like choice. Additionally, competition drives productivity improvement in other sectors of the economy, so why not in the public services? Moreover, as Julian Le Grand argues, however committed the professionals are, "they can never have the degree of concern for users that users have for themselves."[11] The potential benefits for government of putting the user in the driver's seat include not just improved performance, satisfaction, and productivity but also the possibility that the system constantly improves itself and therefore no longer has to be driven ("flogged," as Blair would say) as it does under the command-and-control option. As Blair once put it, "Innovation should come from self-sustaining systems."[12]

The quasi-market system works well in many situations, but certain conditions have to be in place. Consumers of the service need to be able to exercise choice, as they can, for example, in aspects of health care and education. At least a degree of diversity of provision has to be available, for example, in relation to school ethos or specialism, and a range of different competing suppliers needs to emerge.

There are also dangers that need to be avoided. The greatest is that markets will militate against equity, though for most public services equity is a highly desirable outcome. It is for this reason, above all, that the quasi market is "quasi" and not pure. So in Blair's education and health markets, unlike a pure market, the price (of an operation or a school location, for example) is fixed by government rather than by the laws of supply and demand. Moreover, the evidence shows that if quasi markets are to promote equity, the government needs both to regulate more and intervene more than it would in a pure market. In the school reforms, for example, the British government continues to restrict selection by academic ability because the evidence shows that this harms equity. For the health quasi market, the government has provided advice and assistance to patients to enable those with low social capital or low incomes to exercise choice. Through this combination of market forces and regulation, designed to avoid the less desirable consequences of unfettered markets, the aim was to reap the benefits of a market in terms of innovation and productivity while enhancing equity and the other values that are central to public services.

The third paradigm is the combination of devolution and transparency. This is necessary because there are some services and some circumstances where neither command and control nor quasi markets are desirable. That is why Gordon Brown, in his speech to the Social Market Foundation in February 2003, emphasized the need for "non-market, non-command-and-control models of public service reform."[13] Where, for instance, individual choice does not apply, as for example in policing, prisons, or the court service, it is impossible to create quasi markets. The pioneer of devolution and transparency is the New York City police department, which devolved operational responsibility and resources to each precinct commander and then created transparency by publishing weekly crime data precinct by precinct. Precinct commanders were held to account for their performance by the chief of police.[14] The model, though, has wider application, and its influence can be seen in, for example, the reforms of the court service or police in the United Kingdom. As with quasi markets, it unleashes frontline managers to do the job and holds them to account for their performance. Also like quasi-market models, it allows for services to be contracted out. Thus a small number of privately run prisons or privately provided local education authority (LEA) services have been commissioned, resulting in a boost to the performance of the whole system. In other words, beneficial competitive pressure can be introduced even where individual choice does not apply.

I describe these three approaches as paradigms advisedly. They are theoretically different models. In practice, in any given service a combination of the three can be adopted. Thus, for example, in the school system in England, under Blair, failing schools were required to improve under pressure from government (command and control), parents exercised choice and funding followed their decisions (quasi markets), but funding was devolved to the school level, head teachers had extensive operational authority, and their results were published (devolution and transparency). Each of these elements is apparent in the Obama administration's Race to the Top campaign. The key is for those overseeing the reform of a system to be conscious of the paradigms and how they fit together in a specific reform, even if, as in the United States, the ground reality is often highly complex because of the separation of powers at every level and, in some cases, the imposition of court mandates.

This leads us to the three core functions at the base of the fan in figure 10-1. Whichever of the paradigms it chooses (or, if it so chooses, a combination of them), a government retains responsibility for these three major aspects of reform, which cannot be delegated. The first is the capacity, capability, and culture of the system—the quality of its human capital. For example, an individual hospital cannot ensure a continuing supply of good doctors or nurses for an entire country. Neither can it secure the hospital building program overall. Nor can it set the legal framework within which doctors practice, nor shape the overall relationship between that profession, the state, and society. Nor could any U.S. school district, other than, possibly, a very large one, perform these functions in a vacuum. For a public service, only a system-level government can do this, albeit in consultation with others.

The second function is managing the overall performance of the system. Although an individual hospital can be responsible for its own performance, it is not in a position to set the objectives of the system nor to decide how progress will be measured and what data will be published. Nor can it decide who intervenes (or when and how) when the performance of an individual hospital falls below an acceptable standard. Again, the same applies to a U.S. school district. Again, only a system-level government can decide these issues.

Third, in each public service and for the public services as a whole, a strategic direction is required: future trends need to be analyzed and understood; the various steps in a reform program need to be sequenced and their combined efforts understood; and the values that underpin the reform need to be stated and their impact secured. Again, only a system-level government can perform these functions.[15]

The critical question in relation to governance is whether those roles should be played, as in England, by a central or local government or, as in the United States, by federal, state, or district-level authority. Other countries also debate these central questions. Japan, for example, is keen to encourage greater school autonomy and reduce the influence of the center. In the Netherlands, with a strong tradition of school autonomy and quasi-market approaches, policymakers are rethinking the role of the center. For example, in the quasi-market paradigm, who should regulate? In the United Kingdom, government in Westminster is too remote—after all, for most parents, school choice is not a national market but a local one. By contrast, the local authorities are often too small, with the local possible choices often crossing local government boundaries. In the United States, similarly, districts are often too small to manage markets, and state governments often too remote.

The Blair Reforms and Education Governance

Tony Blair inherited an education system that, for all the value of the Conservative reforms, which he did not overturn, was underfunded and underperforming. He said famously that his three priorities were education, education, and education (apparently unaware at the time that he was echoing Lenin) and saw the improvement of the education system as a key element in unlocking individual opportunity and preparing Britain for a globalized world.

In the first Blair term we were unashamedly both centralist—strengthening the power of the Department for Education—and devolutionary—extending further the devolution of budgets and responsibilities to schools. In short, broadly we applied paradigms one and two.[16] The principle we applied to devolution to schools was "intervention in inverse proportion to success."[17]

Central government became more assertive about intervening in cases of failure, whether at the school or the local government level. We developed national strategies for literacy and numeracy in primary schools, which were implemented rapidly across the whole system and, though they were demonstrably effective in improving performance—indeed, Michael Fullan has described these strategies as the first successful whole-system reform[18]—they were also highly controversial because they involved a government-developed and government-imposed (though not technically mandated) pedagogy, including an emphasis on phonics in literacy teaching and mental arithmetic in mathematics.

Regular inspections of schools, on a four-year cycle, by an inspectorate that was independent of government ensured strong accountability, and where schools were found to be seriously underperforming, the local education authority was required to intervene. Schools' results in tests of English, mathematics, and science at ages seven, eleven, and fourteen and national exams at sixteen and eighteen were made public.

Although schools undoubtedly felt the pressure of this sharp accountability during this phase, they also benefited from greater budgetary devolution and greater opportunity to take control of their own destiny, including, for example, managing their own buildings and site.[19] This trend culminated in a decision in 2004 to ring-fence school expenditure (so that local government could not divert any of the education budget to other noneducation purposes) and devolve three-year budgets to schools. Inevitably, the consequence for local government of this combination of centralization and devolution to schools was that it lost discretion. Paradoxically, though, for some LEAs the settlement of the first Blair term was a new clarity of role, which their leaders could exploit effectively—for example, they knew that if they were effective agents of central government in implementing the literacy and numeracy strategies, dealt effectively with underperforming or failing schools, and offered increasingly autonomous schools the advice and support they needed to improve continuously, they could not only succeed but be seen by local people to succeed. As one successful local government leader put it to me after a couple of years, "A year ago we thought you were mad and it wouldn't work. Now we think it will work but we still think you're mad."[20]

In this phase, an LEA that ran an effective operation and built good relations with its schools was able to sustain a significant organization and connect the school system not just to the rest of local government but to local business and other key stakeholders. Well-led LEAs such as the one in Birmingham, led by Tim Brighouse, made tremendous progress.

Toward the end of the first term there were two further significant developments in relation to LEAs. In 1998 we legislated to give central government the power to intervene in ineffective LEAs and require them to outsource their services to private sector companies. It was one of those pieces of legislation that informed opinion assumed we would never use, but from mid-1999 we began to do so, ultimately intervening in about a dozen or so (out of 150) LEAs. Although each of these interventions was acutely challenging to see through effectively, later independent evaluations suggested that their impact was overwhelmingly positive, not just in improving the results in these places but in encouraging other authorities to focus on improvement too. The key in each case—a major communications challenge—was to make clear that the intervention was an attack not on the local schools, still less the local community, but on the inefficient LEA bureaucracy.

The second major development was a policy called Excellence in Cities, which offered extra resources to cities that faced particularly challenging education circumstances on condition they developed a good, evidence-based plan and demonstrated that the schools in their area supported that plan.[21] It was, perhaps, a prototype of the Obama administration's Race to the Top program. It too turned out to be positive and was followed in the second term by even more impactful policy in a handful of major cities, starting with the London Challenge, in which leaders of successful schools took responsibility for improving underperforming schools across the city, regardless of local authority boundaries.

Thus though the first Blair term demanded much of the LEAs, it also provided huge opportunities to demonstrate effectiveness and to prove that the local education authorities could play a decisive role in improving student outcomes. Much of this continued in the second term, but during the second term two developments with ultimately negative consequences (in my view) and one with ultimately positive consequences changed the role of the LEA again and paved the way for the changes made in 2010 and 2011 by the new Conservative-led coalition government.

First, in the early years of the second term the government responded to the reaction from the field against top-down pressure and sharp accountability. Ministers began to soften the emphasis on literacy and numeracy in primary schools and to suggest that the recommended pedagogy be implemented flexibly. They lost the will to intervene further in LEAs—there were no interventions after the end of the first Blair term. The intervention policy was difficult technically and controversial politically, and, influenced by other cabinet ministers who were hearing complaints from political allies at the local authority level, successive education ministers from 2001 onward opted for a quieter life, in spite of the clear benefits that interventions had brought. The result was that the sharp emphasis on student outcomes that had driven up performance in the first term was substantially weakened, as the Programme for International Student Assessment report and other international comparisons revealed in the ensuing years. Nevertheless, local education authorities continued to turn round poorly performing schools highly effectively—this had become a routine.

The second development was a decision taken in the middle of the second term to reorganize all local authority services, on the basis of experiments in Hertfordshire and Brighton, and to merge children's social services, including adoption, child abuse, and looked-after children, with education authorities.[22] The legislation had a strong rationale—seamless provision for families and children. When Gordon Brown became prime minister he extended the logic and reorganized central government, too, merging the Department for Education with parts of the Health Department to create the Department for Children, Schools, and Families.

However, as the new approach was implemented between 2004 and 2010 the theoretical benefits were overwhelmed by the practical implications. The leaders of LEAs (now called children's services departments) inevitably spent more time on their new responsibilities than on the school performance agenda. Moreover, as is well known in the United States, one tragic complex case of child abuse can be so overwhelming in media and organizational terms that there is no energy left for the rest of the work. A particularly devastating case in Haringey, north London—which dominated the headlines for months—left all the directors of children's services watching their backs on child abuse, and the inevitable result was that they took their eyes off the continuing school performance challenge.

An underlying bureaucratic logic drove this shift of focus, too. Because schools were largely autonomous, whereas children's services remained a central part of the overall local authority, directors of children's services had a bureaucratic incentive to focus their attention on the latter. Conversations I had in 2008 with directors of children's services provided strong evidence for this point. Outstanding directors, such as Alan Wood in Hackney, could, of course, succeed across the entire agenda, but the mere mortals who held most of these posts found it challenging and sometimes overwhelming. The job had become too large and too diffuse.

The third development was an increasing focus, starting in the Blair second term and largely driven from 10 Downing Street itself by Blair's highly influential education adviser, Andrew Adonis (who in the third term became an education minister), on the creation of "academies"—independent state secondary schools funded directly by central government and analogous to charter schools in the United States. This was perceived, in part, as a new attack on the competence of local authority—as indeed, to a degree, it was—and therefore some resisted the policy. Others, however, saw it as a new opportunity to deal systematically with school failure—as opposed to dealing with failing schools one at a time—and in the long run the local authorities that took this approach proved highly successful. They realized that whole-system success resulted less from control and regulation than from enabling schools to succeed and building partnerships with schools, communities, and businesses.

When the coalition government took power in May 2010, it took the logic of these developments seriously. Members reinvigorated the focus on student outcomes, began to reverse the integration of children's services and education authorities (starting with the national department, which became the Department for Education again), and extended the academies policy. Moreover, in their determination to bring the country's budget deficit under control, they hammered spending on local government "bureaucracy" and—relatively speaking—protected the budgets that had been devolved to schools.

Their task now is to answer Michael Fullan's challenge in his influential recent paper, "Choosing the Wrong Drivers for Whole System Reform," namely, "When you decentralize, how do you get 'systemness'?"[23] The logic of the new government's approach is to have an effective central department and thousands of autonomous schools that over time will self-organize into chains or networks. The local government or middle-tier role in relation to schools would then be minimal. One sees this most clearly in the 2011 policy on underperforming schools, under which schools below a minimum acceptable performance standard, instead of, as in the past, facing intervention from the LEA, will now be forced to join one of the emerging successful chains of schools. In American terms it is as if a failing school were required to join, for example, the KIPP (Knowledge Is Power Program) chain rather than be "turned round" by the district. The emerging chains in England, unlike KIPP in the United States, have shown a willingness to take on this challenge. There is huge and radical potential here, but when (in Fullan's word) "systemness" is required, as it will be, for example, when England's new standards require implementation across 24,000 schools from 2012 onward, the implementation challenge will be acute. It remains to be seen how it will be handled.

Lessons from Around the World

The strongest lesson about governance from around the world is that there is no simple model that can be said to be demonstrably the best.[24] Finland, Singapore, and Ontario, for example, are all highly successful but have very different approaches to education governance. Finland has a highly consensual approach to policymaking and leaves extensive discretion to its excellent teachers, while Singapore is highly centralized with decisions, albeit based on consultation, shaped and made in the highly competent ministry by, generally speaking, excellent officials and ministers. Equally, there is a great deal of similarity, globally speaking, between governance in, for example, Massachusetts and Delaware, but the difference in performance is substantial.

It makes sense to conclude from this that focusing purely on the problem of governance will not solve the problem of performance; it does not make sense to conclude that, therefore, governance does not matter, particularly if existing governance arrangements have the effect of putting barriers in the way of high performance. Moreover, there is an emerging body of evidence on what some of the characteristics of good governance might be, in terms of effectiveness.

One other note of caution needs to be sounded. The governance of an education system is not just a matter of performance or effectiveness; it is also representative of the values of a society and has a part in its democracy (or lack of it). The challenge in a country such as the United States is to combine its democratic values and local traditions with an approach to education governance that promotes effectiveness—or at least does not get in the way. Countries with highly diverse populations, such as the United States and the United Kingdom, have to secure legitimacy for education policy by being demonstrably inclusive. As the world globalizes this is becoming a major challenge in many countries.

In the United States a model of governance designed in the nineteenth century (and highly effective in enabling the United States to lead the world in public education as it spread across the prairies) has been tested and found wanting in the past thirty years or so. Partly as a result of the need to raise a significant proportion of the funding at district level, the United States is one of only four countries in the 2009 Programme for International Student Assessment sample of more than sixty countries to spend more per student in wealthy areas than in poor areas.[25] Moreover, the relative weakness of both the state and federal governments has meant that the districts have been the driving force of change—and many of them have not seen fit to devolve all that much power and responsibility to the school. So although systems such as Victoria (Australia), New Zealand, and Chile have moved with the trends toward a strong center and substantial school-level autonomy, much of the United States has not. Only in large, well-led urban areas such as New York City, Chicago, and New Orleans have these local constraints been overcome. Finally, because U.S. school boards are directly elected, often on very low turnouts, they have been vulnerable to effective lobbying by minority interests, some of which have defended the status quo highly effectively, even when it is demonstrably indefensible. In some cases, this has even resulted in a teachers union takeover of a school board, occasionally followed by a frankly incestuous contract negotiation.

Each of these barriers to high performance stands in the way of systemwide success in the United States, each often overcome only by courageous leadership of a rare kind. Many other systems are favored by governance arrangements in which the odds are not so heavily stacked against universal success. In the recently published McKinsey study we find, somewhat counter to our expectations, that of key players in our sample of more than twenty much-improved school systems on five different continents, almost all pointed to the vital role of what we call the mediating layer.[26]

It appears that whole-system reform requires improvements both in schools and at the national government level. Unexpectedly, the research shows us that the mediating layers of governance (such as local education authorities in England) also play a crucial role in system reform. Mediating layers perform an interpretative role and provide a channel through which reforms can flow from central government to schools, teachers, and individual pupils.

In most cases, system reform initially focuses on the center of the system and schools. Once a system requires the ability to pass reforms from the center to schools, the mediating layer receives more focus. Where a mediating layer already exists it is often refined and bolstered. Where one does not, it is created to improve the coordination of the reform.

Although mediating layers across the world have a common purpose, they can work in several ways. The approach to the mediating layer varies, but the McKinsey Global Education Practice study shows that the role they play in system improvement is similar.

[Mediating layers] typically have three tasks:
—Providing targeted support to schools.
—Acting as a buffer between the center and the schools while interpreting and communicating the improvement objectives, in order to manage any resistance to change.
—Enhancing the collaborative exchange between schools, by facilitating the sharing of best practices between schools, helping them to support each other, share learning, and standardize practices.[27]

In the study, we did not explore in depth the governance model in each country, but what is clear is that a mediating layer of some kind has a vital role to play. The findings are consistent with and build on the concept of tri-level reform that Michael Fullan and I have written about in the past.[28] In another McKinsey study on school leadership in eight systems around the world, a similar, somewhat extended agenda for the middle or mediating tier emerges.[29]

Increasingly, evidence from case studies shows that the mediating layer, and those leaders within it, can have a powerful impact on learning outcomes. "One major study showed that an effective district superintendent could influence average student achievement by up to 10 percentile points."[30] Kenneth J. Meier reports a similar finding about the effect of management on student outcomes.[31] A strong mediating layer can provide support to leaders in underperforming schools, improve access to and implementation of professional development, help communicate best practice laterally across a system, help to identify future leaders for the system itself, and improve the accountability of the system.

These roles can be considered to be what Fullan calls the collective capacity–building functions of a middle tier.[32] Assuming that this international evidence is significant—and there is reason from Programme for International Student Assessment results and elsewhere to believe that it is—the current coalition government in Britain is left facing three problems with which it is still wrestling.

First, in relation to national strategy, the middle tier can be an asset or a liability. If it is lined up strategically with state or national government, it can be a catalyst; also, sometimes, it can be a shock absorber, adapting and tuning well-intended national programs so that they work in local circumstances; but, as those who have led American state education systems know, this middle tier can also be a bureaucratic barrier that stands in the way of coherent reform.

In England this tends to be how local authorities have been perceived, fairly or not. Squeezed between assertive central government and principals who want autonomy, especially control of budgets, the local authorities have been unable to fully establish the case for their existence. The present government is intent on weakening them further, not least through spending cuts of 20 to 30 percent (as part national deficit reduction) while protecting the school budgets. On the assumption that local authorities are a bureaucratic barrier, this makes sense, but in a country the size of England the roles of catalyst and shock absorber still need to be played. It is, after all, unthinkable that the system can operate at all as a system with more than 23,000 schools and a remote central government in Westminster. So the question arises, if local authorities will not play these vital roles, who will? Crucially, though this question is an immediate practical challenge for Britain's coalition government, it is likely to arise, albeit in a variety of forms, in many jurisdictions around the world. The British government has already in effect decided that the answer to these questions is not the local authority. However, for practical reasons it cannot be either the central government (especially given that the government espouses a strong attachment to localism) or the individual schools.

The emerging answer seems to be a range of branded chains of schools or more informal networks. So far, however, these involve only a minority of schools, and even then not all of them have the capacity to deliver what is required. Whether a radical transformation of the middle tier, such as Joel Klein pulled off spectacularly in New York City, would be possible across an entire country remains doubtful. The government may choose to take the view, for both philosophical and practical reasons, that this problem should be left for the system to sort out for itself. If so, it will be a radical experiment, and the risk to the government's ability to deliver high performance in the short and medium term will be substantial.

Second, where a major national change is made, such as the introduction of new school standards, central government will need agents across the country to secure universal implementation. In the past, the local authorities would have been expected to perform this function. Who will perform it in the new world?

Third, for a government committed to parental choice and encouraging a diversity of supply, there is another important question, too. Who will regulate the emerging quasi market? As noted above, there is clearly not one national market; equally, though, many of the local authorities, especially in urban areas, are too small to manage real markets, even if they have the inclination. Each of these questions has a number of potential answers, but for the moment they remain unanswered.

An Effective Delivery Chain

If reform is to deliver real improvement in students' results, then the intent at the system level has to translate into impact at the classroom level. For this to happen there has to be a delivery chain, defined as follows:

> A delivery chain is the set of *system actors* (people or organizations), and the relationships between them, through which a given system activity will be implemented. A delivery chain has one question at its core: Starting from the policy intent of a leader in your system and ending with the front-line behaviors and practices that this policy is designed to influence, how— and through whom—does a system activity actually happen?[33]

As the extensive literature on the subject makes clear, networks may have an increasingly important role to play, but they do not preclude the need for a re-forming government to work out systematically how its decisions will translate into changes in the classroom and therefore changes in student outcomes. In England and the United States there are significant and contrasting challenges ahead at all levels in ensuring that this delivery chain is effective.

School Level

In many school districts in the United States there is a trend toward devolving budgets and responsibility to school level, but in governance terms the picture remains unclear. Is the principal an agent of the district or a leader of the school? If the interests of the school and the district are in conflict, which side is the principal on? In England this is perfectly clear—the school's governing body represents the principal and only in extreme circumstances of financial irregu-larity or severe underperformance can the local authority intervene. In this sense, every school in England is more like a charter school, with its autonomy defined in law. However, even in the case of charter schools the picture is not entirely clear in some American states. Who can intervene in cases of failure, and in what way, given that these are schools fully funded by public dollars?

The situation appears clearer in England, where the governing body is clearly responsible for the school, but governing bodies raise questions, too. Often quite

large—ten to twenty people, depending on the size of the school—governing
bodies can be cautious, often opting for the safe appointment when the head-
ship (principalship) is open and too often acting as cheerleaders for the school,
regardless of its performance, rather than holding it to account. (A similar effect
is seen in the boards of some charter school authorizers who have failed to can-
cel charters when performance is poor.) In some of the worst cases of failure—
as in the celebrated case of Hackney Downs School in the mid-1990s—the
governing body, far from solving the problem, simply compounds it. So England, too, faces a school governance challenge, but given that governors across
the country make up a volunteer army of around 300,000 people,[34] governments are understandably cautious about embarking on radical reform.

District and Local Authority Level

The governance challenge at the district level in the United States is fully laid bare
elsewhere in this book. The complexities of the problems at the local authority
level have been a major theme of this chapter. The fact remains, though, that
unless these problems are solved on both sides of the Atlantic, successful whole-
system reform, as has been seen, for example, in Ontario and Alberta, will remain
out of reach. Again, for the United States, possible solutions are to be found elsewhere in this book. For the government in England there are the pressing questions mentioned in the previous section.

Another role required at this level has less to do with the practicalities of the
delivery chain than with identity and sense of place. An effective district or local
authority leader, such as Arne Duncan in Chicago or Tim Brighouse in Birmingham, can mobilize an entire city—its voluntary sector, its businesses, and its
citizens—behind a reform. Whatever arrangements are made also need to enable
and encourage the emergence of this kind of leadership.

Interestingly, mayors, in different ways, may be the key on both sides of the
Atlantic. In the United States the experiments with mayoral control in Boston,
New York, Chicago, and the District of Columbia, while by no means perfect,
seem on the whole to have increased the chances of improving urban education.
In England, cities have mostly not had directly elected mayors and have depended
on city councils, but under Blair, and now encouraged by David Cameron, a
number of cities are opting for directly elected mayors who may become leaders
of education reform, as Jules Pipe has become in Hackney and Sir Robin Wales
aspires to become in Newham.

State or System Level

At the system level—which I take to be the state in the United States—there are
contrasting challenges in the United States and England. In the United States,
most states, encouraged by the Race to the Top competition whether or not they

were eventual winners, have been seeking to build their capacity as leaders of whole-system reform and to do so at a time when the fiscal constraints are substantial. The signs are that state leaders such as Paul Pastorek (and, one hopes, his successor) in Louisiana, Mitchell Chester in Massachusetts, and Terry Holliday in Kentucky are demonstrating that this can be done through a combination of effective coalition building within and beyond the education system and a sharp understanding of the increasingly strong evidence base on how systems can and do deliver results. Certainly in the work of the U.S. Education Delivery Institute with state education leaders, there is strong evidence that this is the case.

In England, by contrast, there is no shortage of influence at the central-government level, and the coalition government's secretary of state for education, Michael Gove, is undoubtedly one of its stars. Here the challenge is to deliver across such a large system, with major issues about its middle tier, at a time of fiscal constraint. There is also a philosophical tension—which the Blair administration also faced in its later years—between wanting to devolve power and creating markets, on one hand, and discovering that the only way to do so is an increasing assertion of central authority, on the other. The similarity in the United States and England is that from different starting points, both need to develop an effective understanding among politicians and top bureaucrats of the growing global evidence on what works in whole-system reform, and both need to strengthen the capacity of the delivery chain to function effectively.

The Federal Level

The federal level in the United States is quite different from central government in England and seems, under the Obama administration, to have found a means of powerfully influencing the whole country, albeit with a small percentage of the overall education expenditure. Historically, the U.S. Department of Education has used a combination of financial, regulatory, and legal levers in attempting to improve performance. Although some individual programs have had a positive effect, the overall impact has been slight.

The No Child Left Behind legislation significantly enhanced federal influence, but implementation proved challenging, and the overall impact of the law, though in my view positive because it put equity firmly at the center of the national debate, was uneven, and some of the contradictions inherent in the law eventually came home to roost. Arne Duncan, having learned from the previous decade and carefully listened to the field, has wielded more influence than his predecessors by combining a number of factors:

—a coherent core narrative of what the United States needs in education reform (the Four Assurances)[35]

—powerful use of financial incentives through Race to the Top

—state authority to create coalitions to develop common standards and assessments

—careful building and maintenance of a broad political coalition, at a time when this is far from easy to do[36]

—steady reform of the way the U.S. Department of Education operates, not least through the establishment of the Implementation and Support Unit, which engages in dialogue with states about whole-system reform rather than in a range of separate dialogues about compliance with individual grants

It remains to be seen what impact Duncan's approach will have on the performance of the system, but the signs are promising. This approach exemplifies a key message about governance in any system at any time; namely, that though the form of governance clearly matters, in the end the quality of leadership is decisive.

The best periods of education reform in England's recent past (1987–89; 1997–2001) have coincided with credible, courageous political leadership (Kenneth Baker in the former period, David Blunkett in the latter) sustained for three or more years. Too often, though, changes of minister resulted in quite arbitrary changes in policy or priority, with a result that momentum was lost. This, too, is a clear message in the recent McKinsey study, which shows that, in the world's most improved systems, both political and technical leaders tend to have tenures of more than five years.[37]

Both England and the United States have seen plenty of bold education reform experiments in the past two or three decades, both have made some progress but not enough, and both have significant governance challenges to surmount in the immediate future. Both have shown much more interest in quasi-market solutions to their education problems than most countries, which adds to the complexity of the challenge and, though the evidence for this approach remains limited globally because there is relatively little to go on, consideration of quasi markets may turn out to be a significant strength in the long term.

What both countries need most is a coherent agenda, pursued over several years with courageous leadership, a commitment to building collective capacity at every level in the delivery chain, and, above all, sustained implementation. As Tony Blair said recently, "Effective delivery—it's *the* issue around the world these days."[38]

Notes

1. Hansard, "Education: A Framework for Expansion," Cmnd 5174, London, December 1972 (http://hansard.millbanksystems.com/lords/1973/mar/29/education-a-framework-for-expansion).

2. Sir Robin Auld, *The William Tyndale Junior and Infants' School: Report of the Public Inquiry* (London: Inner London Education Authority, 1992).

3. Prime Minister James Callaghan, "Towards a National Debate," speech, Ruskin College, Oxford University (Times Educational Supplement, October 22, 1976).

4. See Hansard, "Better Schools," 1985 (http://hansard.millbanksystems.com/written_answers/1985/apr/23/better-schools-1).

5. Audit Commission for Local Authorities in England and Wales, *Losing an Empire, Finding a Role: The LEA of the Future* (London: Her Majesty's Stationery Office, 1989).

6. See National Commission for Excellence in Education, *A Nation at Risk: The Imperative for Educational Reform*, 1983 (http://datacenter.spps.org/uploads/SOTW_A_Nation_at_Risk_1983.pdf).

7. I. V. S. Mullis and others, *PIRLS 2001 International Report: IEA's Study of Reading Literacy Achievement in Primary Schools* (Chestnut Hill, Mass.: TIMSS and PIRLS International Study Center, Boston College, 2003); I. V. S. Mullis and others, *TIMSS 2007 International Report* (Chestnut Hill, Mass.: TIMSS and PIRLS International Study Center, Boston College, 2008).

8. Unpublished speech by the author to Blair's cabinet, December 2004.

9. Jim Collins, *Good to Great: Why Some Companies Make the Leap . . . and Others Don't* (New York: HarperBusiness, 2001).

10. Quoted in Michael Barber, *Instruction to Deliver* (London: Methuen Publishing, 2008).

11. Julian Le Grand, *Motivation, Agency, and Public Policy: Of Knights and Knaves, Pawns and Queens* (Oxford University Press, 2003).

12. Tony Blair, prime minister of the United Kingdom, personal communication with author, April 2006.

13. Gordon Brown, *A Modern Agenda for Prosperity and Social Reform* (London: Social Market Foundation, 2004).

14. Barber, *Instruction to Deliver*, pp. 338–39.

15. Ibid., pp. 336–40.

16. During Blair's first term I was chief adviser to the secretary of state for education on school standards.

17. Department for Education and Employment, "White Paper: Excellence in Schools" (London, 1997), Executive Summary.

18. Michael Fullan, *Choosing the Wrong Drivers for Whole System Reform* (Melbourne: Centre for Strategic Education, 2002).

19. National Audit Office, *Report by the Comptroller and Auditor General, Improving Poorly Performing Schools in England* (London: Her Majesty's Stationery Office, 2006).

20. Barber, *Instruction to Deliver*, p. 35.

21. Department for Education and Employment, *Excellence in Cities* (London, 1999).

22. This is the official English designation for children who are being "looked after" by local authorities, either in foster care or residential care. For further discussion of the difficulty in managing networks, see chapter 16 in this volume.

23. Fullan, *Choosing the Wrong Drivers for Whole System Reform*.

24. For further discussion of international comparisons, see chapter 12 in this volume.

25. Organization for Economic Cooperation and Development, *PISA 2009 Results* (Paris, 2010).

26. Mona Mourshed, Chinezi Chijioke, and Michael Barber, *How the World's Most Improved School Systems Keep Getting Better* (London: McKinsey, 2010).

27. Ibid.

28. Michael Barber and Michael Fullan, *Tri-Level Development: It's the System* (Bethesda, Md.: Editorial Projects in Education, 2005).

29. Sir Michael Barber, Fenton Whelan, and Michael Clark, *Capturing the Leadership Premium: How the World's Top School Systems Are Building Leadership Capacity for the Future* (London: McKinsey, 2010).

30. Ibid.

31. Chapter 16, this volume.

32. Michael Fullan, *All Systems Go: The Change Imperative for Whole System Reform* (London: Corwin, 2010).

33. Michael Barber, with Andy Moffit and Paul Kihn, *Deliverology 101: A Field Guide for Educational Leaders* (Thousand Oaks, Calif.: Corwin, 2011), p. 67.

34. A classic example, incidentally, of Edmund Burke's "little platoon." Edmund Burke, *Reflections on the Revolution in France* (Oxford University Press, 1993).

35. In 2009 the U.S. Department of Education defined four uses of education funds disbursed under the American Recovery and Reinvestment Act: adopting rigorous standards, building effective data systems for tracking student and teacher performance, improving teaching quality, and tackling school failure.

36. In February 2011 I had the opportunity to meet with Arne Duncan and the new cohort of governors elected in November 2010. What was striking was the degree of respect for him and his agenda from Republicans and Democrats alike.

37. Mourshed, Chijioke, and Barber, *How the World's Most Improved School Systems Keep Getting Better*.

38. Tony Blair, personal communication with author, London, July 2011.

SANDRA VERGARI

11

Education Governance in
Canada and the United States

How best to assign policy responsibilities in federal systems has long been a concern of scholars and public administrators. In the United States, Alice M. Rivlin has proposed scaling back the federal role in many policy areas and establishing clear divisions of responsibility between the federal government and the states.[1] She argues that such reforms would enhance government effectiveness and accountability. Rivlin recommends that most federal education programs be abolished and that education be treated as a state responsibility.

Education reform involves experimentation, adaptation to local conditions, accountability from officials on the scene, and community engagement, tasks Rivlin thinks can best be performed by state and local governments: "Education in America will not improve significantly until states and communities decide they want better schools. . . . An 'education president' can help focus media attention . . . but he risks diluting state and local responsibility by implying that Washington can actually produce change."[2]

The division of power for education that Rivlin proposes is much in evidence in Canada, where education governance is dominated by the provinces and territories and where there is a weaker accountability regime for public education. Although the federal role in the United States is much stronger, federal power over education is constrained by the states.

This chapter neither rejects nor endorses Rivlin's recommendation that U.S. education policy be assigned to the states. Rather, the findings support Rivlin's observation that subnational commitment to education reform is essential for meaningful improvement. Even with a relatively activist federal role, as long as

This chapter is adapted from Sandra Vergari, "Safeguarding Federalism in Education Policy in Canada and the United States," *Publius: The Journal of Federalism* 40, no. 3 (2010): 534–57.

states are reluctant to reform education, significant improvement is unlikely. In both countries, there have been some voluntary efforts among subnational units to establish national education policy. However, the success of national policy also depends on subnational commitment.

This comparative analysis of Canada and the United States identifies similarities and differences in federal and subnational powers and practices in education policy.[3] The study posed two questions for both countries: What does the balance of government power over public education look like and why? and What governance factors have encouraged and inhibited the development of national education policies (as distinguished from federal government mandates) and why?

Public Education in Canada and the United States

Differences in education governance between Canada and the United States can be partly explained by different histories, values, and social structures.[4] "In Canada, governments have historically been seen as positive and important instruments for achieving social purposes," notes Benjamin Levin, whereas in the United States, there is a strong belief in individual rights and suspicion of government.[5] Equity and accountability are touted as values in both countries. Equity is manifested in school finance and education outcomes more strongly in Canada, while there is a stronger accountability regime in the United States. Table 11-1 presents a summary comparison of education in the two countries.

The Canadian Constitution states that "in and for each Province the Legislature may exclusively make Laws in relation to Education."[6] This provision inhibits broad, direct federal activism in education policy. In contrast, education is not mentioned in the U.S. Constitution, and the U.S. federal government is involved directly in education policy.

Education has often been treated as a "reserved power" of the states under the Tenth Amendment. Until the 1980s, states devolved much of their power over education to local school districts. The tradition of local control of education owes largely to political practice rather than federal or state constitutional requirements.[7] However, as James E. Ryan observes, "The Tenth Amendment is no match for Congress's spending powers."[8] The U.S. Constitution grants Congress power to tax and spend to provide for the "general welfare" and to make all laws "necessary and proper" to do so. These clauses permit broad federal power over education policy.

Federal activism in education has, at times, engendered passionate opposition and charges from state and local interests that the activity is unconstitutional. However, "so long as states accept federal funding, Congress can do pretty much as it pleases with education—even establish a national curriculum and a national exam—without running afoul of the Constitution."[9] States are free to reject many federal education policies if they also decline corresponding funding, but states typically value federal dollars.

Unlike other industrialized federations, Canada does not have a federal department of education. Indeed, there is relatively little federal involvement in elementary and secondary education. The federal government is responsible for and funds the education of Aboriginal students living on reserve, military personnel and dependents, and federal prison inmates. The federal government also supports language education and education research. There is limited additional involvement with education. For example, two federal departments, Industry Canada and Human Resources and Skills Development Canada, have partnered with the provinces and territories to advance information and communications technology in education.

Each province or territory has its own ministry or department of education headed by a minister who is typically a member of the provincial or territorial legislature. The education ministers formed the Council of Ministers of Education, Canada (CMEC) in 1967. They aimed to "provide a forum" in which to "discuss matters of mutual interest, undertake educational initiatives cooperatively, and represent the interests of the provinces and territories with national educational organizations, the federal government, foreign governments, and international organizations."[10]

Most public funding for elementary and secondary education in Canada is derived from the province or territory or through a mix of provincial and local funds. In 2008 the provincial and territorial governments provided 74 percent of school board revenues, 25 percent came from local funds, and less than 1 percent came directly from the federal government. There are jurisdictional differences: the local contribution is less than 1 percent in five provinces or territories and ranges from 25 percent to 44 percent in four provinces.[11]

In the United States, the states have stepped up their role in school finance since the 1970s, but the aggregate local portion is much larger than in Canada. In 2009–10, 12.5 percent of elementary and secondary public education revenue came from the U.S. federal government, 43.5 percent from the states, and 44 percent from local sources. These aggregate data mask state differences.[12]

In 2007–08, per pupil spending in the provinces ranged from C$9,260 in Prince Edward Island to C$11,086 in Alberta. Expenditures ranged from C$10,007 to C$10,996 across seven provinces. The provincial average was C$10,678. When compared with school finance in the Canadian provinces, there is greater subnational funding disparity in the United States. In 2009–10 per pupil spending ranged from $6,064 in Utah to $18,618 in New York. The national average was $10,615.[13]

The Canadian federal government administers a general equalization funding program (that is, the funds are not earmarked for any policy area). This general

Table 11-1. *Elementary and Secondary Education in Canada and the United States*

	Canada	United States
Government type	Parliamentary democracy	Representative democracy
Subnational power	Constitution assigns provinces exclusive power to adopt most education laws	No mention of education in Constitution; tradition of local control; states now primary policymakers
Federal government role	Very limited; no federal department of education	Federal laws, regulations, and funds; federal department of education
Official languages	English, French; federal-provincial cooperation on official languages in education protocol	None; English official language in thirty-one states; federal and state policy to assist English-language learners
School finance	Provinces and territories provide majority of funds; local funds make up 20–44 percent of total in five jurisdictions; relatively strong equity	State and local funding; substantial inequity across jurisdictions; about 10 percent of public school funds provided by federal government
Students, schools, educators	20 charter schools (Alberta); 15,000 traditional public schools; 5.1 million students; 7 percent of students in private or home school; 338,000 public school educators	5,000 charter schools; 93,900 traditional public schools; 49.5 million students, 10 percent of students in private school; 3 percent homeschooled; 3.3 million public school teachers

Curriculum standards	Established by province or territory	Established by states
Standardized testing	Provincial or territorial tests; Pan-Canadian Assessment Program managed by Council of Ministers of Education Canada	State testing required as condition of federal aid; states determine own tests; National Assessment of Educational Progress managed by federal government
Public report cards on school performance	Mandated by some provinces; relatively weak culture of performance reporting	Mandated by state laws and a condition of federal aid; moderately strong culture of performance reporting
Education outcomes	Favorable international ranking; student achievement gaps; relatively high equity	Lagging international ranking; substantial student achievement gaps
Entities facilitating policy learning and development of national policy	Council of Ministers of Education Canada, Canadian Education Association, The Learning Partnership, regional consortiums, Statistics Canada	National Governors Association, Council of Chief State School Officers, Achieve, Education Commission of the States, regional consortiums, federal government

Sources: Alberta Ministry of Education, "Number of Alberta Schools and Authorities," 2012 (http://education.alberta.ca/apps/statistics/numberofschools.asp); Riley Brockington, "Summary Public School Indicators for Canada, the Provinces and Territories, 2005/2006 to 2009/2010" (Ottawa: Statistics Canada, 2011); Canadian Education Association, *Public Education in Canada: Facts, Trends and Attitudes, 2007* (Toronto, 2007); National Center for Education Statistics, *The Condition of Education 2012* (U.S. Department of Education, 2012). See Statistics Canada, "School Boards' Revenue and Expenditures, by Province and Territory," 2010 (www.statcan.gc.ca/tables-tableaux/sum-som/l01/cst01/govt 43d-eng.htm); U.S. English, "U.S. States with Official English Laws," n.d. (www.us-english.org/view/13).

funding emphasizes equity and does not exist in the United States. Payments are provided to six less prosperous provinces to enable them to provide public services that are reasonably comparable to those in other provinces at reasonably comparable tax rates. Provinces may spend the unconditional funds according to their respective priorities, including education. Through this program, the federal government indirectly enhances subnational capacity to adopt similar education policies.[14]

In the United States, the Elementary and Secondary Education Act of 1965 was the beginning of an enduring and expanding federal role focused on improving the education of disadvantaged students. Nonetheless, significant financial inequities across school districts remain.[15]

Both Canada and the United States have education policies focused on language issues. The Canadian Charter of Rights and Freedoms protects the minority language rights of French-speaking students living outside Quebec and English-speaking students living in Quebec. In the United States, there are federal and state policies aimed at assisting English-language learners.

Following passage of the Official Languages Act in 1969, the Canadian provinces and territories have cooperated with the federal government to fund education in English and French. The first Official Languages in Education Protocol, developed in 1983, is significant partly because "it was the first political document to establish pan-Canadian guidelines for federal-provincial cooperation in an area of provincial/territorial jurisdiction."[16] Under the current protocol, the federal government contributes C$1.034 billion over four years to language instruction costs incurred by the provinces and territories, according to separate agreements negotiated with each jurisdiction.[17]

National Policy and Federal Policy

It is useful to consider education governance in federations in terms of factors that promote similar policies across subnational units. Such policies can be called *national policies*, whether they materialize through adoption of similar policies by individual subnational units or through coordinated commitments to adopt uniform policy. In contrast, *federal policies* are formal laws and regulations of the federal government.[18]

What factors encourage the development of national policy? First, when subnational units in a country face common problems and pressures, they may be motivated to adopt common policy responses. One of the foremost challenges confronting education policymakers in both Canada and the United States is economic competition. President Barack Obama has warned that "countries that out-educate us today will out-compete us tomorrow."[19] Global and subnational competition create political pressure for the provinces and territories and states to ensure a well-educated labor pool. Concerns about not falling behind other jurisdictions motivate subnational policymakers to consider similar education policies. Although workforce preparation and economic concerns feature prominently in the discourse in both countries, a well-educated citizenry is also essential to ensuring a thriving democracy.

Second, learning about policies of other governments encourages the development of national policy. Policy ideas float across jurisdictional borders. Subnational governments may be sensitive to one another's actions because they offer examples of how to satisfy voter preferences or serve as benchmarks for citizen assessment of government.[20] Moreover, policymakers may choose to judge policy ideas according to logical criteria other than partisanship.[21]

Entities that contribute to policy learning and development of national education policy in Canada include the Council of Ministers of Education Canada, the Canadian Education Association, and regional curriculum consortiums. All thirteen provinces and territories are members of the CMEC, which calls itself "the national voice for education in Canada."[22] The council fulfills some functions that are comparable to those of the U.S. Department of Education. For example, it administers the Official Languages Program, manages a pan-Canadian student assessment program, develops and reports on education indicators, partners with Statistics Canada to provide education statistics, provides a clearinghouse to facilitate recognition of foreign education and occupational credentials, and consults and acts on issues such as Aboriginal education.

Founded in 1891, the Canadian Education Association sponsors forums, undertakes research, and publishes education resources. Sustaining members are the thirteen provincial and territorial ministries of education and the federal Human Resources and Skills Development Canada.[23]

The Canadian Council on Learning was established in 2004 with a focus on lifelong learning. It was funded through a five-year, C$85 million grant from Human Resources and Skills Development Canada. In 2009 the department announced that the grant would not be renewed, and the council ceased operations in early 2012. According to a Human Resources and Skills Development official, Canada needs better learning information "that is more aligned with labour market demand and takes into account international competitive challenges."[24]

Entities that contribute to policy learning and coordination in the United States include the National Governors Association (founded in 1908 and composed of the nation's governors, it receives state and federal funding), the Council of Chief State School Officers (founded in 1927, members are heads of state departments of education), Achieve (an education reform entity founded in 1996 by governors and corporate leaders), and the Education Commission of the States (an interstate compact created in 1965 that receives state and federal funding).

Preferences for efficiency and economies of scale are a third set of factors encouraging national policy. Subnational governments with similar capacity challenges and policy priorities face incentives to cooperate. They can avoid wasteful duplicative efforts and use resources more efficiently by working together on education policy.

In both Canada and the United States, there have been regional efforts at cooperation on standards, assessments, and other education initiatives. The Western and Northern Canadian Protocol for Collaboration in Education was established in 1993 by the education ministers of Manitoba, Saskatchewan, Alberta, British Columbia, Yukon, and Northwest Territories. Nunavut joined in 2000. The Atlantic Provinces Education Foundation was established in 1995 by the education ministers of Newfoundland and Labrador, Nova Scotia, New Brunswick, and Prince Edward Island. Regional efforts in the United States include the New England Common Assessment Program, a four-state partnership formed in 2002, and the New England Secondary School Consortium, a five-state partnership formed in 2008.[25]

Subnational jurisdictions in Canada and the United States share similarities in required school-year length and years of instruction. During the past two decades in both countries, there have been centralizing trends such as reduced numbers of school boards and expanded provincial or state roles in regulating curriculum, mandating assessments, financing public education, monitoring local compliance, and intervening in local school governance.[26] At least five Canadian provinces have taken steps to remove elected school board trustees from office or place them under provincial supervision. In the United States, about twenty-nine states have laws permitting state takeovers of school districts.[27]

In Canada, movement toward some national education policy has occurred in the absence of federal activism. In the United States, presidents and education department secretaries use the bully pulpit, and the federal government can exercise its power of the purse, to support national education policy. There are also political, economic, and cultural factors that inhibit development of national policy.

Dynamics that encourage national policy are tempered by subnational preferences for policy autonomy. Subnational governments use a variety of means to protect their interests and "safeguard federalism."[28] State resistance to federal education policy and implementation approaches that are less than faithful to policy purposes are salient examples of safeguarding federalism in the United States. In Canada, despite subnational adoption of some similar education policies, some jurisdictions prefer policy diversity on curriculum and accountability matters. Participation in regional curriculum consortium initiatives is voluntary, and Saskatchewan and Yukon have modified centrally defined curriculums in accordance with local values and priorities.[29]

Under federalism, "it can be difficult to create, monitor, and enforce cooperative agreements, especially when states have incentives to shirk, as they often do, and unless there is a body with real enforcement powers."[30] In Canada, the CMEC fulfills a national coordinating role but lacks enforcement power. The ability of the U.S. federal government to enforce its education policies is hampered by politics, capacity limitations, and concerns that withholding funds punishes children who need the aid. Thus states and school districts can often alter the original shape of federal education policy.[31]

Academic Standards, Assessment, and Accountability

Canadian provinces and territories are responsible for their respective curriculums and assessments. There are some similar expectations across the nation. Indeed, "Curriculum standardization enables government authorities to claim that their core curriculum is of equal quality to that offered elsewhere in Canada."[32] Provinces with "quite ideologically divergent governments" have adopted more-rigorous curriculums and more testing.[33] As noted earlier, common challenges and priorities, policy learning, the logical merit of ideas, and efficiency concerns encourage national policymaking.

Despite centralizing trends, jurisdictional differences remain. In some areas of Canada, there is an enduring, significant commitment to local educational freedom that is rooted in variations in culture, economics, geography, history, language, and politics. The Northwest Territories and Saskatchewan, for example, have long supported a flexible curriculum that accommodates local concerns.[34]

The number and types of provincial and territorial assessments in Canada have increased substantially over the past two decades, and there are similarities across jurisdictions. Assessments typically begin at the third or fourth grade and focus on literacy and mathematics; these tend to be formative in nature. There is also a trend of eleventh- or twelfth-grade summative tests linked to student grades and eligibility to graduate. However, key differences exist in the scoring, reporting, and use of assessment data.[35]

The "true character" of an accountability regime resides in "what is measured and reported, by whom, to whom, and the consequences."[36] Each province and territory has stated that at least one of its assessment programs is aimed at enhancing system accountability. However, the programs do not prescribe negative consequences for teachers, schools, or districts based on assessment data.[37] The accountability function occurs primarily through public reporting of assessment data. The exposure of educators to public scrutiny "is the only acute consequence that can potentially affect their professional identity and work."[38]

Newspapers often publish assessment data, and the independent Fraser Institute publishes school report cards for five provinces and Yukon. However, the impact of interest group efforts to promote school accountability is weaker than in the United States, and "the development of performance reporting by schools and districts has not progressed very far in Canada."[39] Instead, there is a "system reliance on local teachers, principals, and district personnel" for accountability.[40]

Despite some similar curriculum and assessment policies, the provinces and territories have displayed a preference for diverse accountability policies. The stronger accountability regime in the United States owes partly to the stronger federal role.

The No Child Left Behind Act of 2001 (NCLB) was adopted by a huge bipartisan congressional majority and signed into law by President George W. Bush in January 2002. U.S. intergovernmental relations experts ranked the act the third most important intergovernmental event of the decade (1995–2005).[41] Under the NCLB, schools must make "adequate yearly progress" in reading and math, as determined by state testing, or face escalating regulations designed to assist students and restructure lagging schools.

The NCLB requires states and school districts to disseminate annual report cards on the performance of schools and student subgroups. School report card data are placed on government websites and published in newspapers. Under the act, states must assess students annually in reading and math in grades three through eight and once in high school. States must also test students in science at least once in grades three through five, six through nine, and ten through twelve. However, states determine their own tests and proficiency standards.

Although the NCLB does not meet the legal definition of a federal mandate, its potential financial impacts on nonfederal parties are similar to laws and rules identified as mandates.[42] The extent to which the act is a burden on states is, of course, a matter of interpretation. Before the NCLB, states had already been developing standards and tests. About half of the states require high school exit exams for graduation, and many use the same exam to fulfill NCLB high school testing requirements.[43]

Many states have exploited the act's loopholes. The NCLB allows states to determine how large a student subgroup must be in order to have student test scores count toward adequate-yearly-progress calculations for a school; some states set low thresholds, others set high ones. States also use disparate methods of calculating graduation rates and student proficiency under the NCLB. More than 50 percent of the states have ignored NCLB guidelines for identifying persistently dangerous schools, and of the nation's 97,000 public schools in 2006–07, states identified only forty-six as persistently dangerous.[44]

States have also safeguarded federalism by engaging in aggressive lobbying of the federal government. State challenges to the NCLB provide leverage in securing bargains and waivers from the federal government.[45] Thus the NCLB shifted from being a policy "imposed equally on all jurisdictions to one dependent on what each state could negotiate with the federal administration."[46] By July 2012, the Obama administration had used its waiver authority to release more than half of the states from NCLB requirements.

Assessment Policies

Both countries have nationwide assessment programs. The Pan-Canadian Assessment Program is developed, administered, and funded by the Council of Ministers of Education Canada. The National Assessment of Educational Progress, also known as "the nation's report card," is sponsored by the U.S. government.

Every three years, the CMEC administers the Pan-Canadian Assessment Program to random samples of schools and eighth-grade students. Each time it is administered, the test emphasizes a different major subject (reading, math, or science), coinciding with the major subject of the Programme for International Student Assessment (PISA), administered two years later. Initiated by the member nations of the Organization for Economic Cooperation and Development, PISA provides international indicators of reading, math, and science knowledge and skills among fifteen-year-olds.

The Pan-Canadian Assessment Program data are calculated at both pan-Canadian and jurisdictional levels. In a context of diverse curriculums and assessments across Canada, the program provides a uniform measure of students' proficiency in reading, math, and science at particular ages. Provinces and territories can validate their respective assessment data against Pan-Canadian Assessment Program and PISA data.

Like the Pan-Canadian Assessment Program, the National Assessment of Educational Progress (NAEP) permits states to compare their performance with state and national data. The assessment tests in reading and math occur at least every two years in grades four and eight; grade twelve tests in the two subjects are administered at least every four years.

In contrast to the Pan-Canadian Assessment Program, a national education policy, the NAEP is a federal policy, and subnational participation is not purely voluntary. States that receive federal Title I education funds are required to participate in the NAEP reading and math tests in grades four and eight. School districts receiving Title I funds and selected for the NAEP must also participate in the four tests.[47]

Since states determine their own exams and proficiency standards, the standards cannot be compared directly. The National Center for Education Statistics analyzes states' proficiency standards against those of the NAEP for grades four and eight in reading and mathematics. The analysis compares state minimum scores for determining student proficiency with the cut points for NAEP Proficient and Basic categories.[48] The study finds substantial variation in the achievement levels that states set for proficient performance. For example, thirty-one states had proficiency standards for fourth-grade reading that were lower than the NAEP Basic level; eight states had proficiency standards for eighth-grade math that were lower than the NAEP Basic standard. The analysis reveals that "students of similar academic skills, but residing in different states, are being evaluated against different standards for proficiency."[49]

National Education Policy Initiatives

In 2008 the CMEC released *Learn Canada 2020*, a framework for improving education. The joint declaration of the education ministers avows commitment to "four pillars of lifelong learning" and objectives in eight "key activity areas." The ministers declare that the initiative "reflects the educational priorities of Canadians" and pledge to report annually on progress.[50] *Learn Canada 2020* also includes assertions about jurisdiction over education, economic issues, and federal obligations to Aboriginals:

> Education in Canada is under the exclusive jurisdiction of provinces and territories. Ministers recognize the national interest in ensuring a healthy economy and the importance of education for economic development. . . . Canada's education ministers will engage [all who] must participate in meeting these goals . . . [including] key stakeholders . . . and other orders of government. We will encourage the federal government to meet its constitutional obligation and work with provinces and territories to provide equality of opportunity for Aboriginal peoples.[51]

The CMEC and the regional curriculum consortiums facilitate voluntary policy coordination among the provinces and territories, thereby enhancing prospects for national education policy. Below, I discuss two American state-led efforts.

In 2005 the fifty state governors signed *Graduation Counts: A Compact on State High School Graduation Data*. The compact embodied several commitments, including a pledge to use a common, four-year, cohort graduation rate formula. In mid-2008 state commitment to timely implementation of the compact was lacking. Only sixteen states reported that they used the compact formula to calculate graduation rates. Five states planned to implement the compact later in 2008, eight states in 2009, nine in 2010, six in 2011, and one in 2012. Five states had no concrete plans to use the formula.[52] Daria L. Hall, of the Education Trust, an entity focused on improving education for disadvantaged students, called this state of affairs "a real problem" and lamented, "This is a commitment that the governors made, and we now see the states walking away from that commitment."[53] As predicted by Hall, however, state reluctance to uphold the compact would soon be moot.

In October 2008 the federal government stepped in with new NCLB rules requiring a uniform method of calculating graduation rates. States must now calculate the percentage of students who graduate within four years of entering high school, akin to the formula governors had agreed on in 2005. States may seek federal approval to use extended-year graduation rates that consider students who obtain a regular diploma within more than four years. However, such rates must be reported publicly and separately from the four-year rate. States are required to hold school districts accountable for graduating the vast majority of students in four years.

The Common Core State Standards Initiative is led by the Council of Chief State School Officers and the National Governors Association, with support from education and business entities. Initiative documents assert that there is "a growing belief" among leaders in state government, education, and business that disparate state standards no longer make sense, given increasing student mobility and global competition. The initiative is intended to "allow students equal access to an excellent education regardless of where they live."[54] By July 2012, all but a handful of states had adopted the Common Core state standards.

Federal efforts to promote national standards during the George H. W. Bush and Bill Clinton administrations encountered formidable political resistance. The Obama administration supports the initiative and has provided federal funds to encourage implementation.[55]

Equity and Education Outcomes

Does the stronger federal role in the United States lead to more equitable education outcomes? A comprehensive examination of education outcomes is beyond the scope of this chapter, but the data reveal both differences between and similar challenges in Canada and the United States.

Among the fifty-seven countries or education systems participating in the 2006 Programme for International Student Assessment, Canadian students were outperformed only by those in Hong Kong and Finland on the combined science scale. Among the sixty-five jurisdictions participating in PISA 2009, four outperformed Canada on the combined reading scale.[56] Although there are significant provincial differences in PISA performance, Canada stands out favorably owing to high performance and high equity across socioeconomic groups.[57]

In contrast to Canada, the United States was outperformed on science literacy by twenty-two other PISA 2006 participating entities, and links between scores and student background were relatively high. On the 2009 PISA, fifteen jurisdictions had higher average scores than the United States on the combined reading scale. Seventeen percent of the variation in U.S. student performance on the test is explained by socioeconomic factors compared with 9 percent in Canada.[58]

The national graduation rate in Canada was 78 percent in 2009–10. The U.S. graduation rate for 2008–09 was 76 percent. Graduation rates across Canada ranged from 87 percent in New Brunswick to 38 percent in Nunavut. Manitoba and the three territories were the only jurisdictions with rates below 70 percent. In the United States, 2008–09 state graduation rates ranged from 91 percent in Wisconsin to 56 percent in Nevada. Rates were below 70 percent in seven states and the District of Columbia.[59]

Graduation rates in both countries vary across demographics. In Canada, the graduation rate in 2008 was 83 percent for females and 75 percent for males. The U.S. female and male rates in 2009 were 76 and 70 percent, respectively. Among Aboriginal Canadians aged twenty to twenty-four living on reserve in 2006, high school completion rates ranged from 28 percent in Manitoba to 59 percent in Yukon; rates for Aboriginals off reserve ranged from 45 percent in the Northwest Territories to 85 percent in New Brunswick. In the United States, 2009 graduation rates for Native Americans, blacks, and Hispanics were 53, 59, and 63 percent, respectively; rates for whites and Asians were 79 and 81 percent, respectively.[60]

There are also achievement gaps between students attending English-language and French-language schools in Canada. Gaps are also seen in graduation rates of English-language learners in the United States, which lag state and national averages.[61]

Challenges of Multilevel Governance

As a diverse industrialized federation without a federal department of education and with relatively favorable education outcomes, Canada offers an important case for analysts of education governance. The Council of Ministers of Education Canada fulfills a coordinating role in education policy and performs some tasks that are comparable to those of a federal department of education. However, a huge difference is that CMEC lacks enforcement authority.

Although there are few federal elementary and secondary education policies in Canada, the CMEC and the regional curriculum consortiums can promote development of national education policy. Rather than having policies imposed on subnational units by a federal government, the education ministers must reach consensus and implement initiatives voluntarily. Should an initiative turn out to be problematic, they have no one to blame but themselves.

On the other hand, a federal government can facilitate implementation of policies that are politically and technically challenging yet in the national interest. The federal government can also advance equity in education with policies designed to be implemented uniformly across subnational units. When subnational officials face stakeholder complaints about a federal policy, they can conveniently deflect blame to the federal government (even though such officials may quietly support all or part of the policy). Intergovernmental complexity in the United States may make it more difficult for citizens to hold education policymakers accountable.

Multilevel governance presents "immense challenges for citizens seeking accountability, clarity, responsiveness and transparency."[62] The lack of a strong federal role in education in Canada suggests a less complex and therefore potentially more accountable education policy arena than in the United States. However, education accountability systems are generally weaker in Canada, and accessing timely, detailed information on education policy and outcomes is easier in the United States. The stronger formal accountability regime in the United States derives in part from federal education policy.

The United States is an intriguing case for analysis owing to the dynamic nature of education policy and the intergovernmental relations resulting from federal and state activism. The federal government has been increasingly active in trying to promote several uniform objectives that are believed by many to be in the national interest. However, the federal government lacks political and technical capacity to implement its education policies and must rely on state cooperation. For their part, the states have shown varying levels of interest in equity and excellence and, as a whole, have worked to safeguard federalism.

Many states were reluctant to implement the Graduation Counts compact in a timely manner. In the end, the federal government used its spending power to require a policy that matched many elements of the compact. The federal government "borrowed strength" and used existing state policymaking as leverage to advance a uniform policy.[63] This federal action is apparently yielding intended results. By April 2012, the District of Columbia and forty-three states had publicly released graduation data in accordance with the 2008 regulations.[64] In contrast, if a policy commitment of the CMEC is not ultimately upheld by each province and territory, the Canadian federal government does not have standing to impose the policy.

The Common Core State Standards Initiative is a substantially broader, more complex effort than the relatively straightforward matter of calculating graduation rates. Given state reluctance to implement Graduation Counts until the federal government took action, it is reasonable to question the extent to which the states will engage in robust implementation of Common Core standards, particularly if federal financial incentives related to the initiative are reduced or eliminated.

Having only thirteen provinces and territories in Canada means that education leaders may be able to meet face-to-face regularly.[65] This factor may facilitate consensus building and development of national policy. However, the cases of Graduation Counts and the Common Core State Standards Initiative suggest that some consensus on education policy may be possible even among a greater number of diverse states, owing to common challenges and priorities, policy learning, and the efficiency benefits of cooperation.

Conclusion

Although Canada and the United States are both industrialized federations, there are significant differences between the two in the limits on federal power over elementary and secondary education. In Canada, the constitution and political practice preclude a strong, direct federal role in education governance. In the United States, the federal government is constrained in enforcing its education policies partly because one of its main powers, the ability to withhold funds, may deny aid to children. Federal policy success depends on state cooperation, and states have worked to safeguard federalism. In both countries, subnational governments enjoy the bulk of power over education. As emphasized by Alice Rivlin, genuine education reform can occur only when subnational governments decide that they want better schools.[66]

This chapter also demonstrates the usefulness of distinguishing between federal policy and national policy. Global economic competition, political pressure for subnational units to rank well against one another, policy learning, the appeal of policy ideas based on logic rather than partisanship, and efficiency concerns are incentives for subnational governments to develop national education policies.

There have been efforts to adopt national education policies in both Canada and the United States. In both countries, the federal government can play a supporting role in national policymaking. Through its general equalization program, the Canadian federal government contributes indirectly to subnational capacity to adopt national education policy.[67] In the United States, the federal government can facilitate national policymaking by supporting state-led efforts such as the New England Common Assessment Program and the Common Core State Standards Initiative.

Federal policy appears to have greater potential for success than national policy because of federal resources and enforcement authority. However, there are explicit constitutional constraints on federal power over education in Canada, and political and technical constraints in both countries. Subnational governments in both countries actively safeguard federalism and protect their autonomy. Thus subnational commitment is essential for the success of both national and federal education policy.

Notes

1. Alice M. Rivlin, *Reviving the American Dream: The Economy, the States, and the Federal Government* (Brookings Press, 1992). While working for President Clinton, Rivlin "did

come to realize that the political obstacles to devolution were daunting" (e-mail communication with author, September 10, 2009). Rivlin still favors "dividing the job." See Alice M. Rivlin, "Rethinking Federalism for More Effective Governance," *Publius: The Journal of Federalism* 42, no. 3 (2012): 387–400.

2. Rivlin, *Reviving the American Dream*, p. 11.

3. "Subnational" refers to provinces, territories, and states. Local school districts fulfill important roles in both countries. The study does not address local issues or post-secondary education.

4. Charles Ungerleider and Ben Levin, "Accountability, Funding, and School Improvement in Canada," in *International Handbook of School Effectiveness and Improvement*, edited by Tony Townsend (New York: Springer, 2007), pp. 411–24.

5. Benjamin Levin, *Reforming Education: From Origins to Outcomes* (New York: RoutledgeFalmer, 2001), p. 32.

6. There is a constitutionally protected right to religious education for Roman Catholics and Protestants when either group is the minority in a community.

7. Richard Briffault, "The Local School District in American Law," in *Besieged: School Boards and the Future of American Politics*, edited by William G. Howell (Brookings Press, 2005), pp. 24–55; James E. Ryan, "The Tenth Amendment and Other Paper Tigers: The Legal Boundaries of Education Governance," in *Who's in Charge Here? The Tangled Web of School Governance and Policy*, edited by Noel Epstein (Brookings Press, 2004), pp. 42–74.

8. Ryan, "The Tenth Amendment," p. 42.

9. Ibid.

10. See Council of Ministers of Education, Canada, "Education in Canada: An Overview," n.d. (www.cmec.ca/299/Education-in-Canada-An-Overview/index.html).

11. See Statistics Canada, "School Boards' Revenue and Expenditures, by Province and Territory," 2010 (www.statcan.gc.ca/tables-tableaux/sum-som/l01/cst01/govt43d-eng.htm).

12. The local share is 58 percent in Connecticut and exceeds 50 percent in eleven other states; the state share exceeds 50 percent in seventeen states. U.S. Census Bureau, "Public Education Finances: 2010" (2012).

13. Per pupil spending was C$20,539 in Yukon, C$18,256 in Northwest Territories, and C$15,610 in Nunavut. Subnational variation is owing partly to different student population sizes and costs. See Statistics Canada, Table A.20.1: "Total Expenditures per Student in Public Elementary and Secondary Schools, Canada, Provinces and Territories, 2001/2002 to 2007/2008 (in Current Dollars)," 2010 (www.statcan.gc.ca/pub/81-595-m/2011095/tbl/tbla.20.1-eng.htm); Census Bureau, "Public Education Finances: 2010."

14. See Canada Department of Finance, "Equalization Program," 2011 (www.fin.gc.ca/fedprov/eqp-eng.asp); Jennifer Wallner, "Beyond National Standards: Reconciling Tension between Federalism and the Welfare State," *Publius: The Journal of Federalism* 40 (Fall 2010): 646–71.

15. See chapter 14 in this volume for further discussion.

16. Council of Ministers of Education, Canada, "Official Languages," n.d. (www.cmec.ca/154/Programs-and-Initiatives/Official-Languages/Overview/index.html).

17. Department of Canadian Heritage and Council of Ministers of Education, Canada, *Protocol for Agreements for Minority-Language Education and Second-Language Instruction*

2009-2010 to 2012-2013 between the Government of Canada and the Council of Ministers of Education, Canada (Ottawa: Government of Canada, 2009).

18. My definitions of *national* and *federal* are rooted in Elmore and Fuhrman's concept of "the national interest" and Fuhrman's description of national policy as "multistate" and distinct from federal policy. Richard F. Elmore and Susan Fuhrman, "The National Interest and the Federal Role in Education," *Publius: The Journal of Federalism* 20 (Summer 1990): 149–62; Susan H. Fuhrman, "Clinton's Education Policy and Intergovernmental Relations in the 1990s," *Publius: The Journal of Federalism* 24 (Summer 1994): 83–97.

19. Barack Obama, Remarks by the President on Race to the Top, Graham Road Elementary School, Falls Church, Virginia (White House Office of the Press Secretary, January 19, 2010) (www.whitehouse.gov/the-press-office/remarks-president-race-top-graham-road-elementary-school).

20. Kathryn Harrison, "Provincial Interdependence: Concepts and Theories," in *Racing to the Bottom? Provincial Interdependence in the Canadian Federation*, edited by Kathryn Harrison (University of British Columbia Press, 2006), pp. 1–23.

21. John W. Kingdon, *Agendas, Alternatives, and Public Policies,* 2nd ed. (New York: HarperCollins, 1995).

22. See Council of Ministers of Education, Canada, "Education in Canada: An Overview," n.d. (www.cmec.ca/299/Education-in-Canada-An-Overview/index.html).

23. Sustaining membership fees are the Canadian Education Association's largest single source of annual revenue. See Canadian Education Association, "About Us," 2009 (www.cea-ace.ca/about-us).

24. Jill Mahoney and Gloria Galloway, "Conservatives Stop Funding for Learning Organization," *Toronto Globe and Mail,* January 8, 2010, p. 1.

25. For analysis of the New England Common Assessment Program, see chapter 7 in this volume.

26. Sonia Ben Jaafar and Stephen Anderson, "Policy Trends and Tensions in Accountability for Educational Management and Services in Canada," *Alberta Journal of Educational Research* 53 (Summer 2007): 207–27; Bonnie C. Fusarelli and Bruce S. Cooper, eds., *The Rising State: How State Power Is Transforming Our Nation's Schools* (State University of New York Press, 2009); Dick Henley and Jon Young, "School Boards and Education Finance in Manitoba: The Politics of Equity, Access, and Local Autonomy," *Canadian Journal of Educational Administration and Policy* 72 (April 2008): 1–25; Benjamin Levin, *Governing Education* (University of Toronto Press, 2005).

27. Ungerleider and Levin, "Accountability, Funding, and School Improvement in Canada"; Todd Ziebarth, *State Takeovers and Reconstitutions* (Denver: Education Commission of the States, 2004).

28. John Nugent, *Safeguarding Federalism: How States Protect Their Interests in National Policymaking* (University of Oklahoma Press, 2009).

29. Ben Jaafar and Anderson, "Policy Trends and Tensions in Accountability."

30. Mark Carl Rom, "Policy Races in the American States," in *Racing to the Bottom? Provincial Interdependence in the Canadian Federation*, edited by Harrison, pp. 229–56, 233.

31. Christopher Cross, *Political Education: National Policy Comes of Age* (Teachers College Press, 2004); Susan H. Fuhrman, "Less Than Meets the Eye: Standards, Testing, and Fear of Federal Control," in *Who's in Charge Here? The Tangled Web of School Gov-*

ernance and Policy, edited by Noel Epstein (Brookings Press, 2004), pp. 131–63; Benjamin Michael Superfine, "The Politics of Accountability: The Rise and Fall of Goals 2000," *American Journal of Education* 112 (November 2005): 10–43; Sandra Vergari, "Federalism and Market-Based Education Policy: The Supplemental Educational Services Mandate," *American Journal of Education* 113 (February 2007): 311–39; Sandra Vergari, "The Limits of Federal Activism in Education Policy," *Educational Policy* 26 (January 2012): 15–34.

32. Ben Jaafar and Anderson, "Policy Trends and Tensions in Accountability," p. 212.

33. Ungerleider and Levin, "Accountability, Funding, and School Improvement in Canada," p. 421.

34. Ben Jaafar and Anderson, "Policy Trends and Tensions in Accountability"; Canadian Education Association, *Public Education in Canada: Facts, Trends, and Attitudes, 2007* (Toronto, 2007).

35. Don A. Klinger, Christopher DeLuca, and Tess Miller, "The Evolving Culture of Large-Scale Assessments in Canadian Education," *Canadian Journal of Educational Administration and Policy* 76 (June 2008): 1–34.

36. Ben Jaafar and Anderson, "Policy Trends and Tensions in Accountability," p. 224.

37. Klinger, DeLuca, and Miller, "The Evolving Culture of Large-Scale Assessments."

38. Louis Volante and Sonia Ben Jaafar, "Profiles of Educational Assessment Systems Worldwide: Educational Assessment in Canada," *Assessment in Education: Principles, Policy, andPractice* 15 (July 2008): 201–10, 207.

39. Ungerleider and Levin, "Accountability, Funding, and School Improvement in Canada," p. 420.

40. Ben Jaafar and Anderson, "Policy Trends and Tensions in Accountability," p. 225.

41. The federal welfare reform act of 1996 ranked first; the September 11, 2001, terrorist attacks ranked second. Carol Weissert, Carl W. Stenberg, and Richard L. Cole, "Continuity and Change: A Ranking of Key Issues Affecting U.S. Intergovernmental Relations (1995–2005)," *Publius: The Journal of Federalism* 39 (Fall 2009): 677–695.

42. U.S. General Accounting Office, *Unfunded Mandates: Analysis of Reform Act Coverage* (2004).

43. Forty-eight states had standards and tests in 2000. Patrick McGuinn, *No Child Left Behind and the Transformation of Federal Education Policy, 1965–2005* (University Press of Kansas, 2006); Center on Education Policy, *State High School Exit Exams: Working to Raise Test Scores* (Washington, 2007).

44. U.S. Department of Education, *An OIG Perspective on the Unsafe School Choice Option* (2007).

45. John Dinan, "The State of American Federalism, 2007–2008: Resurgent State Influence in the National Policy Process and Continued State Policy Innovation," *Publius: The Journal of Federalism* 38 (Summer 2008): 381–415; Bryan Shelly, "Rebels and Their Causes: State Resistance to No Child Left Behind," *Publius: The Journal of Federalism* 38 (Summer 2008): 444–68.

46. Kenneth Wong and Gail Sunderman, "Education Accountability as a Presidential Priority: No Child Left Behind and the Bush Presidency," *Publius: The Journal of Federalism* 37 (Summer 2007): 333–50, 345.

47. See National Center for Education Statistics, "National Assessment of Educational Progress (NAEP): Frequently Asked Questions," 2012 (http://nces.ed.gov/nationsreport card/faq.asp).

48. Proficient refers to "competency over challenging subject matter." Basic refers to "partial mastery of skills necessary for *Proficient* performance." National Center for Education Statistics, *Mapping State Proficiency Standards onto NAEP Scales: 2005–2007* (U.S. Department of Education, 2009), p. 5.

49. Ibid., p. 47.

50. The eight activity areas are literacy, Aboriginal education, postsecondary capacity, education for sustainable development, providing an effective voice nationally and internationally, official languages, assessment and system performance indicators, and nationally and internationally comparable data. Council of Ministers of Education Canada. *Learn Canada 2020* (Toronto, 2008), pp. 2–3.

51. Ibid.

52. The number of on-time graduates in a year would be divided by the number of first-time entering ninth graders four years earlier; the denominator could be adjusted for pupil transfers. Special education pupils and English-language learners could be assigned to cohorts permitting a longer graduation time frame. National Governors Association, *Graduation Counts: A Compact on State High School Graduation Data* (Washington, 2005); National Governors Association, *Implementing Graduation Counts: State Progress to Date, 2008* (Washington, 2008).

53. Quoted in Scott J. Cech, "States' Graduation-Rate Effort Inches Forward," *Education Week*, August 13, 2008, p. 8.

54. The initiative follows the American Diploma Project Network, a thirty-five-state effort to raise standards and align curriculums and assessments with the standards. National Governors Association and Council of Chief State School Officers, *Common Core State Standards Initiative: Frequently Asked Questions* (Washington, 2009), pp. 1, 4.

55. For additional discussion of the Common Core state standards, see chapter 7 in this volume.

56. Shanghai (first-time PISA participant), Korea, Finland, and Hong Kong.

57. Patrick Bussiere, Tamara Knighton, and Dianne Pennock, *Measuring Up: Canadian Results of the OECD PISA Study; The Performance of Canada's Youth in Science, Reading, and Mathematics 2006; First Results for Canadians Aged 15* (Ottawa: Statistics Canada, 2007); Tamara Knighton, Pierre Brochu, and Tomasz Gluszynski, *Measuring Up: Canadian Results of the OECD PISA Study; The Performance of Canada's Youth in Reading, Mathematics, and Science, 2009; First Results for Canadians Aged 15* (Ottawa: Statistics Canada, 2010).

58. Organization for Economic Cooperation and Development, *PISA 2006: Science Competencies for Tomorrow's World: OECD Briefing Note for the United States* (Paris, 2007); Organization for Economic Cooperation and Development, *Strong Performers and Successful Reformers in Education: Lessons from PISA for the United States* (Paris, 2011).

59. The Canadian rate is calculated by dividing the number of graduates by the average of the seventeen- and eighteen-year-old population. The U.S. "averaged freshman graduation rate" is the number of graduates divided by the estimated count of freshmen four years earlier. The freshman count is based on an average of the number of eighth graders five years earlier, ninth graders four years earlier, and tenth graders three years earlier. Riley Brockington, "Summary Public School Indicators for Canada, the Provinces and Territories, 2005/2006 to 2009/2010" (Ottawa: Statistics Canada, 2011); National Center for Education Statistics, *The Condition of Education, 2012* (U.S. Department of Education, 2012).

60. Statistics Canada, *Education Indicators in Canada: An International Perspective* (Ottawa, 2011); Editorial Projects in Education Research Center, "Graduation in the United States: Graduation Rates Rising," *Education Week*, June 7, 2012, p. 26; John Richards, *Closing the Aboriginal/non-Aboriginal Education Gaps* (Toronto: C.D. Howe Institute, 2008).

61. Francine Denomme and Ruth Childs, "Does Ontario Have an Achievement Gap? The Challenge of Comparing the Performance of Students in French- and English-Language Schools on National and International Assessments," *Canadian Journal of Educational Administration and Policy* 71 (March 2008): 1–24; Mary Ann Zehr, "Graduation Rates on ELLs a Mystery: Many States, Districts Don't Track Data," *Education Week*, September 8, 2009, pp. 1, 20–21.

62. Richard Simeon, "Federalism and Social Justice: Thinking Through the Tangle," in *Territory, Democracy, and Justice: Regionalism and Federalism in Western Democracies*, edited by Scott L. Greer (New York: Palgrave Macmillan, 2006), pp. 18–43, 40.

63. See Paul Manna, *School's In: Federalism and the National Education Agenda* (Georgetown University Press, 2006); Elmore and Fuhrman, "The National Interest and the Federal Role in Education."

64. "Title 1: Improving the Academic Achievement of the Disadvantaged; Final Rule," *Federal Register* 73 (October 29, 2008): 64435–513; Sterling C. Lloyd, "44 States Now Using the Same Grad.-Rate Formula," *Education Week*, June 7, 2012, p. 27.

65. Harrison, "Provincial Interdependence."

66. Rivlin, *Reviving the American Dream.*

67. Wallner, "Beyond National Standards."

MICHAEL MINTROM *and* RICHARD WALLEY

12 | *Education Governance in Comparative Perspective*

Political leaders, public intellectuals, and business elites have long recognized the importance of education for social cohesion, the transmission of social values, and economic advancement. This explains the widespread development in the nineteenth century of systems for universal public education and the efforts made worldwide in the twentieth century to emulate, expand, and enhance those systems. The present era shares with the past a relentless quest on the part of governments everywhere to ensure that education of suitable quality is made available to as many children and young people as possible. But the present era is also distinct.

It is now well understood that education is the fundamental driver of economic advancement.[1] Continuous economic advancement predicated on the market system, and the competition engendered by that system, has led to greater integration of local, regional, and national economies with global economic processes.[2] Intensification of economic competition has wiped out much of the stability and predictability that once characterized everyday life in economically advanced democracies. Winning back some of that stability and predictability has become a mandate for political leaders everywhere.

This chapter contrasts developments in education governance in the United States with those in several other countries. Our comparative study shows that distinctly different governance arrangements are equally capable of producing excellent results, as measured by student performance on standardized international tests. This finding is consistent with recent work by John Hattie.[3] Through meta-analyses of student outcome data, Hattie has shown that a variety of classroom-level practices have stronger impacts on student learning than differences in class size and other matters that broadly link to school governance. The evidence suggests that education governance can make a significant difference to student outcomes as long as it supports effective practices in schools and classrooms.

Ways of Thinking about and Comparing Governance

If we want to understand governance struggles in any area of public policy, it is crucial that we appreciate the ways that specific actors can effectively undermine, constrain, or veto decisions made by others.[4] In general, the greater the number of people who are given legitimacy to weigh in on decisions, the greater the number of veto points that any given decision must clear. Given the range of factors to be governed, and the scope of diversity even within jurisdictions, comparing education governance arrangements internationally is a complex undertaking, and we should be suspicious of simple conclusions.[5]

Table 12-1 illustrates the matrix of actors and decisions involved in education governance in New Zealand. Each cell can be thought of as a potential veto point, offering an opportunity for people to wrestle for control in decisionmaking. Actors may be involved in more than one decisionmaking process, and there is no inherent limit to the number of actors who can be involved in a given decision. *Finances* (column 5) may be managed by a parent committee, approved by a local board, and voted on by central government within an existing and possibly quite limiting legislative framework. Moreover, the decision categories are broad. *Curriculum* (column 1), for example, can have a range of meanings, from prescriptive programs of learning to broad frameworks with a great deal of teacher autonomy, sometimes alongside one another with students of different ages or with different subjects.

Additionally, it is a feature of education governance systems, particularly of many Anglo-Saxon systems, that dispersion of control varies across institutions within a jurisdiction. Long-established private schools and newer entities such as academies in the United Kingdom and charter schools in the United States enjoy a greater degree of autonomy than their rule-constrained counterparts. But the payment of fees or close engagement of parents in school decisionmaking changes the balance of what might be called "soft governance"—a degree of influence rather than control.

The nature and circumstance of the unit of comparison—the jurisdiction—has huge implications for thinking about governance. Whether a decision or control is delegated in legislation to a cabinet-level secretary of education or to a bureaucrat within a department of education has implications that are played out in the context of the constitutional arrangements of the jurisdiction itself. Personalities, finely attuned balances of power, and political horse-trading in spheres completely unrelated to education may have profound influences on the style of governance applied to education. Decisionmaking in these jurisdictional units tends to be driven more by individual idiosyncrasies that by structural commonalities. A comparison between a jurisdiction where school curriculum is set at a national level, such as in New Zealand, and one with more locally

Table 12-1. *Actors and Decisionmaking in Education Governance*[a]

Actor	Decision arena								
	(1)	*(2)*	*(3)*	*(4)*	*(5)*	*(6)*	*(7)*	*(8)*	*(9)*
Central government	x	x	x		x			x	
Local government									
Local governance entity (for example, school board)									
Local or central bureaucracy (for example, Ministry of Education)	x	x	x					x	x
School governance entity (for example, United Kingdom governors)	x	x		x	x	x	x	x	x
Principal and head teacher	x	x		x	x	x	x	x	x
School middle management									
Other specialist (for example, financial)									x
Parent		x		x	x	x	x	x	x
Teacher	x								
Student									
Other interested community party									
External specialist (for example, academic)									

a. Column headings are as follows: (1) curriculum; (2) standards and assessment; (3) enrollment; (4) recruitment; (5) finance; (6) operations; (7) management structure; (8) class size and structure; (9) property maintenance. The x represents situations in which different actors (rows) have some governing role over different key education decisions (column).

established curriculums, such as the United States, must take account of the fact that New Zealand, with a school-age population of around 750,000, is smaller than many of the local districts in the United States.

Culture—the finely attuned balance of social norms and expectations that places pressure on individuals and groups to behave in certain ways—plays an enormous part in the successful operation of education governance arrangements. The comparatively greater success of parent education governance in areas of high income or high socioeconomic status is but one indicator of this.[6] Reducing layers of government control of public schools and devolving them to the community or parent level can greatly reduce veto points and, hence, contestation of decisionmaking. It also holds the potential to address concerns about the uneven spread of managerial competencies throughout an education system. During the past two decades, we have seen mayors, state governors, and presidents seeking to achieve greater control over traditional forms of school governance, weakening the influence of actors closer to the schools themselves, such as superintendents and boards.[7]

This leads to a further challenge, the role of soft governance, such as efforts by parents to informally influence school practices by lobbying teachers and principals. In systems as complex as education, one anticipates a wide variety of individual circumstances. Relationships, personalities, incomes, locations, and general predispositions all come into complex play. Frustrating though it might be to those with an appetite for centralized control of schools, in reality a school-level decision on particular testing practices can be influenced by the principal's friendship with a key parent as much as by central-government policy. A simple and common circumstance is practice around enrollment choice. Typically, home location determines eligibility for attendance at a particular school across most jurisdictions. Property values in those areas reflect the ability to enroll a child in a favored school, and this will often in turn be advertised by realtors. Parents with the necessary wherewithal will make these decisions carefully, years in advance. This is a fascinating user-pays situation, where markets assign prices to education through intermediary products and provide some parents with a type of choice where none is supposed to exist. Similar behavior is seen in some parents involved with particular religious institutions to secure enrollments into faith schools.

Finland offers the least school choice of all jurisdictions under discussion. School places are assigned, and that is that. There is a process, however, whereby parents can apply to have the assignment changed, and around a quarter of parents do so. Fifty percent of Finnish principals report that other schools in their locality "compete" with them for students. So clearly some degree of choice (or de facto choice) exists in Finland, but the ability of parents to exercise that choice is limited. How does one characterize this level of choice? Soft governance is also seen in the decisionmaking process in New Zealand, as illustrated in table 12-1. Local government and regional governance entities do not exist in New Zealand. Every school is governed by its own board of trustees consisting of parents, teachers, students in secondary schools and other local luminaries, and the school principal. Ostensibly, the board of trustees runs all aspects of school operations, and the principal acts as a kind of chief executive officer and reports to the board. There is a strong theoretical and legislative underpinning to this arrangement. But real-life examples of differing arrangements abound. Common forms include instances where the principal has captured the board and runs a benign dictatorship with little meaningful parent input. In others, the board works in direct opposition to the principal in dysfunctional arrangements that tend eventually to be dissolved by central-government intervention. Thus local governance of schools tends to be characterized by levels of expertise, the strength of specific personalities, the historic level of board engagement in decisionmaking, and the availability of financial resources.

Contrasting Approaches to Education Governance and Student Performance

This chapter considers six jurisdictions in particular—Australia, Canada, Finland, Korea, New Zealand, and the United Kingdom—as they share broad comparability, in terms of reasonably well developed systems of universal public education (albeit with varying levels of private contribution). It is fundamentally more meaningful in terms of culture and concept to compare the United States with, for example, Australia or the United Kingdom than to Qatar. Nonetheless, one of the recurring themes here is that caution must be exercised in comparison and transposition of results and findings. Small differences play out in large ways.

In exploring the impact of governance on student outcomes internationally, we examined outcome data from the OECD's Programme of International Student Assessment (PISA). The overarching question that arises from this research, and other evidence, is whether the data demonstrate or imply a link between governance arrangements and student outcomes. The data from this program are relatively comprehensive for all comparator jurisdictions.[8] The Programme for International Student Assessment is a series of standardized tests in mathematics, reading, and science administered to fifteen-year-olds in a wide range of jurisdictions. It was first administered in 2000, and four assessments have taken place, the most recent being in 2009. Figures 12-1, 12-2, and 12-3 show mean country scores for our six comparator jurisdictions and the two controls in reading, mathematics, and science from 2000 through 2009.

The figures have two notable features. First, because the means themselves have small standard errors (usually somewhere between two and five points) differences are both substantively and statistically significant. Second, all our jurisdictions appear to perform reasonably well, though the United States and the United Kingdom drop a little below the OECD mean in some years and subjects. With the possible exception of the science and mathematics scores for the United States (figures 12-2 and 12-3), none of these jurisdictions performs beneath the OECD mean, at least in this study. There is no evidence of a crisis in student outcomes. Nonetheless, if keeping ahead of the rest of the world in education matters for economic competitiveness—and evidence increasingly suggests that it does—then there is good reason to avoid complacency and to look for lessons from other jurisdictions that are producing equivalent, or slightly better, education outcomes.

The jurisdictions under study seem to fall into three distinct groups. The United States and United Kingdom hover around the OECD mean in most years and scores, although the United Kingdom appears to have suffered a serious degradation in performance between 2000 and 2006 (no data are available for the United Kingdom in 2003). A mid-high-performance group of jurisdictions, com-

Figure 12-1. *Time Series of PISA Results across Seven Countries and the OECD, Reading, 2000–09*

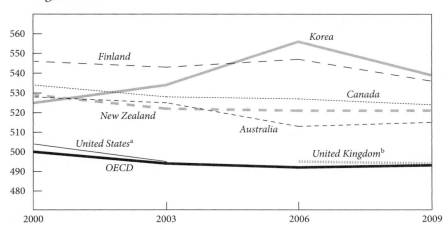

Source: Data from the Programme for International Student Assessment, 2000, 2003, 2006, and 2009 (Paris: OECD).
a. No data for United States for 2006; score equals 500 for 2009.
b. No data for United Kingdom for 2003; score equals 523 in 2000.

prising Australia, Canada, and New Zealand, appears relatively stable, although they fall slightly over time in reading and math. Finally, both Finland and Korea are notable for their consistently high but slightly unstable scores over time.

One factor that seems to merit consideration is the congruence across the three sets of results. It is not the case, for example, that students from Finland seem to be tremendously good at science but suffer in terms of literacy. They appear to be equally good at everything. Equally, the dip and then rise of U.S. performance is common across all three sets of data.[9] There are two possible conclusions to be drawn here. First, something exogenous—about the administration of the test, for example—produces such consistent results across areas that do not need to be consistent. But PISA is a carefully designed study with a large sample size (countries need to assess at least 4,000 students to participate). The other possible conclusion is that there is, indeed, something common about the learning experience of many students participating in the study. Possibly, the education system—and the governance settings of that system—are factors that exert a broad and diffuse influence.

We undertook further efforts to compare PISA data to quantified measures of governance. We considered reading, mathematics, and science scores against three quantified governance measures from PISA 2009: an index of school responsibility for resource allocation; an indicator of school choice, as measured by the percentage of principals who reported that one or more schools in the local area competed for students; and an index of school responsibility for curriculum and

Figure 12-2. *Time Series of PISA Results across Seven Countries and the OECD, Mathematics, 2000–09*

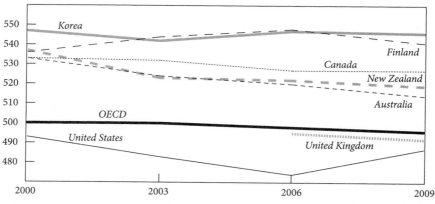

Source: Data from the Programme for International Student Assessment, 2000, 2003, 2006, 2009 (Paris: OECD). Data for United Kingdom for 2003 are unavailable; in 2000 the score for United Kingdom was 529.

assessment. Important caveats come with these measures. We chose them from PISA because they are clear and quantifiable. However, taken on their own, they sometimes disagreed with our assessments of country education systems elsewhere in this chapter. For example, Finland scores relatively low on school curriculum responsibility. We believe this reflects the role of local boards of education

Figure 12-3. *Time Series of PISA Results across Seven Countries and the OECD, Science, 2000–09*

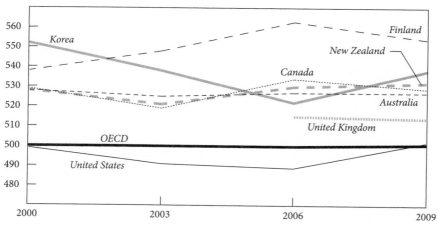

Source: Data from the Programme for International Student Assessment, 2000, 2003, 2006, 2009 (Paris: OECD). Data for United Kingdom for 2003 are unavailable; in 2000 the score for United Kingdom was 532.

as opposed to school-level decisions; but as noted elsewhere, these are small and extremely local entities, and in practice teachers enjoy a great deal of autonomy over these matters. In comparison, New Zealand reports a high degree of curriculum autonomy despite a nationally legislated curriculum and a highly prevalent (although not compulsory) nationally administered senior secondary qualification. This may be because the New Zealand curriculum is a relatively nonprescriptive learning framework, which deliberately grants autonomy to teachers while providing overall national consistency.

Similarly, a high percentage of Korean principals report competition between schools for students, despite the virtual nonexistence of parent choice in the Korean system. This may be more a reflection of the perception of principals than of actual parent discretion. It is but one indication of the influence of culture and local circumstance, which can create distinct gaps between intent and outcome or between technical description and actual experience.

Our findings from this analysis suggest that simple categorizations, and even key indicators and indexes, do not, on the whole, tell a good story about governance. Simply, we do not find any relationship between school governance and student performance, and links to education outcomes remain opaque. Our experience, both of the differences between quantified indicators and broader qualitative analysis and of the lack of insight generated by the quantitative measures, suggests a vital point. That is, we must resist the allure of assuming a clean— but false—relationship exists between reform of governance arrangements and realization of valued education outcomes from school systems.

Although this analysis does not clarify the nature of governance factors that influence student achievement, more can be learned from PISA by examining the impact of the longest-standing alternative governance arrangement—private education. Figure 12-4 provides an illustration. Universal public education for the vast majority of jurisdictions is a relatively recent phenomenon, with a current history of no more than 150 years. Private education has been the predominant form of education for a much greater period of human history, but, for the ages of five to around fifteen in most developed economies, it has been usurped by publicly funded education over the past hundred years. The notion of private education is subject to as many subtleties as education governance, but it is safe to assume that across most jurisdictions, this is a form of education paid for by consumers or their families.

As a broad generalization, private education comes with greater institutional autonomy and greater accountability to those who purchase it. Usually, private schools are more likely to benefit from higher levels of income than their public counterparts and thereby to enjoy better facilities and, sometimes, to offer higher rates of teacher pay. Owing to the relationship between those who purchase the service and those who supply it, and the wide availability of a free-of-charge

Figure 12-4. *Difference in Mean Reading Scores between Students Attending Private and Public Schools*

Percent

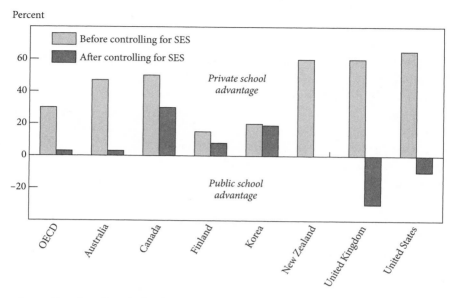

Source: Data from Organization for Economic Cooperation and Development, *PISA 2009 Results: What Makes a School Successful?* vol. 4, *Resources, Policies, and Practices,* 2010 (http://dx.doi.org/10. 1787/9789264091559-en); Organization for Economic Cooperation and Development, *PISA 2009 Results: What Students Know and Can Do,* vol. 1, *Student Performance in Reading, Mathematics, and Science,* 2010 (http://dx.doi.org/10.1787/9789264091450-en); and Organization for Economic Cooperation and Development, "Private Schools: Who Benefits?" *PISA in Focus,* no. 7 (August 2011).

alternative in most jurisdictions, private schools tend to be populated by students from wealthier backgrounds.

The PISA 2009 results contain much cogent information about the effect of private schooling. Most important, across the participant countries there is, on average, a thirty-point difference in reading score, in favor of private schools, between students attending private and public schools. This is approximately equivalent to two-thirds of the difference between the lowest- and highest-performing comparator jurisdictions in 2009 (the United Kingdom and Korea). However, this mean difference between public and private schooling outcomes narrows to negligibly few points when controlling for socioeconomic status.

The OECD suggests a small number of factors of private schooling that account for the remainder of this point difference. These include choice of curriculum, better disciplinary climates, and better resourcing. Across our comparator jurisdictions, the picture is one of highly interesting variance. The two highest-performing jurisdictions, Finland and Korea, show a small but relatively stable advantage in private schooling. The results from the United Kingdom and the United States are different and quite extraordinary, however. In the lowest-scoring comparator jurisdictions, private schooling makes a huge difference, but after controlling for socioeconomic status the difference is negative. An awkward implication that could be drawn is that those private school students would have been better off in a public school (and their parents could have saved a great deal of money). But maybe, more sensibly, what these results tell us is something about the relative success of public school institutions in different jurisdictions in eliminating the disparities that accrue from students' socioeconomic status differentials. These are complex results that deserve further investigation.

Achievement data tell us that these alternative governance arrangements do impact student achievement. However, they do so in a very small (and sometimes negative) way when the much more influential factor of socioeconomic status is taken into account.

The Contrasting Cases of Finland and South Korea

Of all the jurisdictions under comparison, it is Finland and South Korea that tend to attract most comment. Both countries perform consistently well in international evaluations, particularly PISA; South Korea and Finland ranked second and third in the world, respectively, on reading scores in 2009. Both also scored within the top five places in science and mathematics. As to reading scores, they formed a group of three countries (with Hong Kong) whose scores were not statistically significantly different. Fundamentally, the performance of Finland and Korea is comparable.

The PISA assessment divides the tested student population into reading levels ranging from one (the lowest) to six. Both jurisdictions show comparatively few children reading at low levels and comparatively greater numbers of children reading at higher levels. But whereas Finland has more than twice the average percentage of students performing at the highest level in reading, South Korea comes in only just above the OECD average. Finland also enjoys a relatively small spread of scores, suggesting that it experiences consistent success as well as better chances of, on at least one measure, excellence. The characteristics of the systems in these jurisdictions contain interesting similarities as well as differences. In 2009 PISA contained some categorized features of education systems that are worth exploring in these two countries.

Governance

Both South Korea and Finland offer low or nonexistent levels of parent choice of school. In South Korea, children are randomly assigned to both public and private schools. In Finland, few private schools exist, and all are "comprehensive," that is, granted little or no leeway over student selection. An interesting adjunct to this is that, in both jurisdictions, "private" schools are funded by the state. Nonetheless, we must return to earlier caveats about this information; a high percentage of principals in Korea report local competition for enrollments, a fact that may indicate a high level of academic competition between institutions despite a low level of choice.

Both jurisdictions are somewhat decentralized. Through the pressure of successive waves of population growth, South Korea devolved greater degrees of responsibility to municipal authorities, consisting of sixteen provincial offices and 182 local boards. These entities take care of budget and general administration tasks. Control of schools in Finland sits primarily with municipalities, of which there are 336. However, we should be cautious of simple comparisons. The school-age population of South Korea is approximately 7.5 million, compared with approximately 800,000 for Finland. As a consequence, the smallest South Korean administrative entity is approximately twenty times the size of one in Finland. These entities have quite different spans of control. There also appears to be a subtle but important distinction between the drivers of this decentralization. The Finnish system emphasizes local—almost village-level—control of schooling. The historical driver of Korean decentralization, on the other hand, is efficiency, in response to a system that grew too large to be efficiently managed centrally. This decentralized Korean system can also be viewed as simply a centralized system with distributed administrative functions.

The two countries treat curriculum and assessment very differently. The Finnish education system is characterized by something that would be all but anathema to many Western economies—zero state testing until the final secondary level assessment, and indeed very little official testing at all. In contrast, and in common with many developed Asian economies, South Korea tests often and for many purposes, and tests are given as early as elementary school. Much effort is expended studying for the all-important College Scholastic Ability Test (CSAT), but there are many staging posts (albeit nonstandard) along the way.

The curriculum comparison is also revealing. Both jurisdictions ostensibly implement a national curriculum plan. But the on-the-ground approach could not be more different. The South Korean national curriculum appears to be strongly adhered to and includes centrally mandated subjects and textbooks. This assessment should be qualified by reference to recent moves to decentralize some aspects of the Korean curriculum to the school and teacher level.[10] Nonetheless, according to our qualitative assessment, there is a high degree of curriculum homogeneity, mostly enforced by the high-stakes rule of the centrally administered CSAT.[11]

In contrast, the Finnish curriculum is implemented almost entirely at a municipality level, and individual teachers enjoy a high degree of autonomy over curriculum subjects and choice of texts. The OECD notes a positive relationship between low school transfer rates (the rate at which students are moved to different schools, most often owing to behavioral or other academic difficulties) and autonomy in setting curriculum and assessment practices. In fact, autonomy over curriculum across the OECD seems to be a key and important factor correlated with improved reading scores. When we look at the percentage of variation between countries in reading performance accounted for by school system features in the PISA 2009 results, we find a difference of 23 percentage points attributable to autonomy for curriculum and assessment. A difference of 1 percentage point was attributable to responsibility for resource allocation.

Values

In both Finland and Korea, teachers enjoy high professional standing, but, again, there are differences. Finland in particular is often noted as having a carefully selected teaching workforce, qualified to a level equivalent to a U.S. master's degree. South Korean teachers complete a four-year program of postsecondary study, but this does not make them much different from most other developed economies. Teacher pay in Finland is only slightly higher than the OECD average, whereas South Korean teachers are paid at a level second only to educators from Luxembourg (who are generally cited as a high outlier in discussions of teacher pay). What both countries appear to have in common is a culture of respect for the profession of teaching. This cultural factor is often cited as a missing component in a number of midranking education systems, in that the teaching profession is not placed on a par with medicine or law in the social hierarchy.

Both jurisdictions place high value on preprimary education. The PISA data paint something of a counterintuitive picture of preprimary education. Whereas most comparator jurisdictions show significant upward differences in reading scores for children who attended preprimary education, these differences are so small as to be statistically insignificant for Korea and Finland. This could mean that preprimary education adds little to the overall experience, but it could just as easily be seen as a factor of education systems with high consistency of performance and high levels of access to preprimary education—approaching universal. A related feature of the two systems is that, in both jurisdictions, children do not begin formal elementary education until a comparatively late age—seven in Finland and between six and seven in South Korea.

Overall, there is not a great deal to suggest that governance makes a strong difference to education outcomes for children, at least for the international education community's star performers. Nonetheless there are features here that are worth exploring further. If you want to be Finland or South Korea, it would seem to be the case that you should adopt policies that value good teachers; devolve funding and administration to a local level but possibly keep decisionmaking out of the schools themselves; adopt enrollment policies that offer little or no parent choice; and emphasize preprimary education. Although this is not a feature of South Korean governance, judging from broader results, it might also make sense to devolve responsibility for curriculum and assessment to a local level. The overarching message from this examination of high-fliers is much the same as from many other places: teaching matters—pedagogy, curriculum, resources, and assessment. Good governance must support these items as a priority.

Success and Failure: Relationship between Education Governance and Achievement

Another way to consider the relationship between education governance and achievement is to consider the success or failure of schools. The notion of the school as a crucial element in any intervention logic recurs in conversations about education governance. More or less competition could be cited as good or bad for education; but written into the terms of the debate is the idea that it is competition between schools, not between systems or curriculums or theories of governance, that will produce improvements in school performance. In fact, much evidence on academic achievement focuses on the primacy of what happens in the classroom (and, indeed, on the much more influential parent, family, and socioeconomic factors). The 2009 PISA suggests that the greatest variation in performance is within, rather than between, individual institutions and jurisdictions. That is, there is more difference between the worst and best student in any school than between the worst and best schools. Similarly, there is more difference between the individual performance of the worst and best students in any country than between the average performance of the worst and best countries.

Australia, like its federal companions Canada and the United States, has delegated the bulk of education policymaking to its component jurisdictions. Nonetheless, Australian schooling has shown some general trends overall, not least a significant rise in the number of private schools, with those entities accounting for around a third of enrollments. As well as private and government schools, there is a proportion of Catholic schools—essentially private schools run by religiously affiliated trusts or boards.

An analysis of the effectiveness of Australian schools in 2004 goes some way toward confirming the hypothesis that the institution as a whole can in some way be responsible for the results of individuals, even though those individuals experience different teachers and teaching styles. After controlling for social intake, size, location, sector, and achievement on intake, Stephen Lamb and colleagues find a wide variation, both above and below an expected level of performance. This is particularly noticeable at the lower levels of scores; some school scores show several standard deviations both above and below the mean.[12]

However, the links through to governance in this study were diffuse. Overall, around 90 percent of variation in performance was ascribed to factors other than the school as an entity. Of the remaining 10 percent, only small effects were noticeable for differences between Catholic, government, and independent schools. Parent choice—a matter, it appears, of high public policy value in Australia—seems at a macro level to be adding little to individual school performance. We might expect much better results from private schools in a system where choice is so prevalent. This tends not to be the case, at least in Australia.

Studies of the relationship between governance and failing schools tend to tell a different story. There is actually a large body of work on what makes a good school good and on how to rescue a failing school. We do not propose to investigate the issue in depth here. Rather, it is noteworthy that the bulk of advice on the matter deals with leadership and governance as a central theme.[13]

The United Kingdom's National Audit Office, relating well-trodden advice from the Office for Standards in Education, Children's Services, and Skills and similar entities, has established a framework of problems common to poorly performing schools: ineffective leadership, weak governance, poor standards of teaching, lack of external support, and challenging circumstances.[14] In 2006 it noted that 4 percent of primary and 23 percent of secondary schools in the United Kingdom could be described as poorly performing. To explore one aspect in a little more depth, the 2006 report notes the crucial role of governors (volunteer-parent governing committees) in challenging head teachers and senior teaching staff in failing schools.

It appears that an accountability role is important. The centrality of leadership, and the role of the principal as a direction-setting change manager, is also acknowledged. New Zealand's Education Review Office notes leadership as a key factor of successful schools but says little about governance. Its framework for successful schools proposes a focus on the learner, leadership in an inclusive culture, effective teaching, engagement with parents and communities, and coherent policies and practice in a cycle of continuous self-review.[15]

Lessons

Based on the foregoing survey and discussion of education governance and student outcomes across six jurisdictions, we can draw lessons for governance reformers. These lessons address the politics of school governance, diagnostic tools, leadership, classroom practices, and the preparation of students and teachers.

Avoid Costly Political Battles

Transforming education systems requires massive political will that must be sustained over many years. The history of education reform is littered with examples of failed efforts. This is largely because the grammar of schooling has been well established, and as a result a variety of somewhat arbitrary aspects of school systems have been treated as essential elements.[16] Reform efforts that have worked have tended to add new components to school systems, usually leaving other aspects in place. The resulting incrementalism, or tinkering around the edges, has meant that many features of schooling appear the same today as they did a century ago. This kind of system-level resistance to change is not unique to the field of education. Incrementalism has long been recognized as a predominate change dynamic in various areas of government and corporate activity. Getting beyond incrementalism typically involves high levels of coordinated activity led by policy entrepreneurs.[17] In light of this, effective change efforts often involve engagement in local-level experimentation, creation of whole new organizational entities working alongside traditional forms, and efforts to build networks and political coalitions.

When considering education reforms, we suggest that efforts should be made to avoid costly political battles. These can readily suck time and energy away from the focus of change itself. In practice, this suggestion implies that creating coalitions of willing change agents and working around the edges of traditional systems are likely to be the most fruitful ways forward. When sufficient evidence is assembled to support arguments for change, and when prefigurative forms of change have had a chance to flourish, the likelihood of securing major change will increase. Although teachers unions might be considered a powerful brake on reform, there are likely to be ways of presenting reform efforts that will not immediately buy a major fight. In fact, a number of actions that would appear to promote the achievement of valued education outcomes also involve raising the status of teaching as a profession. Distasteful as some might find it, first exhausting those options is probably more effective than going directly into battle with the education establishment. Governance reformers should ask, What changes in governance arrangements are likely to generate valued education outcomes without provoking major political battles?

Use Appropriate Diagnostic Tools

Systems of public education, to be judged as providing adequate return on investment, must produce outcomes of high value to society. Agreement about what outcomes are most valued can be elusive in pluralistic societies that exhibit diversity and multiculturalism. Yet even in societies that are socially and culturally homogeneous, conceptions of valued outcomes are subject to ongoing, incremental change. In the present age, continuous economic transformation is forcing debate about what matters most in education. Kenneth Strike has proposed that states and nations should hold schools and students accountable, using "a high, but narrow bar."[18] For example, all young people, and all societies, benefit when high standards are set regarding the attainment of basic literacy and numeracy. According to Strike, government should not, in the name of pluralism, tolerate either student failure or school failure on these narrow measures. Meanwhile, holding schools and students accountable for performance only in basic literacy and numeracy leaves considerable scope for school leaders and communities to decide what curricular elements matter most to them and how they should be taught. From a governance perspective, test results represent vital indicators of system performance. Testing programs generate the information required to diagnose an education system's performance. Aside from giving a picture of overall system performance, diagnostic tools are most useful when they can identify areas of the system that are not performing well.

We advocate use of appropriate diagnostic tools, such as measures of student gain scores, because they can greatly assist in the allocation of resources across a public school system. Implementation of sound testing systems should therefore precede more comprehensive changes in education governance. Governance reforms and related efforts to achieve greater control over public schools make sense only when clear evidence exists that schools are performing poorly. No priority should be given to governance reforms that affect schools currently producing good outcomes. Governance reformers should ask, What changes in current governance arrangements are likely to generate better information on education outcomes and assist in prioritizing areas for reform efforts?

Recognize the Power of Leadership

Discussions of education governance typically circle around big questions of structural design and control. Although there is certainly value in exploring ways to achieve better structural design, we should not neglect the power of leadership to make things happen in change-resistant environments. For example, Richard E. Neustadt has made a classic argument that, given the separation of powers in the United States system of government, the most important power of presidents is the power to persuade.[19] Subsequent studies of U.S. presidents in power and presidents in the making illustrate how people's ability to span structural boundaries and master the rules of the game are crucial to achieving significant change in a system that routinely stymies change efforts.[20] Studies of agenda setting and policy entrepreneurship further confirm that effective leadership efforts can make change happen, seemingly against the odds.[21] This suggests that, for people interested in securing better education outcomes, finding ways to effectively empower locally led change processes can be productive. Such efforts, carefully orchestrated, offer the promise of creating new coalitions that could ultimately support ambitious efforts to better align governance structures with the pursuit of valued education outcomes.

Some recent studies of leadership in schools have explicitly explored how the practices of people in leadership positions, such as school principals, can produce gains in student learning. These studies recognize that classroom interactions are central to the production of valued education outcomes. For example, Richard Elmore proposes that in education, "leadership is the guidance and direction of instructional improvement. This is a deliberately deromanticized, focused, and instrumental definition."[22] Such a focused definition resonates with notions of leadership as the promotion of creative problem solving within collectivities.[23] Based on a meta-analysis of prior research, Viviane Robinson identifies five school-level leadership practices that impact positively on student outcomes. These are establishing goals and expectations, effectively organizing resources for the attainment of valued goals, planning and evaluating teaching and the curriculum, promoting and participating in teacher professional development, and ensuring an orderly and supportive environment.[24] Among these, the practice that appears to have the most impact on student outcomes is promotion and participation in teacher learning and development. These findings support arguments that value can be gained from efforts to distribute leadership throughout schools. Such efforts empower teachers and promote learning conversations among stakeholders.[25]

Effective school leaders also tend to build inclusive relations with members of the broader school community. When managed carefully, such efforts can scaffold student learning.[26] Insights from research on the power of leadership have led to the development of programs in New Zealand and elsewhere that train school principals to serve as effective leaders. Governance reformers should ask, What changes in current governance arrangements are likely to support school leadership that contributes to better education outcomes?

Focus on Classroom Practices

In the context of discussions of education governance, focus on classroom practices may seem misplaced. Yet in the cases of Korea and Finland we can see that valued education outcomes can be broadly generated by two national school systems that display almost polar-opposite governance mechanisms. The focus on the classroom leads us to consider what elements of a governance system matter—and which do not—for promoting improvements in student learning. Fundamentally, education outcomes are the products of the interactions that occur between teachers and students. Anecdotally, most people who have attained success in their lives can recount turning points that occurred through their engagement with specific teachers or mentors.[27] More formally, systematic observations of teachers in classrooms confirm that appropriate application of specific practices can have profound effects on student learning. Consider, for example, the giving of feedback to students. When carefully managed and given in a constructive fashion, feedback can strongly support progress in student learning.[28]

Indeed, a meta-analysis of evidence reveals that an array of classroom practices, appropriately applied, can have much more influence on student learning than politically charged factors such as class size and the financial resources available to a school.[29] Richard Elmore's classic discussion of backward mapping and his more recent considerations of school reform confirm the importance of elevating classroom practices in discussions of education governance.[30] Governance reformers should ask, What changes to current governance arrangements are likely to have the most impact on improving classroom practices?

Attend to Student Preparation

The value students gain at any step in their education depends greatly on what they bring to it. This raises several matters for consideration. On a somewhat negative note, we need to be sensitive to the limits of what schools can do when working with students. Certainly, there is plenty of evidence that specific attributes of family and social settings affect individual education outcomes.[31] However, we verge on despair when we view these deficits as fixed and when teachers treat them as insurmountable barriers to student success. "Deficit thinking" assumes that factors such as family poverty, instability in housing and family relations, learning disabilities, and parents' limited education present obstacles to student learning.[32] But too much focus on student deficits can become an excuse for teachers to assume that any efforts to promote learning are bound to fail.[33] Emerging evidence on effective teaching strategies and the results of school efforts to engage families and communities as partners in student learning suggest that many deficits can be turned around.[34] Schools and teachers need to figure out what they can do and to employ teaching practices that add value to students, even in the face of troubles that are beyond the control of individual teachers and schools.

Longitudinal studies comparing students who experienced high-quality early childhood education with those who did not clearly demonstrate the positive impact of early interventions that improve student preparation for subsequent schooling. The most powerful evidence to date has been summarized by James Heckman.[35] The clear message here is that investments in high-quality early education serve to promote student performance in subsequent years of schooling and well beyond. Additionally, evidence from the OECD's PISA studies, among others, confirms that education outcomes for students at age fifteen are positively influenced by their previous exposure to preschool education programs. Governance reformers should ask, What changes in current governance arrangements are likely to help give students strong foundational experiences in life that will enhance their ability to make the most of their subsequent education opportunities?

Attend to Teacher Preparation

After investigating characteristics of top-performing national school systems, Michael Barber and Mona Mourshed conclude that "the quality of an education system cannot exceed the quality of its teachers," and "the only way to improve outcomes is to improve instruction."[36] Our discussion of the education systems in Finland and South Korea supports these observations. Strong empirical evidence offers further confirmation. For example, analyses of longitudinal data from the Tennessee Value-Added Assessment System offer clear evidence of the powerful effects that good teachers can have on student outcomes. Paul Wright, Sandra Horn, and William Sanders report that good teachers appear to be effective with students at all achievement levels, regardless of the amount of heterogeneity in their classrooms. And if the teacher is ineffective, students will achieve inadequate progress academically, regardless of how similar or different they are regarding their academic achievement. These researchers conclude that serial exposure to effective teachers can have dramatic effects on student outcomes.[37] These findings suggest the importance of using diagnostic tools that allow for school-level identification of failing teachers and focusing efforts on ways to either improve their performance or remove them from teaching. This is different from placing a focus on schools as failing organizations.

Building on findings of this kind, Linda Darling-Hammond has used state-level evidence from multiple states in the United States to demonstrate gains in student performance that flow from enhancements in teacher preparation.[38] Darling-Hammond notes that although the states that have aggressively pursued investments in teacher knowledge and skills have equal or higher levels of student poverty than nearby states that pursued other, distinctively different reform strategies, their students subsequently achieved at higher levels. Although all of the states in her study had increased teacher salaries during the previous decade, only those that insisted on higher standards for teacher education and licensing realized gains that were not made by states that maintained or lowered their standards for entering teachers. Following from this research, Linda Darling-Hammond and Gary Sykes propose that the achievement of highly qualified teachers in the United States requires a national teacher supply policy.[39] Our assessment of education systems in a collection of other countries has indicated that setting high standards for entry into teacher training is a vital ingredient for enhancing education outcomes.

However, a focus on the initial preparation of teachers should not lead to neglect of the potential contribution of ongoing professional development of teachers. Helen Timperley and Viviane Robinson have documented how professional development can advance teachers from deficit thinking to a more reflective consideration of the way their own practices can change student performance.[40] Governance reformers should ask, What changes in current governance arrangements are likely to systematically improve the quality of teaching where it is likely to have the most significant effects on education outcomes?

Conclusion

Political leaders everywhere face strong incentives to achieve greater returns on public investments in education. Given this, it is tempting for many to seek radical changes in governance arrangements, with the intention of gaining greater control over what happens in schools and in classrooms. Although we can certainly see the merits in pursuing governance reforms, we also recognize that such actions often create major political battles that deflect attention from the core business of improving student outcomes. For this reason, we suggest that would-be reformers seek to achieve changes both by working with people in the current system and by looking for ways to introduce changes that challenge the hegemony of traditional schooling arrangements. With respect to working the inside track, a lot could be gained by improving the information available to administrators regarding student performance, by directing teachers to focus on outcomes for students, and by ensuring that students are appropriately prepared for each level of education. Changes along these lines could be achieved through efforts that recognize teachers as professionals and that involve getting resources to the places where they can make significant differences to student outcomes. Evidence on major reform efforts suggests that when political leaders take the risk of tying their reputations to achievement of specific changes, those changes can happen rapidly.[41] Of course, major risks accompany such a strategy. But if public leaders are not prepared to stake their fortunes on creating significant system improvements, then it is unlikely that anyone else will. With respect to working outside the present system, we suggest that efforts to promote experimentation in schooling can do a lot to inform practices within traditional schooling systems. However, in such cases, effort must be made to ensure that experiments are effectively evaluated and that knowledge of their effects is adequately disseminated to others who could use it.

Notes

1. Elhanan Helpman, *The Mystery of Economic Growth* (Harvard University Press, 2004).

2. Thomas L. Friedman, *The World Is Flat: A Brief History of the Twenty-First Century* (New York: Picador, 2007).

3. John Hattie, *Visible Learning: A Synthesis of over 800 Meta-Analyses Relating to Achievement* (New York: Routledge, 2009).

4. Thomas Konig, George Tsebelis, and Marc Debus, eds., *Reform Processes and Policy Change: Veto Players and Decision-Making in Modern Democracies* (New York: Springer Press, 2010).

5. This point resonates with evidence in Barry Rabe's contribution in chapter 13 of this volume, where the focus is placed on governance issues in the distinctly different areas of health care and environmental protection.

6. Viviane Robinson and Lorrae Ward, "Lay Governance of New Zealand's Schools: An Educational, Democratic, or Managerialist Activity?" *Journal of Educational Administration* 43, no. 2 (2005): 170–86.

7. Ann Allen and Michael Mintrom, "Responsibility and School Governance," *Educational Policy* 24 (May 2010): 439–64.

8. The Progress in International Reading Literacy Study and Trends in International Mathematics and Science Study, two other significant international assessment programs, do not feature comparable data from all comparator jurisdictions.

9. The only counterfactual here is Korea, whose performance in reading seemed to peak in 2006 but at the expense of science.

10. Soon Nam Kim, "The Developmental Directions and Tasks of the School Based Curriculum Management System in Korea," *Asia Pacific Education Review* 6, no. 1 (2005): 41–49.

11. Wonsuk Lee, "Perceptions of High School Students, Their Parents, and Teachers on the Factors Determining the Effects of the Essay Test on the Curriculum of High Schools in Korea," *KEDI Journal of Educational Policy* 7, no. 1 (2010): 209–32. See also Hoi K. Suen and Qiong Wu, "Psychometric Paradox of Very High-Stakes Assessment and Solutions;" *KEDI Journal of Educational Policy* 3, no. 1 (2006): 113–29.

12. Stephen Lamb and others, *School Performance in Australia: Results from Analyses of School Effectiveness* (Melbourne: Department of Premier and Cabinet, 2004).

13. Viviane M. J. Robinson, *Student-Centered Leadership* (San Francisco: Jossey-Bass, 2011).

14. National Audit Office, *Improving Poorly Performing Schools in England* (London: Stationery Office, 2006).

15. Education Review Office, *Evaluation at a Glance: What ERO Knows about Effective Schools* (Wellington, U.K.: Education Review Office, 2011).

16. David Tyack and Larry Cuban, *Tinkering toward Utopia: A Century of Public School Reform* (Harvard University Press, 1995).

17. Michael Mintrom, *Policy Entrepreneurs and School Choice* (Georgetown University Press, 2000).

18. Kenneth A. Strike, "Centralized Goal Formation, Citizenship, and Educational Pluralism: Accountability in Liberal Democratic Societies," *Educational Policy* 12 (January 1998): 211.

19. Richard E. Neustadt, *Presidential Power: The Politics of Leadership* (New York: Wiley, 1960).

20. Robert A. Caro, *The Years of Lyndon Johnson,* vol. 3, *Master of the Senate* (New York: Knopf, 2002); Robert A. Wilson, ed., *Power and the Presidency* (New York: Public Affairs, 1999).

21. John Kingdon, *Agendas, Alternatives, and Public Policies,* 2nd ed. (Boston, Mass.: Little, Brown, 1995); Mintrom, *Policy Entrepreneurs and School Choice.*

22. Richard F. Elmore, *School Reform from the Inside Out: Policy, Practice, and Performance* (Harvard Education Press, 2004), p. 57.

23. Ronald A. Heifetz, *Leadership without Easy Answers* (Belknap Press of Harvard University Press, 1994); Karl E. Weick, "Leadership as the Legitimation of Doubt." In *The Future of Leadership*, edited by Warren Bennis, Gretchen M. Spreitzer, and Thomas G. Cummings (San Francisco: Jossey-Bass, 2001).

24. Robinson, *Student-Centered Leadership.*

25. James P. Spillane, *Distributed Leadership* (San Francisco: Jossey-Bass, 2006).

26. Carolyn J. Riehl, "The Principal's Role in Creating Inclusive Schools for Diverse Students: A Review of Normative, Empirical, and Critical Literature on the Practice of Educational Administration," *Review of Educational Research* 70 (Spring 2000): 55–81.

27. K. Anders Ericsson, Michael J. Prietula, and Edward T. Cokely, "The Making of an Expert," *Harvard Business Review* 85 (July–August 2007): 115–21; Howard Gardner, *Creating Minds: An Anatomy of Creativity Seen through the Lives of Freud, Einstein, Picasso, Stravinsky, Eliot, Graham, and Gandhi* (New York: Basic Books, 1993); Ken Robinson, *The Element: How Finding Your Passion Changes Everything* (New York: Viking, 2009).

28. John Hattie and Helen Timperley, "The Power of Feedback," *Review of Educational Research* 77 (March 2007): 81–112.

29. John Hattie, "The Paradox of Reducing Class Size and Improving Learning Outcomes," *International Journal of Educational Research* 43, no. 6 (2005): 387–425; Hattie, *Visible Learning.*

30. Richard F. Elmore, "Backward Mapping: Implementation Research and Policy Decisions," *Political Science Quarterly* 94 (Winter 1979): 601–16; Elmore, *School Reform from the Inside Out.*

31. Larry Cuban, *Why Is It So Hard to Get Good Schools?* (Teachers College Press, 2003); Christopher Jencks and Meredith Phillips, eds., *The Black-White Test Score Gap* (Brookings Press, 1998).

32. Shernaz B. García and Patricia L. Guerra, "Deconstructing Deficit Thinking: Working with Educators to Create More Equitable Learning Environments," *Education and Urban Society* 36 (February 2004): 150–68; Richard R. Valencia, ed., *The Evolution of Deficit Thinking: Educational Thought and Practice* (Washington: Falmer Press, 1997).

33. Helen S. Timperley, "Instructional Leadership Challenges: The Case of Using Student Achievement Information for Instructional Improvement," *Leadership and Policy in Schools* 4 (January 2005): 3–22.

34. Steven B. Sheldon and Joyce L. Epstein, "Involvement Counts: Family and Community Partnerships and Mathematics Achievement," *Journal of Educational Research* 98 (March 2005): 196–206; Frances L. Van Voorhis, "Interactive Homework in Middle School: Effects on Family Involvement and Science Achievement," *Journal of Educational Research* 96 (July–August 2003): 323–38.

35. James J. Heckman, "Skill Formation and the Economics of Investing in Disadvantaged Children," *Science* 312 (June 2006): 1900–02.

36. Michael Barber and Mona Mourshed, *How the World's Best-Performing School Systems Come Out on Top* (London: McKinsey, 2007).

37. Paul S. Wright, Sandra P. Horn, and William L. Sanders, "Teacher and Classroom Context Effects on Student Achievement: Implications for Teacher Evaluation," *Journal of Personnel Evaluation in Education* 11 (April 1997): 57–67.

38. Linda Darling-Hammond, "Teacher Quality and Student Achievement: A Review of State Policy Evidence," *Education Policy Analysis Archives* 8 (2000): 1–44.

39. Linda Darling-Hammond and Gary Sykes, "Wanted: A National Teacher Supply Policy for Education: The Right Way to Meet the 'Highly Qualified Teacher' Challenge," *Education Policy Analysis Archives* 11 (2003): 1–55. See also Linda Darling-Hammond and John Bransford, eds., *Preparing Teachers for a Changing World: What Teachers Should Learn and Be Able to Do* (San Francisco, Calif.: Jossey-Bass, 2005).

40. Helen S. Timperley and Viviane M. J. Robinson, "Achieving School Improvement through Challenging and Changing Teachers' Schema," *Journal of Educational Change* 2 (December 2001): 281–300.

41. Michael Fullan, *Change Leader: Learning to Do What Matters Most* (San Francisco: Jossey-Bass, 2011).

BARRY G. RABE

13

Governance Lessons from the Health Care and Environment Sectors

Hope springs eternal for finding the right governance mix of political will, policy tools, and administrative capacity to address serious education policy problems. A staggering body of publications continues to emanate from an ever-proliferating set of think tanks, advocacy organizations, and schools of education. Many constitute a direct response to the decades-long lamentation that American public education performs at a disappointing level when compared with other nations. They join the quest for, in David Tyack's words, the "one best system," often focusing on a singular element that might propel America from the middle toward the top of the international pack in terms of student performance.[1] In recent years, that quest has included intensified federal and state efforts to improve performance through expanded use of standardized tests, a flurry of related incentives and sanctions linked to performance measures, continuing debate over such school choice options as expanded charters and vouchers, and even transformational use of technology in pedagogy.[2]

The analysis of education policy and governance is often written as if this area is unique, almost sealed hermetically from direct comparison with other policy areas. Much of the best research is presented at conferences and in journals that are exclusively devoted to education; they rarely acknowledge (much less explore) comparisons with other areas of policy. Some of this analysis clearly reflects key education governance elements, including a strong legacy of locally based political control through more than 14,000 elected school boards, strong emphasis on professional service delivery, and traditionally modest encroachment by federal legislation on subfederal preferences. The federal government has been seen as "borrowing strength" from states to secure a significant role, unlike its more dominant posture in other areas.[3] Indeed, Jeffrey Henig notes that American education policy has been traditionally addressed as "a thing apart," though he also suggests that the possible end of "educational exceptionalism" means that "education is becoming more like other domestic policy arenas."[4]

For better or worse, there are strong parallels between education policy and governance and other major spheres of domestic policy that are rarely bundled together in comparative analysis. Parallel arenas include delivery of medical care to the poor and air quality protection. Despite their many particular differences, these two arenas have moved from state and local dominance toward greater federal influence through landmark legislation in recent decades. They reflect some continued mixture of federal, state, and local responsibilities as opposed to some form of pure centralization and have developed governance mechanisms to attempt to handle these intergovernmental dynamics. Unlike education policy, however, they have a longer history of substantial federal engagement. Thus they may offer some particular insights about navigating governance challenges embedded in federalism during a period in which the federal role in education policy has begun to expand.

Health Care and Air Quality, American Style

Much as in education, governmental roles in health care or air quality protection in the United States were long deemed the exclusive province of local and state governments. In both cases, local and state health departments were dominant players between the 1870s and the middle of the twentieth century, with significant input regarding basic service delivery to the poor, children's health programs, and mental health services.[5] These were highly professionalized units that drew staff almost exclusively from accredited medical and public health degree programs. They generally functioned without elected governing bodies such as school boards and with only limited mayoral direction. Such health departments often took the lead role in overseeing service provision in public hospitals and clinics. These facilities provided a range of health care services to those deemed eligible according to some measure of poverty while leaving large sectors of society without anything approaching modern coverage.

Local health departments also embraced a disease prevention mission by assuming a lead role on air and water pollution. Much of this activity was largely hortatory, though some local departments did begin to make inroads on intensive coal use in some densely clustered residential areas and direct sewage release to public water bodies. Environmental health units within local health departments remained heavily professionalized and data driven. They relied substantially on disciplines such as epidemiology and biostatistics to examine health and disease trends, they used key findings to make the case for intervention to local elected officials, and they clung to close professional ties with regional schools of public health and medicine to preserve professional autonomy and influence.

During this extended period, many states gradually played a secondary role, usually confined to matching-fund programs rather than firm regulatory standards. In health care, this often included some form of state fund–matching share for provision of large public hospitals that offered care to those who lacked insurance or the capacity to pay for care. In air quality, a series of disasters in the 1940s and 1950s led to expanded roles in particular states. For example, a 1948 air inversion resulted in prolonged exposure to smog in a small Pennsylvania community named Donora with an economic dependence on the mining and burning of coal.[6] This episode led to twenty fatalities and nearly 6,000 cases of illness, prompting the state legislature in Harrisburg to rapidly establish air emissions guidelines. Some other states followed this pattern, though state engagement moved earlier and more rapidly on water pollution than air quality, perhaps in part owing to more direct detection of the impact of contamination on human health. But most of these policies were quite modest in scope and essentially deferred decisionmaking to local bodies such as health departments.

Any federal role was quite modest through the middle of the twentieth century, much as was the case in education policy. But some early problems at the local level did trigger federal scrutiny. In the Donora case, for example, the U.S. Public Health Service conducted an investigation and concluded in 1949 that "we can now say positively what couldn't be said before with scientific proof—that contamination of air in industrial areas can cause acute disabling diseases." Federal hackles were also raised in medical care amid reports of poor service delivery in some local public hospitals, again leading to some form of federal agency analysis and expression of concern.[7]

All of this contributed to a flurry of congressional hearings on health care and air quality in the 1950s and early 1960s. But any federal role was largely confined to highlighting concerns with local governance and finding some modest way to offset some of the costs for research or service delivery. In health care, a set of grant-in-aid programs provided supplemental funding to local communities to expand hospital capacity and medical care. The focus in both cases was to provide a broad set of funding that essentially could provide some tangible support to nearly every congressional district. There was a slight redistributive edge, with hospital expenditures (under the so-called Hill-Burton Hospital Survey and Construction Act) concentrated in areas of highest need. Similarly, supplements for health insurance were concentrated on lower-income groups (under the so-called Kerr-Mills Act), most notably the elderly, who appeared most vulnerable to limited access to care. In air quality, Congress passed five versions of legislation between 1955 and 1967, which tended to set broad and nonbinding clean-air goals that served essentially as financial conduits to underwrite local and state research and experimental program costs. In both cases, grant structure bore significant resemblance to federal forerunners to the 1965 Elementary and

Secondary Education Act, with some effort to concentrate resources on high-need populations and areas but considerable federal caution in trying to use those funds to alter dominant modes of governance, propel local reforms, or improve performance.[8]

This intergovernmental management arrangement was comfortable on all sides, giving the federal government some visibility and state and local counterparts new forms of revenue with few strings attached. But this kind of classic cooperative federalism partnership was relatively short lived, as the Johnson and Nixon eras ushered in major new pieces of federal legislation in health care and air quality that fundamentally challenged the prevailing order of governance. This legislation was in response to growing concerns about empirical trends such as limited access to quality medical services among the elderly and the poor and deteriorating air quality levels in many major urban areas in the Northeast, Midwest, Southeast, and Southwest. These new laws went far beyond the Elementary and Secondary Education Act in carving out a major federal regulatory role and, in the case of medical care, a major funding role, as well. Indeed, similar kinds of intergovernmental tensions, now manifest in education policy through federal legislation, such as the 2001 No Child Left Behind Act (NCLB), emerged decades earlier through the enactment of programs such as Medicaid and the Clean Air Act. These highly complex and durable pieces of federal legislation and key features of their governance hold potential lessons for education policy.

The Medicaid Era, 1965–Present

Medicaid was enacted only a few months after the 1965 Elementary and Secondary Education Act. It was inserted into the same bill that launched the Medicare program. Both Medicare and the education act overshadowed Medicaid in public visibility during the launch of the Great Society; Medicaid was, in many respects, an "afterthought," an incremental extension of an existing block-grant program that provided some federal funds to assist states in extending health care to low-income citizens.[9] Medicare has become a massive program, whereby the federal government provides health care and hospital insurance to all senior citizens, largely bypassing state and local governments. But Medicaid rapidly emerged as the "big sleeper" of the Great Society, reflected in both enrollment and cost. Citizen eligibility has grown steadily throughout the life of the program, including a jump from 35.7 million participants in 1992 to 58.1 million in 2008. During those years, expenditures soared from $177 billion to $339 billion when measured in 2008 constant dollars. Among the nearly 1,000 separate federal grants-in-aid programs, Medicaid consumes nearly one half of all federal expenditures for these kinds of programs.[10] Approximately two-thirds of its enrollees are children and families with low incomes, although these individuals incur only about one-third of total program costs. In contrast, the elderly poor (primarily through nursing home care) and individuals with mental and physical disabilities represent only about one-third of enrollees but incur nearly two-thirds of all costs.

Part of the extraordinary growth in expenditures is linked to the very generous terms the federal government offers to participating states. Quite unlike the far more modest federal matching shares in programs such as the Elementary and Secondary Education Act and the Individuals with Disabilities Education Act, Medicaid offers 50 to 83 percent coverage of state expenditures. The actual level of federal financial support is linked to state per capita income, with larger shares allocated to lower-income states. The federal government outlines a set of basic services that all participating states must provide to those deemed eligible, as well as a list of optional services that states can add. In both cases, states then receive federal reimbursement for the provision of these services. Medicaid thus does not provide services directly but rather assumes a role as bill payer or insurer of state-eligible activity and determines what services will be covered. It also establishes an extensive set of regulations to oversee many facets of the state-based programs. States thus have tremendous incentive to leverage federal dollars, although they also face growing challenges in covering their share. Indeed, Medicaid has been called the PAC-man of state budgets and consumes an average of one-quarter of total state government spending a year.

The Clean Air Act Era, 1970–Present

The federal government ultimately settled on a strategy to promote air quality that was far more reliant on the stick of regulation than on the carrot of money in securing state cooperation. The 1970 Clean Air Act ushered in the modern era of federal clean air standards and created a regulatory framework that remains substantially in place today. Whereas Medicaid covers well over half of total state expenditures, federal support to states for clean air program implementation has generally hovered between 20 and 25 percent. Total federal and state enforcement costs were approximately $2 billion in 2010, with the vast majority of total program costs imposed on regulated parties. Federal legislation established national ambient air quality standards, outlined a range of emission standards for industrial facilities and motor vehicles, and created mechanisms to determine whether various regions were in "attainment" of federal standards.

States were responsible for developing state implementation plans that would outline their emission reduction strategies and report on their progress. These plans required federal approval through the U.S. Environmental Protection Agency (EPA) before states would be delegated authority to proceed. Relatively few federal takeovers have occurred through full rejection of state plans, but this option has remained a possibility throughout the life of the program. It puts considerable pressure on states to perform according to federal standards if they want to maintain oversight authority. Each subsequent round of the legislation (in 1977 and 1990) has tended to set more ambitious emission reduction targets, add "emerging contaminants" to the list of air pollutants that must be addressed, and specify enforcement provisions that include financial and criminal penalties for noncompliance.[11]

Overarching Governance Features

Despite their considerable structural and technical differences, Medicaid and the Clean Air Act share a set of common governance features that have been hallmarks of their entire existence. Indeed, these features seem to only gain strength with the passage of time and may position the two programs for far more expansive roles in the coming decades.

Durability

First, both programs have demonstrated extraordinary durability and retain many key design elements from their initial enactment decades ago. Indeed, the ten-page version of Medicaid enacted in 1965 and the forty-seven-page version of the Clean Air Act enacted in 1970 remain entirely recognizable in current, albeit much lengthier, successors. Consequently, these "first drafts" have proved extremely difficult to alter in fundamental ways, despite numerous hearings in numerous Congresses that have explored far-reaching reforms. In the case of Medicaid, significant congressional coalitions have emerged on at least three occasions (early 1980s, mid-1990s, and early in the new century) to convert the program into a block grant. In each such case, Congress offered a quid pro quo to states; this entailed capping total federal expenditures, thereby ending the open-ended entitlement provision, in exchange for a substantial increase in state latitude to spend federal matching dollars as states saw fit. At one point, President Ronald Reagan embraced this strategy and then reversed course by proposing a full federal takeover of Medicaid in exchange for devolution of dozens of other federal programs, including several major education programs. None of these proposals were enacted, and much of Medicaid's initial framework remains intact. The Clean Air Act has also faced a number of legislative challenges, including proposals for far-reaching shifting of authority to states and elimination of so-called command-and-control regulatory provisions in favor of far more flexible mechanisms. As in the case of Medicaid, all such proposals have been soundly defeated, and the core of the 1970 version endures.

This pattern, of course, reflects a general pattern in American politics that notes partisan gridlock, proliferation of veto points, and the absence of a "compromise mindset" in either enacting new domestic legislation or undertaking major revisions of existing programs.[12] Many have characterized the 1990 passage of the Clean Air Act Amendments as a "political fluke," reflecting a one-time convergence of unique factors that allowed significant new provisions while retaining many core features of the 1970 version.[13] No subsequent amendments to the legislation have passed in the past twenty-one years, and none are in the offing, consistent with the pattern in other areas of environmental protection. Despite the attendant controversy in both of these established programs, Medicaid and the Clean Air Act have strong interest group bases of support, established intergovernmental management routines, and consistent measures of support in public opinion surveys.

The resulting durability of these programs underscores a possible consideration for education policy: initial passage of major legislation may not be followed by a rapid sequence of legislative amendments. Consequently, a major legislative breakthrough may represent a one-time-only coalition that is not easy to sustain and leaves future rounds of revision highly uncertain. Just as the Elementary and Secondary Education Act and the Individuals with Disabilities Education Act have proved difficult to modify by legislative amendment since their initial enactment several decades ago, legislation such as the NCLB may defy any major congressional overhaul for some time to come. Many factors may deter further reform, including the creation of established governance routines that may prove increasingly resistant over time to proposals for major alterations. That may limit future reforms to such options as incremental changes through bureaucratic channels or entrepreneurial efforts by one branch or level of government to foster more substantial reform.

The Administrative Presidency and Executive Federalism

Elected executives at both federal and state levels have emerged as major drivers behind many of the most significant changes that have occurred in Medicaid and the Clean Air Act in recent decades. At the federal level, this follows the general tenets of the "administrative presidency" model. Under this construct, presidents of both parties attempt to maximize their leverage over policy interpretation and implementation and may indeed be particularly inclined to pursue these approaches, given the high hurdles of gaining congressional support.[14] Tools for the administrative presidency may include executive orders, directives, and reallocation of discretionary funds. But they may also extend to tools that allow presidents and their agents to directly negotiate particular terms with individual states. Intergovernmental waivers have been a staple feature in Medicaid, whereas state implementation plans continue to serve a somewhat comparable role in the Clean Air Act.

Of course, the presidential role often looms large in landmark domestic legislation. It is indeed difficult to envision either Medicaid or the Elementary and Secondary Education Act without Lyndon Johnson's aggressive entrepreneurship. In turn, Richard Nixon's imprint was evident in the initial Clean Air Act, just as George W. Bush was a decisive architect in the enactment of the NCLB. But the administrative presidency role channels presidential influence in new directions, often taking advantage of legislative inertia and the need to translate or redirect established legislation into a particular context. Consequently, it is not surprising to see the Obama administration increasingly turning to similar methods. The administration is unilaterally attempting the largest expansion of the Clean Air Act since the 1990 amendments, through executive determination that carbon dioxide meets the flexible criteria that determine whether a substance constitutes an air contaminant. After prolonged legislative gridlock over climate legislation, the EPA is now retrofitting the 1990 air legislation to extend to major carbon dioxide sources such as electric utilities and oil refineries. It also negotiated a major intergovernmental agreement in 2009 to expand air quality standards to cover carbon emissions from vehicles through 2016 and then two years later to set even higher standards through 2025. None of this has involved any consent from Congress, generating considerable interbranch and interparty tension on the matter. This has led to expanded committee oversight hearings but has not deterred the administration from moving rapidly into implementation. Perhaps similarly, President Obama and his education secretary, Arne Duncan, have begun to outline possible new executive interpretations of the NCLB, given the possible absence of major legislative amendments. One option under active consideration includes application and potential application of negotiated waivers with states, building directly on experience gained by former presidents in Medicaid.

Presidents, of course, are not the only elected executives in American federalism. Jeffrey Henig notes the recent proliferation of education governors, and a similar phenomenon has emerged in medical care for the poor and air quality.[15] Governors such as Mitt Romney (Massachusetts), Peter Shumlin (Vermont), and John Kitzhaber (Oregon) have emerged as major national figures on the basis of state policy innovations that are directly linked to Medicaid, in some cases pushing the federal government not only to give them latitude for state implementation but also to consider their particular approach as a possible national model. In air quality and the related issue of climate change, a wide range of governors have also gained national notoriety, and in some cases a direct line to the White House, in advancing new policy initiatives. These include figures such as Arnold Schwarzenegger (California), Deval Patrick (Massachusetts), and George Pataki (New York).

These entrepreneurial governors have pushed the envelope for policy innovation, often seeking maximum latitude from the federal executive branch in going their own way. Unlike other federal systems of government, such as Canada and Germany, the United States does not operate a system of executive federalism that brings all elected federal and subfederal executives together on a regular basis to negotiate terms of key intergovernmental policy decisions. Organizations such as the National Governors Association often play some role in convening states, and a president will occasionally sit down with such a group of governors or even invite them to a special conference, as did George H. W. Bush with the 1989 Education Summit convened in Charlottesville, Virginia. But much of the federal-to-state dynamic in program implementation and exploration of innovation involves bilateral exchanges between the federal executive branch and its counterparts in individual states. Consequently, governors and their senior advisers have emerged as primary point persons in responding to administrative presidency initiatives. Some may embrace them, others may seek some form of supplemental federal compensation to secure cooperation, and still others may openly rebel and refuse to cooperate. In turn, many governors may pursue unilateral experiments under the larger umbrella of a federal policy.

In these cases, federal and state legislatures are hardly irrelevant, yet their roles may be marginalized to hearings and some form of executive oversight in the absence of their own ability to forge legislative coalitions and issue clear directives through legislation. This results in an increasingly executive-to-executive form of governance in both medical care for the poor and air quality, with potential parallels to the area of education, as programs such as the NCLB may increasingly operate without periodic legislative tune-ups.

Reasonable Outcomes

The durability of Medicaid and the Clean Air Act and the growing tendency to defer major policy steps to executive leaders may further stem from the fact that both programs can boast rather solid performance records. In the two decades in which performance management has emerged as a focal point in American governance, essentially all policy areas have come under scrutiny to systematically measure outputs and, to the extent possible, outcomes and larger impacts.[16] Indeed, concerns about the performance of K–12 students across the United States, as measured in standardized test scores, has been a central impetus in much recent federal and state policy reform, perhaps most notably the NCLB.

Neither Medicaid nor the Clean Air Act have spotless performance records, yet a substantial body of formal analysis indicates that they have gone some distance in responding to the outcome goals set forth in statute. Medicaid has actually contained costs more effectively on a per capita basis than either employer-provided insurance or other public programs such as Medicare. In turn, there are considerable differences in health outcomes between those eligible for Medicaid and comparable citizens without medical insurance. Medicaid enrollees receive more care than the uninsured, including preventive care, outpatient visits, and prescription drugs. Results are mixed in assessing the impact of this coverage on health outcomes, although Frank Thompson's careful review of the available literature notes that "available studies indicate that Medicaid enrollment yields better health outcomes than being uninsured."[17] Although the costs have been staggering and there have been many implementation controversies, proponents of sustaining Medicaid (or expanding the program) have a considerable body of evidence to advance in suggesting that the program has made some constructive impact in the lives of millions of Americans.

In the case of the Clean Air Act, the EPA has maintained and released detailed annual measures of overall air quality trends and air emission levels for a range of individual contaminants. The trend line for all of the major emissions cited in federal legislation, including carbon monoxide, ozone, lead, nitrogen dioxide, particulate matters, and sulfur dioxide, points to fairly consistent improvements in air quality and a steady decline in emissions rates. The agency regularly presents and frames these data in making the case that it continually performs at a high level and that Clean Air Act outcomes are among the more positive of any federal government initiatives of the past half century. In fact, the celebration of the fortieth anniversary of the agency, which was created by President Nixon in 1970 through executive order, emphasized air quality measures as a prime indicator of overall agency performance. A 2011 EPA summary on the Clean Air Act's impact notes that "between 1980 and 2009, gross domestic product increased 122 percent, vehicle miles traveled increased 95 percent, energy consumption increased 22 percent, and U.S. population grew by 57 percent. During the same time period, total emissions of the six principal air pollutants dropped by 57 percent."[18] Air quality improvements have been particularly significant in specific states and regions, perhaps most notably California.

The EPA has repeatedly attempted to use this aggressive presentation of outcome data to buttress its own economic impact analysis demonstrating achievement of these emission gains. This routinely leads to agency interpretations that implementation costs have proved far lower than initial industry projections, though a good deal of this analysis is disputed. At the same time, the agency has been quick to highlight areas where it feels it has not been able to perform effectively owing to lack of a legislative charge. For example, the same reports that highlight air quality performance gains also note that growth in greenhouse-gas emissions has been steady during this period, almost inviting the kind of presidential intervention that has occurred in giving the EPA a charge in this area in the absence of new legislation.

Both cases demonstrate that performance-based evidence can be marshaled to advance the cause of sustaining or expanding existing programs, following a pattern that has also emerged in some other policy areas.[19] This is clearly at variance with developments in education policy, in which performance measurement frequently produces an assessment that is mediocre or worse and thus gives rise to exploration of options that might lead to more salutary outcomes. Indeed, poor performance may open the doors to critical questioning of existing governance arrangements. In turn, individual states or school districts that produce significant performance improvements are less likely to face governance scrutiny.

Aversion to Embracing Market Strategies

All three policy areas discussed in this chapter have faced considerable political pressure to shift toward governance strategies energetically embraced by a significant body of policy analysts, particularly from the discipline of economics. In health care and education, this would entail a shift toward direct transfer of government funds to individuals, who would then purchase their own insurance or tuition plan from a public, private, or nonprofit provider.[20] In air quality, this would entail the use of market-based trading of emissions rather than command-and-control regulation that requires identical use of technology and application of emission standards across sources.[21] These approaches have been lauded by proponents as mechanisms that would maximize flexibility, achieve performance goals in a cost-effective manner, and reduce the need for more complex governance mechanisms.

In practice, the recurrent chorus of support for such shifts has gathered limited momentum in actual policy development, with considerable resistance to embracing these approaches on any large scale. At the same time, the limited experimentation that has occurred suggests that implementation may be more complex than anticipated and that governance results may be rather mixed at best. In Medicaid, the George W. Bush administration did allow for some experimentation with vouchers, most notably through the Florida Consumer Choice program that the president negotiated with his executive federalism partner, and older brother, Governor Jeb Bush. This program was heralded as a major breakthrough and perhaps a stepping-stone toward a national model. But its first half decade of experience suggests problems that include limited public awareness of the option and unexpectedly low rates of participation among eligible citizens. A much-expanded version of this plan, proposed in 2010 by Republican congressman Paul Ryan, would expand this model to much of Medicaid and Medicare; the House passed the bill, placing tight caps on inflation adjustments. But the proposed plan remains highly controversial and would likely constrain the capacity of those eligible to enter the private insurance marketplace and secure coverage that included such options as long-term care. The future of such an approach is highly uncertain.

In air quality, the Clean Air Act Amendments of 1990 did authorize an emissions-trading program for one major air contaminant, sulfur dioxide. This established a national trading system for these emissions from large power plants and has commonly been praised for securing significant reductions at relatively low cost. However, this case is in many respects an outlier among air emissions, as a readily available alternative to high-sulfur coal was commonly available, namely, low-sulfur coal mined largely in Western states. Such a convenient and inexpensive substitution is rare in environmental emissions, and the sulfur dioxide–trading program may have had the perverse incentive of making it cheaper than anticipated to continue to burn coal as opposed to alternative sources that might have a more benign impact on air quality. Nonetheless, this case has been used repeatedly in proposing new forms of air quality regulation, including application to the issue of reducing greenhouse-gas emissions. Massive legislation that would establish a national cap-and-trade system for carbon dioxide emissions did pass the House in 2009 but collapsed in the Senate in 2010. Many opponents questioned whether a trading model that might have worked for a narrow range of pollutants with an energy alternative readily available could indeed be transferred to the sprawling issue of carbon sources.

Even before the national debates over federal cap-and-trade policy, previous efforts to extend these general principles to other conventional air contaminants proved problematic. Despite the considerable powers of the administrative presidency, Congress repeatedly blocked proposals by President George W. Bush to extend the emissions-trading provisions for sulfur dioxide to other contaminants. Much of the opposition questioned whether this shift would actually achieve statutory emissions reduction goals and whether it could be successfully implemented for more complex contaminants.

Indeed, the three regional plans to establish multistate carbon cap-and-trade zones have struggled mightily to move from the drawing board into full governance mode. A number of governance problems have emerged to delay implementation in these cases, including shifts in political support amid gubernatorial changes, the enormous complexity of measuring all covered carbon sources and establishing a viable trading oversight mechanism, and securing the transparency and cooperation from the various governmental agencies that are necessary to ensure the proper functioning of such a market. Much as is the case in education policy, enormous effort is expended to study and promote market-based alternatives that would involve governance arrangements that are fundamentally different from the existing order. But these alternatives continue to face difficulty in securing political support through new legislation, at either federal or state levels. They also pose a number of governance challenges that have tended to be ignored by proponents, who contend that market-based programs will simply self-implement. Moreover, there may be some parallels in the challenges experienced in early experiments with market-based approaches in health care and air quality and the evolving experience of charter schools. These alternatives have been aggressively advanced by their proponents, in part for their market-sensitive qualities, but serious questions have arisen concerning their capacity for effective governance and demonstrable performance improvements.

State Experimentation: Beneath a Strong Federal Framework

Both Medicaid and the Clean Air Act share governance dynamics that feature a significant federal framework that sets forth national requirements and standards but also allows for a fair amount of state-specific experimentation as long as it is consistent with federal expectations. Medicaid clearly gains the attention of states through its sizable assumption of program costs and set of regulatory expectations that states must fulfill to secure federal funds. The Clean Air Act is far more reliant on the tool of regulatory standards, as its intergovernmental share is far more modest. But it also has set forth regulatory expectations that must be met if states are to avoid enforcement actions that could go so far as to include a federal takeover of all state program operations. These policies engage states in very different ways, highlighting different governance details.

Nonetheless, both programs have consistently used a federal mechanism that outlines program requirements for all states and collects data on a national basis to measure performance. Both programs have consistently been designed to reward states that comply with federal standards and make life more difficult for those that evade compliance. This is fundamentally different from the pattern in education policy, whereby broad national goals are set but states and localities have far more latitude in setting actual standards, even to the extent of reserving authority to select their own preferred standardized test that will be central to any potential evaluation of their performance in comparison with other states. Of course, the NCLB and federal education policies generally lack the strong federal presence of Medicaid and the Clean Air Act, setting up an intergovernmental governance mechanism that gives states far more autonomy in setting their own course, despite the continuing attraction of securing federal funds.

State Waivers: Experimentation in Medicaid

Formal waivers can serve as a temporary learning device for governance, enabling states to use their status as intergovernmental laboratories to explore innovations that can be closely monitored by other states and federal counterparts for lessons and ideas. They can also serve as a formal strategy at the federal level in pursuing a particular goal or standard but without attempting to impose some universal rubric on how each and every state will meet that goal or standard. Moreover, they potentially play an expanding role as executive authority mounts at federal and state levels and presidents and governors increasingly dictate key governance features. Nonetheless, the use of waivers as an approach to intergovernmental management has received remarkably little scholarly scrutiny, although Medicaid offers a substantial body of evidence on how the mechanism operates.[22]

One prominent form of Medicaid waiver involves federal efforts to outline areas where it would most likely endorse proposals for a targeted type of innovation. Approval of a state proposal would still be conditional on formal review but with the understanding that this general approach was entirely consistent with federal principles. Medicaid amendments in 1981, through the Omnibus Budget Reconciliation Act, gave the program expanded authority in this area. This included waivers to allow states to promote a transition from providing long-term care in institutionalized settings toward maximum use of home-based and community-based alternatives. The initiative responded both to growing concern about the mounting costs of institutionalized care and to a sizable body of research that argued that a more localized approach to such care was likely more compassionate and effective than predominant institutional approaches.

This ushered in a process of so-called 1915(a) waivers, whereby the federal government outlined its goals and expectations for state acquisition of a waiver, leaving states the option of doing nothing, seeking a partial (or experimental) waiver, or pursuing multiple waivers to attempt far-reaching change. This process began somewhat slowly in the 1980s but accelerated dramatically during the presidencies of former governors Bill Clinton and George W. Bush. By 2008, approval had been granted to 280 separate 1915(a) waivers, with at least one for every state, serving nearly 1.2 million people at a cost of $27 billion. This waiver program continues, and 2005 deficit reduction legislation gave added latitude to states in this arena. Performance assessments have noted that cost reductions have been considerably lower than anticipated and that many states have had to ration access to home- and community-based services, given high—and growing—demand. Nonetheless, one careful review of this experience concludes that this waiver program "has in all likelihood had a positive impact on the health of the elderly and people with disability as well as the quality of their lives."[23]

A second prominent form of Medicaid waivers involves so-called demonstration grants. These are general-innovation waivers, designed to allow states to make their case that the federal government should give them particular latitude to experiment. States must demonstrate to the satisfaction of Washington that proposed innovations respect federal Medicaid standards and also offer the prospect of superior outcomes if approved and implemented. This option has been open to the federal executive branch since the inception of the program, drawing on section 112 of the 1962 Social Security Act. But its use has expanded markedly in recent decades, with the Clinton and George W. Bush presidencies most active and enthusiastic about this approach. These demonstration waivers have taken many forms, with large numbers focused on transition toward managed care, reallocation of services to concentrate greater resources on preventive care, and cost containment. Perhaps the most famous waiver involved the proposal by Massachusetts governor Mitt Romney to transition toward a state mandate to require purchase of health insurance, with an expanded role for Medicaid in providing coverage options. Indeed, this waiver was instrumental in the design of 2010 federal health reform legislation and figured prominently in the 2012 presidential campaign, given the Romney candidacy for the Republican nomination.

It is more difficult to evaluate the collective experience of these demonstration waivers, given their diverse scope and intent. But it is important to note their continuing role as a central method for retaining federal standards while attempting to allow flexible and innovative state responses to those standards. The role of waivers is quite different in education policy, where the federal role is not as fully developed and waivers are commonly seen as a threat rather than a tool of innovation. This is reflected in former education secretary Rod Paige's 2002 denunciation of the very idea of waivers: "And if anyone comes to me to appeal for a waiver from the federal requirements, I hope to be very pleasant as I firmly say, not in this century. Not in this country."[24] Indeed, somewhat similar sentiments were expressed in 2011–12 as the Obama administration suggested that some form of waiver process may be necessary to give state and local school districts more latitude in meeting coming deadlines that are likely beyond their capacity. One additional point of contention concerning this intergovernmental governance tool is the substantial authority that waivers would likely extend to the executive branch of the federal government in the absence of legislation that establishes the kind of national standards operational elsewhere. This has been evident in Republican congressional responses to Secretary Duncan's proposals for expanded use of waivers under the NCLB as well as possible Obama administration waiver expansion in medical care and air quality.

State Implementation Plans: Experimentation in the Clean Air Act

The federal government, through the EPA, does indeed set a national definition of miles per gallon under fuel economy as well as closely related air emission standards set under the Clean Air Act. In fact, all air emission standards and regulatory requirements in that legislation operate on a national basis. This includes empirical measures of emission release and limits for each regulated contaminant as well as detailed provisions on what kinds of pollution abatement approaches (known as "best available control technologies") should be used nationwide. At the same time, the Clean Air Act operates in a federal system and not a unitary one. The EPA has not used waivers for air quality to nearly the extent that the Department of Health and Human Services has under Medicaid, but it has long relied on a set of negotiated agreements with each state known as a state implementation plan. A state implementation plan outlines the terms whereby the federal government delegates most regulatory oversight decisions to lead state environmental agencies. This may include room for program experimentation or special flexibility in unique circumstances.

Much of the intergovernmental negotiation over these plans involves the regional offices of the EPA, which divides the nation into ten zones that hold nearly two-thirds of the overall agency workforce. Regional oversight is thought to provide a better federal understanding of particular state and local circumstances than a central agency trying to negotiate with fifty state units at the same time. The past decade or more of experience with state implementation plans suggests considerable room for innovation, if states want to push the issue. This includes some far-reaching experimentation with the issuance of air quality permits for large industrial facilities, offering greater flexibility in technical compliance in exchange for demonstrable superior performance.[25] In the 1990s the Clinton performance management push included federal encouragement of states to think outside the conventional implementation box, to look across an array of contaminants and devise creative strategies that would adhere to legal requirements but potentially lead to superior environmental outcomes at lower overall costs. This also offered possible financial incentives, including more flexible use of categorical program funds through performance partnership grants. In New Jersey, for example, the state Department of Environmental Protection secured supplemental—and more flexible—federal funds and compliance flexibility in exchange for expanded efforts to integrate permitting across environmental media, inclusion of greenhouse-gas emission reductions to state air plans, and other innovations. In many respects, this comes closer to the Medicaid demonstration model than the more-targeted 1915(a) waivers program but more fully illustrates that this general approach of blending federal oversight with state flexibility is not confined to medical care, though it is not clear how readily this would translate to education policy, given the more modest nature of the federal government's role.

State Grant Competition: Racing to the Top in Air Quality

Implicit in both the Medicaid waiver and Clean Air Act state implementation plans are attempts to allow and encourage individual states to reach higher performance goals through innovation. Many areas of the Clean Air Act allow states to go beyond federal standards if they so choose, in many instances by setting more rigorous emission reduction levels. About two-thirds of the states have pursued this option; the remaining third either have banned such a step or simply have not pursued the option. One additional effort to allow for "racing to the top" has entailed a decades-long agreement between the EPA and the State of California. Under this arrangement, the federal government recognized that California has had particularly severe air quality problems and established an extensive air quality regulation program well in advance of federal legislation.

This agreement allows California to establish more rigorous standards. The process formally functions as a waiver, as the EPA must approve the proposal. But all the hundreds of known requests of this sort have ultimately been approved, many quite rapidly, suggesting that California has an enormous degree of latitude in this area. At this point, however, the remaining forty-nine states are provided with a choice, namely, to join sides with California and adopt its regulation or to adhere to the more modest federal standard. In many instances, this has led to considerable intergovernmental negotiation and pressure on the federal government to adopt the California-plus-others levels in an upward bidding war.[26]

The EPA-California arrangement varies markedly from the more recent attempt to adopt a Race to the Top approach in education, through Secretary Duncan's creation of a competition for funding among state contenders. As Kenneth Wong notes, applicants were evaluated on a number of criteria, including a commitment to promote teacher accountability and professional development, expand the number of eligible charter schools, and increase student eligibility for school choice programs.[27] The initial round triggered forty-one state applicants, of which sixteen were finalists and two were recipients (Delaware and Tennessee). A second round produced a larger set of recipients.

It is too soon to assess the impact of this approach, but the differences with the air quality case are significant. Under the Clean Air Act approach, California receives an ongoing invitation to propose modification that, if approved, can then be joined by other states. Under the education policy approach, a large source of funding is created, but it is one with an uncertain future and several broad goals, and it includes a state competition process with many likely losers. This latter approach is more like a project grant, albeit one with relatively few likely winners, that could be terminated at any point, as opposed to a longer-term commitment directly related to meeting established federal standards. This comparison further underscores the firmer foundation beneath federal efforts in the medical care and air quality cases and, in turn, the more fragile federal foundation in the case of education policy.

Mission Creep: Expanding beyond Capacity?

The resiliency of programs like Medicaid and the Clean Air Act in concert with the difficulty of enacting new federal legislation to address emerging problems opens the possibility of grafting major expansions onto existing structures. In both cases, major federal reform initiatives during the Obama presidency have relied heavily on using these established programs and governance arrangements to tackle vast new responsibilities. On one hand, their rather strong intergovernmental footing could provide a base for new departures. On the other, the possibility of adding far-reaching and highly controversial responsibilities could indeed impose a set of expectations beyond the capacity of the established program structure to deliver.

The case of turning to the Clean Air Act as a second best option for establishing greenhouse-gas emission permits represents an example of a move by a rather desperate administrative presidency in reaction to a failed legislative effort. The Clean Air Act has never been widely seen as a vehicle for regulating a wide range of greenhouse-gas emissions, in part because of the vast number of societal sectors that produce significant emission levels. Instead, respective Congresses spent much of a decade looking at a new form of legislation that would use emissions trading, working perhaps in partnership with the Clean Air Act but moving in independent directions and relying heavily on collaboration with other governing units such as the Department of Energy, the Department of Agriculture, and the Department of Transportation. This is consistent with Kenneth Meier's observation that "network management" can emerge as a major governance challenge.[28]

The Obama administration first proposed in 2009 the idea of developing greenhouse-gas reduction permits under the Clean Air Act, but this was largely viewed as a threat to prod Congress into agreement on comprehensive legislation. When legislative deliberations collapsed, the president carried through on his threat, leaving the EPA with an exceptionally complex and contentious policy development operation. The EPA continues to attempt to use state implementation plans and related provisions and has tried to ease implementation by delaying any official launch until 2013 and concentrating initially only on a small set of very large industrial facilities. It has also tried to use performance negotiations, including offers to give more latitude to states that make demonstrable early emission reductions or program commitments. Nonetheless, this will be a massive undertaking and require considerable elasticity in extending regulatory provisions that were designed exclusively for conventional contaminants. States such as Texas and Virginia have actively refused to cooperate with the EPA in any fashion and have taken the lead in multistate litigation trying to thwart the greenhouse-gas emissions reduction effort.

All of this looks like child's play in comparison to the 2010 Patient Protection and Affordable Care Act. This legislation was enacted under highly contentious circumstances, even though one of its core provisions borrows from the insurance purchase–mandate approach pioneered in Massachusetts through Medicaid waiver.[29] The act proposes to reduce dramatically the number of Americans without health insurance, with an anticipated transfer of at least 34 million uninsured Americans to the ranks of the insured. This 1,912-page bill is among the most complex pieces of legislation enacted in American history, with a vast range of regulatory provisions. It also includes what would clearly be the largest increase in the scope of Medicaid since its 1965 creation. Indeed, at least one-half of the newly insured under the act would transition into eligibility for Medicaid. The federal government would initially pledge to paying a share for added costs well above the standard program share, but this share would decline over time. There are considerable concerns about overall costs for both federal and state governments and questions about the need to modify Medicaid governance to accommodate such a potential surge of new enrollees. As in the EPA case, multiple states launched litigation efforts to repeal all or portions of the legislation, though these were largely rejected by a historic Supreme Court decision. However, states did win some added protection against possible losses of Medicaid funds in this case. In turn, at least seven states have given consideration to withdrawing formally from the entire Medicaid program, and still others are weighing significant service cuts in anticipation of the expanding coverage requirements.[30] Ironically, the recipient of the Medicaid waiver that launched the insurance mandate process, Mitt Romney, subsequently endorsed federal waivers under Medicaid to allow any state to withdraw from the new federal legislation.

The continued ability of Medicaid and the Clean Air Act to operate with a reasonable level of resilience, intergovernmental collaboration, and performance effectiveness is clearly challenged by these new developments. If these are at all a model, it is conceivable that established federal education programs, including the NCLB and the Individuals with Disabilities Education Act, could also become magnets to dramatically expand or reshape their mission. Given the challenges of enacting comprehensive legislation, the Clean Air Act serves as a reminder that a new president can rather dramatically shift the course of an existing program. Given the challenges of unmet public policy goals, Medicaid serves as a reminder that new policies can graft substantial new goals on established ones, whether or not they are ready for that role. In the case of education policy, this challenge becomes potentially more daunting, given the rather modest nature of the federal funding role when weighed against ambitious federal goals and aspirations that presidents and Congresses might like to set for the future.

Looking Abroad

Intergovernmental governance is a common thread that connects the cases of Medicaid, the Clean Air Act, and federal education policies such as the NCLB. The Medicaid and Clean Air Act cases suggest that it is possible to devise federal policy that produces reasonably coherent governance structures that foster some degree of federal and state collaboration. These programs have proved highly resilient and have demonstrated some significant performance-based achievements. They have also shown some capacity for adaptation and innovation, in some instances actively engaging states in a creative approach to intergovern-mental management. All of this takes place, however, under a clear federal state-ment of what is expected of states, whether this involves adherence to the core federal tenets of Medicaid in order to ensure reimbursement or state imple-mentation plans to retain oversight of the Clean Air Act.

Establishing a comparably clear federal framework in education will remain challenging, given the nation's enduring history of rooting education governance at the state and local levels. Nonetheless, as Kathryn McDermott and Kenneth Wong note, the intergovernmental partnership in education is currently in flux.[31] In particular, the Common Core State Standards Initiative provides a potentially powerful mechanism for creating a clearer and more stable framework that could serve as a basis for future intergovernmental collaboration. Such a transition, if it fully materializes, will not have emerged through federal commands, as in the Medicaid and Clean Air cases, but rather from state government initiatives to cre-ate a common framework capable of being embraced enthusiastically (as has the Obama administration thus far) by the federal government.

There may also be some merit to consideration of models and examples from outside the American experience, particularly through review of comparable policies in other federal or multilevel governance systems. A common theme in two prominent examples, one from health care and the other from air quality, has some parallels with the very features evident in the American Medicaid and Clean Air Act experiences. These ground a central-government role that imposes clear standards and expectations on state or equivalent units, including measures of performance. But they also give those subcentral jurisdictions a fair amount of latitude in discerning how best to meet central expectations and opportunity to receive any financial awards or benefits that may be available. In medical care, Canada's approach remains intriguing. Its federal government has long since established a series of national principles that provinces must address in exchange for substantial intergovernmental revenue transfer. These include public admin-istration, comprehensiveness, universality in coverage, portability, and accessi-bility. Each principle is accompanied by relatively straightforward descriptions of what Ottawa expects in return for funding through a fixed national budget-ing system, which places a cap on total expenditures. This process and the Cana-dian system generate numerous questions and criticisms, perhaps most notably timeliness of service delivery. But its comparative performance in terms of per capita costs, health quality performance indicators, and public support indicate that this kind of system has considerable merit.[32] There may, in fact, be some par-allels between the Canadian approach of combining core principles, performance expectations, and budgetary controls with some of the more successful state health care experiments of the past two decades in the United States, including those discussed under the umbrella of Medicaid.

Climate policy in North America and around the world is more mixed than the intergovernmental train wreck in the United States. In the European Union, the emissions-trading system was riddled with problems in its initial years of operation, from 2005 to 2007. These included lack of a central accountability system, which inadvertently allowed member states to literally set their own emission targets and self-allocate supplemental allowances, thereby skewing the proposed carbon market. But the European Union treated this as a period of experimentation and policy learning, using this round to make major modifications that secured a clearer set of central expectations and metrics and thereby transformed the system in more functional ways in recent years.[33] Under the latest round of operation, Brussels measures all emissions and allocates allowances to member states, much like a central banker overseeing a common currency. But within this system, each nation and each regulated emission source has considerable latitude to find the most cost-effective strategy to reduce emissions and maintain compliance. The American state and regional programs that are now moving toward implementation of their own carbon cap-and-trade programs are attempting to learn lessons from this very experience in Europe. California is planning to use 2013 as a practice round for its own initial carbon-trading initiatives, possibly in concert with state and provincial partners. At the same time, the ten-state Regional Greenhouse Gas Initiative in the Northeast is attempting to build on its initial years of experience to better link emission allowance adjustments with actual emissions, given unexpected dislocations in the American economy and electricity demand.

These examples serve as a reminder that there are lessons to be drawn for U.S. consumption from beyond American shores, much as Michael Mintrom and Richard Walley note, comparing the experience of various nations in education policy.[34] A common challenge in all of these cases, as well as the examples of medical care for the poor and air quality in the United States, is finding the best possible ways to craft a federal and state partnership that can prove reasonably functional and effective over time. These American case reviews suggest at least some success in sustaining that relationship over several decades through models such as Medicaid and the Clean Air Act, perhaps with some lessons for possible next steps in the education policy arena.

Notes

1. David Tyack, *The One Best System: A History of American Urban Education* (Harvard University Press, 1974).

2. Paul E. Peterson, *Saving Schools: From Horace Mann to Virtual Learning* (Belknap Press of Harvard University Press, 2011).

3. Paul Manna, *School's In: Federalism and the National Education Agenda* (Georgetown University Press, 2006).

4. Chapter 9, this volume.

5. Carol S. Weissert and William G. Weissert, *Governing Health: The Politics of Health Policy* (Johns Hopkins University Press, 2003); George Pickett and John J. Hanlon, *Public Health: Administration and Practice* (St. Louis, Mo.: C. V. Mosby, 1990).

6. J. Clarence Davies III, *The Politics of Pollution* (Indianapolis: Bobbs-Merrill, 1970).

7. Cited in Pickett and Hanlon, *Public Health*.

8. Paul E. Peterson, Barry G. Rabe, and Kenneth K. Wong, *When Federalism Works* (Brookings Press, 1986).

9. Frank J. Thompson, *Health Policy and the Bureaucracy: Politics and Implementation* (MIT Press, 1981).

10. Frank J. Thompson, *Medicaid Politics: Federalism, Durability, and Health Reform* (Georgetown University Press, 2012).

11. Gary C. Bryner, *Blue Skies, Green Politics: The Clean Air Act of 1990 and Its Implementation.* (Washington: CQ Press, 1995).

12. Amy Gutmann and Dennis Thompson, "The Mindset of Political Compromise," *Perspectives on Politics* 8 (December 2011): 1124–43.

13. Richard E. Cohen, *Washington at Work: Back Rooms and Clean Air* (Boston: Allyn and Bacon, 1995).

14. Richard P. Nathan, *The Administrative Presidency* (New York: Wiley, 1983); Barry G. Rabe, "Environmental Policy and the Bush Era: The Collision between the Administrative Presidency and State Experimentation," *Publius: The Journal of Federalism* 37 (Summer 2007): 413–31.

15. Chapter 9, this volume,

16. Donald P. Moynihan, *The Dynamics of Performance Management: Constructing Information and Reform* (Georgetown University Press, 2008).

17. Thompson, *Medicaid and Health Reform,* p. 19.

18. U.S. Environmental Protection Agency, *Air Quality Trends* (www.epa.gov/airtrends/aqtrends.html).

19. Shelley Metzenbaum, "From Oversight to Insight: Federal Agencies as Learning Leaders in the Information Age," in *Intergovernmental Management for the 21st Century,* edited by Timothy J. Conlan and Paul L. Posner (Brookings Press, 2009): 209–42.

20. Alain C. Enthoven, *Health Plan* (Reading, Mass.: Addison-Wesley, 1980).

21. Barry G. Rabe, "The Aversion to Direct Cost Imposition: Selecting Climate Policy Tools in the United States," *Governance* (October 2010): 583–606.

22. Carol S. Weissert and William G. Weissert, "Medicaid Waivers: License to Shape the Future of Fiscal Federalism," in *Intergovernmental Management for the 21st Century*, edited by Conlan and Posner, pp. 156–76.

23. Thompson, *Medicaid and Health Reform*, p. 197.

24. Paul Manna, *Collision Course: Federal Education Policy Meets State and Local Realities* (Washington: CQ Press, 2011), p. 43.

25. Daniel J. Fiorino, *The New Environmental Regulation* (MIT Press, 2006).

26. Barry G. Rabe, "Contested Federalism and American Climate Policy," *Publius: The Journal of Federalism* 41 (Summer 2011): 494–521.

27. Chapter 8, this volume.

28. Chapter 16, this volume.

29. John Dinan, "Shaping Health Reform: State Government Influence in the Patient Protection and Affordable Care Act," *Publius: The Journal of Federalism* 41 (Summer 2011): 395–420.

30. Thompson, *Medicaid and Health Reform*, p. 275.

31. Chapters 7 and 16, respectively, this volume.

32. Gerald W. Boychuk, *National Health Insurance in the United States and Canada* (Georgetown University Press, 2008).

33. Jorgen Wettestad, "European Climate Policy: Toward Centralized Governance," *Review of Policy Research* 26 (May 2009): 311–28.

34. Chapter 12, this volume.

PART IV

PATHS FORWARD

CYNTHIA G. BROWN

14

Toward a Coherent and Fair Funding System

The public education system in the United States has long been marred by inequity. African Americans, Hispanics, American Indians, English-language learners, students with disabilities, and low-income students historically have borne the brunt of inequitable treatment, and many continue to do so today. On national reading and math assessments in 2011, these students scored at least two grade levels behind their more advantaged peers.[1] The historical tension in this country over the purpose of public education, whether for democratic citizenship or for vocational and economic security, continues today, But it is undeniable that inequitable schooling undermines our children's opportunity for successful employment and economic security and denies them the tools necessary for political engagement and civic participation.

In the not too distant future, students of color will be the majority of U.S. public school students and will ultimately dominate the workforce of tomorrow. This will create an even more urgent need for the nation to make sure all our children, especially children of color, have access to a high-quality education.

The development and governance of our public school systems, and particularly their funding, have supported and exacerbated these inequities. Although the structure of public education has evolved, equality of opportunity remains elusive. A rational governance structure could improve student outcomes for historically disadvantaged students and make possible the success of numerous other schooling reforms.

History can tell us how our unaligned, dysfunctional, and inequitable school governance structures evolved, but to understand the current dimensions one needs to follow the money. Indeed, public decisionmakers have usually shortchanged certain groups of school children, whether through formal segregation or by employing different expectations for rural and immigrant students. But the most egregious inequity is the persistent imbalance in financial investments to public education.[2]

Access to resources is about governance, and the nation will not be able to resolve persistent inequities among student groups until it addresses the flaws of a diffuse, disjointed, and fundamentally incoherent governance structure that drives its public school funding. Without such reform, directing more money through the current governance system is unlikely to result in the substantial improvements in student achievement needed to reach national performance goals. Indeed, researchers have found that throughout the world, resource allocation policies that do not induce changes in behavior are unlikely to improve education results.[3]

For this author, equitable funding does not mean equal funding per student. Students' needs and schools' operational costs vary. And funding streams from all levels of government should take this into account. In an earlier chapter in this volume, Marguerite Roza describes in more detail the mechanisms of school funding. This chapter focuses on the equity implications of those arrangements.

Consequently, the chapter recommends a state-based system of school financing—though not necessarily state governance of school operation and design—one that eliminates local funding while increasing state and federal funding to make up the difference. It advocates that state legislators adopt weighted student funding schemes, built on a foundation of basic quality, for districts and for schools within districts. It calls for Congress to redesign the major federal funding formula and to close a federal law loophole that permits school districts to fund their schools unequally with state and local dollars. And it advocates that state and federal legislators develop and adopt measures of school district return on education investment and productivity.

Such legislative action will take an extraordinary amount of political will from officials at various levels in the fractured governance system, will far from evident today. But if all U.S. students are to have the same opportunity for successful futures in a globally competitive society, such political will must emerge. The imperative is ours.

How the U.S. School System Came to Be

From the country's beginning, the financing and operation of schooling was unequal. As early as the eighteenth century, colonial governments established schools along with laws and financial schemes to sustain them. These schools were often built on religious traditions and supported by landowners through "the coercive force of [property] taxes," which were eventually enshrined by states in compulsory taxation.[4] Lawmakers then grouped schools into school districts run by elected community leaders. Some districts were more financially advantaged than others. Indeed, decisionmakers held wildly different educational expectations for separate groups of students based on their race, national origin, and poverty status and consequently invested unequal amounts of money per student in their education. They completely ignored differences in students' educational needs that might translate into extra resources for some.

Early Years

The U.S. system of public schools that we know today evolved over the nineteenth century as the American public became concerned about both the quality of the minimal education in rural areas and the fast growth of cities populated by new arrivals from farmlands and foreign countries. Education had come to be recognized as a major gateway to more favored positions and wealth in society. Rural schools began as village centers, and city schools grew up in small communities usually populated predominantly by distinct groups identified by race, U.S. region, or country of origin. Poverty was widespread, but the promise of better opportunities beckoned. One group, African Americans, when given access to education at all, was usually forced to attend segregated and grossly under-resourced schools.

Local leaders governed schools in rural villages and small communities. School board trustees taxed their fellow property owners, hired teachers, and bought textbooks. Public investments in schooling were quite uneven, and there were virtually no attendance policies. This all changed quickly with urbanization and the growing complexity of American society and occupations. Soon control of school governance transferred from laymen to education professionals, though they still usually worked under the direction of elected lay school boards.[5]

From the earliest days of school systems, there were struggles between advocates for local school control and those for centralization. This was especially true in the new cities, where chaotic growth created challenges to the provision of basic services, including education, and where ethnic, class, and race disharmony was rife. As David Tyack has noted, "Convinced that there was one best system of education for urban populations, leading educators sought to discover it and implement it."[6] But to these educators, the one "best system of education" was never intended to provide equality of opportunity for all who attended school.

Neighborhoods or loosely confederated wards initially operated urban schools, and any centrally collected funds were allocated unequally depending on the relative power of local leaders. In the second half of the nineteenth century, city leaders began to appoint superintendents to oversee groups of schools, slowly creating central bureaucracies. The challenges were enormous. The first Chicago superintendent, appointed in 1854, oversaw two dozen teachers with an average of 100 students in each of their classrooms.[7] Even then, investments in city schools were unequal. In New York City, just a few years later, "a group of black leaders told a state investigating committee about the wretched condition of . . . segregated schools" and that "the board of education had appropriated one cent per Negro child and sixteen dollars per white child for sites and school buildings, even though there were 25 percent more black children attending school in proportion to their total population than white."[8]

Early twentieth-century reformers were successful in bureaucratizing the provision of public education. Experts now administered schools with an unprecedented level of centralized authority. The U.S. Congress even got involved, presenting a federal program for vocational education in 1917.[9] Between 1930 and 1970, two-thirds of schools and nine of every ten U.S. school districts were eliminated in a process of consolidation.[10] But the boundaries of many thousands of districts remained, drawn to preserve the education funding advantage for middle- and upper-income communities.

The centralizing trends were encouraged by state officials, who spearheaded initiatives to consolidate local schools as part of broader efforts to expand state control over public education. Not only was local control over education weakened by the elimination of many elected school boards, but also the authority of the remaining boards was eroded as state governments gradually extended their authority over issues such as district accreditation, school curriculum, and teacher certification.[11]

These more centralized local school districts and newly involved state governments were led by elites who firmly subscribed to notions of race-, ethnic-, and class-based differences and learning expectations for students. These officials put in place student-tracking systems and differentiated curriculums and assigned students based on their anticipated place in the workforce. And they invested fewer dollars in the education of those groups of students whom they considered inferior. Clearly, the "democracy" of democratically elected representatives governing education was incompatible with equity in education. These decisionmakers made investments and policies that reinforced rather than mitigated the educational disadvantage of poverty.

For a century, a wide variety of education reformers, including teacher groups and business organizations like the National Association of Manufacturers and the Chamber of Commerce, as well as African American leaders and their allies, decried the unfair and underfunded state of American education. The alliance was based on the confluence of concerns about civil rights and national economic development—an alliance that continues today on most K–12 education issues with the exception of tax revenue. Politically and in court, the reformers secured victories that resulted in greater state and local investment in schooling, especially teacher salaries and increased support for schools for black students, including, sometimes, integrated schools. But as Tyack points out, as late as the mid-1950s "the disparities in educational expenditures between states and between communities in states, and even within socioeconomic neighborhoods of the same districts . . . remained shockingly high, belying the goal of equality of opportunity revived by reformers at the close of World War II."[12] This pattern continues today.

Federal and State Action in the Mid-Twentieth Century

During the 1950s and 1960s opinion leaders and ultimately a significant portion of the public expressed growing concern about the deplorable state of schools with large concentrations of low-income students and those that were racially segregated. The 1954 Supreme Court decision in *Brown v. Board of Education* called for the end to legal segregation of public schools. However, little action to desegregate actually ensued, because local decisionmakers, having virtually total control over the operation of schools, enthusiastically chose to fund black schools at much lower levels than white schools. The federal government had no enforcement tools, and state governments had no motivation to act. In the meantime, the civil rights movement blossomed, and African Americans peacefully demanded the end to segregation at all levels of government. A decade after *Brown*, Congress finally acted with the passage of the Civil Rights Act of 1964, a far-reaching law with an immediately visible effect on public accommodations and schooling.

At the same time, there was also growing recognition that some states and districts were much poorer than others in terms of their tax bases and their much larger populations of low-income children. In 1965 Congress passed the Elementary and Secondary Education Act (ESEA) as a part of President Lyndon Johnson's War on Poverty. The act provided a federal contribution to public education, but it was a modest amount. Still, it sent out funds based on each state's number of low-income children using a flawed adjustment for cost-of-living differences. It also provided a vehicle to enforce the desegregation requirements of *Brown* and the 1964 Civil Rights Act by enabling the federal government to threaten to and actually withhold ESEA funds if desegregation did not move forward.

Title I, section 201, of the ESEA set forth as its categorical purpose to "provide financial assistance . . . to local educational agencies serving areas with concentrations of children from low-income families to expand and improve their educational programs . . . to meet the special educational needs of educationally deprived children." Although the act's intentions were good, local governing arrangements that federal policy relied on enabled many districts' administrators to undercut federal goals.

Local educators welcomed direct federal funding of public schools, but they were unaccustomed to federal directions on how to spend government money, and they championed local control. Rather than spending this $1 billion in high-poverty schools on the neediest students, they often used it for the general needs of schools and districts. Federal auditors documented the abuses, but no action was taken. A new breed of federally focused civil rights advocates uncovered the auditors' reports and in 1969 produced a widely publicized study, *Title I of ESEA: Is It Helping Poor Children?*[13] As Phyllis McClure makes clear, the "free-wheeling spending practices of school officials . . . made the case for strong federal guidelines that would lead to curbing the abuses and establishing comparability requirements that state and local funded services for schools receiving funds under Title I be equivalent to such services for schools that do not receive Title I funds. Not only was federal money being spent on the general needs of school systems (general aid), it was also paying for goods and services that had previously been purchased with state and local funds."[14]

The documented abuses in Title I spending led Congress in 1970 to give federal overseers more power in relation to state and local governments by enacting amendments that restricted how school districts could spend Title I funds. One major change was adoption of the comparability provision. Section 105(a)(3) said that "state and local funds will be used in the local educational agency to provide services in project areas which, taken as a whole, are at least comparable to services being provided in areas in such district which are not receiving funds under this title." But from the beginning, because of the push from the powerful Chicago congressman Roman Pucinski, the U.S. Office of Education regulations established a major loophole by excluding teacher "longevity pay," increases in pay solely attributable to years of teacher experience, from calculations of comparability.

Pucinski wanted to protect the ability of urban districts to permit more-experienced teachers to transfer to higher-income and lower-minority schools but still show comparability—an ability that would have been significantly undermined had districts been required to consider actual teacher pay when showing comparability of services. Of course, including the loophole allowed districts to assign the weakest and poorest-paid teachers to predominantly African American or Hispanic schools.[15] Thus the intent of federal law was subverted to benefit the status quo. It is an example of the general weakness of the federal government vis-à-vis states and localities in directing public education and the incoherence and misalignment of our current governance structure that works to perpetuate funding inequities.

States gradually assumed a greater share of school funding, but the patterns of inequity continued. The 1972 report of the bipartisan Select Committee on Equal Educational Opportunity of the U.S. Senate observed that "in nearly every state the highest spending school district spends at least twice as much as the lowest spending school district. Variations of 3-, 4-, and 5-to-1 are not uncommon and at the extreme—in Wyoming and Texas—the highest spending school district spends more than 20 times as much as the lowest."[16] Table 14-1 illustrates some comparable data. No one had ever seen numbers like these before the 1970s.

The committee noted that comparison of expenditures among states did not present an accurate picture of school finance disparities. More important were the intrastate differences in per pupil expenditures. The committee went on to say

Table 14-1. *Interstate Disparities in Per Pupil Expenditures, 1969–70*[a]
Dollars

State	High	Low	High-to-low index[b]	State	High	Low	High-to-low index[b]
Alabama	581	344	1.7	Missouri	1,699	213	4.0
Alaska[c]	1,810	480	3.8	Montana[e]	1,716	539	3.2
Arizona	2,223	436	5.1	Nebraska[e]	1,175	623	1.9
Arkansas	664	343	2.0	Nevada	1,679	746	2.3
California	2,414	569	4.2	New Hampshire	1,191	311	3.8
Colorado	2,801	444	6.3	New Jersey[f]	1,485	400	3.7
Connecticut	1,311	499	2.6	New Mexico	1,183	477	2.5
Delaware	1,081	633	1.7	New York	1,889	669	2.8
District of				North Carolina	733	467	1.4
Columbia	n.a.	n.a.	n.a.	North Dakota[g]	1,623	686	2.3
Florida	1,036	593	1.7	Ohio	1,685	413	4.0
Georgia	736	365	2.0	Oklahoma	2,566	342	7.5
Hawaii	n.a.	n.a.	n.a.	Oregon	1,432	399	3.5
Idaho	1,763	474	3.7	Pennsylvania	1,401	484	2.9
Illinois	2,295	391	5.9	Rhode Island	1,206	531	2.3
Indiana	965	447	2.2	South Carolina	1,741	350	5.0
Iowa	1,167	592	2.0	South Dakota	610	397	1.5
Kansas	1,831	454	4.0	Tennessee	700	315	2.4
Kentucky	885	358	2.5	Texas	5,334	264	20.2
Louisiana	892	499	1.8	Utah	1,515	533	2.3
Maine	1,555	229	6.8	Vermont	1,517	357	
Maryland	1,037	635	1.6	Virginia	1,126	441	
Massachusetts	1,281	515	2.5	Washington	3,406	434	
Michigan	1,364	491	2.8	West Virginia	722	502	
Minnesota[d]	903	370	2.4	Wisconsin	1,432	344	
Mississippi	825	283	3.0	Wyoming	14,554	618	

Source: Select Committee on Equal Educational Opportunity, *Toward Equal Educational Opportunity: The Report of the Select Committee on Equal Educational Opportunity*, U.S. Senate, pursuant to S.R. 359, 92 Cong., 2 sess. (U.S. Government Printing Office, 1972).

a. Data are not fully comparable between states since they are based entirely on the data included in state's analysis of per pupil expenditures.

b. Empty cells appear in the original Select Committee document for an undetermined reason.

c. Data represent revenue per pupil.

d. Does not reflect subsequent reforms.

e. Data are high and low of average for districts grouped by size.

f. Data are for fiscal year 1969, since fiscal year 1970 data were not yet available at the time of this writing.

g. Data are averages of expenditures of all districts within county.

that the "most immediate impact of school expenditures occurs in individual schools," although few districts broke down their expenditures on a school-by-school basis. It then cited the District of Columbia case of *Hobson* v. *Hansen* (1967). Julius Hobson, a local community activist, testified before the committee that in 1970, three years after the court decision, the spending differential between the lowest-funded "black-dominated" and the highest-funded "affluent white" elementary schools in Washington had increased from $411 per pupil in 1967 to $506 in 1968 and the gap between the lowest- and highest-funded elementary schools was as much as $1,719 by 1970.[17]

President Nixon issued an executive order in 1970 that established the President's Commission on School Finance. The commission issued its report and recommendations in March 1972, nine months ahead of the Senate committee. Its major finding was that "the financial problems of education derive largely from the evolving inabilities of States to create and maintain systems that provide equal educational opportunities and quality education to their children."[18] The 157-page report is chock full of recommendations that eerily track today's education reform debates. But most significant for this discussion is the call for "full state funding of elementary and secondary education"; the report recommends that

—"State governments assume responsibility for financing substantially all of the non-federal outlays for elementary and secondary education with local supplements provided up to a level not to exceed 10 percent of the State allocation"

—"State budgetary and allocation criteria include differentials based on educational need, such as the increased costs of educating the handicapped and disadvantaged, and on variations in educational costs within various parts of a State"

—there be enacted a "general purpose Federal incentive grant that would reimburse States for part of the costs of raising the State share of total State and local educational outlays above the previous year's percentage . . . contingent on the submission by a state of a plan for achievement of full State funding over a reasonable period of time"[19]

Of course, these commission recommendations had major implications for the balance of power in school governance among local, state, and federal levels. Here a federal body is recommending state control of school financing, with other operational controls sure to follow. Sadly, the commission's recommendations got little attention and gained no traction.

A year later the U.S. Supreme Court ruled in *Rodriguez* v. *San Antonio* that there is no federal constitutional right to an equal educational opportunity, thereby relieving pressure on states to take action. Today, forty years after bipartisan efforts to address the inequitable financing of public education, those concerns remain largely unaddressed by state and local as well as national decisionmakers.

State and Local Court Activity since 1970

Over the past forty years, lawsuits challenging state education finance systems have been brought in forty-five states, with plaintiffs succeeding about half the time.[20] These lawsuits attack unfairness in state funding that results in different investments in students based on where they live, not their educational needs or a sufficient level of spending for all. In most states, the battle has been over whether state funding should make up for inequitable wealth across local school districts, where those with more property wealth could tax themselves at lower rates and still raise substantial sums. Schools in property-poor districts received less support and usually had disproportionate numbers of low-income and minority students. In other states, the issue has been whether states provide enough resources to operate schools with an adequate level of quality.

But success in many of these cases has been short lived, replaced by several years of wrangling within state legislatures (for example, Texas, New Hampshire, New York) or voter revolt through public referendums placing caps on property taxation (for example, California's Proposition 13 in 1979, following the state supreme court's 1976 decision in *Serrano* v. *Priest*). In California, the governance relationships are particularly convoluted. Californians often use the ballot initiative process, "the most democratic and purely majoritarian form of policymaking."[21] This has resulted in regular conflicts between the courts and voters. Sometimes ballot initiatives are challenged to keep them off the ballot, but usually the challenges are made in state or federal courts after voter approval. Initiatives are allowed to amend the state constitution but may not fundamentally revise it.[22]

Perhaps the most famous state finance–equity suit is *Abbot* v. *Burke* in New Jersey. The *Abbott* case began in 1981 when the Education Law Center challenged the New Jersey public education finance system on behalf of four school districts. In 1990 the state supreme court upheld an administrative law judge's finding of inequity on behalf of twenty-eight and eventually thirty-one "poorer urban" districts. Action shifted to the state legislature to provide a more equitable and adequate funding scheme and then back to the courts when plaintiffs concluded that the legislature's actions were insufficient. The ping-pong game among the plaintiffs, courts, legislature, and governor continues to this day. Along the way, important remedies have been adopted, perhaps the most significant being preschool for disadvantaged children and desperately needed school construction in low-wealth districts. Indeed, "New Jersey was the first state to mandate early education, starting at age 3, for children at risk of entering kindergarten or primary school cognitively and socially behind their more advantaged peers."[23]

Although the results of school finance litigation have certainly been less than desired, the same can be said of a handful of school desegregation cases that involved state financial investments. The U.S. Supreme Court limited state responsibility in desegregation cases when it ruled in its 1974 decision in *Milliken v. Bradley* that because there was no evidence that the fifty-three surrounding school districts had contributed to the segregation of Detroit schools, those districts did not need to assist in their desegregation. The court also emphasized local control over the operation of schools.

Federal courts have at times found evidence of state complicity in the segregation of schools. And they have ruled that states must make financial commitments to right these wrongs. But the results have rarely been positive. A Kansas City, Missouri, case exemplifies the worst distortions of the law's intent. Plaintiffs filed suit in 1977 alleging that Kansas City, Missouri, schools were illegally segregated. In 1984 a federal district court judge ruled in the plaintiffs' favor, establishing that the Kansas City School District and the State of Missouri were liable for illegal segregation of schools. Although the ruling appears not to have reflected the actual hopes of the predominantly African American community, between 1985 and 2003 federal judges ordered more than $2 billion in state and local dollars for the school district to be used to encourage desegregation. The decision

> turned every high school and middle school (as well as half the elementary schools) into "magnet schools," each with a distinctive theme—including not merely science, performing arts, and computer studies, but also classical Greek, Asian studies, agribusiness, and environmental studies. The newly constructed classical Greek high school housed an Olympic-sized pool with an underwater observation room, an indoor track, a gymnastic center, and racquetball courts. The former coach of the Soviet Olympic fencing team was hired to teach inner-city students how to thrust and parry. The school system spent almost a million dollars a year to recruit white kids from the suburbs, and even hired door-to-door taxi service for them.[24]

Not surprisingly, the $2 billion investment showed no gains in performance or integration. Test scores continued to decline. Schools became more racially isolated. And eventually the African American community pushed for a return to neighborhood schools.

Some school desegregation cases have been affected by state action that changed the governance situation but left funding inequity unaddressed. Results were predictable. Chicago, Illinois, is a case in point. Most experts have concluded that Illinois today has the most inequitable state funding system in the country, despite efforts by bipartisan groups of advocates like the Center for Tax and Budget Accountability to correct it. It is likely that racial politics has played a role in the state funding pattern, particularly in Chicago.

The creation and maintenance of segregated schools is not unique to Chicago, but the city is a particularly grim story. African Americans migrated to Chicago in two waves—after World War I and during World War II. In the second wave the African American population more than tripled to more than 1 million. Racist real estate policies confined blacks to the South Side and eventually the West Side. Temporarily integrated schools soon became segregated. In the 1960s African Americans and biracial groups mounted substantial protests, a congressional committee held a highly publicized hearing on de facto segregation in the city, and the federal government attempted to intervene, ultimately unsuccessfully. Despite the maintenance of segregated schools in Chicago, the flight of the white population exploded as it did in many of the nation's cities. The Chicago school board made a few weak attempts at voluntary integration, but mostly it engaged in active gerrymandering of school boundaries and confinement of black students to overcrowded schools next to underenrolled predominantly white schools and built whole schools of temporary buildings—called Willis Wagons, after Superintendent Benjamin Willis—on vacant lots. In the late 1970s the federal government tried again to address school segregation in Chicago. Although the U.S. Department of Education held up federal funding and ultimately the Department of Justice took Chicago officials to federal court, the action came too late. There were too few white students left in the city to integrate many schools. (Indeed a new group of students, Latinos, had arrived in substantial numbers.)[25]

During the years of the Chicago desegregation struggles, the state remained mostly uninvolved in school governance, other than shortchanging the system in funding. But that changed in 1979, when the Chicago school district declared bankruptcy. The white-run school system had run up a $400 million debt— more than $1.2 billion in 2011 dollars. The legislature established the School Finance Authority, whose members were jointly appointed by the Illinois governor and the Chicago mayor, that bailed out the system but drastically cut funds for schools. It forced the superintendent, Joseph Hannon, to resign. The mayor and the school board initiated a national search for his replacement and in 1981 chose Ruth Love, Chicago's first African American superintendent. Love was handed an impossible job. The district did not return to financial stability until 1991, three years after she left office.[26]

The state continued to shortchange the city. For example, in the 1990s the formula used to calculate state school aid was supposed to equalize funding throughout the state and make up for low tax bases and large numbers of low-income students. However, state legislators arbitrarily decided that only 23 percent of Chicago students were from low-income families, whereas in fact, "at least half of the children in the Chicago public schools are poor," and, because of these purposely erroneous calculations, "schools in the six-county suburban area [surrounding Chicago] got the full benefit of their 7 percent poverty children," while inner-city schools did not.[27] Finally, state officials concerned about the quality of Chicago schools put the schools under mayoral control in 1995. Although school performance has improved to some degree, the district still suffers from serious financial challenges with little help from a continuing inequitable state funding scheme.

Given the U.S. system of school organization, with its approximately 15,000 school districts and the constitutional requirement that states provide public education, any hope of fair financial treatment must rely on state action. The 1972 reports of the Senate Select Committee and the Nixon Commission on School Finance concluded the same. The 1973 *San Antonio* v. *Rodriguez* case in Texas, and the subsequent Supreme Court decision, locked the door on federal action under the U.S. Constitution, though the Supreme Court affirmed that school finance cases could be successful in state courts. However, state litigation successes have been modest, and many states continue to operate systems with great funding disparities across their school districts. State revenues and funding schemes often do not fully remedy and may even exacerbate inequities among districts owing to their location in richer or poorer parts of a state.[28]

Education Governance in the United States Today

While Americans have awakened to the fact that their country is losing ground internationally, their elected officials fight most proposals for change. After a bruising fight over health care reform in 2010 the United States moved closer to, but still far distant from, the health care systems of other advanced countries. As for public education, the past decade has seen significant movement on reforms, particularly with regard to common nationwide standards and policies that enhance the teaching workforce. As policymakers ask schools to produce more students prepared to go on to postsecondary education and employment training, the public and their representatives have developed, to some extent, a sense of urgency to improve the education system for all students. Indications that two-thirds of future jobs must be filled by workers with a postsecondary degree or credential contribute to this feeling.

The move to common standards and assessments under the same governance systems for public schools makes no sense. Equal achievement outcomes, or at least much smaller gaps in achievement, will not be attained if state and local governments invest less rather than more in minority and low-income students relative to their educational needs. But that is what is done across the country. Today's national demands for better public schooling are built on anachronistic funding schemes that work in different ways at local, state, and federal levels.

Does money really matter in education quality and student outcomes? A war among researchers over this question has raged for years. As more has been learned about education expenditures, and with troubling, public examples of large sums seemingly wasted or put to poor use, there seems to be a consensus that money is necessary but not sufficient. Erik Hanushek, the strongest critic of claims that education resources lead directly to achievement outcomes, states that "providing resources without changing other aspects of schools . . . is unlikely to boost student performance."[29] Changing other aspects of schools is essential, but many of the most important strategies for turning around low-performing schools require increased funding. Policymakers now agree that the public education sector must start paying attention to the return on investment in public schooling.

Local Funding Inequity

About 40 percent of public school funding across the country is generated at the local level, mostly by property taxes. But in any given state the percentage of funds that is raised locally can range from 3 percent (in Hawaii) and 8 percent (in Vermont) to more than 60 percent (in Illinois and Nevada).[30] Critics and advocates have decried inequitable state funding of school districts for decades, but the inequitable distribution of resources within school districts has become well understood only in the past decade. Why? Because school-level budgeting or consideration of per pupil expenditures by school was never really done, and so there were no data to present to the public. Instead, districts typically sent resources to schools through staff allocations (for example, number of teachers or guidance counselors per set number of students), for specific programs (for example, advanced placement classes, prekindergarten, band, magnet schools), or in response to requests from schools that had an understanding of the funding process. As a 2006 Fordham Institute report notes, "A dirty secret is that schools often get a good bit of their funding by asking for it—and some schools are better than others at asking."[31]

There had not been any sort of translation of the value of investment in staff and programs or even perks into actual dollar figures. Now that skilled researchers and experts like Marguerite Roza and Karen Hawley Miles have examined actual spending school by school in several large school districts, the gross underinvestment in schools with large concentrations of low-income students and students of color has become clear. With few exceptions, these schools receive lower per pupil allocations of nonfederal funds than schools with less poverty, and they rarely receive funding with extra weighted dollars provided on the basis of students' extra needs or the concentration of such students. It is quite likely that this pattern has prevailed since school systems began; it was simply not documented.

Although the documentation of inequitable resources among schools is relatively recent, knowledge of the situation is not. Indeed, the federal government has condoned inequitable spending in low- and high-poverty schools within school districts for decades, undermining the congressionally stated goal that federal elementary and secondary school funds supplement state and local funds in high-poverty schools.

The primary inequity in school funding across schools is teacher salaries. As Marguerite Roza has pointed out, "Inside nearly every urban school district in the country, teachers are paid more to teach middle- or upper-class students than to teach high-poverty students."[32] The reason for this is twofold: the single-salary scale used to pay teachers and the concentration of less experienced teachers in high poverty schools. Under the single-salary schedule prevalent in the vast majority of school districts, teacher pay increases with experience and postgraduate credit. More-experienced teachers often transfer to less challenging schools and are given priority in transfer requests and assignments.

Historically, decisions about teacher pay have been made by local school boards. In most of the North and West, school boards negotiate salaries and benefits with teacher unions and enter into collective bargaining agreements. Although it is not a formal process, school boards in the South usually make compensation decisions through similar processes. States have also enacted compensation policies. However, as research over the past decade has documented the wide variations in teacher effectiveness,[33] legislators and advocates alike have questioned the logic of paying teachers the same regardless of success with their students or their assumption of additional responsibilities. In many places, courageous and innovative union leaders have entered into negotiations and agreements to alter compensation systems. The federal government—both the Bush and Obama administrations and Congress—has also encouraged such change through the federal Teacher Incentive Fund program that has allowed numerous districts and sometimes states to develop and experiment with new pay plans and evaluation systems that reward effective teachers and give assistance to improve those who are struggling.

State Funding Inequity

States today pick up slightly more than 50 percent of the cost of public education, on average, but the split between local and state share varies greatly among states. Most states use sales and income taxes to finance schools, and a few add lottery funding. Advocates and litigators for poor and minority students have battled for more than forty years in the courts and legislatures about the fairness of state funding systems.

Although these battles continue today, some progress has been made in the many states that have increased their investments in the neediest students. In a recent survey and report, Deborah Verstegen finds that thirty-four states support programs for at-risk children and thirty-seven provide aid for English-language learners. She concludes that "this is a notable departure from the past as states are recognizing the high costs and needs of students who come to school without functional literacy in the English language, which is the language of instruction. Only four states do not provide any additional assistance for either low income/at-risk students or English learners."[34] Still, in many states, legislators remain slow to respond to the needs of growing numbers of disadvantaged students in their states; in a few, they have actually retrenched.

California is the starkest example of backsliding. Although California legislators equalized funding across school districts to a large extent after the *Serrano* decision, the adoption of Proposition 13 began a downward spiral in statewide education spending and the resumption of interdistrict funding inequity. Today, California spends much less than the national average on per pupil expenditures and has one of the highest costs of living. In a recent paper for the Center for American Progress, Frank Adamson and Linda Darling-Hammond find that in California,

> the range of instructional expenditures now exceeds a 3-to-1 ratio between low- and high-spending districts, both on an adjusted and unadjusted basis. This is true even when the highest-spending districts, which are often quite small, sparsely populated, or otherwise unusual, are excluded from the analysis. Unadjusted spending per pupil ranges from about $6,000 to $18,000 (using the 95th percentile district as the top of the scale to eliminate the atypical outliers). Strikingly, adjusted spending shows an even wider gap, ranging from about $6,100 to $23,500 per pupil—a ratio of nearly 4-to-1.[35]

Adamson and Darling-Hammond show that the school district salaries of teachers with comparable education and experience varied by a ratio of more than two to one in 2009, a substantial increase from the year 2000. And the range of teacher salaries increased after adjustments were made for labor market conditions, high-salary districts spending more than twice as much as low-salary districts for beginning teachers and nearly three times more for more-experienced teachers with similar experience and education levels.[36]

It is relatively easy to argue that California public school students attend grossly underfunded schools generally and that low-income students are concentrated in school districts that receive the smallest shares of state and local funds. California students are also low achievers. California students were the lowest-performing students outside the South on eighth-grade math and eighth-grade reading portions of the 2011 National Assessment of Educational Progress. (New Mexico scored lower on fourth-grade math and Alaska scored lower on fourth-grade reading.) Indeed, California scored lower on this assessment in both these grades and all courses in 2009 than Arkansas, Florida, Georgia, Kentucky, North Carolina, South Carolina, Texas, and Virginia.[37]

The New Jersey story was more promising by the end of the 1990s. Its legislators adopted, by force of law, a needs-based approach to remedial and supplemental programs and reforms, with attendant financial investments, that resulted in more equitable state funding of education. Since then, National Assessment of Educational Progress results show progress in closing achievement gaps and improving education outcomes in reading and math. For example, between 2003 and 2007, all New Jersey students improved their fourth-grade reading scores, and the gap between African American and white students continued to narrow through 2011. On eighth-grade math, all students in New Jersey improved between 2003 and 2011, and achievement gaps were narrowed for African American but not for Latino students.[38]

But there is a troubling side of the New Jersey fiscal equity story. The average per pupil expenditure in school year 2008 in New Jersey was $16,163, whereas the California average was $9,706. Well-known *Abbott* districts, such as Newark, spent $23,500 per pupil in 2008. Others, such as Asbury Park, spent an average $33,225 on each student. What do these particular districts have to show for the investment in terms of student-achievement gains? Very slow improvement. To be sure, other *Abbott* districts, such as Union City, have taken advantage of the injection of resources. The 12,000-student system, which spent $18,739 per pupil, is now the highest-performing New Jersey city district.[39] That the district improved the alignment of goals and funds by implementing school-based budget modeling certainly played a part.[40]

The fact remains, however, that many *Abbott* districts are poster children for the fact that money alone cannot turn around low-performing schools and districts. New Jersey taxpayers are getting a low return on their investment in these districts.

Successful state court challenges in the past usually sought financial remedies with little or no attention to policies that could make a difference in school quality and thus outcomes. This has undermined the credibility of these efforts, in New Jersey and other states. A recent study by Ulrich Boser reports that inefficient school systems, among other things, represent a significant reform opportunity. Low productivity is costing the nation's school system as much as $175 billion a year. Without clear controls on how additional school dollars are spent, more education spending will not on its own improve student outcomes.[41]

What is needed is clear, but in tough economic times the political will to correct inequity is even scarcer than the historical pattern of inaction in better times. Still, given the urgent need to better prepare all students, particularly the economically disadvantaged, to become part of a future workforce that demands better preparation, state policymakers and advocates need to embrace a measure of intrastate equity to promote discussion and reform. Ultimately, they will need to tackle issues of efficiency and productivity as well, but this should not be done before equitable funding systems are adopted.

Diana Epstein has made key recommendations about fiscal equity: that states "should employ progressive school finance systems so districts with high percentages of low-income children receive more resources than those with fewer low-income children. Those states without progressive finance systems should therefore undertake reforms, a process that is both technically difficult and politically challenging since it is likely to create funding winners and losers as funds are distributed in new ways." She also says that "a useful fiscal equity measure should express the relative level of funding inequity in a state, adjust for local cost differences and include weights for extra student needs, capture whether or not a state's school finance system is progressive or regressive (providing more or less funding to districts with a high percentage of low-income children), and be relatively simple to use and explain." Epstein concludes by acknowledging that states may resist such reform and that the federal government should consider incentivizing states to take action to reform their school finance systems.[42] This may well be necessary because state legislators will most likely have to deal with hold-harmless provisions for districts slated to lose funding during a phase-in period in order to gain enough support for this kind of change. Such provisions might require extra funding, but in the long run they are really about the reallocation of resources.

Rhode Island, the last state without a state school funding formula, recently reformed its state school finance system. Kenneth Wong details how this came about and notes the stimulus for action provided by the availability of federal competitive funds through the Race to the Top program. He concludes, "The reform process itself was successful because of effective leadership and mutual trust, the prominent role played by independent expert analysis, a fiscally responsible approach that focuses on students and their needs, and a data system that is transparent and publicly available."[43]

Federal Funding Inequity

In the United States, in contrast to other advanced countries, the federal government supplies a small portion of the funds used by public schools, just around 9 percent. The primary purpose of the funding is to provide extra resources for the students and schools with the greatest educational needs. Essentially, it is weighted student funding. Federal funds play virtually no role in eliminating inequity between states in education expenditures. A much greater federal investment in education could be used to improve interstate equity, but this idea faces two obstacles. The most obvious is resource constraint, a theme put into high relief by political brinksmanship in the summer of 2011 around the issue of raising the country's debt ceiling.[44] But the other obstacle stems from the same politics that shaped existing federal funding streams. In general, to gain majority votes, members of Congress have adopted formulas to distribute federal funds in ways that spread the money around to large numbers of school districts in all states.

The major federal programs, the Elementary and Secondary Education Act and the Individuals with Disabilities Education Act are theoretically designed to provide extra dollars for disadvantaged students. But both have shortcomings. Title I of ESEA, the largest federal funding source, presents the greatest problems. Its formula—actually four formulas—is supposed to target funds, through states, to schools with the greatest need based on student poverty. But the formula does not do this well. The four formulas have been cobbled together and layered on top of one another since enactment of the ESEA in 1965. These formulas are complex, but, in brief, there are three major problems.

The first is that though money is directed to districts based on the number of low-income children who reside in them, to account for variations among states in the cost of providing education, state average per pupil expenditure was originally used as a proxy for that variation in cost, and it continues to be used today. Perhaps using this proxy made sense fifty years ago, when measures of the cost of providing education were crude, but today it represents a bias in favor of wealthy states. There is no need to continue the bias. Better measures of cost, such as the Department of Education's comparable wage index, which also captures variations within states, are now available.

A second problem is that, as Raegen Miller notes, just one of the four formulas accounts for states' fiscal effort, that is, their expenditures for education relative to their fiscal capacity to support schools. This oversight means that the federal government subsidizes wealthy states that tax themselves at relatively low rates while failing to reward low-wealth states that choose to tax themselves at relatively high rates. For example, California has more children in poverty than any other state and operates large schools with an average enrollment of more than 650 students. A high-poverty school in California, Miller observes, "could easily receive more than $200,000 less than it would receive if it were in Maryland. The cumulative shortfall for California amounts to $532 million, a sum worthy of concern."[45] Clearly, the formulas that produce these allocations are out of sync with fairness and common sense. Much stricter attention to fiscal effort would be required to support a federal role in improving interstate equity, but in the meantime, fiscal effort, along with the cost of providing education, can serve as a ready framework for assessing the shortcomings of the Title I formulas.

The third major problem with the Title I formulas is their use of two alternate approaches to weighting the number of low-income children that drives funds to districts. The upshot of the two approaches is that large school districts receive disproportionately larger allocations of Title I funds, on a per low-income child basis, than medium-size and small, often rural, districts. For example, in fiscal year 2009 each low-income child in the Flint, Michigan, school district generated $1,984 in Title I funds, while those in Detroit drew $2,266. Detroit's 19 percent advantage over Flint is greater than the difference in these districts' values on the comparable wage index. Yet, in that year, Flint and Detroit served roughly the same concentration of children in poverty—38 and 39 percent, respectively, but Flint served 9,577 low-income children while Detroit served 80,289 low-income children.[46] The funding advantage comes purely from Detroit's size.

A significant revision of the ESEA Title I formula could address these inequities. But formula fights in the U.S. Congress are historically raucous affairs, pitting regions of the country and states against one another. The Center for American Progress recommends that there be one formula and that it focus on concentrations of children from low-income families, not on raw numbers of children in poverty; account for states' fiscal effort, that is, the extent to which a state leverages its own resources to finance public schools; and use the comparable wage index to measure cost differences across and within states.[47] The center's recommendations would increase the intensity of congressional formula debates since school districts themselves would join the fray with states and battle especially based on their size and concentration of child poverty. But such a debate would be a more genuine, honest exchange, and, one might hope, lead to a fairer result. That said, however, the United States will never approach the equitable national funding systems of its higher-performing peers until it invests more federal funds in supporting public education, since at its current levels it cannot make up for the interstate differences in child poverty and taxable wealth. Alas, an increased proportion of such federal funding seems an unrealistic expectation for the next decade or two.

Another serious problem with federal action—really inaction—concerns the federal Title I comparability provision. This provision in theory requires that state and local funding amounts be comparable per pupil between Title I and non–Title I schools before the federal funds are added to a school's budget. Although this provision always contained a loophole, over time it has been weakened further. As Ross Wiener has pointed out, "Today, school districts need only have a single-salary schedule for all teachers and policies that ensure equivalence among schools for teachers, administrators, and other staff, and for instructional materials. The law previously required equivalence with regard to student-staff ratios *and* per-pupil instructional staff expenditures, but it now allows school districts to choose between [those options] and affords them other options for determining comparability."[48]

Today, most large school districts take advantage of these weak federal provisions and do not allocate their state and local dollars equitably in real dollars to high- and low-poverty schools. This has now been well documented. An especially graphic example is Jennifer Cohen and Raegan Miller's study of the lack of comparability in Florida districts.[49] Using school-level data on Florida's sixty-seven school districts over seven years, Cohen and Miller find salary differences that corresponded to school poverty levels. "Holding all else equal," they conclude, "a 10 percentage point increase in the student poverty rate corresponds to a $213 decrease in average teacher salary. This means teachers in a school with a 70 percent student poverty rate make, on average, $1,067 less than teachers in an otherwise identical school with a 20 percent student poverty rate. This relationship is wiped out, however, when they account for schools' average level of teacher experience. A one-year increase in average teacher experience translates to a $523 increase in average teacher salary. This pattern conforms to expectations and corroborates prior research on hidden salary gaps."[50]

Especially troubling are Cohen and Miller's findings for a couple of Florida districts where even with the addition of Title I funds—which of course are supposed to provide extra funding—the per pupil expenditures of high- and low-poverty schools are barely equal. Polk County exhibits the greatest inequity. Its lowest-poverty schools outspent its highest-poverty schools, despite the addition of supplemental Title I funds. Osceola County was not much better. Cohen and Miller report that "the average regular per pupil expenditure among the highest-poverty schools in Osceola was just $101 more than among the lowest-poverty schools. This difference corresponds to about a quarter of the approximately $380 per student Title I allocation the county's highest-poverty schools received during the period studied, so it is also dubious to conclude that Title I funds played a supplemental role in Osceola's Title I schools."[51]

Some observers fear that requiring the equal expenditures of state and local dollars before the addition of federal funds will have adverse consequences. Specifically, they fear the forced transfer of more-experienced and higher-paid teachers to high poverty schools where they may not want to work. Advocates for closing the comparability loophole, however, believe that forced transfers should be prohibited as a means for school districts to come into compliance with the comparability requirement and that full compliance should be phased in. Comparability is about financial resources, not personnel. Extra dollars for the most challenging schools might be used to reward more effective teachers, employ master and mentor teachers to work with novice teachers and those who are struggling, expand learning time for students, and numerous other programs and activities that can support needy students.

The Obama administration and several members of Congress—notably Representative Chaka Fattah (D-Pa.) and Senator Michael Bennet (D-Colo.)—have made closing the comparability loophole a priority. Indeed, the proposed reauthorization of the ESEA adopted in October 2011 by the Senate Health, Education, and Pensions Committee contained loophole-closing language. However the full Senate never voted on the bill.

Education Systems in High-Performing Countries

Systems of public schools in Europe and Asia, like that in the United States, developed in the nineteenth century. Today, however, virtually all high-performing countries, as measured by the Programme for International Student Assessment and the Trends in International Mathematics and Science Study, have more-centralized systems of education governance and financing than does the United States.[52] Most are national systems, and a few—Canada, Australia, and Germany—have state-based systems, similar to that in the United States. They do not have local school districts governed by elected school boards. These high performers do many things differently with regard to schooling, including how they fund schools. As Andreas Schleicher, head of the Indicators and Analysis Division for the Directorate for Education of the Organization for Economic Cooperation and Development, points out, "Spending patterns in many of the world's successful education systems are markedly different from the U.S. These countries invest the money where the challenges are greatest rather than making resources contingent on the economic context of the local communities in which schools are located, and they put in place incentives and support systems that attract the most talented school teachers to the most difficult classrooms."[53]

Many of the high-performing nations were not always so successful educationally or economically. Several countries in Europe and Japan were in ruins after World War II. Finland was a wood-based economy under Russia's thumb until the breakup of the Soviet Union. And South Korea and Singapore became economic powerhouses only in the past two decades. Yet these countries broke with their pasts, embraced the national redesign of their centrally operated school systems, and instituted fairer funding schemes. And they did this quickly over twenty and thirty years.

Interestingly, even in European countries that are today struggling politically and socially with large immigrant populations of different racial and religious backgrounds, legislators continue to invest disproportionately greater resources in education of immigrant students. The Netherlands is a case in point. Despite recently adopted national policies that would be viewed as discriminatory in the United States and major incidents of immigrant harassment, the Dutch system of school financing remains a system of weighted student funding based on student needs. (Although all schools in the Netherlands are fully publicly funded, there is also complete freedom of choice of schools, including religious and private schools.) Between 1985 and 2006 there were two major categories of weights: 0.25 for native Dutch students whose parents had little education and 0.9 for immigrant students from non-Western countries, including Morocco, Turkey, Surinam, and the Antilles.[54] In 2006 legislators changed the weights for political rather than technical reasons. They eliminated both major weights and replaced them with two new weights phased in over time: 0.3 for students whose parents have low education and 1.2 for students whose parents have very low education. The latter weight continued to favor immigrant students.[55]

In their recent study of weighted student funding in the Netherlands, Helen F. Ladd and Edward B. Fiske conclude that "some Dutch policymakers and researchers view closing achievement gaps, rather than equalizing school quality, as the main goal of weighted student funding." Ladd and Fiske add that money alone was by no means the sole policy lever used to address achievement gaps. But, they report, between 1994 and 2004, "the gaps for the immigrant groups, but not for the disadvantaged Dutch, narrowed quite substantially."[56]

The Contrast between the United States and Higher-Performing Countries

Radical change in the design of public education—in either the three-tiered governance structure or in funding—has never taken place in the United States. The question is why? My view is that progress has been blocked by challenges associated with the racial diversity—Caucasians, African Americans, and Native Americans—present in the United States since its most formative days, compounded later by large growth in the immigration of multiple ethnicities, and with ongoing class differences. Elites and decisionmakers at all levels embraced education as a sorting mechanism and invested inequitably, usually in different per pupil amounts with little or no regard for the extra costs of educating disadvantaged students. Eventually, decisionmakers came to see the economic need to provide a good education to a greater proportion of U.S. students. But the successful European and Asian countries, with their much more centralized governments, got there first. They, too, once had large low-income populations and tumultuous class conflicts, but they did not have the racial diversity of the United States. By centralizing governance, they were able to cope with the educational and social needs of their less diverse populations. None of them today have the wide gaps in distribution of wealth prevalent in the United States (though their wealth gaps are now growing), and most are as economically successful.

Although the extent of its racial and ethnic diversity makes this country unique, so do other aspects. Most high-performing nations, with the qualified exception of Australia and Canada, were never as wide open in space and have much longer histories of developing as societies, with rules of behavior and with governments that provide substantial social and educational safety nets. Americans have always believed deeply that the nation offers limitless opportunities to succeed and have never looked to centralized government at the state or federal level for adequate, sustained support. The great expanse of land, a wealth of natural resources, and a common language contribute to this belief, as do stories of successful individuals. These beliefs transcend race and national origin. Horatio Alger may have been white, but the well-known histories of Oprah Winfrey and Barack Obama are similar.

Americans believe hard work alone brings rewards and that people are entitled to keep most of what they earn. Too few question the great inequities in their salaries and in the U.S. tax structure. They do not expect or believe that government at any level should intervene. Many believe that poor people are either directly responsible for their condition or are unlucky; in either case, they should be given some help, but not too much. This belief often carries racial undertones. There is a fairly widespread belief that low-income minorities are either innately or culturally inferior and that low-income whites are more likely to be unlucky. Today, this bad luck seems to include unemployment owing to the outsourcing of jobs overseas and the lack of adequate education and training to adjust.

Conclusions and Recommendations

Looking at efforts to provide quality education to low-income and otherwise disadvantaged students in the United States, the problem of inequity seems virtually intractable. Yet there has been considerable progress. A substantial middle-income population of African Americans and Hispanics emerged with the elimination of previously legal discrimination in schooling and job opportunities. There is a much stronger presence of elected officials of color at all levels of government. Large numbers of students with disabilities who were historically excluded from school are now receiving an education. However, progress in narrowing achievement gaps—though rapid until two decades ago—has now slowed, and current trends indicate that large inequalities are likely to persist well into the future.

A change in education finance governance will go some way to achieving equity of opportunity. Without fair access to adequate resources, schools serving disadvantaged students will never reach the level of success required to keep the national economy strong. Equitable access to resources is about governance driven by a sensible scheme and decisionmaking process of distribution.

Christopher Edley, the dean of the Boalt Law School and cochair of the U.S. Commission on Equity and Excellence, recently said of school finance policy,

> There is no area of public policy that better illustrates the contemporary chaos of our federalism [characterized by] federal, state, and local [governments, including] 15,000 local school districts plus 3,000 charter school

entities . . . property taxes but also state revenues and some federal revenues . . . [and] utter confusion in the minds of the public as to which level of government is responsible for particular policy choices, particular failures, particular successes. . . . The school finance reform issue brings into high relief this conflict over roles, responsibilities, and accountability. . . . Our local system of finance and our continuing commitment to a nineteenth century model of local control, challenge our notion of one nation.[57]

It is hard to imagine that the United States would ever adopt a national system to fund education, as so many of its advantaged peers have over the past two centuries. But a fifty-state system of school funding would be a vast improvement. Such a system might include five measures.

First, states should assume the entire cost of their public schools, except for minimal federal help, and adopt systems of funding whereby weights are assigned to students with extra educational needs—low-income students, English-language learners, and students with disabilities. There should be extra weights for students in schools with large concentrations of low-income students. And there should be federal financial incentives to stimulate state action to establish such systems. States should ensure that districts allocate resources to schools in terms of real dollars and in amounts that reflect student needs. Each state should develop a measure of return on investment and hold local educators accountable for the productivity of their districts through public reporting of efficiency metrics. A wide variety of governance arrangements—charter schools, districts in which noncontiguous schools share curriculums and pedagogical approaches, virtual schools, districts organized to further economic and racial-ethnic integration of schools, transformation of low-performing schools into state-operated districts, and so on—should be responsible for the design and operation of schooling, using the dollars allocated under a state funding system. The state role in operational matters would vary from state to state.

This is basically the 1972 recommendation of President Nixon's Commission on School Finance. The commission also recommended a general-purpose federal incentive grant to assist in meeting additional costs of the changed system.[58]

Second, local districts should no longer have the power to use local property tax revenue to fund schools. All revenue supporting public schools should come from states and the federal government. This, too, was a recommendation of the Nixon commission. States will need to raise additional revenue through any number of tax strategies, for example, state property taxes, income taxes, sales taxes, or others, to make up for the loss of local revenue and to add revenue to level up schools and districts previously shortchanged. Parents and other community members should be allowed to provide up to 10 percent of a school's overall budget in additional financial assistance to support special programs beyond a basic, high-quality education.

Third, federal funds should financially assist those states with insufficient wealth to generate necessary funds for schools as long as they meet a baseline level of tax effort. To be politically viable, federal funds will need to reach every state and support schools with high concentrations of low-income students, as does the current ESEA Title I. However, Congress should redesign the four Title I formulas into one formula. That formula should drive funds based on concentrations of children from low-income families, not on raw numbers of children in poverty. It should also include some measure of fiscal effort and a measure of the cost of schooling.

This recommendation does not really change the current federal role in supporting public education. Many argue that the proportion of federal funding support should be substantially increased. This may be viable once more federal revenue is available. But it makes no sense for Congress to supply greater amounts of funding if it continues to do so inequitably.

Fourth, Congress should close the ESEA Title I comparability loophole that endorses the local practice of often providing lesser amounts of state and local funds per pupil to Title I than to non–Title I schools. It should also prohibit the forced transfer of teachers to meet the comparability requirement. In addition, in exchange for Title I funding, the federal government should make permanent the reporting of school-level expenditures, which was mandated as a one-time requirement under the American Recovery and Reinvestment Act of 2009.

Fifth, the federal government should provide competitive incentive grant funds to states and a few districts to develop and experiment with education reforms such as adopting weighted school funding systems, designing model measures of return on investment, and providing a level ground of academic content and expectations across states and districts. This could lead states and districts to adopt more equitable funding systems and to engage in much needed innovation.

Ultimately, we must recognize that our current governance structure is not working. It both allows and creates significant inequity in our public schools. Substantial, maybe even massive, changes in the way we view and handle governance in education are needed, and we must be open to addressing all aspects of our current system, regardless of their entrenched or historical nature. Adopting the changes above would result in a more coherent way to govern education finance, one that would produce greater funding equity in the United States and move us toward equal educational opportunity for all children. But regardless of the approach states take, the end goal must be to produce a governance system that ensures all schools have the resources they need and power to spend them wisely.

Notes

1. National Center for Education Statistics, "National Assessment of Educational Progress Subject Areas," 2011 (http://nces.ed.gov/nationsreportcard/subjectareas.asp.).

2. For a more detailed accounting of how financial inequity within schools takes place, see chapter 3 in this volume.

3. Eric A. Hanushek, "School Resources," in *Handbook of the Economics of Education*, edited by Eric A. Hanushek and Finis Welch (Amsterdam: Elsevier, 2006).

4. See Institute for Educational Equity and Opportunity, "Education in the 50 States: A Deskbook of the History of State Constitutions and Laws about Education," 2008 (www.ifeeo.org/sitebuildercontent/sitebuilderfiles/edureportexcerptfinal2.pdf).

5. David B. Tyack, *The One Best System: A History of American Urban Education* (Harvard University Press, 1974).

6. Ibid., p. 28.

7. Ibid.

8. Ibid., p. 119.

9. The Smith-Hughes Act of 1917, Pub. L. 64-347.

10. Christopher Berry, "School Consolidation and Inequality" in *Brookings Papers on Education Policy: 2006–07*, edited by Tom Loveless and Frederick Hess (Brookings Press, 2007).

11. Ibid.

12. Tyack, *The One Best System*.

13. Ruby Martin and Phyllis McClure, *Title I of ESEA: Is It Helping Poor Children?* (Washington: Washington Research Project and Southern Center for Studies in Public Policy and the NAACP Legal Defense and Education Fund, 1969).

14. Phyllis McClure, "The History of Educational Comparability in Title I of the Elementary and Secondary Education Act of 1965" (Washington: Center for American Progress, 2008).

15. Ibid.

16. Select Committee on Equal Educational Opportunity, *Toward Equal Educational Opportunity: The Report of the Select Committee on Equal Educational Opportunity,* U.S. Senate, pursuant to S.R. 359, 92 Cong., 2 sess. (U.S. Government Printing Office, 1972).

17. Ibid.

18. President's Commission on School Finance, *Schools, People, and Money: The Need for Educational Reform* (U.S. Government Printing Office, 1972), p. 10.

19. Ibid., pp. 60–61.

20. Eloise Pasachoff, "How the Federal Government Can Improve School Financing Systems" (Brookings Center on Children and Families, 2008).

21. Craig B. Holman and Robert Stern, "Judicial Review of Ballot Initiatives: The Changing Role of State and Federal Courts," *Loyola of Los Angeles Law Review* 31, no. 4 (1998): 1240.

22. Ibid., p. 1244.

23. See Education Law Center, "The History of *Abbott* v. *Burke*," 2011 (http://staging.edlawcenter.org/cases/abbott-v-burke/abbott-history.html).

24. See R. Shep Melnick, "The Two Billion Dollar Judge: A Review of *Complex Justice: The Case of Missouri* v. *Jenkins*," *Claremont Review of Books,* Spring 2009, pp. 13–15.

25. Dionne Danns, "Northern Desegregation: A Tale of Two Cities," *History of Education Quarterly* 51 (February 2011): 77–104.

26. Ibid.

27. Patrick T. Reardon, "School Board Axes $42 Million in Jobs, Programs," *Chicago Tribune*, September 1, 1991.

28. Diana Epstein, "Measuring Inequity in School Funding" (Washington: Center for American Progress, 2011).

29. Eric A. Hanushek, *Courting Failure: How School Finance Lawsuits Exploit Judges' Good Intentions and Harm Our Children* (Stanford, Calif.: Education Next Books, 2006), p. 270.

30. See National Center for Education Statistics, "Total Revenues and Percentage Distribution for Public Elementary and Secondary Schools, by Revenue Source and State: School Year 2007–08," 2008 (http://nces.ed.gov/programs/coe/tables/table-sft-2.asp).

31. Thomas B. Fordham Institute, *Fund the Child: Tackling Inequity and Antiquity in School Finance* (Washington, 2006), p. 16.

32. Marguerite Roza, *Educational Economics: Where Do School Funds Go?* (Washington: Urban Institute Press, 2010), p. 7.

33. *Learning Denied: The Case for Equitable Access to Effective Teaching in California's Largest School District* (Oakland, Calif.: Education Trust West, 2012); Eric A. Hanushek and Steven G. Rivkin, *The Distribution of Teacher Quality and Implications for Policy* (Palo Alto, Calif.: Annual Review of Economics, 2012).

34. Deborah A. Verstegen, "Public Education Finance Systems in the United States and Funding Policies for Populations with Special Educational Needs," *Education Policy Analysis Archives* 19 (July 2011) (http://epaa.asu.edu/ojs/article/view/769).

35. Frank Adamson and Linda Darling-Hammond, *Speaking of Salaries: What It Will Take to Get Qualified, Effective Teachers in All Communities* (Washington: Center for American Progress, 2011).

36. Ibid.

37. See National Center for Education Statistics, "State Education Data Profiles," 2011 (http://nces.ed.gov/programs/stateprofiles/).

38. National Center for Education Statistics, "Achievement Gaps: How Black and White Students in Public Schools Perform in Mathematics and Reading on the National Assessment of Educational Progress" (U.S. Department of Education, 2011).

39. See Edutopia, "From Failing to Model District," 2003 (www.edutopia.org/media/3313_systemreform/html/uc_overview.html).

40. Anthony N. Dragona, "Tuning the Tin Ear: In Search of Fiscal Congruency," *School Business Affairs* 77 (January 2011): 23–26.

41. Ulrich Boser, *Return on Educational Investment: A District-by-District Evaluation of U.S. Educational Productivity* (Washington: Center for American Progress, 2011).

42. Diana Epstein, *Measuring Inequity in School Funding* (Washington: Center for American Progress, 2011), p. 1–2.

43. Kenneth K. Wong, *The Design of the Rhode Island School Funding Formula: Toward a Coherent System of Allocating State Aid to Public Schools* (Washington: Center for American Progress, 2011), p. 21.

44. Federal law restricts the amount of debt the federal government can amass. When we reach this statutory limit, like we did in 2011, Congress must either raise the debt

ceiling, in effect, giving itself permission to spend more than it raises in revenue, or balance the federal budget by cutting all spending that the government cannot pay for solely from revenue.

45. Raegen Miller, *Secret Recipes Revealed: Demystifying the Title I, Part A Funding Formulas* (Washington: Center for American Progress, 2009), p. 4.

46. Raegen Miller, *Softening the Blow: Toward A Fairer Allocation of Title I Funds* (Washington: Center for American Progress, 2011), p. 1.

47. Ibid.

48. Ross Wiener, "Strengthening Comparability, Advancing Equity in Public Education" (Washington: Center for American Progress, 2008).

49. Florida school districts are not unique in funding schools inequitably. It is just easier to document in Florida because Florida is ahead of its peers in reporting actual school expenditures, including measures of actual average teacher salaries and per pupil expenditures, in total and by clusters of programs—regular, exceptional, vocational education. Regular expenditures include those funded by Title I.

50. Jennifer Cohen and Raegen Miller, *Evidence of the Effects of the Title I Comparability Loophole: Shining a Light on Fiscal Inequity within Florida's Public School Districts* (Washington: Center for American Progress, 2012), p. 3.

51. Ibid., p. 18.

52. The Program for International Student Assessment is a test of student knowledge and skills that is administered every three years by the Organization for Economic Cooperation and Development on behalf of participating governments in seventy countries. Trends in International Mathematics and Science Study is an international mathematics and science assessment that allows the United States to compare the achievement of our 4th and 8th graders to that of students in other countries. It is administered every four years.

53. Andreas Schleicher, "The Importance of World-Class Schools for Economic Success," testimony before the Senate Health, Education, Labor, and Pensions Committee, March 9, 2010 (http://help.senate.gov/imo/media/doc/Schleicher.pdf).

54. Adding weights for a given category allocates more resources for students in that category—usually because those students require additional resources. The weight is a multiplier of the basic per pupil allocation that is provided on top of it. The higher the weight the more additional resources are allocated for a given child.

55. Helen F. Ladd and Edward B. Fiske, "Weighted Student Funding in the Netherlands: A Model for the U.S.?" *Journal of Policy Analysis and Management* 30 (Summer 2011): 470–98.

56. Ibid., p. 491. For further discussion of education governance in other countries, see chapters 10, 11, and 12, this volume.

57. Christopher Edley, remarks at Center for American Progress event, "School Finance Reform: Impacts on Equity and Lessons from Rhode Island," Washington, August 3, 2011 (www.americanprogress.org/events/2011/08/schoolfinancereform.html).

58. For a similar state funding proposal, see chapter 15 in this volume.

PAUL T. HILL

15

Picturing a Different Governance Structure for Public Education

Education governance is always difficult in the United States.[1] Although K–12 education is administratively set apart from other public services, it is subject to the vagaries of school board elections and the pressures of interest-group politics.

Subjecting education to electoral and interest-group politics has consequences. Winners at the ballot box and in the struggle for control of bureaucracies try to dominate schools with policies and mandates.[2] School heads and teachers, as the lowest-ranking bureaucrats in a tall stack of policymakers and administrators, face many constraints as they try to meet the needs of the children in front of them. Depending on one's point of view, a particular mandate might be benign or necessary. But in the aggregate the constraints imposed by governance—about what must be taught, who may teach, what books and other materials may be used, how schools and classrooms are organized, and when schools will open and close—force particular allocations of time and money and limit problem solving at the school level.

The politics of education in the United States can be nasty, and conflict is constant. The roots of conflict are easy enough to see. The beneficiaries of primary and secondary education, especially small children, cannot effectively assert their own interests. The adults who care about education have interests of their own that conflict with those of other adults and are not perfectly aligned with those of children. The interests of different adult groups naturally grind against one another.

These conflicts are endemic to the education of young children, but many other countries (and private schools in the United States) manage them more smoothly. In those other contexts professional elites are in charge of education policy and professionals run schools. Parents, free to choose schools, have real but defined options. These arrangements do not eliminate the intrinsic conflicts among adults, but they do keep the lid on them—until, that is, low performance or patterns of discrimination (or the entry of an unassimilated minority, such as the Muslims in Europe) undermines the legitimacy of current arrangements. Then, the education politics of private schools or other countries can become as noisy and intrusive as our own.

Can Americans deal with the intrinsic conflicts around public education in a different way, one that buffers if not totally insulates schools from the shifting winds of politics and interest-group conflict? That is the challenge of this chapter.

Why Rethink Governance?

In the United States, every level of government—federal, state, and school district—can impose controls of some kind on schools, on how funds will be used and accounted for, what jobs teachers may and may not do, how many students may be assigned to a teacher in an hour or a day, how space and equipment will be used, what parent groups must be consulted before decisions are made, what facilities schools may occupy, and so on.[3] School boards can intervene in almost any detail of school operation and district human resource management under the guise of casework for constituents.[4] Teacher collective bargaining agreements, court orders, and individualized education plans for students with special needs are also part of governance. So are licensing policies that exclude many people with relevant skills from working in schools, and school district control over school buildings, which favors some schools with free facilities and forces others, for example, charter schools, to pay.

As Richard Weatherly and Michael Lipsky have shown, the requirements affecting teachers and principals are so complex that no one can abide by them all simultaneously.[5] Although every rule was made for a reason, no one has carefully considered whether individual rules conflict with one another. As in other politically governed organizations, practitioners must choose between working to rule—that is, following all requirements scrupulously until the enterprise grinds to a halt—or selecting which rules to follow and which to ignore.

Weatherly and Lipsky argue that the existence of conflicting regulations liberates "street-level bureaucrats" such as teachers and principals by allowing them to choose which directives they will follow. In practice, however, overregulation creates a threatening environment in which actions taken by street-level actors to fulfill one requirement can put them out of compliance with another.[6]

Our governance system can make it impossible for the people at the interface between the school and the pupil to act on what they know: parents who know what their children need, principals who are able to identify a teacher who can be effective in a particular school, teachers and school leaders who know what a school's needs are and therefore how it should spend its budget, teachers who know what their students have and have not mastered. Instead, our system acts as if the exercise of discretion is dangerous.

Even in school districts that now threaten to close low-performing schools or to fire ineffective teachers, much of the old governance structure remains in place. This means that regular public schools must try to improve performance while still carrying all the old compliance burdens; it also means that educators can still hope a good compliance record might help them survive a poor performance record.

Such rules have profound effects on what students experience and what schools can produce. Both singly and in combination, they privilege some practices over others, force schools to waste time and money, and prevent innovation. Yet many educators and elected officials support them, claiming that the rules are the price of using public money and educating all children.

Governance constraints facing U.S. public schools do not merit the deference they get. Most if not all are results of interest-group advocacy (for example, for special programs) that define groups of students, instructional fads, or employment security. As Terry Moe has shown, temporary majorities control future actions by encoding them in rules and bureaucratic structures.[7]

Yet publicly funded education for children up to the age of eighteen is impossible without some form of governance. Compulsory school attendance and taxpayer investment in K–12 education are premised on the idea that not all parents would or could invest enough in their children's education to ensure full preparation for remunerative work and effective citizenship. Expenditure of public funds always requires some accounting and therefore some rules. In the field of education, chief among these rules is that discrimination against students by race, sex, language group, or income cannot be allowed.

The question about governance is how to meet the inevitable requirements for compliance with civil rights laws, state accountability requirements, and proper management of public funds without driving out within-school problem solving, adaptation to natural variations in student need and interests, and innovation. I argue here that public education governance can be rationalized so that it increases the degree to which educators can focus on learning rather than the demands of regulation and politics. However, no governance arrangement can totally eliminate interest-group advocacy or change the fact that the beneficiaries of public education, children, do not understand their long-term interests but contending adult groups think they do.

How to fix public education governance in the United States is not a new question. Analysts have suggested many alternative forms of governance intended to eliminate many of the inequities and inefficiencies built into the system. Milton Friedman ushered in an era of governance reform thinking. He argues for eliminating regulation and bureaucratic provision in favor of a government-funded marketplace in which parents are free to enroll their children in any school and entrepreneurs are free to run any school they like.[8] John Chubb and Terry Moe suggest a regulated market, in which families have free choice and providers need to get a license and abide by civil rights laws.[9] I have argued for a contracting regime in which public authorities contract with independent parties to provide schools and also close low performers; public funds would follow students to the schools in which they enroll.[10] Others have suggested leaving a government-operated school system intact but putting different people—mayors, appointed boards, or state officials—in charge or using performance standards to focus the attention of educators on student learning, not distracting rules.[11]

These proposals, all of which incorporate one or more of the possible "control processes" identified by Joseph Murphy (state, citizen, professional, community, and market control) all have been tried in limited ways.[12] However, none has been fully implemented because the political processes that created our current governance system also shore it up.

Why add further to this literature? There are two reasons. First, the politics are changing so that proposals that generated lethal opposition in the past might get a more serious look today.[13] Increasing numbers of large-city school systems are experimenting with new school creation, use of charters and contracts, and experimentation with new sources of teachers and recruitment and rewards systems for educators. Teachers unions, once able to block such initiatives, though still powerful, are beset with criticism from former allies and their own members. Second, the foregoing ideas are not the only ones possible. As Terry Moe and I have argued, there is no reason to insist, as some earlier proposals do, that there is no real role for government in the oversight of public education.[14] It is possible to formulate new hybrid proposals that balance the roles of public and private actors that might be both more acceptable and more effective than any tried before.

Criteria for Possible Governance Systems

I propose five criteria that any U.S. public education governance system should be designed to meet: elected representation; professional and executive freedom to act; intolerance of inequity and neglect; efficiency; and responsiveness to performance and adaptability to new needs and possibilities.[15] These criteria naturally arise from criticism of the existing system. It is only from understanding the consequences of particular arrangements that we can identify the need for something better.

These criteria will be debated and might be improved. But the concerns integrated into these criteria are the ones that must be dealt with; no other desiderata are as important as those raised here. The criteria are not all perfectly aligned. There are tensions, for example, between representation and professional freedom of action, and in some cases between equity and efficiency. It is impossible to eliminate these tensions entirely by clever design of a governance system; thus a governance system must be able to manage, not hide, conflicts. Any governance system will have its risks and challenges. Our current education governance system, however, fails badly on most of the criteria.

Elected Representation

In America, elections confer legitimacy. This does not mean that Americans expect to vote on every issue or want elected representatives only to take actions that are immediately popular. Instead, Americans want to think their representatives owe them their jobs and always question whether they are retaining citizens' confidence. There is considerable latitude in the design of representative institutions and in what powers elected representatives can wield. There is also tolerance for suspension of some powers of elected representatives in emergencies, for example, following Hurricane Katrina. But the inexorable pressure toward elected representation now evident in the demands to restore local control of New Orleans's schools indicates that stable governance solutions must ultimately include representative elections.

Representation can backfire if elected officials become beholden to particular groups and are able to remain in office despite showing bias. But representatives can play indispensable roles in balancing competing interests and resisting poorly informed mass opinion. Representation has its risks and benefits; other aspects of a governance system can affect the likelihood that representation will be genuine and resist capture.

Executive and Professional Freedom

The second principle is in tension with the first. Elected representatives need to oversee the system, but no one benefits from having the schools so dominated by rules that professionals cannot do their best for children or subjected to such intrusive oversight that school leaders cannot focus on instruction. The same is true at the system level. Superintendents and other top administrators need the freedom to attack problems quickly and decisively.

Today, the traditional education profession is under attack, as analysts question the effectiveness of education school training, traditional licensing of teachers and principals, and seniority-based teacher pay schemes. There are movements to remove education schools as gatekeepers to teaching and school leadership, allow lateral entry for people from other professions, and link pay and promotion to measures of performance on the job.

These developments question whether the profession as currently defined is as good and effective as it could be. But they do not assume that just anyone could do the job of a teacher or principal. On the contrary, they seek to staff schools with the most competent and effective people possible, assuming that decisions made by principals and teachers are all important.

Thus despite the contention over training, licensing, and pay, there is no real dispute over the importance of getting excellent teachers into jobs and giving them the freedom to do their best. The question is whether current barriers to entry into teaching, and the way we now pay teachers and estimate the value of their contributions, give us the best possible teaching force.

Intolerance of Inequity and Neglect

Since 1964, American public education has been required, both by law and public expectation, to avoid assigning poor and minority students to inferior schools, to avoid admissions discrimination based on race, and to close gaps in achievement and opportunity. Later laws also established the rights of handicapped children to appropriate services and, when possible, full inclusion in mainstream classes.

In practice, public school systems do not always meet these expectations. School quality, teacher experience, central-office services, and education dollars are all unevenly distributed; schools in the poorest neighborhoods often get the least of everything. Special-education service requirements also strain budgets and force trade-offs between groups of students. Core aspects of the current governance system, including collective bargaining–based placement and retention privileges for senior teachers, also prevent effective action in many cases.

But the expectation remains. A desirable future governance system must not just make formal promises of equity; it must be designed to keep them.

Efficiency

Public education uses two kinds of scarce resources, children's precious time and taxpayers' precious money. Children have only one chance to be, say, nine years old; and once spent, taxpayer dollars cannot be spent again. Although there are disputes about how much to emphasize efficiency, Americans are not happy to learn about a teacher who was paid despite being demonstrably incompetent or about other wastes of public funds. The current recession has created a new awareness of the need to get the most possible out of time and money. This represents an evolution in expectations. In earlier, flusher times, principals and teachers were not expected to worry about costs or make program decisions on the basis of demanding cost-benefit comparisons. Critics of spending decisions could be labeled enemies of public education. Now, careful marshaling of public resources is both necessary and legitimate.

Efficiency, like equity, is a goal always to be sought. Although it makes sense to assume that the governance system that maximizes efficiency will spend as much as possible on instruction and as little as possible on administration, nobody knows enough about these figures to mandate a universal solution.

Performance and Adaptability

Consistent with the two previous criteria, it is not enough for public education to offer schools that look well staffed and equipped. A good school is one that works for the children who attend it, and a good system is one that makes sure every child is in a school that works for him or her. There is real uncertainty about what constitutes a good school, especially for the low-income and minority children whom no state or locality has been able to bring up to the levels that guarantee high school education and college admission.

A good system must therefore be one that seeks high performance and admits uncertainty. School effectiveness is to be sought, not assumed. For governance, this means that the system is naturally skeptical, not cocksure, and seeks and uses evidence about what is working and what is not. The governance system, including the elected officials at the top, must not be so constrained by politics as to be unable to change course in search of better performance.

Public school systems, especially in big cities, often find themselves saddled with contracts and spending commitments that stifle problem solving: buildings they no longer need, financial commitments (such as obligations to retirees that must be paid from current revenues) that they can no longer meet. The "one best system"[16] constructed after World War II worked well enough when student enrollments and per pupil funding were constantly growing, but contemporary conditions discredit its assumptions of permanence and universality. Public school systems need the freedom to experiment with instructional and staffing strategies, including greater use of online instruction.

Permanent commitments constrain and in many cases prevent the search for efficiency and performance. Although total flexibility is not possible—skilled professionals need competitive pay and reasonable job security, and buildings and equipment can be obtained only through multiyear leases—the governance of public education must not make permanent arrangements when more flexible ones are possible.

The Current System in Light of the Five Criteria

Our current governance system does not fare well in light of the foregoing criteria, as summarized in table 15-1. In general, the current system does offer elected

Table 15-1. *The Current System and Governance Criteria*

Criterion	Current system
Based on representation	Elected school boards are nominally representative, though susceptible to capture by organized groups
Open to strong executive and professional action	Traditional superintendents are often outsiders with weak political bases, and are easily disposed of by school boards. Principals' authority over hiring, spending, and instructional decisions is tightly circumscribed. Superintendents and principals gain freedom of action only when normal politics are suspended.
Intolerant of inequity and neglect	The system is, by intent, dedicated to equity and remedying achievement gaps, but is often constrained from agressive action by policies, labor contracts, and funding commitments.
Efficient	Inflexibility works against new uses of resources and search for continuous improvement.
Performance based and adaptable	Governance focused on inputs, not results, constrains the search for high performance, abandonment of ineffective commitments, and search for options.

representation, though its susceptibility to capture by well-organized groups, especially teachers unions, can undermine its legitimacy. It fails, in most cases badly, on the other four criteria. It comes down consistently on the side of representation as against professional freedom of action. It enunciates strong principles of equity but neither allocates resources in ways that allow fulfillment of those promises nor admits that some equity principles can be in conflict. It works against efficiency and strong professional action by tying up money in state and local central-office bureaucracies, making compensation and program continuation decisions on bases other than performance, and keeping decisions about resource use out of the hands of the people who are directly responsible for children's education. It limits the search for new options to those controlled by and acceptable to bureaucracies and dominant interest groups[17] by rewarding rule following and preventing innovation via controls on hiring, purchasing, school structure, and resource use. Is there a better way to govern schools, or are these deficiencies the inevitable results of tensions among the five criteria?

Common Proposals for Alternative Governance Systems

In trying to distill the main alternative governance models from the current literature and policy debate, I come up with seven alternative models. These are vouchers; a choice system, overseen by the state's governor; a board of experts, with only periodic oversight; control by local central government; local site councils; charters; and a recovery school district. I also suggest a hybrid system that combines these models.

Model 1: Vouchers and Market Governance

Milton Friedman has proposed that taxpayer funds be allocated to families through education vouchers.[18] Parents could redeem the vouchers for instruction in any school. Any entity, for-profit or nonprofit, could operate a school. A school could operate as long as it could pay its bills, which would depend on whether parents chose to enroll their children. Friedman argues that market forces would govern education perfectly well. Parents would see that students who attended some schools did much better than others (for example, according to college admissions, ability to earn income) and would abandon less successful schools in favor of more effective ones. Because there would be no barriers to the formation or expansion of a school, better providers would come to educate the majority of students. Fee-based advisory services, which would help parents analyze school outcomes data and make good choices, would come into being. Schools might be tempted to beat the competition by fudging performance data, but advisory services and normal legal penalties against fraudulent claims would punish the frauds.

Friedman's claims have been hotly contested on grounds that schools would compete not on effectiveness but on the ability to attract easy-to-educate students. Critics claimed that schools would control performance data, so that all but the savviest parents would be forced to choose schools without access to good information. Although other schools would probably arise to serve less able students, the result would be a publicly funded education system stratified by class and race. Schools that served the most challenging students would have little incentive to serve them well. Some parents might choose foolishly, on grounds other than the best academic match for their children. Achievement gaps would widen, and social stratification would increase.

Many have been unconvinced by Friedman's answers to his critics—that if every child were bringing the same amount of money to a school, competition would be strong enough in the long run to punish abusers, so that some schools would specialize in effective instruction for the disadvantaged. However, in light of the high levels of abuse and neglect in the current system, where children are supposedly protected by governmental oversight, Friedman's proposals merit more serious consideration. Market-based governance could hardly lead to more inequitable outcomes than we now observe, and it could reward innovation and productivity in schools, setting off a continuous improvement process that would benefit all students.[19]

Model 2: System of Choice with Governor Oversight

Chester E. Finn Jr. has proposed a governor-managed statewide system of autonomous schools, each funded entirely on the basis of student enrollment. A state's governor would promote formation of voluntary support networks to help schools obtain needed education and business services, and they would see to it that ineffective schools and networks were closed. As Finn concludes, "If people are not satisfied with their schools or their results, they would have three main options: move their kids to different schools, move their families to a different state, or elect a different governor."[20]

Presumably, governors or their delegates would have funding to run analyses and reporting systems to help parents understand the strengths and weaknesses of particular schools. Presumably also, these governors would have some resources to encourage formation of new schools and networks in localities where students have no good choices. Finn does not say, but it is safe to assume, that governors could create special oversight organizations for schools in troubled cities and other areas where school providers are reluctant to operate. Given local differences in needs and in access to talent, costs, geography, and facilities, it is hard to imagine how education in a whole state could be overseen centrally. A governor would probably have to divide the state into localities of manageable sizes. These could be run by administrators appointed by the governor and need not have the political complexity of today's school districts. But the governor would end up delegating a great deal of authority to officials whose views and capacities could vary tremendously from place to place, which could mean that schools could be more efficient and equitable in some localities than in others.

This proposal combines strengths of market-based government with the advantages of some public oversight. It resembles the governance of the charter school sector that has emerged in New Orleans since Hurricane Katrina.

Finn's proposal is new and has not been widely criticized. Fleshing it out, including making provisions for quality control, oversight of fair admissions, and creation of autonomous schools on a statewide scale, might make the proposal seem less simple.

Model 3: Expert Governance with Only Periodic Oversight

Ted Kolderie and others have argued that education is a technical field requiring unfettered application of expertise, subject only to occasional reviews by voters or elected officials.[21] A public education system cannot serve children well if competing adult interests and arguments over funds and instructional methods constantly intrude on schools' operation. Although experts (which, under Kolderie's plan, means traditionally qualified teachers governing their schools as cooperatives) need the ultimate sanction of approval by elected officials, constant oversight and political buffeting is counterproductive. Experts should be left alone for long periods of time, free from the need to satisfy interest groups in the short run; politics should affect their actions only gradually, and with significant time lags.

By this argument, public education should be treated more like the judiciary, the Federal Reserve, the Federal Aviation Administration, or even the armed services. These entities operate without constant political oversight, in part out of deference to expertise, but they remain democratically overseen institutions because elections and deep shifts in public sentiment ultimately affect them. Boards of experts, with long, staggered terms so they cannot be completely transformed all at once, would run public education systems.

Critics note that that control of public enterprises by professional "experts" is often far from ideal.[22] This is so even in fields such as medicine, where expertise is generally acknowledged. It is even more problematic in education, where expertise is openly contested. Another objection against expert control is that it would deny families and neighbors the ability to deliberate over their children's education. However, nothing would prevent the experts in charge of education from listening to parents. A combination of governance of individual schools by experts and family choice would maintain expert control over schools but impose a market discipline—the need to pay attention to family concerns and a school's appeal relative to others in the same area—on school leaders.

Like the voucher proposal, this plan might not work well by itself. It could, however, be an important element of a hybrid governance system, as is discussed below.

Model 4: Control by Local General Government

There is growing support for the idea that public education should not be governed as a separate enterprise but should be controlled by elected officials of general government, for example, mayors and governors.[23] In many ways the rationale for these proposals resembles that for governing education as an expert structure. This proposal adds a political dimension. Mayors and high-level elected officials serve broader constituencies than superintendents and school boards. Compared with school boards, which are usually disbanded or stripped of their powers under mayoral control, higher-level elected officials should be less subject to capture by powerful education interest groups such as teachers unions.

In practice, however, mayors and others delegate responsibility to administrators (for example, Joel Klein in New York City, Michelle Rhee in the District of Columbia), who can act aggressively with their boss's support. Thus mayoral takeover, in effect, becomes an expert structure (one in which expertise is contested) backed up by political muscle.[24]

General government control is subject to the same kinds of criticisms as expert control. Opponents cite Klein in New York City and others as people who relied too much on the mayor's support and did not listen closely enough to teachers, parents, and interest groups that expected to have influence over public education. Others would claim that these administrators listened and understood what established groups told them but acted in ways they thought necessary to get better outcomes for disadvantaged children.

In political discourse, the charge "You didn't listen" often means "You must not have listened, because if you had listened you would see it my way." Under general government control, leaders are empowered to see things differently, which is both an advantage and a liability. Options can be considered that the core education interest groups would have kept off the table, but dedicated opposition from those same groups can threaten a superintendent's or even a mayor's job.

Model 5: Community Deliberation

In 1988 the Illinois state legislature committed Chicago schools to radical decentralization of decisionmaking to local site councils elected by neighbors, parents, and teachers. These councils had control over principal hiring and discretionary budgets averaging $500,000 a year. Although many vestiges of the old centralized system remained in place (including union contract provisions on teacher hiring and transfers and central-office control of professional development programs), local site councils had real power.

The underlying idea, as explained by Anthony Bryk, was democratic localism. Intense deliberation at the local level would unite teachers and parents, help educators adapt to neighborhood norms and culture, and increase parents' appreciation for the work done in schools. Low-income and minority parents, relatively voiceless in Chicago's bureaucratic school system, would be heard, so their trust and support for schools would grow. The result would be more-focused instruction, more parental support, and fewer disruptions by the district central office and disgruntled parents.

After years of study, Anthony Bryk and his colleagues concluded that Chicago's experiment in democratic localism led to improvement in about one-third of the city's schools, but an equal number of schools, those with the most-divided parent bodies and the weakest community leadership, declined even further.[25] Schools whose student bodies included groups that had serious political clashes in the broader community (for example, African Americans and Hispanics in poor areas of Chicago) were often deeply divided. Subsequent Illinois legislation strengthened the hand of the mayor in imposing strong academic standards and transforming and replacing the weakest schools. Chicago's local site councils still exist, and work as advertised in many cases, but the mayor's initiatives trump local council prerogatives in schools with low test scores, graduation rates, and student attendance.

Theorists from other cities, particularly Philadelphia, have also envisioned public school governance based on grassroots deliberation and have called other reforms that lack these features undemocratic. Deliberation proponents often criticize mayoral and state takeovers for locating decisions too far away from neighbors and parents.[26] Some also criticize initiatives that involve family choice, saying that they substitute consumerism for citizenship.

Although many excellent schools in the United States and abroad are governed by active groups of parents and teachers, performance failures occur, and when they do, higher authorities eventually intervene, imposing external standards and, in some cases, dissolving and replacing schools. For the governance of a large public school system, community deliberation is an option that can be pursued conditionally; officials in charge of the broader system must have other options as well.

Model 6: Chartering by Multiple Independent Authorities

State charter school laws establish an escape route from the dominant governance system. A limited number of schools in each of forty-one states are able to escape many of the regulations and hiring constraints that apply to district-run schools. These schools operate under charters, which are essentially three- to five-year contracts that spell out a school's mission, objectives, rights to funding, and criteria for renewal. Charter schools are funded based on enrollment, a set amount for each child.

In most states, groups that hope to obtain a charter and operate a school can apply to more than one designated authorizer, often including the state department of education, county offices of education, colleges and universities, and local school boards. Charters can be canceled for low student performance, financial malfeasance, failure to comply with applicable laws, or failure to attract enough students to pay school costs. State charter laws were not written to supplant the dominant K–12 governance system. Charters exist alongside district schools and in many cases compete with them for students (and the public funds students bring) and space in school buildings. However, there are proposals to eliminate firm caps on the number of charter schools allowed in a state, allowing every public school to operate under a charter.[27] School districts could continue to run schools directly, but charter schools' advantages—far fewer constraints on hiring, use of time, teaching methods, technology, and facilities—could cause schools to migrate to charter status.

Critics think even limited chartering creates opportunities for more privileged families to escape from public schools and threatens to resegregate schools. Others fear that teachers unions and other left-leaning institutions will be weakened at the expense of more business-oriented and entrepreneurial organizations, which will, in turn, emphasize competition over communitarian values.

Proposals for unlimited chartering raise further fears. One is that charter schools will "forum shop" among possible authorizers, to find those whose demands about student performance and equitable admissions are easiest to meet.[28] Another is that the possible elimination of school districts in favor of multiple charter authorizers means that there will be no one responsible for making sure all the children in a locality have a good school to attend.

Model 7: A State-Administered Recovery School District

Louisiana's state recovery school district (RSD), a state entity established by law that could take over and operate or charter out any consistently failing school in the state, made possible the quick reestablishment of public education in New Orleans after the devastation of Hurricane Katrina. The RSD had taken over seventy low-performing schools before the storm hit and created a new system of schools. Most of these schools were chartered, but a few were directly run by the RSD. The Louisiana RSD also exercised its authority to take over failing schools throughout the state, transforming troubled schools in Baton Rouge, Shreveport, and other cities.

Other states (for example, Michigan, Tennessee, New Jersey) are establishing similar authorities. A recovery school district can permit massive intervention in a locality where the school district has largely failed (for example, Detroit). It can also serve as a sanction against any district in the state that neglects or fails to improve consistently unproductive schools. It can therefore attach real district-level consequences to a state performance accountability system: either fix a struggling school or lose it.

Louisiana's RSD is not a whole alternative governance system. It coexists with conventional school districts and with independent charter schools. Its threat to take over particular schools whether the local district consents or not can create a serious political backlash, but it signals that the state will not tolerate district negligence.[29] Combined with other new governance reform models, however, the RSD opens up new possibilities.

Combining Models

These models present a range of difference on two dimensions: who governs public education and what powers the governing institution can exercise. The latter issue is seldom addressed in discussions of education governance because school boards, as elected bodies, are assumed to be able to control any aspect of district policy. The idea that the powers of an elected body could be strictly circumscribed is not new to American government, but it has not been applied to the governance of K–12 school systems.

Each of these models offers something that the current system of governance by local school boards does not. However, each has serious problems, particularly if considered as a total replacement for the current system. Table 15-2 rates each of the governance models and the existing system against the criteria derived above.

Table 15-2. *Alternative Governance Models, by Five Criteria*

Criterion	Model[a]							
	Current	1	2	3	4	5	6	7
Elected representation	+	−	−	−	+	?	−	−
Executive and professional freedom	−	+	−	+	+	−	+	+
Intolerance of inequity and neglect	−	−	−	?	?	?	−	+
Efficiency	−	+	−	?	?	−	?	?
Responsiveness and adaptability	−	+	+	+	+	−	+	+

a. The models are (1) vouchers and markets, (2) choice with governor oversight, (3) expert governance, (4) local general government, (5) community deliberation, (6) chartering, and (7) state-administered recovery school district.

All of the alternatives merit more pluses than the existing system in table 15-2, except possibly model 5 (community deliberation), but each fails in particular areas. None, other than the state recovery school district (model 7), wins high marks on equity, because there is nothing to prevent the dominant forces in any governance structure from neglecting those with the least political influence. The RSD option at least provides a check: if the local governance structure consistently tolerates schools that do not teach students effectively, an outside force can seize control, transform, or replace them. There is, of course, no absolute guarantee that a state RSD will exercise its powers or succeed when it tries to provide more effective schools.

The presence of many question marks in table 15-2 reflects the limitations of any governance structure. The results are not predetermined but would depend on personalities and implementation.

With the exception of the market and governor-overseen choice (models 1 and 3), none is more likely than the current system to be efficient. All the others could privilege some uses of funds over others, require extremely complex decisionmaking processes and unstable policies, and resist new ideas.

The potential complementarities among different governance models are obvious from table 15-2. The plus marks across the columns suggest that a combination of an elected board, nearly unfettered leadership by experts, elements of a market or choice system, and a state RSD in the background might meet all the criteria.

A Possible New State and Local Governance System

Is there a way to synthesize the strengths of multiple models into a governance system that would be superior to any single one of them?[30] Although the new governance system I propose might retain some trappings of traditional district governance, the resemblance is at most skin deep. It gives elected officials important but defined and limited roles to play, but it prevents empire building and capture by status quo interest groups. It includes strong sanctions against elected officials and administrators who shrink from the hard work of closing less effective schools and commissioning promising new ones. It creates a stable funding and oversight environment for high-performing schools but also builds in a constant search for better options. The system is open to creative uses of technology, new teacher roles and school staffing schemes, and imaginative use of technology. Finally, this new governance system guarantees that families have choices in their neighborhoods, outside traditional school district boundaries, and in higher education and cyberspace.

Elements of the new governance system would include, in each district, the following:

—an elected board of representatives (five, seven, or nine members) with staggered four-year terms

—a chief executive officer (CEO), appointed by the board, to serve a term longer than any elected representative

—a funding system would send dollars to the schools that students attend and hold back limited amounts of money to support data- and performance-assessment systems and salaries for immediate staff members for the board and CEO

—school operators under charter and performance contracts, plus independent charter and cyber schools

—a set of independent school support networks funded by school purchases and voluntary membership fees; essentially, no services infrastructure in the district central office, with the possible exception of new service providers that could be temporarily incubated before being spun off as self-supporting nonprofits

—freedom for parents to choose any school in the district or any school in any other district to which they could gain admission and transport their children

—a state recovery school district that could take control of consistently unproductive schools that the local board had refused to close or replace

The state superintendent could also disband a negligent board and call for new elections or assign schools formerly overseen by a local board to other localities.

The respective roles and powers of the board and CEO would be set by law as follows:

—The board's powers would be "constitutionally" limited. It would have only two powers: to appoint the CEO and to approve an annual slate of actions proposed by the CEO to manage the local supply of schools. By approving creation of new schools the local board would become a charter authorizer. It could also choose to authorize schools that would operate in other localities.

—The board could not employ any persons other than the CEO and a small number of staff for board meetings. The board would approve the CEO's proposed annual budget, but no less than 90 percent of all funds available from state, local, and federal sources must follow children to the schools in which they enroll, and those funds would be in the form of cash.

—The board would not own any school facilities and could enter into contracts only for the CEO's employment and for the operation of particular schools, in the form of performance contracts. The board could not contract for any school for more than five years.

—Schools would rent school facilities. Communities could set up independent real estate trusts to own, develop, acquire by lease, buy, sell, and rent out buildings for the use of schools.

—For any school in any year, the CEO could propose to sustain, expand, transform, close, or replace it with new organizations operating in the same space. All schools would be chartered or run under performance contracts.

—The CEO must publicly announce criteria for closure or replacement of school providers by fall of the preceding school year. Criteria would consider student achievement gains and other measures of student outcomes (for example, normal progress toward graduation, graduation rates, graduates' abilities to pass key courses at the next level of education) as well as school climate and enrollment.

—The CEO would manage an annual parent information plan and student enrollment process in which all overenrolled schools would run their lotteries on the same day. Schools might, based on their charter or terms of reference set by either the school board or the CEO, provide admissions weights for children living in particular neighborhoods.

—The CEO would form or work with an independent organization to manage a risk pool from which all schools could draw funds for special education. At the CEO's discretion this risk pool could charge different per pupil amounts to schools based on past rates of expenditures for special education.

Table 15-3 summarizes board and CEO powers.

Families would have different options under the new governance system. They could choose any school approved by the local board or the board of any other locality, run as a charter under state law, or licensed by the state as a cyber school. And they could join with other families to petition for a charter to operate a new school.

The function and power of the state RSD would increase under the new system. A local CEO who identified a low-performing school and recommended its closure could, if the board refused to close it for two years, ask the RSD to take the school away from the district. The same could happen if a CEO failed to recommend changes in a failing school (as defined by a combination of student achievement levels and annual growth rates) for two years. After a period of five years, the RSD could return a school to the control of any school district in the state.

Table 15-3. *Powers and Prohibitions in the Proposed Education Governance System*

	Elected board of representatives	*Chief executive officer*
Can	Authorize all schools Approve closure criteria Review school performance Approve funding formulas Hire and fire chief executive officers	Design student-based funding formulas Propose school openings and closures Run fair admissions
Cannot	Employ teachers or principals Keep bad schools open Own school buildings	Invest in assistance providers Build a big central office

The state would take on new roles:[31]

—It would create a student-based funding scheme in which every student carried a backpack of funds—actual dollars—to the schools or online programs he or she attended.[32] The amounts in the backpack could be weighted to give schools extra money to meet the needs of disadvantaged students or those with disabilities. The state could also require that districts allocate dollars to schools on a similar per pupil basis.

—It would set student achievement standards.

—It would maintain a student-identified linked file on every student in the state, with student attributes, schools attended, test scores, and credits gained.

—It would help smaller districts by providing at least annual analyses of student and school performance and gain rates.

—It would offer a "catastrophic insurance" plan into which individual schools could pay against the possibility of enrolling a special-education student whose individualized education plan required services that cost much more than the average per pupil expenditure in the state. (Many states already do this in some form.)

Roles and powers of school operators of charter management networks would be as follows:

—Schools would be free to use their budgets as they chose to support their instructional programs but could not pay for benefits for anyone not currently employed. Individual schools would also be the employers of teachers and would set pay and benefits. Any grants of tenure would be null and void when the school granting it was closed.

—Schools could form or join support organizations and pay fees for any externally provided services they choose, including instruction.

—Schools could be owned by boards of directors, teacher cooperatives, or sole proprietors.

Roles of the school district central office and independent support organizations would be as follows:

—The CEO could establish central office units (for example, to attract high-quality educators to the locality, analyze student outcome data, provide information to parents, deliver services to schools) for a period of no more than five years. At the end of five years the unit must become a nonprofit and rely on school-paid fees or philanthropy.

—No person other than the CEO could work for the school district for more than five years. (This would not apply to teachers and principals, who would be employed by schools, not the district.)

—The district central office could not own any school buildings. Existing buildings would be sold to an independent trust that would rent space to schools at common published rates, develop buildings for rental by schools, and sell or lease out space not claimed by schools.

This governance system would be profoundly different from the one common today. It would closely resemble the system being built to oversee New Orleans schools returned to local control by the Louisiana RSD. Elements of this system were introduced to Oakland schools when the city was taken over by the state of California and are also being built in New York City, Denver, Chicago, and other emerging "portfolio districts."[33] As table 15-4 shows, the new system can meet all the criteria set forth at the beginning of this chapter.

This system could work in any city, town, or major suburb. It might also work in more sparsely settled rural areas if the state created large districts that encompassed twenty or more schools. If it proved impossible to eliminate school boards in localities that have only one to three schools, local boards could get permission to operate schools directly.[34] However, their state funding should be on the same per pupil basis as that of other localities, and their pupils should be free to attend cyber or conventional schools run by other districts or independent organizations.

The new system would require changes in state law to redefine the roles and limitations of local school boards, free up funding so that virtually all dollars followed children to the schools in which they enrolled, and eliminate the principles of virtually unconditional lifetime employment in schools and school districts. It would require development of new institutions—risk pools for special-education services and independent trusts to own, manage, and rent out school buildings for starters—and would require new skills at every level.

Would the new system work as intended? Nobody can be sure until it is tried. What is clear from this perspective is that such a system would not work as advertised if it were implemented only halfway—if, for example, elected boards had no constitutional limitations and could manipulate school staffing or spending, if the state or district hired teachers and purchased assets and assigned them to

Table 15-4. Rating of Proposed New Governance System on Five Criteria

Criterion	How criterion is met
Elected representation	Elected boards with real though definitively limited powers.
Executive and professional freedom	Strong CEO able to take initiative and press the board for action. RSD powers buttress CEO against a recalcitrant board.
Intolerance of inequity, neglect	Board's greatest real power is to approve efforts to improve options for children in unproductive schools. RSD role sanctions any board negligence.
Efficiency	Expensive central-office units are forbidden, and all money goes to the schools. Schools are driven to seek efficiency by competition; and schools have the freedom to adapt their staffing and use of technology in search of efficiency.
Performance-based and adaptability	Governance system seeks student outcomes above all else, is able to abandon less effective schools and methods and to innovate. Everything is flexible and contestable. New ideas, people, methods, organizations, and technology applications are all welcome, as are education providers from outside the locality. Parents' ability to choose schools out of the district, including cyber schools, creates incentives to innovate.

schools, if school providers with new ideas were kept out, or if elected boards were under no external pressure to search for options for children in consistently unproductive schools.

This is certainly not the only possible alternative governance system for K–12 education. It is, however, difficult to see how any system without a mixture of markets and public oversight and a constitutionally limited elected board could meet all the criteria as well.

Transition Scenarios

How might such a dramatic change in governance come about? There are some plausible scenarios, but most of them involve the gradual spread of an idea from a few exemplars rather than sudden universal policy changes.

The barriers to rapid change are clear. Incumbent school superintendents are unlikely to urge the school board that hired them to redefine their own powers so dramatically. Central office employees, teachers and principals unions, and neighborhood politicians who win support by arranging constituent jobs in the school system would consider their positions threatened. Liberal bloggers would characterize such changes as abandonment of efforts to serve the public interest. Parents and teachers who were unhappy with the way the current system operates might support such changes, but they would not lead them.

Dramatic changes in governance are possible at times of physical or economic disaster, as indicated by the experiences of New Orleans, Newark, and Detroit. We can be thankful that such events are rare, and they are too rare to bring about governance changes in many cities.

However, combinations of low school performance, financial stresses caused by overcommitment and declining enrollment, and active state leadership can lead to dramatic changes in governance. Already, collaborations between state officials and local educators and foundations have put new definitions of school board roles on the agenda in Ohio and Indiana.[35] In those states and others (for example, Tennessee and New York), governors and state superintendents are working to redefine the roles of state boards, state education agencies, and local school boards in favor of greater use of chartering as a form of public oversight and more thorough experimentation with online and "blended" models of schooling.[36]

In still other states, key cities like Denver, Chicago, Oakland, and Philadelphia have adopted portfolio strategies that can set the pattern for governance changes in other cities. Legislation passed to enable a portfolio strategy in one city (for example, Colorado's Denver-focused Innovation Schools Act) can be used in another. Similarly, staff with experience in portfolio management in one city can move to another and lead a similar approach. This is evident in Los Angeles, whose district leadership team is populated by senior staff members who developed their ideas and skills in Oakland.

Finally, there is nothing to prevent a new school board, elected on a promise to look at every plausible approach to improvement, from redefining its own role and recruiting a superintendent and leadership team who know how to pursue a portfolio strategy. This can lead to imitation by other cities and ultimately to changes in state law. Even if states create policies that facilitate use of this governance model, they are likely to differentiate between school districts in urban and suburban areas, where it makes immediate sense to open up school and service provision to the many unused resources available there, and rural areas, where few such resources exist. However, even rural areas can benefit from governance schemes that are open to greater use of online resources and the introduction of blended schooling models.

Conclusion

The new system sketched here opens up new possibilities, especially for big cities. Even modest-sized cities are a generous source of scientific, artistic, and management talent, but traditional school districts keep these resources at arm's length. A different governance system, one built around a constant search for the best possible learning experiences for children, would need to be much more flexible than the system we have. To attain such a system, Americans would need to subject political control of schools to strict limitations based in state law. The powers and limitations of school boards, would, in effect, define a new constitution for school districts. No one, not even an elected local board, would have the power to award anyone a permanent job or contract.

The system would allow a constant search for improvement. In so doing it would also sponsor some false starts and failures. It would require changes in state laws that set the missions of school districts and state education agencies.

These ideas are new and will be controversial. But the governance system described here is not completely new; it is made up of familiar parts, which are used in the governance of other public sector enterprises, including school districts such as New York City, New Orleans, and Denver.

Despite the political and implementation challenges it will inevitably raise, the new system will be worth the pain of transition. It will allow Americans to answer the question, "Are we doing absolutely the best we can for our children?" in the affirmative.

Notes

1. In my definition, *education governance* is the creation of rules for publicly funded education and use of these rules as the basis of oversight by elected or appointed public officials. In the United States, public education governance constrains educators' actions by means of established policies and routines, distributed powers, required consultations, and multiple independent reviews and approvals. Governance is distinct from *leadership*, the use of discretion by officials to cause change in the organizations they head.

2. On the consequences of teachers union domination of school board elections, see Terry M. Moe, *Special Interest: Teachers Unions and America's Public Schools* (Brookings Press, 2011), pp. 112–54.

3. For extensive critiques of existing governance arrangements, see Noel Epstein, *Who's In Charge Here? The Tangled Web of School Governance and Policy* (Brookings Press, 2004); Dominic Brewer and Joanna Smith, *Evaluating the "Crazy Quilt": Educational Governance in California* (Palo Alto, Calif.: Stanford Institute for Research on Education Policy and Practice, 2006).

4. For a review of school board duties as assigned by state legislation, see Paul T. Hill and others, *Big City School Boards: Problems and Options* (Seattle: Center on Reinventing Public Education, 2003).

5. Richard A. Weatherly and Michael Lipsky, "Street-Level Bureaucrats and Institutional Innovation: Implementing Special Education Reform," *Harvard Educational Review* 47 (Summer 1977): 171–97.

6. See, for example, John Meyer, Richard Scott, and David Strang, "Centralization, Fragmentation, and School District Complexity," *Administrative Science Quarterly* 32 (June 1987): 186–201.

7. Terry M. Moe, "The Politics of Bureaucratic Structure," in *Can the Government Govern?* edited by John E. Chubb and Paul E. Peterson (Brookings Press, 1989), pp. 267–329.

8. Milton Friedman, *Capitalism and Freedom* (University of Chicago Press, 1962).

9. John Chubb and Terry M. Moe, *Politics, Markets, and America's Schools* (Brookings Press, 1990).

10. Paul T. Hill, Lawrence Pierce, and James Guthrie, *Reinventing Public Education* (University of Chicago Press, 1997). See also Paul T. Hill, "School Boards, Focus on School Performance Not Money and Patronage" (Washington: Progressive Policy Institute, 2003).

11. Kenneth Wong and others, *The Education Mayor: Improving America's Schools* (Georgetown University Press, 2007). See also Kenneth Wong and Francis Shen, "City and State Takeover as a School Reform Strategy," 2002 (www.ericdigests.org/2003-2/city.html); Chester E. Finn Jr., "Reinventing Local Control," *Education Week*, January 23, 1991; Jennifer A. O'Day and Marshall S. Smith, "Systemic Reform and Educational Opportunity," in *Designing Coherent Education Policy: Improving the System,* edited by Susan H. Fuhrman (San Francisco: Jossey-Bass, 1993), pp. 250–312.

12. Joseph Murphy, "Governing America's Schools: The Shifting Playing Field," *Teachers College Record* 102 (February 2000): 57–84.

13. See, for example, Amy Bingham, "Teachers' Union Endorses Obama Despite Hating His Policies," *ABC World News with Diane Sawyer,* July 6, 2011 (http://abcnews.go.com/Politics/obama-passes-teachertestbarely/story?id=14003658).

14. Terry M. Moe and Paul T. Hill, "Governments, Markets, and the Mixed Model of American Education Reform," *Education Week*, April 20, 2011.

15. I do not know enough about foreign cultures or political systems to assert that the same criteria would apply to publicly funded elementary and secondary education systems elsewhere.

16. David Tyack, *The One Best System: A History of American Urban Education* (Harvard University Press, 1974).

17. In a companion piece to this chapter I show how the current funding system for public education privileges established practices and incumbent groups and works against innovation. See Paul T. Hill, *School Finance in the Digital Learning Era* (Washington: Thomas B. Fordham Institute, 2011).

18. Friedman, *Capitalism and Freedom.*

19. Paul T. Hill, "Baselines for Assessment of Choice Programs," *Education Policy Analysis Archives* 11 (2003) (http://epaa.asu.edu/ojs/article/view/267).

20. Chester E. Finn Jr., "How to Run Public Schools in the 21st Century," *Defining Ideas*, June 22, 2011 (www.hoover.org/publications/defining-ideas/article/83137).

21. Ted Kolderie, *Creating the Capacity for Change: How and Why Governors and Legislatures Are Opening a New-Schools Sector in Public Education* (Washington: Education Week Press, 2007).

22. For an influential version of this critique, see Harold J. Laski, *The Limitations of the Expert* (London: Fabian Society, 1931).

23. See, for example, Wong and others, *The Education Mayor*. Jeffrey Henig discusses this model in detail in chapter 9 in this volume.

24. Are Joel Klein, his successor Dennis Walcott, Michele Rhee, Paul Vallas, and his successor John White in any sense experts? None are traditionally educated as teachers and superintendents, but with the exception of Rhee all are experts at public management, and

in the cases of Klein and Walcott, local politics. These forms of expertise are clearly relevant to the reform of big urban districts, but leaders with such qualifications must also rely on education experts in many ways. For much more on this point see Paul Hill and others, *Portfolio School Districts for Big Cities: An Interim Report* (Seattle: Center on Reinventing Public Education, 2009).

25. The Consortium on Chicago Schools Research has created the world's deepest and best literature on efforts to reform a major urban school system. Anthony S. Bryk and his colleagues have pulled this work together in two books, *Charting Chicago School Reform: Democratic Localism as a Lever for Change* (Los Angeles: Westview Press, 1999), and *Organizing Schools for Improvement: Lessons from Chicago* (University of Chicago Press, 2010).

26. See, for example, Eva Gold, Jeffrey Henig, and Elaine Simon, "Calling the Shots in Public Education: Parents, Politicians, and Educators Clash," *Dissent*, Fall 2011, pp. 34–40.

27. See, for example, Andrew J. Rotherham, *Smart Charter School Caps* (Washington: Education Sector, 2007).

28. Chester E. Finn Jr., Terry Ryan, and Michael B. Lafferty, *Ohio's Education Reform Challenges: Lessons from the Front Lines* (New York: Palgrave Macmillan, 2010).

29. Paul Hill and Patrick Murphy, *On Recovery School Districts and Stronger State Education Agencies: Lessons from Louisiana* (Seattle: Center on Reinventing Public Education, 2011).

30. The work in this section is a preliminary result of a new grant to the Center on Reinventing Public Education from the Laura and John Arnold Foundation.

31. Relative to school district governance, thinking about alternative state roles is not well developed. A new organization of state superintendents, Chiefs for Change, has formed to advance a similar agenda, which is also gaining some traction among members of the more traditional state leaders' organization, the Council of Chief State School Officers. A forthcoming Center on Reinventing Public Education study by Patrick Murphy and Lydia Rainey provides new analysis of possible state roles that could complement the new district governance structure proposed here.

32. For more on the backpack concept, see Hill, *School Finance in the Digital Learning Era*.

33. Hill and others, *Portfolio School Districts for Big Cities*. See also Center on Reinventing Public Education, "Portfolio Schools Project," n.d. (http://www.crpe.org/cs/crpe/view/projects/7?page=initiatives&initiative=30).

34. States could adopt their own version of a portfolio strategy, overseeing districts run in multiple ways but holding all to common performance standards and constantly reserving the right to assign a lagging district to new management.

35. See, for example, Public Impact, *Creating Opportunity Schools: A Bold Plan to Transform Indianapolis Public Schools* (Indianapolis: The Mind Trust, 2011).

36. In a blended school, students study under direct adult supervision but make heavy use of online instructional materials and diagnostics. These schools employ fewer teachers, but teacher jobs are focused on enrichment, diagnosis, and remediation.

KENNETH J. MEIER

16

From Theory to Results in Governance Reform

Structural change that creates environments or processes that generate better outcomes is the holy grail of governance reform. One reason that structural governance reforms are attractive to education policymakers is that they might be a solution to Elmore's paradox, that almost every education reform works with thirty students, but nothing works with 30,000.[1] The advantage of structural reforms is that they are scalable; that is, they work at the macro level by changing the environment or processes for all individuals within the system. Such is the promise of governance reform in education, but for such reforms to succeed they must change what students are taught in the classroom. They have to lock in some values or create some incentives that generate better education.

The effort to reform the governance structure of U.S. education has a great deal of promise, but it is not without limits. Structure matters in public policy, including in education, but it is not determinative. The logic of education governance reforms must be solid, and changes must lead to improvements in how and what children are taught. These changes need to be convincing on their face to both scholars and public policymakers. Structural governance reform will not be easy; and, most important, the results will not be immediate but rather will accumulate slowly over time as the governance structure generates the incentives that are needed. As a result, would-be reformers need to be confident in the governance reforms that they propose. At the same time, that is not a reason to shy away from debating the reforms or even considering and adopting them. In the coming years, reformers will continue to offer proposals to improve education governance, often focusing on structural issues. Although those changes may be useful, thinking about structural reform must also consider the talents and limits of the people who govern as well as how the constellation of policies that reside outside these structural reforms, but nevertheless orbit them, will help shape the outcomes that any system of governance produces.

The first question in evaluating governance reforms should be, What do the data show? Unfortunately, as Michael Mintrom and Richard Walley conclude, in many cases the data do not exist, or the data arrive at inconsistent conclusions in regard to governance reforms.[2] In the absence of data, a particular governance reform must be examined and assessed along other dimensions. In this chapter I do this by looking at governance reform through five theoretical lenses: as a structural problem, as an oversight problem, as a political problem, as a network management problem, and as an incentives problem. Following the assessment of reforms via these lenses, the essay goes on to use these perspectives to suggest some alternative reforms that can also change the values inherent in educational governance.

Many of the examples and illustrations in this chapter are taken from Texas simply because of my extended research on Texas education.[3] Although Texas is by no means a microcosm of the United States in terms of education, it is a highly diverse state with a twenty-five-year history of efforts aimed at improving educational performance. Much of what is true of Texas is true of other jurisdictions as well.

The Problem

The U.S. education system has extensive variation, perhaps more variation than any other national system of education, as a result of its fifty-one state education systems. These systems vary greatly in terms of powers and orientation. In the United States, the nearly 14,000 local school districts generally have the freedom to decide issues of curriculum, personnel, and so on. In assessing educational performance, we need to recognize both means and variances. Within the U.S. system, performance varies widely. Some districts and schools are spectacular successes, producing well-educated, engaged citizens, often within disadvantaged populations; but clear failures populate the other end of the spectrum. Can the successes be transported to the failures? Can the failures be turned around? Governance reformers assume that they can.

The current governance system has locked in not just a grammar of education and an implementation process but also a political process.[4] Taking education "out of politics," as nineteenth-century reformers advocated, did not really mean out of politics, it meant out of certain types of politics. Partisan politics and the interests of immigrants, minorities, and the poor were disadvantaged; and the politics of business, professionalism, and local centralization were advantaged. Students of race and education well understand that this is not an apolitical system but merely a different form of politics.[5] The independent school district biased the policy process against mass participation in education governance by structuring a system with low turnout and few incentives for politicians or aspiring politicians to participate and substantial professional barriers to participation entry. As a structural-political manipulation it worked very well, but it did not work perfectly. No one predicted the rise of teachers unions as a political force or the emergence of education as a partisan political issue.

As an education reform, however, the independent school district has to be credited as one of the most effective reforms of the nineteenth century in that it moved local education from a patronage-ridden dumping ground to a system capable of producing a well-educated citizenry. At the same time, this reform, by reifying local control of education, has generated the tremendous variation in education quality that we see today. Within this variation there are substantial failures, and virtually every student of U.S. education policy recognizes that the consequences of education failure for economic outcomes, crime, and democratic participation are massive. As a result, the incentives to seek comprehensive reforms are compelling.

The Dimensions of Governance Reform

No attempt to group educational governance reforms can do justice to the bewildering array of proposals. At the risk of oversimplification, many reform proposals can be classified along two dimensions—centralization versus decentralization, and a broad versus narrow scope for educational institutions. At the extreme end of centralization reforms are national control of education via standards, performance systems, funding, and even personnel. In the U.S. federal system, reforms can also centralize at the state level; and though states vary substantially in their degree of centralization, the trend since *A Nation at Risk,* the 1983 report on education commissioned by President Reagan, has been more state control.[6] Local control of education has led to independent school districts and districts with separate sources of funds (and discretion in using those funds). Finally, the ultimate manifestation of decentralization in education is the passing of control of education to parents through market or quasi-market mechanisms such as vouchers or charters. Reformers argue variously that some functions (testing, standard setting) be centralized at the national level, other functions be centralized at the state level (funding), and still others be decentralized (curriculum) or left to the market.[7] Governance reforms focused on centralization or decentralization will privilege those values and incentives that dominate the specified locus of control (federal, state, local).

The scope of education reform considers whether education should be a separate autonomous entity with responsibility for education only or should be integrated into existing governance structures. This integration can take two forms. First, the independent school district can be replaced by control by a more general political entity such as the mayor or governor. Second, school functions can be limited solely to education or expanded to a wide variety of health, welfare, and safety issues. Governance reforms focused on scope essentially address the range of values that one would like to see considered in public education.[8]

Current Governance Structures

Some of the variation in political governance at the local level already exists. Although the overwhelming majority of schools are governed by independent school districts, there are both common school districts with different governance structures (county school districts in Alabama) and dependent school districts that vest power in more generalist politicians. Can one make an argument that dependent school districts perform better?[9] I have not seen any systematic evidence, and the general view is that they do not, but answering this question would require dealing with a significant selection bias problem in terms of the types of systems that retained the dependent school district.[10]

Still, there are sound reasons for thinking that governance structures in education matter a great deal. Even a simple difference in electoral structure, such as single-member districts versus at-large elections, matters in terms of representation and in terms of advocacy. With the exception of African Americans in districts outside the South, single-member districts provide more representation for racial and ethnic minorities; and those representatives appear to be able to influence the relative quality of education for minorities.[11] Recent work by Curtis Ellis, Alisa Hicklin, and Rene Rocha also finds that single-member districts generate a more equitable distribution of resources within school districts, separate from any racial impacts.[12]

Because governance reform promises a great deal, it is important to clarify the nature of the arguments made and whether the hypothesized relationships are direct or contingent. In many cases, one sees the argument that governance structure B outperforms governance structure A, that is, $B > A$, when the actual situation indicates that governance system B outperforms system A when certain conditions (C) are met, that is, $B|C > A$.

In practice, for example, some might argue that having mayors directly involved in the administration of education (B) is better than an independent school district (A), if the mayor finds that education is a salient issue and can appoint effective managers (C). In cases such as this, we need to be careful about whether or not structure B is the causal variable or whether C (interest and effective managers) is the causal variable—and thus whether C can work without the presence of B. It might also be the case that C is more likely to occur under B than under A, that is,

$$P(C|B) > P(C|A).$$

In this case, if mayoral control increases the probability of effective managers, and effective managers are important, then mayoral control is to be preferred. We also need to be concerned about selection bias, particularly because many arguments sample on the dependent variable. Just because C worked or worked in the presence of B in a given district does not necessarily confirm the hypothesis. This situation needs to be compared with other situations with C alone or with C in the presence of B.[13]

Governance Reform as a Structural Problem

Fortunately, as Barry Rabe notes in chapter 13, the governance question in education is similar to a number of other governance questions, and those literatures provide some insight into how governance reform can affect education. The governance question that we are addressing can be related to a classical debate in public administration—is the problem the structure or the people? The answer must be that it is the structure, at least in part, for the solution to be structural reform. Yet this academic debate has raged for ninety years, ever since the Hawthorne experiment first divided scholars into organizational sociologists and organizational psychologists.[14] The debate also raises the question of how structure changes the incentives of the individuals.

Jack Knight notes that all structures create biases.[15] Most formal scholars of politics contend that structures are ways to solve collective action problems, to overcome the limits of individual rationality, and to contribute to some aspect of collective rationality.[16] There are multiple ways, however, to solve any collective action problem with a structure-induced equilibrium. Structures privilege some values (biases) more than others, and the choice of specific structures is crucial. The question for education governance structures is, How can structure create incentives and biases for quality education (putting aside for now what we might mean by quality)?

A change in governance structure generates changes in goals and processes and creates potentially different incentives for the actors. The central importance of governance systems is not without challenge; structures can influence results but they clearly do not determine them. As an example, Richard J. Daley was one of the most powerful mayors in U.S. history, yet he governed in a weak-mayor system that allowed the mayor few formal powers relative to the city council. The dominant governance structure at the local level in the United States is the independent school district, yet there is wide variation in the quality of education produced by what are similar governance systems. Accordingly, we might heed Alexander Pope, who stated, "For forms of government, let fools contest, whatever is best administered is best." Similarly, if we look at municipal governments in general in the United States, we have fairly extensive research on how the structure of local governments matters, and the answer appears to be "not much."[17] These municipal governance structures mimic the types of structures one might design based on Finn's notion that we need to include more generalist politics into education.[18] Consistent with these findings, Michael Mintrom and Richard Walley's cross-national assessment concludes that links between governance and student achievement are weak.[19]

Governance Reform as an Oversight Problem

A clear weakness of the current education governance system is its inability to address the failure of schools.[20] This highly political decision in our current governance system is generally vested in civil servants who lack the autonomy or the political support to take independent action. For the most part, the governance system simply ignores failures. This problem was clearly part of the motivation for the transfer provisions of the No Child Left Behind Act (NCLB). At the present time, when charter schools fail, the students are simply dumped back into the public school system (even though dissatisfaction with public schools might have been the reason for seeking out a charter school) or their parents are left to seek a different charter school. Little focus on any special remediation for these students is apparent.

The situation with traditional public schools is no better. Arne Duncan, the U.S. secretary of education, is credited with turning around the Chicago Public Schools, something Paul Vallas was credited with a few years earlier. One wonders how much real improvement there is in these cases or whether we are seeing what the stock market mavens call a "dead cat bounce." Texas is currently seeking to close the North Forest School District, but rather than seek a creative solution to the problem (such as the post-Katrina New Orleans reforms), the state proposes to simply consolidate North Forest with the Houston Independent School District, a district with more than enough pressing problems without the addition of 7,400 new students from North Forest.

The evidence clearly indicates a need for some type of government regulator to make quality judgments and decide whether to close schools. Despite the incentives for transfer built into the NCLB, not enough parents are willing to make these judgments and undertake the transfer of their children.[21] At the same time, one can question the will of either politicians or bureaucrats to make the tough decisions that are needed if one is to rely on governance reforms that encourage experimentation and innovation.[22] This is especially the case since even terrible schools seem to generate some vigorous support from parents and community leaders. Do we have other examples of government regulators in different policy areas who are willing to police based on quality and take action against poor performers? Examples such as home mortgage financing, medical malpractice, and child protective services suggest that this is a valid question, and it is important to evaluate the capacity of state departments of education, the most likely regulators, in this regard. Logic and examples from other policy areas suggest that capacity will vary a great deal, and in many areas the capacity will be limited to nonexistent.[23]

An important question is whether, in an era of long-term economic scarcity, political decisionmakers are willing to allocate funds to oversight and regulation rather than to simply funding services. Opting for services over administrative capacity, some might say bureaucracy, is politically popular, but without efforts at quality control we know that some funds spent on services will be wasted. Because administrative capacity is also useful in dealing with crises or the need to change, failure to invest in such capacity puts limits on how good an education system can become.

Governance Reform as a Political Problem

One theme of the proposed governance changes proposed by Chester Finn and Michael Petrilli and others is to vest additional powers in more general elected officials—governors, mayors, and so on—rather than in independent school boards, which often are dominated, particularly in small districts, by the superintendent.[24] The idea is that generalist politicians are not captured by the biases in existing governance systems and will bring in values that emphasize quality education.[25] Injecting more politics into education is not necessarily a bad thing.[26] Much of the pressure for racial equity came through either the political process or outside pressures;[27] and the Texas reforms of the mid-1980s, which transformed what was a poor education system to one that is at least above average, had political origins and was led by Governor Mark White with the assistance of H. Ross Perot.[28]

Moving authority for education to more generalist politicians makes elections more important for education policy, but it also muddies the electoral incentive. Under a single-function education governance system like the independent school district, the electoral issues should all be linked to education. In a multifunction governance system such as a state, issues vary in importance across both space and time. Economic growth, jobs, taxes, and other issues can easily drive education off the agenda.

Governance systems that privilege the interests of generalist politicians are simple enough to design. There are currently several dependent school districts in the country. In other cases, school board elections are made more salient and more contestable as partisan elections, or elections are held during the regular November election period; both are partial steps toward privileging generalist politicians.[29] Kenneth Wong and Francis Shen provide extensive detail on recent mayor-centric governance and find its impact is highly variable.[30] In the United Kingdom, school districts are simply another unit of local government and are subject to the inputs of the local government council.[31] Even in such systems, however, the salience of education policy for politicians is highly variable. Generalist politicians appear to care about education policy either when there are dwindling resources or when there is an immediate crisis that cannot be avoided, such as the property tax lawsuits of a few decades ago.[32] The current recession appears to have pushed education issues off the agenda of many governors or transformed them into other issues that have created additional crises for education (for example, the Indiana property tax cap in 2010 and the 2011 Michigan law that reduces state aid to school districts that pay more than a certain dollar amount for health insurance for employees).

The ebb and flow of political attention to education policy can be starkly illustrated by the sources of funding for Texas schools. A decade of court battles and support from politicians, including Governor George W. Bush, increased the state contribution to K–12 education to 44 percent of the total in the 1999–2000 school year; under Governor Rick Perry, that percentage dropped to a low of 34 percent in the 2004–05 school year before making a modest comeback. The contrast between political attention and its benefits for public education is especially clear in Texas when one compares Governor White to both George W. Bush and Rick Perry. Although Bush offered few innovations during his two terms, he did continue and even augment the level of financial support for education. In contrast, Rick Perry has advocated a dramatic reduction in education expenditures (including a 6 percent reduction in 2011 with the endorsement of the legislature) and has proposed only one structural reform—the requirement (not passed) that 65 percent of school district employees be in the classroom. The 65 percent requirement has its origins in the positive correlation between the percentage of employees in the classroom and test scores. Unfortunately, systematic examination of the causality between these two variables provides strong evidence that bureaucracy is the result of poor performance rather than a cause as schools take efforts to correct the problem.[33] In addition, the operation of administratively lean school districts appears to work relatively well until there is some type of crisis (budget cuts, large influxes of students, natural disasters such as hurricanes, and so on), when such districts suffer substantially greater reductions in performance than those districts with more managerial capacity.[34]

In other cases, the quest for quality education can be trumped by the politics of revelation. Texas, which elects its state board of education, has seen a public fight to require that science texts allow for revelation as a source of knowledge in addition to or in place of observation and experimentation.[35] In his campaign for the Republican nomination for president in 2011, Governor Perry explicitly endorsed the teaching of creation science in public schools. Politicians adopt issue positions for electoral reasons; some of these issue positions on education, if adopted, will not improve U.S. education.

Governance Reform as a Network Management Problem

The reality of U.S. public schools is they are not walled off from other units of government. They operate in a complex network of other governmental units, nonprofits, and for-profit organizations that deal with health care, vocational training, safety, and other issues. Managing this network takes substantial time and resources.[36] According to the 2009 Texas Superintendent Management Survey, 79 percent of school superintendents interacted with county or city government on at least a monthly basis; 71 percent with local police and fire departments; 52 percent with nonprofit organizations; and 87 percent with local business leaders.[37] This level of interaction occurs because schools are the institution with the greatest contact with adolescents.

The question needs to be raised whether we want to further increase the demands on schools for issues that are not directly related to education. In organization theory, multiple-function organizations are characterized by goal ambiguity, that is, a plethora of goals that often conflict and as a result undermine the organization's core function.[38] Students of bureaucracy frequently contend that the way to create successful programs is to establish clear goals for the bureaucracy, provide sufficient resources, and allow professional autonomy.[39] Education administrators are particularly likely to resist this governance change. When presented with the statement, "School districts are asked to do too many things; we should focus more on education," 39 percent of Texas school superintendents in 2009 strongly agreed and an additional 48 percent agreed.

Governance Reform as an Incentives Problem

One objective of education governance structures is to change the incentives of politicians, educators, and parents. Finn and Petrilli discuss the impact of governance reform on the incentives of politicians.[40] The incentives needed to attract and retain talented teachers and administrators are as important as the incentives needed for parental involvement. At the same time, the education policy literature has not sorted out the proper role of incentives in education policy. On one hand, many current reforms such as pay-for-performance systems for teachers and administrators seek to increase incentives for test-score performance. In a

2009 survey fully 95 percent of Texas school superintendents reported using performance appraisal data to make personnel decisions.[41] On the other hand, some of the true success stories of the charter school movement, such as KIPP (the Knowledge Is Power Program) and YES Prep, pay less than public schools and demand substantially more hours, thus eschewing monetary incentives for normative ones.[42] The management literature suggests that altering the array of incentives affects both who seeks certain jobs and what type of effort they make once they are hired.[43] The increase in performance appraisal systems and monetary incentives could well discourage those who seek intrinsic rewards from becoming teachers.

The broader question of teacher incentives, however, is how to attract the best-qualified persons to enter a profession that in the United States is characterized by modest pay and only average social status.[44] National studies generally show that education majors are not among the best students in college.[45] In earlier times, gender segregation resulted in a more selective group of teachers, but that impact has declined in importance.[46]

The same issues can be raised about who goes into education administration. Some districts have substantial performance clauses in their contracts for administrators, but little is known about their effectiveness. In 2009 the principal of a college-prep high school in the Houston Independent School District (HISD) transferred to Sam Houston High, a school that had been rated academically unacceptable two years in a row. The obvious reasons for taking such an assignment were both the direct incentives that HISD offered and the long-term career payoff that a successful turnaround would bring.[47]

Informed and active parents could be a dramatic force for quality in education. Large percentages of parents, however, do not seem to pay much attention to education, to want to exercise educational choices, or to want choices in the first place. Mark Schneider, Paul Teske, and Melissa Marschall present some modest evidence that forcing parents to select among schools has some benefits.[48] An important question is what types of governance can increase the amount of parental involvement.

Finally, the incentives for individuals to undertake governance reform are important. To succeed in reforming education governance systems, we need reformers who are willing to invest their careers and substantial resources in advocacy and in implementation. Reforming schools is a long-term and continuous process. We might heed George Washington Plunkitt's statement that reformers were "mornin' glories—looked lovely in the mornin' and withered up in a short time." Leadership is quite likely the biggest challenge to reforming education governance.

Some Alternative Proposals to Change Education Governance

Changes in governance structure seek to alter the processes, values, and incentives involved in education policy. There are many potential structural governance reforms that could be adopted, but the results they produce may be contingent on several other factors and on the working out of the various governance problems noted above. This suggests that there might not be a single governance reform that is the solution but rather that governance reform should incorporate a variety of different approaches that seek to create incentives for quality education. In those broad terms, there are other macro-level reforms that could attain the same objective of improving the quality of education. Some of these deal with changing inputs to education, some deal with the grammar of education, and some are more systemic changes that can influence education. Six of these are particularly worthy of note.

Take Size Seriously

One disincentive to governance reform is the massive effort needed to address difficult, if not intractable, problems. As a result, the incentives for leadership in the area of class size are insufficient to attract the needed level of effort. One option is to cut down on the size of the problem. The optimum size of schools is subject to some debate, but the gains of a larger school in terms of specialization and the ability to offer a greater range of academic subjects are clearly subject to diminishing marginal returns. It is hard to justify high schools with 3,000 or more students (there are thirty-seven such schools in the state of Texas, the largest of which is Houston's Westfield High, with 4,872 students). Such institutions, often motivated by issues of athletics rather than pedagogy, limit student participation, decrease student contact with faculty and counselors, and often have major issues of student safety.

Similarly, school districts are too large. I have met many individuals capable of running a 10,000-student school district but few capable of running a 150,000-student school district. Whether the size problem is a problem in itself or large mega-districts tend to be inner-city school districts with greater problems is not completely clear; but downsizing problems would increase the approaches to education reform and allow greater crafting of solutions to local needs.[49] Downsizing can also make the problems more tractable and the consequences of failure less severe.

Move to an Effective and Efficient School Finance System

Despite active political efforts and a full decade of legal action, the local property tax remains an integral part of school finance in many states. This vestige of nineteenth-century governance makes little sense in a globalized economic system for a country that has vast differences geographically in wealth. These inequalities in wealth translate frequently into inequities in education and its contribution to human capital. Cynthia Brown's chapter is an effective critique of the reliance on the local property tax as a funding mechanism for public schools.[50] Clearly, money is not the only thing that matters in education policy, but money in the hands of competent educators provides the opportunity to generate positive results. Any governance reform needs funding to succeed, and rationalizing the education finance system will give any adopted reforms a better chance of success.

Use Markets Effectively

Local control of education, something that is much criticized and accounts for substantial variation in the quality of education in the United States, has the advantage of creating a Tiebout market for education.[51] Parents can vote with their feet and can select local jurisdictions that provide them the tax and services benefits that they seek. Although this is a sluggish market with substantial transactions costs, it is still a market. Restricting local control of education places additional barriers to full functioning of this market. This should be seriously considered by those who would limit local control of education.

All markets have structure and rules that generate incentives, and that is clearly the case in education, particularly among charter schools. At the present time, charter schools are the cutting edge of market-based reforms; but to paraphrase Dickens, charter schools are the best of schools, they are the worst of schools. The top end is indicated by the positive publicity garnered by the success of charter schools in a wide variety of locations.[52] Of the nineteen school districts in Texas with a 2010 Texas Assessment of Knowledge and Skills (TAKS) pass rate of 95 or above, seven are charter schools. (Texas treats charters as districts for administrative purposes.) At the same time, fifty-three of the sixty-three districts with pass rates below 50 percent, which I take as an obvious failure, are charters. Although a direct comparison of test scores in Texas is misleading because charters are designed to serve disadvantaged populations, in 2010 charter schools scored a full twelve points below public schools on the Texas Assessment of Knowledge and Skills. This gap remains at eight points when one controls for poverty.[53]

Another indicator of problems on the low end involves state monitors. The Texas Education Agency assigns monitors to problem schools and districts. Monitors can be assigned for performance or financial reasons or for failure to comply with federal and state education regulations. If schools fail to improve after the assignment of a monitor, they can be and sometimes are closed. In the current school year, the agency has eighty-six monitors assigned to schools or districts (some schools have more than one monitor). The 1,049 public school districts that educate 4.7 million students have thirty-two monitors, while the

200 charter schools, educating 119,000 students, have fifty-four. An examination of the documentation for taking action as well as other performance data on Texas schools convinces me that this is not selective enforcement but that the cases are meritorious.

The charter school challenge, therefore, is how to generate more YES Preps (TAKS pass rate of 92 percent) and fewer Houston Can Academies (pass rate of 23 percent). In this process, it is important to remember that markets have a supply side as well as a demand side. A successful charter needs an education entrepreneur with a vision to build an effective school, a quality faculty, and an administrative apparatus that avoids waste, fraud, and corruption. The role of a charter school superintendent or principal is much different from that of a public school superintendent or principal, according to surveys of Texas school administrators.[54] Charter superintendents spend far more time than public school superintendents in managing the school's external environment relative to internal management of the school. They also focus more on raising private funds and generate networks that are less political than public schools'.

Charters are also limited by the supply of talented teachers and face a major labor pool challenge. The average teacher turnover in Texas charter schools in 2010–11 was 32.9 percent, compared with 14.3 percent in public schools. Even highly successful charters such as KIPP (28.8 percent) and YES Prep (30.0 percent) have staggering turnover rates. Charters seek talented teachers yet pay approximately 10 percent less than the public schools (average $39,544 versus $44,019), and teachers can expect a far heavier workload;[55] instruction time was 1,735 hours last year at KIPP, approximately 20 percent more time than at the nearest Houston Independent School District high school (and 38 percent more than the state minimum), and KIPP requires that teachers provide their cell phone numbers to parents.

The data on performance and teacher turnover suggest that Texas, with a modest number of charter schools (versus, for example, Arizona, where the requirements to start a charter are much easier), appears to have reached a critical limit in the talent necessary to start and operate a charter school.[56] Although it is clear from the examples of other states that more charters could be issued if there were no state cap on the number, it is not clear that more quality charters would be provided at current reimbursement rates.

The increase in choice options is directly linked to the problems with monitoring schools and dealing with failures. Ideally, education problems would be met with a rapid response, but the reality is that it takes time for a new school to develop the skills and talents to educate children well, particularly with any experimental effort. Too quick a response will stifle innovation, whereas too slow a response will endanger children.

Create an Efficient Accountability System

Current accountability systems are cumbersome and rife with measurement error, and they impose substantial dead weight costs by shifting resources from teaching to compliance. My interviews with superintendents before the implementation of the NCLB suggest that administrators were more concerned with how to comply with the administrative requirements than they were with how to improve the education of their students. The current accountability system was designed in an ad hoc manner as different issues became salient; new requirements were usually added on top of old ones rather than replacing them.

Part of the logic behind charters is the expectation that they are free from some of the rules and regulations that govern public schools. A model charter law could be used, one that specified the minimum elements of an effective accountability system and provided the crucial information to parents and regulators but did nothing else.[57] Given that possibility, one might ask why the public school accountability system needs to be more burdensome than one for the system for charter schools. Successful implementation of any governance reforms will require that resources be committed to the actual process of education; any resources focused on compliance with accountability systems limit the resources that can be used to improve education.

An efficient accountability system must also either fix or close down failing schools. I have little faith that state departments of education will be effective regulators of school quality and have the political will to close failing schools. The same can be said for charter school authorizers in cases where units other than the state department of education can authorize a charter school.[58] One real loser in this is charter schools, since every positive example can be countered with three or four negative ones. One can easily illustrate this. In 2010 there were 26,508 children in Texas attending district schools in which fewer than 50 percent of students passed the statewide exam; 23,501 of these students were enrolled in charters. As a result, states will be hesitant to remove the caps on the number of charter schools.

At the same time, charter schools, and perhaps only charter schools, can solve this problem by engaging in vigorous self-regulation. If charter schools or a foundation created an accrediting agency staffed with independent regulators and created their own quality control, then states could opt to follow this lead, funding any accredited charter and withdrawing funds from any charter that lost its accreditation. There might be a type of probationary period to permit new charters to get up to speed, but after this period funding would be contingent on accreditation. States should be attracted to this option, since it would free up a great deal of oversight time, as long as they could be convinced that the accrediting agency was truly independent (the basic auditor problem in principal-agent models). Quality charter schools should strongly support this option because it generates an independent assessment of quality and distinguishes the job they do from others that cannot perform. In short, charter schools need to deal with governance reform as an oversight problem.

Abolish the Education Degree

State boards of education or state teacher standards boards set the criteria for who can be a teacher. Such standards are often a reflection of the values of schools of education and the higher education governance system. Although standards are a good thing, they beget rigidity and limit the ability of schools to attract teachers with the needed skills. The state of Texas has abolished the education degree; prospective teachers must major in the subject they want to teach; the policy further limits individuals to no more than eighteen credit hours in education. The policy goes so far as to prohibit public colleges in Texas from offering the degree. The logic for this policy is that education degrees have little content and that subject knowledge is the value that should be maximized. This effort is consistent with the substantial effort to permit alternative teacher certification in the United States and create incentives for teachers to bring substantive knowledge to the classroom. Although I have not seen a systematic evaluation of the Texas policy, it clearly has not led to any systemic declines in performance. The suggestion here should also imply that reexamining the curriculum in education administration, a field that seems divorced from other fields that specialize in administration and management, is also worthwhile. Changing the process of training teachers and administrators seeks to alter the incentives of those seeking a career in education and improving the skills of those individuals.

Defining the Federal Role

Education organizations face a severe multiple-principals problem; federal, state, and local officials (often both politicians and bureaucrats) all play a role in education governance. The goals of these principals frequently conflict and work at cross-purposes. Expanding the federal role can create greater goal consistency, but at the same time it raises the stakes for decisions about education, since both successes and failures will have greater consequences. Although my own view is that the federal government could and should play a definitive role in setting standards (allowing states to set widely varying standards makes little sense), the federal government should not micromanage schools. Perhaps more promising is an effort to delineate in clear terms what the federal role will be relative to education; and that effort should be discussed at the state level as well.

The federal role in education should also address the immigration question. According to our research, the best teachers in Texas appear to be Latinos.[59] Why? Essentially, this is a function of a segmented labor market and the type of person who aspires to a teaching job. The reality of teaching is that it does not pay especially well, and in the United States the social status of the job is modest at best. As a result, it does not appeal to middle- and upper-class individuals. At the same time, it is an attractive position for first- and second-generation immigrants. These individuals tend to be highly motivated—after all, they did immigrate, either legally or illegally, looking for opportunities. Economic immigrants, especially those from families without advanced degrees, are unlikely to have aspirations to become doctors, lawyers, or research scientists; but they see teachers in their communities and that is a profession that offers them upward mobility. Immigration reform by the federal government, such as creating a process of legalization of current residents, a guest worker program that allows children access to higher education, or passing the Dream Act and applying it to individuals who go into teaching, could all improve the quality of the teaching corps in the United States.[60] Such a change would significantly increase the number and quality of individuals seeking careers in education and thereby address the incentives problem in governance reform.

Returning to the Basic Academic Question

This book demonstrates that individual governance reforms do not consistently produce the same results. Reformers need to consider the organization theory issue of whether performance is improved by changing the structure or by changing the people. I return to that issue both to plug (shamelessly) *Public Management: Organizations, Governance and Performance* and to report on its findings, which are relevant to this debate.[61] Despite the generic title, 90 percent of the empirical analysis in the book examines school superintendents and how they manage their districts. The project estimated a series of education production functions; and, unlike most efforts in the literature, explicitly measured the management activities of superintendents. Not only did management significantly affect education performance, but the effect size of these impacts was cumulatively estimated to make up 20 percent of the variation in school district performance across the more than 1,000 districts in Texas.

What did the managers do? First, they built networks of private sector actors (local business leaders, education technology consultants), other government organizations (local police forces, public health programs, city government), nonprofit organizations (after-school programs, Planned Parenthood), and parent groups. They used these networks to buffer political demands (keeping the political pressures out of the schools) and at times to craft programs to benefit schools. They also used these systems to deal with other crises such as natural disasters and significant budget cuts. Second, they developed human resources. They knew that teacher effects are massive, so they recruited, encouraged, and supported teaching—many times a particular style of teaching—often by freeing teachers from administrative burdens and absorbing these burdens into administration. They also developed human resources—principals, curriculum leaders, and so on. Third, they provided stability in terms of long-term leadership focused on key goals and in curriculum; they did not churn.[62] This stability, in particular, matters more for disadvantaged children. Fourth, they made good decisions on everything from integrating the curriculum to selecting principals to motivating teachers. What we really do not know is whether these good decisions are actually exogenous or whether or not it is the human resources that have been developed that produce good decisions. Nothing we found was a magic bullet, but cumulatively what we uncovered made a great deal of difference. If one could add this 20 percent performance boost to the weakest school district, it would probably be the most effective education reform ever attempted.

Because management appears to matter in a wide range of school districts with different types of students and different organizational structures, it should also be effective in a variety of governance structures. Governance structures create biases and incentives that provide the environment of the organization. A good manager works within these structures to generate organizational performance.

Conclusion

Although governance reform of education holds a great deal of promise, the specific payoff of individual reforms in practice is less clear. Although education is governed in a wide variety of ways cross-nationally and, in a more limited extent, within the United States, in many cases the data are lacking or the results do not point to consistent conclusions.[63] Returning to the formal logic expressed earlier, we have little evidence either empirically or based on the causal logic that one type of governance structure in all circumstances outperforms another governance structure, at least in terms of those considered here and those generally in operation. At the same time, there are clear differences in performance and multiple paths to this end. Logically, this implies that effective performance requires both a given governance structure and something else.

The role of the governance structure, as a result, may well lie in its bringing reforms to scale, creating the structures for macro change so that other types of reform (technology, leadership, quality of teachers) can generate the greatest impact over the widest range of circumstances. A second implication is that reform might mean the adoption of multiple governance reforms, each targeting a different causal path to improve the quality of classroom instruction. A third implication is that any governance reform will be affected by the people who set education policy, the people who manage the schools and districts, and the people who actually teach the students.

Notes

1. Richard F. Elmore, "Getting to Scale with Good Educational Practice," *Harvard Educational Review* 66 (Spring 1966): 1–27.

2. See chapter 12 in this volume.

3. Laurence J. O'Toole and Kenneth J. Meier, *Public Management: Organizations, Governance, and Performance* (Cambridge University Press, 2011).

4. David Tyack, *The One Best System: A History of American Urban Education* (Harvard University Press, 1974).

5. See, for example, Kenneth J. Meier and Joseph Stewart Jr., *The Politics of Hispanic Education* (SUNY Press, 1991).

6. Kenneth K. Wong, *Funding Public Schools: Politics and Policy* (University of Kansas Press, 1999).

7. See chapters 2, 12, and 14 in this volume.

8. On the values of American education, see Frederick M. Wirt and Michael W. Kirst, *The Political Dynamics of American Education* (Berkeley, Calif.: McCutchan, 1997).

9. Jeffrey R. Henig and Wilbur C. Rich, eds., *Mayors in the Middle: Politics, Race, and Mayoral Control of Urban Schools* (Princeton University Press, 2004).

10. Dependent school districts avoided much of the nineteenth-century education reform movement, and therefore we should expect that they are different from those districts that adopted the independent school district governance system.

11. Meier and Stewart, *The Politics of Hispanic Education;* Kenneth J. Meier, Joseph Stewart, and Robert England, *Race, Class, and Education: The Politics of Second Generation Discrimination* (University of Wisconsin Press, 1989); Kenneth J. Meier, Meredith Walker, and Sadé Walker, "Political Structure and the Quality of Representation: The Puzzle of Black Education Politics," paper prepared for the annual meeting of the Midwest Political Science Association, Chicago, 2008.

12. W. Curtis Ellis, Alisa Hicklin, and Rene Rocha, "The Effects of Electoral Structure and Minority Representation on Public School Inequality," paper prepared for the Underrepresented Groups in Subnational Policy Conference, Rice University, Houston, 2009.

13. Alternatively, one needs to sample a second time on the dependent variable and determine that C is not present or that C and B are not present in situations of poor performance.

14. Chris Argyris, *The Applicability of Organizational Sociology* (Cambridge University Press, 1972); Charles Perrow, *Organizational Analysis* (Belmont, Calif.: Wadsworth, 1970).

15. Jack Knight, *Institutions and Social Conflict* (Cambridge University Press, 1992). For a parallel view linking structures to different values, see chapter 15 in this volume.

16. Kenneth Shepsle, "Studying Institutions: Some Lessons from the Rational Choice Approach," *Journal of Theoretical Politics* 1 (April 1989): 131–47.

17. David R. Morgan and John P. Pelissero, "Urban Policy: Does Political Structure Matter?" *American Political Science Review* 74 (December 1980): 999–1006; Robert L. Lineberry and Edmund P. Fowler, "Reformism and Public Policies in American Cities," *American Political Science Review* 61 (September 1967): 701–16.

18. Chester E. Finn Jr., "How to Run Public Schools in the 21st Century," *Defining Ideas,* June 22, 2011 (www.hoover.org/publications/defining-ideas/article/83137).

19. See chapter 12 in this volume.

20. See chapter 15 in this volume.

21. How well parents can evaluate the quality of a school is subject to debate. An analysis of New York City school data finds positive correlations of parental evaluations of schools with test scores, audit reports, and ratings after controlling for various inputs. The study also shows that expectations for schools vary by race and shows positive relationships between parent evaluations and both school safety and teacher assessments of quality. See Nathan Favero and Kenneth J. Meier, "Evaluating Urban Public Schools: Parents, Teachers, and State Assessments," paper prepared for the annual meeting of the American Political Science Association, Seattle, September 2011.

22. One superintendent, whose name is long since forgotten, remarked something like, "The state thinks it can run my district better than I can? Well, come on down."

23. See Kenneth J. Meier, *The Political Economy of Regulation: The Case of Insurance* (SUNY Press, 1988) for examples.

24. See chapters 2 and 6 in this volume. See also Henig and Rich, *Mayors in the Middle*.

25. See chapter 9 in this volume.

26. For a counterargument, see John E. Chubb and Terry M. Moe, *Politics, Markets and America's Schools* (Brookings Press, 1990). Terry M. Moe, "The Politics of Bureaucratic Structure," in *Can the Government Govern?* edited by John E. Chubb and Paul E. Peterson (Brookings Press, 1989), pp. 267–329.

27. Stephen S. Smith, Karen Kedrowski, and Joseph Ellis, 2004, "Electoral Structures, Venue Selection, and the (New?) Politics of School Desegregation," *Perspectives on Politics and Political Science* 2 (December 2004): 795–802; Meier, Stewart, and England, *Race, Class, and Education.*

28. Questioning whether such governance reforms worked is fair. Unfortunately, National Assessment of Educational Progress (NAEP) scores do not start until 1992, several years after many of the reforms were adopted. Since 1992, Texas students have gone from 1 point below the national average to 1 point above. Eighth-grade math scores increased from 4 points below the national average to 5 points above. Reading scores in grade four have gone from 2 points below the national average to 1 below, and eighth-grade reading scores were 1 point above the national average and are now 2 points below. Except for the eighth-grade math scores, one would have to conclude that, since 1992, Texas has kept pace with national gains but no more than that. Another significant reform from a politician was the Zell Miller reforms in Georgia in 1993. That reform involved the passage of a state lottery with the proceeds to fund a prekindergarten voucher program, college scholarships for high-performing Georgia students, and investment in technology. The NAEP provides some evidence here. Fourth-grade math scores from 1992 (before the reforms) dropped by 1 point by 1996 (versus a national rise of 3 points) but gained 4 points by 2000 (versus 7 nationally) and 20 points in 2009 (also 20 nationally). The Georgia gains on the eighth-grade math score were 3, 7, and 29 points, respectively, versus national gains of 4, 7, and 15 points for the same years. Fourth-grade reading scores in Georgia fell two points in 1992 and rose 3 and 6 points, respectively, in 1996 and 2000, compared with no change in 1992 and gains of 2 and 5, respectively, in 1996 and 2000. In short, the Miller reforms did not distinguish that state's performance from national trends. To be fair, there were a great many state-level reforms during this period that could have affected the scores of other states.

29. See chapter 6 in this volume.

30. Kenneth K. Wong and Francis X. Shen, "Mayoral Management: Sustaining Effects of Mayoral Control on School Spending in Urban Systems," paper prepared for the annual meeting of the American Political Science Association, Seattle, September 2011.

31. That is not so broad a power wielded by school boards in independent school districts in the United States, since national government standards and requirements circumscribe the authority of these local districts.

32. Sheila E. Murray, William N. Evans, and Robert M. Schwab, "Education-Finance Reform and the Distribution of Education Resources," *American Economic Review* 88 (September 1998): 789–812.

33. Kenneth J. Meier, Robert Wrinkle, and J. L. Polinard, "Bureaucracy and Organizational Performance: Causality Arguments about Public Schools," *American Journal of Political Science* 44 (July 2000): 590–603.

34. Kenneth J. Meier, Laurence J. O'Toole Jr., and Alisa K. Hicklin, "I've Seen Fire and I've Seen Rain: Public Management and Performance after a Natural Disaster," *Administration and Society* 41 (January 2010): 979–1003. School districts in general are very lean in terms of administration. In 2010 only 1.95 percent of employees in the average Texas school district were in central administration, and only 2.93 percent in school administration. Charter schools in Texas are far more bureaucratic, with 3.13 percent of employees in central administration and 6.52 percent in campus administration. These highly significant differences are not a function of economies of scale (which exist in education administration) but remain after controls for total enrollment.

35. This is a slight exaggeration, but it is clearly the implication of the teaching of creation science.

36. O'Toole and Meier, *Public Management*.

37. See Breanca Thomas, Meredith Walker, and Kenneth J. Meier, "Texas Superintendent Management Survey, 2009" (College Station, Tex.: Project for Equity, Representation, and Governance, 2009) (http://perg.tamu.edu/PERG/Home_files/2009%20 Results.pdf). There is additional contact by other school system members. The 2011 Texas Principals Survey finds that 22 percent of principals made at least monthly contact with county or city government, 49 percent with police and fire departments, 31 percent with nonprofits, and 24 percent with health-related organizations, though the last was not asked of the superintendents.

38. Young Han Chun and Hal G. Rainey, "Goal Ambiguity and Organizational Performance in U.S. Federal Agencies," *Journal of Public Administration Research and Theory* 15 (October 2005): 529–57.

39. Moe, "The Politics of Bureaucratic Structure"; Kenneth J. Meier, "Bureaucracy and Democracy: The Case for More Bureaucracy and Less Democracy," *Public Administration Review* 57 (May–June 1997): 193–99.

40. See chapter 2 in this volume.

41. See http://perg.tamu.edu/PERG/Home_files/2009%20Results.pdf. Actual use varies, from real pay-for-performance systems in some districts to a more general consideration of results in paying bonuses or setting wages. The practice appears to be used more frequently for managers than for teachers.

42. My knowledge of these two organizations is limited to their schools in Houston.

43. See Hal G. Rainey, *Understanding and Managing Public Organizations* (San Francisco: Jossey-Bass, 2009), pp. 273–82.

44. See chapter 12 in this volume. I do not address the question of teachers unions in this chapter, but I point out that many of the high-performing European education systems are both heavily unionized, even at the management level, and exceptionally rule bound.

45. Parmalee P. Hawk, "A Comparison of Education and Non-Education Majors in General College Courses," paper prepared for the annual meeting of the American Association of Colleges for Teacher Education, Washington, February 1999.

46. Sean P. Corcoran, William N. Evans, and Robert M. Schwab, "Women, the Labor Market, and the Declining Relative Quality of Teachers," *Journal of Policy Analysis and Management* 23 (Summer 2004): 449–70.

47. By all indications, this move was successful. Sam Houston attained an acceptable rating within one year. Most striking is the degree of discretion that the principal had; she replaced 140 of the previous teachers at the high school.

48. Mark Schneider, Paul Teske, and Melissa Marschall, *Choosing Schools: Consumer Choice and the Quality of American Schools* (Princeton University Press, 2001).

49. I agree with Chester Finn and Michael Petrilli (see chapter 2 in this volume) on the need for some consolidation. Of the eleven worst school districts in Texas, according to the statewide 2010 exam results, one has 1,110 students, one has 611, and the rest have 300 or fewer.

50. See chapter 14 in this volume.

51. Charles M. Tiebout, "A Pure Theory of Local Expenditures," *Journal of Political Economy* 64 (October 1956): 416–24.

52. One needs to be careful about accepting the spin that schools put on their performance. Although KIPP and YES Prep are good schools, comparisons with top public HISD schools DeBakey (a health sciences magnet) and Bellaire (a comprehensive high school) indicates they are not spectacular. Below are the schools' scores on the Texas Assessment of Knowledge and Skills (TAKS; the statewide level), percentages of students at the much higher commended level, average SAT and ACT scores, and the percentages of students who score at 1,110 or above on the SAT or its ACT equivalent.

High school	TAKS	Commended	SAT	ACT	1,110+
KIPP	79%	15%	958	n.a.	8.1%
YES Prep	92%	22%	933	19.8	12.4%
DeBakey	99+%	57%	1,207	27.2	83.5%
Bellaire	78%	19%	1,156	25.0	25.0%

53. These differences are strongly statistically significant. The gap between charter schools and public schools is 7.2 points for African American students, 9.5 points for Latino students, and 9.0 points for low-income students. An elaborate assessment of Texas charter school performance based on the matching of propensity score concludes that, on average, there were no differences in performance between charter schools and comparable public schools. See Lori Taylor and others, *Evaluation of Texas Charter Schools* (College Station, Tex.: State of Texas Education Research Center at Texas A&M University, 2011). The stress should be on the term "on average," since the study compares the means, not the distributions. The study also finds that a set of sixty-one public school campuses that are operated as charters by the school districts also performed equally well.

54. We have always included charter school superintendents in our surveys, even though little of the analysis included the charter school managers. Initially, this decision was made because charters were new, and we felt had to develop some capacity before meaningful comparisons with public schools could be made. Recent work has begun to use these data.

55. Taylor and others, in *Evaluation of Texas Charter Schools,* place the difference at 12 percent but then incorporate local wage rates and suggest the gap is approximately $10,000, or 24 percent. An interesting statistic is that charters also pay campus administrators about 10 percent less than public school administrators, but pay scales for central administrators are the same when one controls for the smaller size of charters.

56. Some additional supply of personnel can be recruited from public schools, but generally charters do not pay as well as public schools. At the same time, other incentives can be offered. In the fall of 2011 there appeared to be a bit of a hiring war going on between KIPP and HISD for administrative talent. Generally, the administrators who leave the independent district for KIPP note that they desire more autonomy rather than a higher salary.

57. This could be done by state education officials, the National Conference of State Legislatures, or through amendments to the NCLB. Each choice brings a different set of values.

58. Kathryn McDermott, *High-Stakes Reform: The Politics of Educational Accountability* (Georgetown University Press, 2011).

59. Kenneth J. Meier and others, "Zen and the Art of Policy Analysis," *Journal of Politics* 63 (May 2001): 616–29.

60. Two additional pieces of evidence indicate the potential payoff here. Texas has a severe teacher shortage, estimated at approximately 16,000 teachers each year. This shortage exists in all areas of the state except along the Rio Grande valley, where well-qualified teachers take positions as substitute teachers in hopes of getting hired for a permanent job in their home district, to make a salary that is $15,000 a year less than they could earn in Dallas. Texas school districts are also one of the largest users of H-1B visas. Many aggressively recruit teachers, particularly math and science teachers, from other countries.

61. O'Toole and Meier, *Public Management.*

62. Frederick M. Hess, *Spinning Wheels: The Politics of Urban School Reform* (Brookings Press, 1999).

63. See chapter 12 in this volume.

PAUL MANNA *and* PATRICK MCGUINN

17

The Tall Task of Education Governance Reform

Education governance in the United States is fundamentally broken. On that point the authors in this volume—along with many others across the ideological spectrum, including scholars, policymakers, education leaders, school officials, teachers, and parents—readily agree. Several decades of intense school reform efforts in the United States have produced at best marginal gains in student achievement, and there is a mounting sense that the nation's unique and fragmented system of education governance may well pose a major barrier to greater improvement. A recent report by the National Center on Education and the Economy, for example, concludes that the country's education system is neither coherent nor likely to see great improvements based on current approaches to reform.[1]

This volume makes three fundamental arguments. First, existing education governance arrangements have impeded the quest for school reform and improvement. Second, these arrangements have received inadequate attention from scholars and policymakers. Third, a variety of potentially promising governance reforms have emerged here and abroad that offer viable alternatives to the status quo. Reforming education governance will not solve all the problems that plague education. However, there is deep and varied dysfunction in how the United States allocates decisionmaking authority for elementary and secondary schools. So while improving governance of K–12 education may not be sufficient on its own to improve the management and performance of America's schools, it is a necessary precondition for the kind of transformative change and improvement that has to date proved so elusive.

Taken together, we see three sets of takeaways from the previous chapters. Although not all our authors may agree with our specific conclusions, these are the main points that we, as editors, see emerging from the volume. The first set centers on the problems associated with current governing arrangements. The second draws our attention to important tensions that confront potential governance reformers who wish to offer new approaches. The third involves some important design principles that, if embraced, could help to improve the chances that future governance reforms will succeed.

Problems Created by the Nation's Education Governance System

Although prior chapters document numerous problems created by the nation's system of education governance, they tend to be of three different types. Governance by multiple masters creates incoherence in elementary and secondary school systems; makes it difficult for innovators to innovate, leaders to lead, and teachers to teach; and, though it provides many opportunities to foster democratic participation and outcomes, in practice it undercuts these goals.

Governance by multiple masters creates incoherence in the nation's elementary and secondary school system. Separation of powers and federalism have combined with an attachment to local control to produce a cacophony of actors and institutions with some power over American schools. As a result, no single leader (or even a small number of easily identifiable leaders) has the ability to lead effectively or is held accountable for results. No one can reasonably claim that "the buck stops here," for in reality the buck stops everywhere and thus nowhere. The virtue and vice of this system is the multiple points of access that it grants to a wide variety of viewpoints and preferences. Some have argued that this arrangement is both inevitable and desirable in a democracy, yet it has clearly produced a system of decisionmaking at all levels that is neither coherent nor effective. Basic principles of management, in the public, private, and nonprofit sectors, dictate that leaders and staff are most likely to succeed when goals are clear and operational discretion exists for managers and frontline employees to discover the most effective ways of reaching those goals, with all involved in the work being held accountable for their performance.

But none of these basic pillars of sound management appear to be in place in American schools. School leaders are expected to pursue oodles of education goals, many of which are in tension with one another, such as differentiating instruction to meet student needs while simultaneously showing that all students are making progress on standardized measures of achievement. In addition, the existence of multiple masters has led to the gradual accretion of statutory and regulatory mandates, court rulings, and contractual stipulations that dramatically circumscribe the range of action for principals and superintendents and make it nearly impenetrable for education outsiders to understand what is going on. Another consequence of a fragmented governance system is that it simultaneously imposes multiple, differing visions of education, which creates the layering effect that Kenneth Wong and Jeffrey Henig highlight. This problem is exacerbated in the accountability era as the different layers craft and push forth different preferred measures of performance and consequences for failing to meet performance standards.

The arena of school finance vividly illustrates another consequence that fragmented and layered governance can create. As Marguerite Roza shows, inside this $600 billion industry the myriad different education funding streams often flow in narrow, self-contained channels and remain disconnected from outcomes. In addition, across and within states how and how much schools are funded varies tremendously, as do the rules governing the way federal, state, and local education dollars are spent. The tangled web of funding streams and reporting mandates has limited school and district leaders from directing monies flexibly and with an eye toward innovation or improving performance while simultaneously creating a time-consuming focus on fiscal accounting and paperwork.

Historically, a significant barrier to any rethinking of school districts or other major restructuring of education governance has been the absence of a common metric—within and across states—that could permit transparency, comparability, and accountability of student performance from schools operated in different locales or by different providers. As a result, the development of national standards and assessments that could provide such information has the potential to be a governance game changer. As Kathryn McDermott notes, the current push by the Council of Chief State School Officers and the National Governors Association to develop common academic standards and the work of two different assessment consortiums illustrate the increasing level of coordination among states. These new, albeit fragile, forms of state and interstate governance have provided strong challenges to the norm of local control and, if sustained, could promote greater coherence within and across states.

All the research on effective organizations emphasizes the importance of mission clarity and operational flexibility to achieving successful outcomes. Yet when schools or districts fail the tendency is to replace local discretion with centrally mandated and often layered fixes.[2] Getting out of this box is crucial to creating greater coherence and more effective governance in education. As the former Louisiana superintendent Paul Pastorek commented at a conference where our authors presented drafts of their chapters, "There is a silver bullet. The silver bullet is coherence."[3]

Governance by multiple masters makes it difficult for innovators to innovate, leaders to lead, and teachers to teach. The existence of so many different layers of authority in the American education system has produced stifling mandates and ossified funding streams that dramatically shackle innovative leaders and teachers, preventing them from serving students well. Inertia and incentives built into the current system encourage school leaders to continue past practices without reflecting on whether they serve present needs and emerging priorities. In an era when the nation increasingly holds local leaders and schools accountable for results, commensurate substantive changes in governance that could facilitate good management have not been forthcoming. Michelle Davis's interviews reveal the palpable frustration that principals, superintendents, and chief state school officers express over this situation. In many school districts across the country, education leaders are often frustrated by challenges they have no power to control or systems that prompt district responses that often fail to account for what could best serve students. This frustration has led a number of individual leaders, in places such as Indiana, Oregon, and Louisiana, to begin to create new governance structures, though their efforts as of yet remain largely isolated and incomplete.

The current fragmented governance and funding regime in American education stymies not only reformers working from inside the traditional K–12 system but also, as Steven Wilson makes clear, those entrepreneurs working from the outside to offer new ideas or technologies that could productively challenge the current order. Given the multiple veto points in the system, its tangled finances, and the complex regulatory web, including variability across state and district lines, these entrepreneurs face barriers that limit the reach or impact of potentially promising innovations. Although governance reform alone cannot ensure that sufficient leadership capacity or courage will emerge—either inside or outside traditional public schools—it can create the conditions that permit and encourage leaders to lead effectively.

Ultimately, teachers feel the pinch of multiple masters in their classrooms each and every day. Local initiatives or teachers' own professional instincts that may stress offering individualized attention to each student or family clash with state and federal testing and accountability mandates that create incentives to increase the number of students proficient in key subjects, a demand that often leads to a focus on students on the cusp of passing—undercutting opportunities to bring up those who struggle most and to catapult forward the school's highest academic flyers. For those teachers who manage to create space for curricular risk taking or enrichment, the need to jump through bureaucratic hoops to try an innovative technique, explore an engaging but controversial topic, or plan and carry out field trips or visits from guest speakers can involve navigating districtwide rules that are layered with requirements from state boards or legislatures that have passed policies to ensure safety or (owing to interest group pressure) prevent students from being exposed to materials deemed inappropriate.

In theory, today's system of education governance provides many opportunities to foster democratic participation and outcomes, but in practice the system undercuts these goals. The ideal of local control by democratically elected school boards is a powerful and enduring image that has enjoyed much support. Historic efforts to maintain local engagement, ensure that schooling is responsive to local geographically variant norms, and establish governing arrangements so that policies influencing children remain close to home all helped establish the thousands of school boards that we see today. These arrangements are backed by long histories and vocal constituencies. Clearly, among the defenders of local control are powerful interests that seek rents and disproportionately benefit from such arrangements, but other defenders support these arrangements because philosophically they see fragmented, locally dominated governance as the approach that is most democratically responsive to citizen preferences.

Although Jeffersonian notions of locally governed school districts provide a compelling vision of what education governance could be, in practice the reality in most school districts veers far from the ideal. Chester Finn and Michael Petrilli and also Frederick Hess and Olivia Meeks show how the efforts of the Progressive Era to remove education from politics merely shifted the lines of battle rather than inoculating the system from political influences and power. The effect of instituting nonpartisan, off-cycle elections for school boards has been to discourage voter turnout and to empower powerful organized interests that have a material stake in the outcome and can make campaign contributions and mobilize votes. The result is that parents and children, especially disadvantaged children, wield the least power in the current system of education governance, especially in the local politics that orbit the selection of school board members. These political problems are further exacerbated by the district-based structure of American education. The drawing of district lines has resulted—often quite consciously—in the segregation of students by race and class. Long-standing student assignment processes that confine students to the nearest neighborhood school have further locked in these patterns. The lack of choice in the district-oriented governance model has created an education monopoly in which pressures to respond to family preferences or the power to mobilize funding and parent choices to reduce inequity are generally absent.

The enormous complexity of America's education governance system makes it extremely difficult for citizens, even the most interested ones, to track school or district performance and to hold elected officials accountable for the results they produce, as would occur in an ideal Jeffersonian world. The multiple masters and incoherence described above makes transparency of inputs and outputs extraordinarily difficult to achieve. Cynthia Brown emphasizes the ways in which current governance arrangements in education have been especially harmful for the most disadvantaged children in the United States and, alternatively, how poor and minority children have the most to gain from a redesign of the ways that the nation governs its public schools. Existing governance arrangements ensure that poor and minority children will receive fewer resources—and fewer excellent teachers—than children living in middle- and upper-class communities, make it less likely that the resources they do have will be spent in effective ways, and restrict the availability of school choice, typically to parents who can afford private school tuition or can move into higher-quality public school districts.

Rather than attenuating broader societal inequalities that correlate with race, class, and zip code, today's system of education governance tends to exacerbate them, meaning that some students leave school less equipped to become full participants in the nation's economic and democratic life. A look at the latest figures from the U.S. census reveals that huge demographic changes are producing ever larger numbers of students who are members of traditionally disadvantaged groups.[4] If these students continue to be left out, then the nation's current gigantic set of challenges associated with serving them well will only get worse in the future. And the nation's democracy will suffer as a result. Surely, fixing education governance will not eliminate these inequalities overnight. But it could go a long way toward creating conditions more conducive to reform and thus helping the nation's schools contribute to more democratic outcomes.

Tensions That Emerge in Thinking about Governance Reform

It is rather easy to state the problems associated with today's system of education governance. It is much harder to propose alternatives that are not themselves magnets for broad criticism. That is the reality in a large and diverse democratic society such as the United States, where any governance system must try to reconcile numerous inevitable tensions. We identify three in particular that emerge from the previous chapters.

How are we to balance the demands of rival interests that have some stake in how the nation's education system is governed? Debates about education governance often assume that the central problem is rationalizing structures to more effectively pursue agreed-on ends, such as raising student achievement or closing achievement gaps. But as our authors note, citizens disagree not only about how to pursue education goals but also about what those very goals should be. Attempts to reach a consensus on the purpose of education in diverse communities with different religious, racial, ethnic, ethical, and economic preferences may well be impossible. And even if consensus is possible, many compromise solutions are likely to contribute to the incoherence in the system.

An alternative to compromise, of course, would be differentiation, something that a decentralized system of governance organized not around local school districts but by consumer choice could attain.[5] That approach itself poses a challenge because getting to such a model would be a dramatic break with current governance practice and, as Barry Rabe notes, is an approach typically not embraced in other sectors in such a robust form. It is important to recognize that different governance arrangements will privilege not just the material interests of different actors or groups (such as teachers unions, technology providers, textbook and testing companies, and numerous others) but also quite different visions of schooling.

At first glance, some of these actors and groups, in particular students and their families, seem to have the most direct claims on what the education system should do and, by implication, how it should be governed. But although families are perhaps the most proximate interest when it comes to schools and their governance, even families in the same community often disagree about which approaches should prevail. Teachers themselves, already a powerful and well-organized group, raise their own sets of issues and priorities, some of which may align with what students need, including the provision of adequate classroom materials for teaching and learning, but others of which may not, such as last-in first-out hiring processes. And what of taxpayers who foot the bill for all this? They are perhaps the most distal interest in this bunch, but without their support and confidence that the system is producing educated citizens prepared for life in a modern economy and democracy, their patience to fund this enterprise we call public education, in whatever form one might imagine, could run short.

Today, one prominent approach designed to reform governance, which advocates suggest can cut through the interest group thicket that ensnares potentially promising initiatives, is to concentrate decisionmaking power for education in a smaller number of institutions, levels of government, or individual actors. Mayoral control of schools is a leading example here. Such consolidation of authority can promote greater decisiveness, coherence, and accountability but by definition excludes or weakens some stakeholders. However, consolidation certainly eliminates some existing vetoes, but it does not solve the question of which level, institution, or actor should possess the power to govern.[6]

Two extreme options for governance are top-down authoritarian systems, in which the central government makes all of the decisions in a stated attempt to maximize the public good, and the bottom-up libertarian approach, whereby basically public governance gives way to private preferences and choices as parents take public money to purchase a good such as education. It is between these two extremes (and overlapping with America's governance system writ large) that the debate about education governance tends to reside. Which system can adjudicate disagreements in the most efficient way and lead to the best outcomes on both public and private fronts? Is our current system really the best way to deal with all of that? Or is there something else out there that might work better? No doubt, it too will be messy. But can we not find something at least marginally better? To date, the nation's institutions that govern education have made little progress on these fronts, although some authors have proposed models for improvement.[7]

How can we balance a desire for governance that enhances stability yet takes time to cultivate, against the need for rapid, transformative change when failure is persistent? Many of the authors in this volume characterize the nation's current education system as ossified and averse to change and argue that major shocks or disruptions are required to redirect prevailing efforts.[8] But disruption often emerges from battles that produce clear winners and losers. Michael Mintrom and Richard Walley argue that such battles can alienate the street-level bureaucrats (teachers, principals, administrators) needed to implement reforms effectively and sustain them over time. It is difficult work to build reform coalitions, what Clarence Stone has called "civic capacity," that can be wide and deep enough to sustain systemic change.[9] Developing consensus about broad principles or goals and then acceptance of concrete plans of action among citizens, school personnel, interest groups, and policymakers in support of a particular school reform can be a difficult and lengthy process.

Governance that promotes stability can be good, but it also can undercut the ability to change when needed. Parents who lament the performance of their children's schools—and policymakers who believe the education system is in crisis—typically demand immediate changes. Systems that promote too much stability or provide too many veto points can throw up harmful roadblocks to innovators operating inside and outside district schools, as Davis and Wilson highlight. How do we set the accelerator right so that the system can be resilient enough to resist flavor-of-the-month reforms but flexible enough to adjust quickly when needed? When people think schools or school systems are failing there are both political and substantive reasons to try something new. But in places where perceived or actual failure persists, this can create what Hess elsewhere calls "spinning wheels," where there is too much rather than too little reform, which is exacerbated by the constant turnover in superintendent and political leadership, especially in urban districts.[10] Yet the research demonstrates that new reforms need time to take root and deliver improvements. One important point made by Sir Michael Barber is that major governance reform cannot occur overnight. Rather, it takes time to implement properly, and furthermore, one should expect a considerable amount of trial and error in the process.

What should be the relationship between geography and governance? One of the most interesting issues this volume raises for debate is the idea of detaching education governance from geography and instead organizing schools or districts around individual households (as with parent choice), virtual schools or districts, or crosscutting alliances and consortiums. Historically, the nation has organized and mostly funded schools on a local basis, creating a school district around a particular municipal entity such as a town or county and sometimes in geographical units that crisscross these same town and county lines. Four trends in education, however, are challenging such an approach: emerging interstate collaboration, greater parental demand for school choice, the rapid growth of national charter school management organizations, and the growth of virtual schooling. Broader societal changes, too, including population mobility and the emergence of sometimes overlapping yet geographically untethered social networks, further undercut the claims that local governance of education, delivered mainly by traditional school districts, should retain its privileged status.

As Paul Hill as well as Hess and Meeks observe, seeing governance of the nation's education system through the popular lens of geography, rather than the lens of function, common approach, or common need, as in Louisiana's recovery school district, potentially limits the range of approaches that might better meet student needs. It is increasingly clear that the geographic basis of school assignment policies and the drawing of district lines exacerbates performance and equity problems and stymies reform. But Americans are attached to notions of the neighborhood school and the common school for a reason. What do we sacrifice by decoupling the education space from place? Proposals for a new geography or organizing frame for education governance will have to grapple with that question.

Design Principles to Help Guide Future Governance Reforms

At the present time, education governance arrangements vary widely around the world. No single model is necessarily preferred by citizens or produces clearly superior outcomes. Even in the United States, with all of the governance problems this book discusses, one can identify public school districts that contain outstanding leaders and teachers who help all children succeed. The trouble is that as we turn the page of the first decade of the twenty-first century, such places remain too few even as the nation's education challenges—made especially acute given global economic competition, our own rapidly diversifying society, and widening gaps between the haves and the have-nots—are mounting. Given that complexity and the humble recognition that there are no governance silver bullets, we close with a list of principles that any governance reformer should consider.

There are numerous ways to work out the details, as other chapters suggest. Hill, for example, emphasizes that a key issue to consider is not simply who should govern but, more specifically, which powers should be entrusted to which of the institutions or actors who might potentially govern. He lays out a particular answer to that question, which, he argues, goes a long way toward eliminating confusion over the allocation of power while simultaneously reducing regulatory confusion in the nation's schools. Other proposals may slice this apple in different ways. Yet all could benefit, we think, by engaging the issue of education governance reform in ways that remain attentive to these closing principles in order to root out their strengths and weaknesses and applications to particular contexts.

In addition, much debate about governance and how to change it has centered around whether our education system should be more or less centralized. However, the chapters in this volume argue that the real issue is not decentralization or centralization but which kinds of education decisions should be made at which level of society and by what types of institutions or individuals, be they public, nonprofit, or private. The following principles should help advocates for governance reform identify the nuances involved in these sorts of issues as they craft and seek support for their own proposals for change.

How one conceptualizes the governance problem will influence the solutions that one chooses while creating inevitable blind spots. There is not a single education governance problem reformers must confront but rather several challenges that emerge in different ways across numerous contexts. Depending on how one approaches the issue, some things will become more salient and others less so, which suggests that any particular governance approach will have blind spots that create unintended consequences. Furthermore, given on-the-ground realities, defeated ideas and interests will not simply go away but will seek alternative avenues of influence in new systems of governance that privilege other priorities.[11] Kenneth Meier helps illuminate the challenges by articulating five ways to define the governance problem: as a problem of structure, oversight, politics, network management, or incentives. Reinforcing Mintrom and Walley's cross-national analysis, Meier notes that there are multiple paths to improving education governance and school outcomes.

Battles over how to define the governance problem become intense as different groups that have a stake in the outcome maneuver to advance their own interests. One of the most significant developments in education governance in recent years has been the end of what Jeffrey Henig calls "education exceptionalism." Education governance has begun to veer away from Progressive Era assumptions, which stressed the need for insulation from the larger political sphere, to become reabsorbed into more general all-purpose government. This is a major shift as presidents, governors, and mayors have devoted an unprecedented amount of attention to school reform and assumed prominent roles in education policymaking. Operating in different institutional venues, these "education executives" come to the issue of school reform with different perspectives, powers, and constituents from those who inhabit traditional structures, such as school boards. The result has been an increase in mayoral control, state takeovers, and recovery districts and new federal approaches such as competitive grant programs.

Although such changes may have increased the pace of reform, it is important to note that the greater involvement of executives in governance could potentially exacerbate the layering problem in education and that research on the impact of these approaches is mixed. Put differently, governance approaches such as mayoral control or greater empowerment of governors are not reforms in themselves. Rather, they create new possibilities, yet everything still depends on the choices leaders make and the subsequent groups that those choices empower. Thus there is no guarantee that conceptualizing the problem of education governance as emerging from weak executive leadership and empowering new education executives to act will necessarily produce desirable outcomes across the board.

Governance systems interact with policy and capacity, both human and institutional, to produce results. Arguing that governance is crucial means that it is an essential place to start, not end, the conversation about school reform. A related point is that reforming governance does not guarantee the adoption and implementation of more effective policies, it only creates conditions that increase the likelihood that such policies will emerge and succeed. The ultimate effectiveness of any particular governance system depends on the interaction between the institutions and the leaders who inhabit them.

It is thus imperative to build human capital and institutional capacity across all of the different nodes of education governance, be they located inside or outside government. At the present time, the country lacks sufficient numbers of high-quality teachers, principals, and superintendents as well as adequate staff, resources, and technical expertise in local and state agencies to support their work. In his comments at the conference of our authors before publication, discussant Marc Tucker noted the degree to which education ministry officials are revered in high-performing countries around the world, yet similar officials working in states or the federal government in the United States often are criticized or lampooned. The chapters in this volume emphasize the crucial and changing role that state departments of education must play in education governance. Our authors also document how agency staff are struggling to shift from their traditional role as grant administrators and compliance officers to a new role as performance monitors and technical assistance providers. We need to think more deeply and strategically about the kinds of structures, capacities, and resources that state governments need to fulfill their more demanding governance role in the twenty-first century.[12]

Christopher Cerf, New Jersey's education commissioner, has already initiated such an effort by creating a completely revamped organizational and staffing chart that is focused on what he sees as his department's four core missions.[13] The new assistant commissioner positions—chief academic officer, chief performance officer, chief talent officer, and chief innovation officer—are intended to shift the department's resources from compliance-related activities to support for the work of schools and districts. But the New Jersey education department, like state education agencies across the nation, has seen its budget and staff shrink in recent decades even as the demands placed on it have increased dramatically. Students of bureaucratic politics can recount numerous analogous changes in other units of government that in the end produced little substantive change, despite the reshuffling and renaming of subagencies with catchy titles that embrace the buzzwords of the day. The chapters by Barber and by Mintrom and Walley, as well as Tucker's published work, highlight the tremendous skill and knowledge of people working in the education ministries of high-performing education systems around the world and the large talent gap between those agencies and their counterparts in the United States.[14] Redesigning and reinvigorating state and local capacities must be an essential step in future governance reform. The pace at which a governance change can lead to improvement will be determined in part by how fast these human and institutional capacities can be built. This suggests a role for investments by foundations and governments alike as complementary solutions to the broader governance challenge.

The focus of the school reform movement on enacting new policies has ignored the fact that the ultimate success or failure of any particular policy, no matter how promising, is dependent on the governance context in which it will be implemented. Take charter authorizing, for example. Charter schools are often described as a market-based reform, and the model is predicated on independence and differentiation from the regulations and practices of traditional school districts. Yet public authorities continue to govern charter schools because in most cases they remain public schools under the control of the district. As Wilson and Hill clearly demonstrate, charter school authorizing, financing, and supervision greatly influence their potential for success regardless of the efficacy of the underlying model. Most state charter laws have established school districts themselves as the primary (or only) charter authorizer, an odd arrangement to say the least since that gives them the authority to restrict the entrance and operations of their own competition. Other states have enacted laws that either directly or indirectly seek to make charters operate more like district schools, as is the case when states require them to adhere to collective bargaining contracts. At the other end of the spectrum, some states have essentially opted out of charter school oversight and permitted poorly designed charters to open and poorly performing charters to continue operating. Just as good governance can be undermined by bad policy, good policy can be undermined by bad governance. Cultivating human and institutional capacity can go a long way toward ameliorating both problems.

Different sectors of government and society have different governance comparative advantages. The intensive period of school reform over the past twenty years has begun to clarify or suggest appropriate roles in education for local, state, and federal governments, as well as private and nonprofit actors. Based on his experience in England, Barber emphasizes the idea of comparative advantages. Different levels of the education "delivery chain," including the important "mediating layer," bring different capabilities and limitations to the table. Although the nation's current hodgepodge system of governance empowers every level of government to have a say over virtually every aspect of education policy, some decisions and functions are better assigned to certain venues and not others. Consider some examples.

The federal role in education has grown dramatically since the 1965 passage of the Elementary and Secondary Education Act and especially in the wake of that law's revision as the No Child Left Behind Act. However, though the federal government can force states to do things they quite likely would not do on their own, it generally cannot force them to do those things well. So what role might the federal government play in education governance in the twenty-first century? Rationalizing the fiscal, statutory, and regulatory barriers to reform that have accrued since 1965 would be one great place to start. Relaxing the prevailing assumption that federal education programs should be organized around flows of funds from Washington to state education agencies, then on to local school districts through formula grants based on educational "need," could also help. Kenneth Wong shows how these familiar mechanisms are ill suited to drive innovation and improvement in district schools or to support alternative models.

What about the states? These governments play an important substantive role, which is growing more potentially consequential owing to the emergence of state collaborations. In the nation's federal system, states play a pivotal role as overseer of local districts but also as the translator of federal programs and demands into more specific policies that school officials can then carry out in local contexts. There is a dynamic exchange here between these levels of government. Perhaps ironically, heavy hands from Washington sometimes can strengthen the weaker hands of state or local reformers contemplating similar policies, because leaders closer to home can disavow responsibility for a difficult reform, telling their constituents that the feds are making them do it. In this scenario, fragmented governance actually provides useful political cover that can break policy logjams in states and local districts. Furthermore, as Brown argues, states may also be the best positioned unit, along with federal assistance on the margins, to minimize funding and other inequities that persist across local school district lines. Growing energy at the state level (emerging with some support from the federal level) for more coherent standards and expectations as well as the development of data capacities that help monitor and track system performance means that state governments and their capacity will remain crucial elements that can help foster coherence in the nation's education system. Assertive states working together could begin to mimic the collaborative efforts of Canada's provincial education ministers that Sandra Vergari illustrates.

Finally, the demands of the local or operational level, as Davis and Wilson illustrate, argue for governance arrangements that foster greater flexibility to meet pressing needs and seize emerging opportunities. Depending on local contexts, preferences, and the political will of local leaders, those arrangements might involve dramatic breaks with the school district model of governance, as a robust local collection of charter schools or a geographically unbounded recovery district could create, or they might work within a refashioned district model, as Hill suggests, but with dramatically redefined governance roles. Whatever governance arrangement takes hold, it also should recognize the advantages to be reaped by local partnerships with private and nonprofit groups, including community organizations, technology companies, traditional and alternative teacher preparation programs, and even private foundations. These actors can help inject resources and valuable human, material, or financial capital as well as other ideas that, if adapted well, could meet local needs. Supporting that end could be federal and state governments. Together, those higher levels can provide an overarching strategic vision and specific support for research and capacity building that can help local (or virtual, even) communities identify education practices and organizational forms that research suggests have great potential for improving student learning.

The landscape sketched here identifies but a handful of the actors that are likely to play some meaningful role in education governance into the future. Considering the comparative advantages of each and then fashioning lines of command, control, and communication—sometimes in hierarchical arrangements, but probably more often in flexible networked designs—is an important task for governance reformers to consider.

Governance systems that provide strong substantive oversight but few operational constraints are more likely to produce better outcomes. When thinking about how education governance systems should connect different layers of government as well as innovators and service providers in the private and nonprofit sectors, it is useful to consider how the system handles the important task of oversight. A crucial function of a governance system in any policy area is to provide valuable supervision so that citizens and elected officials can be kept abreast of whether the nation is achieving its policy goals and whether governments are good stewards of scarce tax dollars. But how one pursues oversight can have powerful impacts on results. We stress a difference between substantive oversight, which focuses on accountability for valued student outcomes such as whether schools are helping young people acquire the skills and knowledge needed to participate in the nation's economy and democracy, and operational oversight, which emphasizes how districts and schools pursue those outcomes through funding certain programs or activities.[15] A governance system that focuses on substantive outcomes rather than the details of operations could help the nation move closer to accomplishing its educational goals.

American education governance, at every level, generally seems to have inverted the proper mix of operational and substantive oversight. In Washington edu-speak, this issue has become known as the "tight-loose" problem. The federal test-based accountability system at the heart of No Child Left Behind was loose on how states defined and measured education outcomes but tight on how they should achieve them. It allowed states to set their own academic standards, tests, and definitions of student proficiency but mandated a lot of operational oversight, including the grades in which students must be tested and a prescriptive set of policy mandates (choice, supplemental services, corrective action, restructuring) that struggling schools and districts had to enact. Although the program is not without some accomplishments, after a decade of No Child Left Behind it seems that most states responded by gaming the system through lowered expectations for students and that many of the law's policy mandates were either ignored or ineffective (and in some cases even damaging). States and districts also tend to focus on statutory, regulatory, and contractual mandates that restrict the ability of leaders to lead and teachers to teach without much meaningful accountability for student outcomes. Teacher policy is a great example of this, as principals in most states are constrained in how they hire, train, evaluate, compensate, assign, and dismiss teachers.

Although it may seem contradictory to think that strong oversight can coexist with few constraints, such strategic governance is both possible and desirable, as many of Mintrom and Walley's education examples from around the world reveal and as Rabe's analysis of Medicaid and the Clean Air Act demonstrate. Even with the presence of many similar challenges to the education sector, Rabe shows that these two programs have produced significant performance-based achievements as well as some capacity for adaptation and innovation. An important lesson from these other sectors is that governing layers from above can impose clear standards and expectations yet give implementers at the intermediate and ground levels latitude to act. Still, whatever mix of operational and substantive oversight is chosen, and whoever is chosen to pursue it, government must maintain high interest and involvement in helping supply a steady stream of institutional and human capacity, monitoring the overall performance of the system, and providing strategic direction. Thinking about governance in this way argues against models that rely exclusively on market forces or impose heavy operational constraints, as in the current system.

Conclusion

Today, the United States continues to govern its schools based primarily on principles and institutions, particularly the local school board, that were developed during the Progressive Era of the early twentieth century. However, these old principles and institutions are ill suited to the United States of the twenty-first century, which faces radically different education challenges and opportunities. In 1983, the education report *A Nation at Risk* helped unleash and accelerate a thirty-year frenzy of school reform activity, but these efforts focused on creating new policies and programs without rethinking the underlying governance system that would implement them. A variety of new actors, particularly state and federal governments, have expanded their role in education governance since then, but they have done so largely by layering new decisionmakers atop the old architecture. Not surprisingly, the result has been to accelerate fragmentation and incoherence but not, unfortunately, to produce dramatic gains in performance.

Citizens, scholars, and policymakers vary widely in their vision of the purposes of American schooling and the best arrangements to deliver that vision. It is increasingly clear, however, that the way we currently govern education—how we allocate decisionmaking authority across different actors, institutions, and levels of policymakers, both inside and outside government—presents a major barrier to systemic improvement of education. Collectively, the chapters in this volume make two somewhat incongruent points: that traditional K–12 education governance institutions are undergoing an unprecedented period of reform and experimentation, and that the scope and pace of the transformation under way is unlikely to be sufficient to meet the nation's ambitious education goals of achieving excellence and equity. A more comprehensive effort to rationalize our education governance system is long overdue, and we hope that this volume, which draws lessons from a wide variety of perspectives and contexts, can help lead the way in diagnosing the dysfunction in current arrangements and highlighting promising alternative approaches. The challenge is tall. Yet the work absolutely must be done if the nation's democracy and economy are to thrive in the years and decades to come.

Notes

1. Marc S. Tucker, *Standing on the Shoulders of Giants: An American Agenda for Education Reform* (Washington: National Center on Education and the Economy, 2011).

2. See James Q. Wilson, *Bureaucracy: What Government Agencies Do and Why They Do It* (New York: Basic Books, 1989). This is also the argument in the seminal work on systemic reform by Marshall S. Smith and Jennifer O'Day, *Putting the Pieces Together: Systemic School Reform*, CPRE Policy Brief RB-06-4/91 (New Brunswick, N.J.: Consortium for Policy Research in Education).

3. Paul Pastorek, discussant comments at Rethinking Education Governance for the Twenty-First Century conference, sponsored by the Thomas B. Fordham Institute and the Center for American Progress, Washington, December 1, 2011.

4. William Frey, "A Demographic Tipping Point among America's Three-Year-Olds," *State of Metropolitan America,* no. 26 (February 7, 2011).

5. Of course, such a choice-driven system still could be guided by overarching standards or broad goals, such as guaranteeing equitable access to schooling or increasing college attendance.

6. Joseph Murphy, "Governing America's Schools: The Shifting Playing Field," *Teachers College Record* 102 (February 2000): 57–84.

7. Paul Hill, *Reinventing Public Education* (University of Chicago Press, 1997).

8. Baumgartner and Jones seem to suggest as much, too, about the policymaking process more generally. See Frank R. Baumgartner and Bryan D. Jones, *Agendas and Instability in American Politics* (University of Chicago Press, 1993).

9. Clarence N. Stone and others, *Building Civic Capacity: The Politics of Reforming Urban Schools* (University Press of Kansas, 2001).

10. Frederick M. Hess, *Spinning Wheels: The Politics of Urban School Reform* (Brookings Press, 1998).

11. Terry M. Moe, "The Politics of Bureaucratic Structure," in *Can the Government Govern?* edited by John E. Chubb and Paul E. Peterson (Brookings Press, 1989).

12. For more on this topic, see Cynthia G. Brown and others, "State Education Agencies as Agents of Change: What It Will Take for the States to Step Up on Education Reform," Center for American Progress and American Enterprise Institute, Washington, 2011.

13. John Mooney, "The Man with the Plan . . . to Reorganize the Department of Education," *N.J. Spotlight,* July 14, 2011 (http://www.njspotlight.com/stories/11/0713/2249).

14. Marc Tucker, ed., *Surpassing Shanghai: An Agenda for American Education Built on the World's Leading Systems* (Harvard Education Press, 2011).

15. These ideas have been described in different ways by several authors. Wilson's *Bureaucracy* uses the notion of outputs versus outcomes; others have embraced the metaphor of imposing minimal operational constraints as steering but not rowing. See David Osborne and Ted Gaebler, *Reinventing Government: How the Entrepreneurial Spirit Is Transforming the Public Sector* (New York: Penguin Books, 1993).

About the Authors

SIR MICHAEL BARBER is chief education adviser at Pearson and the founder of the U.S. Education Delivery Institute. Previously, he served as the head of McKinsey's Global Education Practice and as cochair of the Pakistan Education Taskforce. Sir Michael's advice on public policy has been sought by governments in more than twenty countries as well as by major international organizations, including the Organization for Economic Cooperation and Development, the World Bank, and the International Monetary Fund.

CYNTHIA G. BROWN is vice president for education policy at the Center for American Progress and served as director of the Renewing Our Schools, Securing Our Future National Task Force on Public Education, a joint initiative of the center and the Institute for America's Future. Previously, she served as director of the Resource Center on Educational Equity of the Council of Chief State School Officers. She was appointed by President Carter as the first assistant secretary for civil rights in the U.S. Department of Education (1980). Before holding that position, she served as principal deputy of the Department of Health, Education and Welfare Office for Civil Rights. She has also worked for the Lawyers' Committee for Civil Rights under Law and the Children's Defense Fund. Brown has a master's in public administration from the Maxwell School at Syracuse University and a bachelor's from Oberlin College. She serves on the board of directors of the American Youth Policy Forum and the Perry Street Preparatory Public Charter School.

MICHELLE R. DAVIS is senior writer for *Education Week Digital Directions* and has tackled subjects ranging from the use of technology in education and online learning to teachers unions and community colleges. Previously, Davis was a staff writer for *Education Week,* where she covered federal issues, including the

U.S. Department of Education, Congress, and the White House. She spent the first half of her career as a political journalist for daily newspapers and came to Washington to cover Congress for *The State*, South Carolina's largest newspaper. Her work has appeared in many publications, including the *Washington Post Magazine Education Review*, *EducationNext*, and *Teacher Magazine*.

CHESTER E. FINN JR. is president of the Thomas B. Fordham Institute. He is a scholar, educator, and public servant who has been at the forefront of the national education debate for thirty-five years. Born and raised in Ohio, he received his doctorate from Harvard University in education policy. He has served as a professor of education and public policy at Vanderbilt University, counsel to the U.S. ambassador to India, legislative director for Senator Daniel Patrick Moynihan, and assistant U.S. secretary of education for research and improvement. A senior fellow at Stanford's Hoover Institution and chairman of the institution's Koret Task Force on K–12 Education, Finn is also senior editor of *Education Next*. The author of nineteen books and more than 400 articles, Finn is the recipient of awards from the Educational Press Association of America, *Choice Magazine*, the Education Writers Association, and the Freedoms Foundation at Valley Forge.

JEFFREY R. HENIG is professor of political science and education at Teachers College and professor of political science at Columbia University. He is the author or coauthor of eight books, including *The Color of School Reform: Race, Politics, and the Challenge of Urban Education* (Princeton, 1999) and *Building Civic Capacity: The Politics of Reforming Urban Schools* (Kansas, 2001), both of which were named—in 1999 and 2001, respectively—the best book written on urban politics by the Urban Politics Section of the American Political Science Association. *Spin Cycle: How Research Gets Used in Policy Debates; The Case of Charter Schools* (Russell Sage, 2008) won the American Educational Research Association's Outstanding Book Award, 2010. Most recently, he is coeditor and contributor to *Between Public and Private: Politics, Governance, and the New Portfolio Models for Urban School Reform* (Harvard Education Press, 2010).

FREDERICK M. HESS is resident scholar and director of education policy studies at the American Enterprise Institute. He has written influential books on education, including *The Same Thing Over and Over*, *Education Unbound*, *Common Sense School Reform*, *Revolution at the Margins*, and *Spinning Wheels*. He also writes the *Education Week* blog, *Rick Hess Straight Up*. His work has appeared in scholarly and popular outlets such as *Teachers College Record*, *Harvard Education Review*, *Social Science Quarterly*, *Urban Affairs Review*, *American Politics Quarterly*, *Chronicle of Higher Education*, *Phi Delta Kappan*, *Educational Leadership*, *U.S.*

News and World Report, Washington Post, and *National Review.* He has edited widely cited volumes on education philanthropy, stretching the education dollar, the impact of education research, education entrepreneurship, and No Child Left Behind. He serves as executive editor of *Education Next;* as lead faculty member for the Rice Education Entrepreneurship Program; on the Review Board for the Broad Prize in Urban Education; and on the Boards of Directors of the National Association of Charter School Authorizers, 4.0 SCHOOLS, and the American Board for the Certification of Teaching Excellence. A former high school social studies teacher, he has taught at the University of Virginia, the University of Pennsylvania, Georgetown University, Rice University, and Harvard University. He holds a master's and doctorate in government, as well as a master of education in teaching and curriculum, all from Harvard University.

PAUL T. HILL is founder of the Center for Reinventing Public Education at the University of Washington. A political scientist, he has spent the past twenty-three years trying to answer the question, "How can we create a system of public oversight that supports, rather than interferes with, school effectiveness and innovation?" Through a series of books and articles, starting with *Reinventing Public Education* (University of Chicago Press, 1997), he has tried to open up new possibilities for K–12 governance, family choice, educator freedom of action, and equal opportunity for disadvantaged students.

PAUL MANNA is associate professor of government and public policy at the College of William & Mary. His research and teaching center on policy implementation, federalism, bureaucracy, and applied-research methods. Manna has published articles and book chapters on topics including federal education policy, school choice, and state education governance. He is the author of *School's In: Federalism and the National Education Agenda* (Georgetown University Press, 2006), which examines the evolving relationship between federal and state education policy since the 1960s, and *Collision Course: Federal Education Policy Meets State and Local Realities* (CQ Press, 2011), which assesses No Child Left Behind's implementation from 2002 to 2009, early Obama administration initiatives, and potential future directions for federal policy. After graduating with his bachelor's in political science from Northwestern University, Manna taught high school social studies for three years before earning his master's and doctorate in political science from the University of Wisconsin.

KATHRYN A. MCDERMOTT is associate professor of education and public policy at the University of Massachusetts, Amherst, where she holds a joint appointment in the School of Education and the Center for Public Policy and Administration. Her main research interest is education equity and the various federal, state, and local policies intended to produce it. Recently, she has focused on intergovernmental relations and accountability in education policy. She is the author of *High-Stakes Reform: The Politics of Educational Accountability* (Georgetown University Press, 2011), an analysis of the politics behind enactment of state-level accountability policies based on test results, and of several journal articles on state accountability policies. *High-Stakes Reform* grew out of research she conducted while she was a participant in the Advanced Studies Fellowship Program at Brown University. Her previous book, *Controlling Public Education: Localism versus Equity* (University Press of Kansas, 1999), highlights the ways in which local control of public education produces challenges for equity in education.

PATRICK MCGUINN is associate professor of political science and education and chair of the political science department at Drew University. His research and teaching focus on national politics and institutions, education and social welfare policy, American political development, federalism, and the policymaking process. McGuinn previously held fellowships at the Institute for Advanced Study in Princeton, the Taubman Center for Public Policy at Brown University, and the Miller Center for Public Affairs at the University of Virginia and was a visiting scholar in the Education and Politics program at Teachers College, Columbia University. His first book, *No Child Left Behind and the Transformation of Federal Education Policy, 1965–2005* (Kansas, 2006), was honored as an outstanding academic title by the American Library Association. After graduating with his bachelor's in government and history from Franklin and Marshall College, Patrick taught high school social studies for three years before earning his doctorate in government and master's of education in education policy from the University of Virginia.

OLIVIA M. MEEKS is a research and evaluation coordinator at District of Columbia Public Schools, where she manages the value-added data for the IMPACT teacher evaluation system and serves on the district's Research Review Board. Before working at District public schools, she served as a research assistant for Frederick M. Hess in the education policy studies department at the American Enterprise Institute. During her tenure at the institute, she cowrote several national reports on education reform, including "School Boards circa 2010: Governance in the Accountability Era," for the National School Boards Association, and "The Case for Being Bold: A New Agenda for Business in Improving STEM Education," for the U.S. Chamber of Commerce. Her research focuses on collective bargaining, customized schooling, and education governance. She is an honors economics graduate of the University of Arkansas, where she was named a Harry S. Truman Scholar in 2008.

KENNETH J. MEIER is distinguished professor of political science and Charles H. Gregory Chair in Liberal Arts at Texas A&M University and Professor of Public Management at the Cardiff University School of Business (U.K.). He is a student of organizations and how they affect equity. Much of his work focuses on public education. He is the author of *Race, Class, and Education: The Politics of Second Generation Discrimination*; *The Politics of Hispanic Education*; and *Public Management: Organizations, Governance and Performance*. The latter reports on twelve years of research on the management of public schools. He is currently engaged in multiyear studies on education policy in the Netherlands and Denmark.

MICHAEL MINTROM is the ANZSOG professor of public sector management with Monash University and the Australia and New Zealand School of Government. His most recent book is *Contemporary Policy Analysis* (Oxford University Press, 2012). Michael is the author of *Policy Entrepreneurs and School Choice* (Georgetown University Press, 2000). He has written extensively on issues to do with school reform in the United States, and his articles on this topic have appeared in various journals, including *Educational Policy*, *Administration and Society*, *State Politics and Policy Quarterly*, and *Publius: The Journal of Federalism*. Early in his academic career, Michael held a tenured position at Michigan State University and was the recipient of a National Academy of Education/Spencer Foundation Postdoctoral Fellowship.

MICHAEL J. PETRILLI is executive vice president at the Thomas B. Fordham Institute, where he oversees the organization's research projects and publications and contributes to the *Flypaper* blog and weekly *Education Gadfly* newsletter. He is also a research fellow at Stanford University's Hoover Institution and executive editor of *Education Next*, where he writes a regular column on technology and media, as well as feature-length articles. Petrilli has published opinion pieces in the *New York Times* and the *Wall Street Journal* and appears regularly on NBC Nightly News, ABC World News Tonight, CNN, and Fox. He's been a guest on several National Public Radio programs, including All Things Considered, Talk of the Nation, and the Diane Rehm Show. He is the author, with Frederick M. Hess, of *No Child Left Behind: A Primer*. Previously, Petrilli was an official in the U.S. Department of Education's Office of Innovation and Improvement and a vice president at K12.com. He started his career as a teacher at the Joy Outdoor Education Center in Clarksville, Ohio, and holds a bachelor's degree in honors political science from the University of Michigan.

BARRY G. RABE is the Arthur Thurnau professor, Gerald Ford School of Public Policy, at the University of Michigan. He also holds appointments in the

Department of Political Science, the Program in the Environment, and the School of Natural Resources and Environment and serves as a nonresident senior fellow in Governance Studies at the Brookings Institution. Much of his research has focused on governance issues outside the arena of education policy, including a range of environmental protection concerns, with a particular emphasis on intergovernmental relations in the United States and Canada. Rabe's most recent book, *Greenhouse Governance: Addressing Climate Change in America*, was published in 2010 by Brookings. He is currently examining the conditions under which market-based policies are adopted in environmental protection and energy policy.

MARGUERITE ROZA is research associate professor at the University of Washington's College of Education and senior scholar at the university's Center on Reinventing Public Education. Her research work has focused primarily on education finance and the effects that fiscal policies at the federal, state, and district levels have on resources in classrooms and schools, as well as the direct impact that education policies have on education budgets and spending inside schools and within districts. Her calculations of dollar implications and cost-equivalent trade-offs have prompted changes in education finance policy at all levels in the education system. She has also been engaged in additional research that explored fiscal trade-offs of wages and layoffs, cost implications of digital learning, likely results of proposed changes to Title I, and state-by-state projections of education spending. Her recent works include *Educational Economics: Where Do $chool Funds Go?* by Urban Institute Press, and pieces published by Education Sector, *Phi Delta Kappan*, and others.

SANDRA VERGARI is associate professor in the Department of Educational Administration and Policy Studies at the State University of New York at Albany. She is a political scientist with a focus on local, state, and federal K–12 education reform politics and policy. Her areas of expertise include charter school dynamics and federalism and education policy. Her current projects include comparative analysis of education governance in Canada and the United States. Vergari's research has appeared in policy reports, academic journals, and books.

RICHARD WALLEY is senior policy manager at the New Zealand Ministry of Education, currently with responsibility for early childhood education policy. As a practicing public policy specialist, his career has covered a range of subjects and disciplines, including education governance, civil justice, regulatory reform, special education, and, most recently, early childhood education, for both the United Kingdom and New Zealand governments.

STEVEN F. WILSON is founder and president of Ascend Learning, a charter school management organization in New York City, and senior fellow at Education Sector, in Washington, D.C. Formerly, he was executive vice president for product development at Edison Schools and a senior fellow at the Center for Business and Government of the John F. Kennedy School of Government at Harvard University. His book *Learning on the Job: When Business Takes on Public Schools* examined the first decade of private management of public schools and earned the Virginia and Warren Stone Prize. Wilson founded and served as chief executive officer of Advantage Schools, an urban charter school management company that enrolled 10,000 students. Before founding Advantage, he was special assistant for strategic planning for Massachusetts governor William Weld. He advised the governor on education policy during the passage and implementation of the state's comprehensive education reform act and assessment system. Earlier Wilson was executive director of the Pioneer Institute for Public Policy Research. His first book, *Reinventing the Schools: A Radical Plan for Boston,* led to the establishment of the Massachusetts charter school law, which he drafted. He is a graduate of Harvard College.

KENNETH K. WONG holds the Walter and Leonore Annenberg Chair in Education Policy, directs the graduate program in Urban Education Policy, and chairs the Education Department at Brown University. Professor Wong is a national figure in shaping the research and policy agenda on urban education reform, equity issues, and governance. He is the 2010 recipient of the Colton Award for distinguished contribution to the Politics of Education Association and the recipient of the 2007 Deil Wright Best Paper Award given by the American Political Science Association for his research paper on education innovation. His recent books include *The Education Mayor: Improving America's Schools* and *Successful Schools and Educational Accountability.* His research has received support from the National Science Foundation, the Institute for Education Sciences, the U.S. Department of Education, and several foundations, including the Joyce, Spencer, Broad, and Rhode Island foundations. He was the key architect in redesigning the school funding formula in Rhode Island that was enacted into law in 2010.

Index

Page references followed by *t* and *f* refer to tables and figures respectively.